Silberberg

P9-BJH-371

GAY SUNSHINE INTERVIEWS

VOLUME 2

PHOTO BY STEVEN LAFER

BIOGRAPHICAL NOTE ON THE EDITOR

WINSTON LEYLAND was born in Lancashire, England, in 1940 but has lived in the United States since childhood. M.A. (history) from UCLA. He has been editor of *Gay Sunshine Journal* since 1971 and editor/publisher of Gay Sunshine Press books since the mid-1970s. He is responsible for twelve anthologies published by the press: *Angels of the Lyre: A Gay Poetry Anthology* (and contributor), 1975; *Orgasms of Light*, 1977; *Now the Volcano*, 1979; *Straight Hearts' Delight: Love Poems and Selected Letters* of Allen Ginsberg/Peter Orlovsky, 1980; *Meat: True Homosexual Experiences from S.T.H.*, Vol. 1, 1981; *Flesh*, Vol. 2, 1982; *Sex*, Vol. 3, 1982; *Physique: A Pictorial History of the Athletic Model Guild*, 1982; *The Disrobing* by Royal Murdoch, 1982; the two volumes of *Gay Sunshine Interviews*, 1978, 1982; and an anthology of Latin American gay short fiction, 1983.

He writes: "I see Gay Sunshine Press as a catalyst in the evolving Gay Cultural Renaissance and myself as deeply involved in that process."

Gay Sunshine Interviews

Volume 2

EDITED BY WINSTON LEYLAND

Gay Sunshine Press
San Francisco

First Edition 1982
Published in hardcover and paperback; there is also a lettered, specially bound hardcover
edition of 26 copies, signed by the editor.

Gay Sunshine Interviews Volume 2: All interviews, except Broughton, Duncan, and
Wieners, copyright © 1982 by Gay Sunshine Press Inc. All rights reserved. Broughton
interview copyright © 1982 by James Broughton. Duncan interview copyright © 1982 by
Robert Duncan, Steve Abbott and Aaron Shurin. Wieners interviews I & II copyright
© 1982 by Charley Shively.

Except for brief passages quoted in a newspaper, magazine, radio, or television review, no
part of this book may be reproduced in any form or by any means, electronic or mechanical, including photocopying and recording, or by any information storage and retrieval
system, without permission in writing from the publisher.

Cover design: Speros Bairaktaris

Publication of this book was made possible in part by a grant from the California Arts
Council.

Library of Congress Cataloging in Publication Data:

Main entry under title:

Gay Sunshine interviews. (Volume 2)

1. Artists—Interviews.   2. Homosexuals—Interviews.
I. Leyland, Winston, 1940–
NX163.G39 700'.92'2 [B] 78-8722
ISBN 0-917342-62-3 (v. 2)
ISBN 0-917342-63-1 (pbk. : v. 2)

Gay Sunshine Press
P.O Box 40397
San Francisco, CA 94140
Complete 22-page illustrated catalogue of titles: $1 ppd.

CONTENTS

Introduction 6

HARRY BRITT 7
   Interviewed by Winston Leyland

JAMES BROUGHTON 23
   Interviewed by Robert Peters

KIRBY CONGDON 39
   Interviewed by Maurice Kenny

MARTIN DUBERMAN 55
   Interviewed by George Whitmore

ROBERT DUNCAN 75
   Interviewed by Steve Abbott and Aaron Shurin

KENWARD ELMSLIE 95
   Interviewed by Winston Leyland

TAYLOR MEAD 109
   Interviewed by John Giorno

ROBERT PETERS 123
   Interviewed by Don Mark

ROGER PEYREFITTE 143
   Interviewed by D. W. Gunn

EDOUARD RODITI 159
   Interviewed by Winston Leyland

NED ROREM 191
   Interviewed by Winston Leyland

SAMUEL STEWARD 219
   Interviewed by Winston Leyland

MUTSUO TAKAHASHI 243
   Interviewed by Keizo Aizawa

JOHN WIENERS 259
   Interviewed by Charley Shively

JONATHAN WILLIAMS and THOMAS MEYER . 279
   Interviewed by John Browning

INTRODUCTION

I N 1973 San Francisco's *Gay Sunshine Journal* initiated its now celebrated series of in-depth interviews. *Gay Sunshine Interviews* Volume I reprinted twelve of these in book form. This second, and final, volume includes sixteen interviews (counting the two separate ones with John Wieners). Thirteen appeared originally in the pages of *Gay Sunshine Journal* 1973–1980. Three are printed here for the first time (Congdon, Steward, Wieners II). All but one are with men deeply involved in the arts: there are eight poets (Congdon, Duncan, Peters, Roditi, Takahashi, Wieners, Williams, Meyer); one actor (Taylor Mead); one librettist-poet (Kenward Elmslie); one poet-filmmaker (James Broughton); one historian-playwright (Martin Duberman); one writer–tattoo artist (Samuel Steward); and one progressive politician (Harry Britt).

As general editor of the series (and interviewer in eleven cases) I have been personally responsible for the form they have taken. Along with other interviewers, I have emphasized the cultural *and* the personal, engendering from the artists reflections and insights into the connections between sexuality and creativity as well as in-depth discussions of literary techniques, styles, personalities. Critical response has been positive. *New Age* wrote: "Many of the interviews transcend mere 'people journalism' and emerge as first-class literary and social criticism on their own, almost creating a new genre of commentary on life and letters."

The interviews in the two volumes demonstrate the existence of a definite gay sensibility in the arts. Its modern genesis is to be found in the works of writers such as Walt Whitman, Oscar Wilde, John Addington Symonds, Edward Carpenter, Constantine Cavafy, Adolfo Caminha. The current gay liberation movement, which received its impetus from New York's Stonewall demonstrations in 1969 and similar manifestations in the San Francisco Bay Area, was especially catalytic for this gay sensibility. The rise and spread of post-Stonewall gay consciousness had a deep effect on many writers, freeing them from societal or self-imposed restraints. See, for example, the work of Royal Murdoch *(The Disrobing,* Gay Sunshine Press, 1982) who wrote most of his poems on gay themes in the 1970s when he himself was in his seventies; or the work of Jim Everhard *(Cute and Other Poems,* Gay Sunshine Press 1982) which "brings together a body of poetry dramatizing the evolution of gay awareness over the past decade with both wit and passion." I doubt that most of the subjects would have been as frank as they are here, if the interviews had been conducted prior to 1970.

I would like to thank all the interviewees and interviewers in these two anthologies for so generously giving their time and energy to this project. They are, I believe, crucial volumes for understanding and evaluating gay artistic sensibility and seminal contributions to the ongoing Gay Cultural Renaissance.

WINSTON LEYLAND

PHOTO © RINK 1982

HARRY
BRITT

HARRY BRITT was born June 8, 1938, in Port Arthur, Texas. He received a B.A. (1960) from Duke University and a B.D. (1963) from Perkins School of Theology, Southern Methodist University. He did graduate study at the University of Heidelburg (1963-1964), University of Chicago (1964-1966), and SMU (1968-1969). During his seminary studies he served as assistant pastor of Wesley Methodist Church in Dallas (1960-1961). During the seminary school year of 1962-1963 he had a fellowship and taught New Testament Greek. He was ordained minister and served as pastor of Central Park Methodist Church, Chicago, 1965-1966, and Community United Methodist Church, Chicago, 1966-1968. He resigned his ministry and moved to San Francisco in the early 1970s.

Britt is currently a member of the Board of Supervisors (eleven in number) which, together with the mayor, is the chief legislative body for San Francisco. He was appointed to the position by Mayor Dianne Feinstein in January 1979 after the public slaying of his predecessor, gay activist Harvey Milk. Britt won election to the office in his own right in November 1979 with the support of a majority of his fellow gays and other minorities in his District—an area which includes the Castro, heavily populated by gays. He won election again in city-wide elections in November, 1980. Since taking office he has proved to be one of the most progressive politicians in San Francisco, responsive especially to the needs of minorities, the disabled, and the elderly.

THE PRESENT INTERVIEW was conducted at Britt's Castro area apartment in May, 1980. The interviewer is Winston Leyland, editor of *Gay Sunshine*. It appeared originally in *Gay Sunshine* 44/45 (1980).

Winston Leyland interviews
HARRY BRITT

LEYLAND: I know a little about your background—that you were a minister for several years. In fact, I've a similar background myself: I was a Roman Catholic priest and left the structure of the Church in the late sixties because I was muzzled after speaking out publicly against the Vietnam War, and also because I wanted to be an open gay person. Could you talk a little about your own experiences in the ministry?

BRITT: I'm never sure whether I'm out of the church or not; I'm not sure whether that's possible. On the whole I feel that my background in religion was very valuable to me, partly as an inoculation against the serious perversion of the mind that religion can do to people who are not aware of how it works, but also because there are within the Jewish-Christian tradition extraordinary resources for people who are trying not only to find meaning but also to restructure society in more human ways. Now that I have access to church situations I've used those and I think I can authentically speak as an heir of the tradition.

LEYLAND: What religious tradition do you come from?

BRITT: Middle-class cultural Christianity: the United Methodist Church in Texas. But it was really the church that brought me beyond the cultural monotony of the middle-class South. I was born in Port Arthur, Texas, a small industrial city on the Gulf Coast and best known as Janis Joplin's home town. Janis and I reacted to the same kind of environment in different ways: she stomped her foot and screamed; I did the opposite and just embodied in myself the values I was raised with and then, I hope, moved beyond that. It was really the church that took me out of the Texas culture and exposed to me realities such as racism and economic injustice, enabling me to form within myself an independent sense of what's more important than what else. Then, I think, by trying to take the church's message very seriously I discovered that the church was not able to deal either with my sexual feelings or with my intellectual discoveries or with my sense of what's important. The church that I experienced was essentially a support system for values that I found to be inappropriate within the terms of this tradition. There were a lot of young ministers in the sixties—when I was in Chicago—who felt that the church was an inappropriate vehicle with which to create more human structures. The turning point for me was the murder of Martin Luther King in 1968, and the reaction to that murder of the so-called Christians that I was serving. The fear and the lack of sensitivity to the meaning of that event for the black people really convinced me that not only had I failed to reach my congregation, but my predecessors, whom I knew to be competent and faithful ministers, had also failed. I increasingly felt that the church was a salvation army, dealing with victims and not with problems. And also I was unable any longer to conceal from myself my homosexuality.

Any historian of the Church knows when the church cannot deal with the prophetic voices that are arising within history, it is the church that's on trial, it's not the heretic. One of the exciting things about being gay right now with a religious background is that the church is just beginning to deal with the issue of homosexuality. There's no question whatsoever that they're going to have to deal with the issue and that the message that we are speaking to them will, at some point, be heard. I would say at this point that we're more a problem for the church than the church is for us.

LEYLAND: I would only partially agree with your last point. There are still many people within the structure of the church who are in a state of fear, not able to explore their sexuality because many churches hold a homosexual life-style to be sinful. The situation is beginning to change slightly in the United States, but it's still rigid in other parts of the world, Latin America for instance. And then in the Catholic Church we have the pronouncements on sexuality of that charismatic reactionary John Paul II who seems bent on cancelling out the little progress that has been made since John XXIII, returning to the pious platitudes of earlier days.

BRITT: Right! In terms of the personal desire to be accepted by the structure it's extremely painful. But people within the church who see their lives as ignition for change can, I think, confidently believe that their work is going to bear fruits very soon. A lot depends on which tradition your're talking about. Within the Roman Catholic church it's hard to see beyond the pompous hypocrisy and moral irrelevancy of the pope to a Catholicism that embraces sexual freedom. But if you look at the churches which usually have been less protective of the past and more open to the future (the United Church of Christ, the Episcopal Church), the process is clearly moving. Where the Episcopalians are now, the Presbyterians will be three or four years from now. And again if the church can't deal with us, that's not the end of the world.

LEYLAND: Was the Methodist Church at that time somewhat more progressive than say the Baptist churches in the South, or other churches?

BRITT: It had less content; it was a more "do unto others as you would have others do unto you" church, with very few commitments to anything beyond being a support group for middle-class values. We weren't allowed to drink or smoke. But that was not much of a price to pay for the benefits of being good. I think the main difference between the Methodists and the Baptists where I was raised was that the Methodists were a small notch above on the economic ladder, while the Baptists were a rural-based, working-class church.

LEYLAND: Were you aware of your gay feelings at this time? Or had you sublimated them?

BRITT: I don't think the word sublimate is relevant here. I can recall having homosexual fantasies as early as the age of five, but there was nothing in my history that offered me any sort of guidance as to how to deal with those. I never recall making any decisions not to act on them; that never was an alternative for me. I assumed I was the only person who had these fantasies and it was best not to allow the world to see them. But I was never aware that there were gay people who lived, who had sex with each other. At the point when I became aware of that I was as revolted by it as everyone else and did not believe that I could be attracted to someone who was homosexual. I assumed that gay people fit all of the stereotypes and could not bring myself to finding that sexually attractive. So I was thirty-four years old before I had my first gay experience; and again not as a result of any conscious decision not to, but simply because there was nothing in my environment that made that a real choice. The real choices were always "How do you play all these games that are not natural to you in a way that conceals the fact that they're not natural to you?" And I was fairly resourceful at that. I was president of my social fraternity in college. The personality that I created as a way of relating to the world was a very acceptable one to most people and produced all kinds of rewards. But it just had nothing to do with me at all. And I really have very little faith in closet existence in terms of the psychological possibilities inherent in it. I think if I were pope and gay, I would resign the papacy.

LEYLAND: Well, you know, both John XXIII and Paul VI were supposedly gay. Paul is supposed to have taken his papal name from that of one of his former lovers, an actor. And, interestingly enough, both popes at least generally kept their mouths shut regarding the "sin of homosexuality" as compared to this new Polish pope who seems determined to condemn openly everything except the "heterosexual missionary position" without contraceptives.

BRITT: Right. [*Laughter.*] I can't conceive of a job that I would not give up if, in order to keep it, I had to deny my sexuality.

LEYLAND: One of the reasons I left the structure of the church was that I did not want to lead a double life and be in the closet about my gayness.

BRITT: The stereotype that gay people are mentally disturbed is essentially correct, in the sense that to live in a closet *is not* healthy mentally. I don't want to make moral judgments, or any other kind of judgments, about people who do that. But I do feel I can say with some conviction after knowing quite a number of gay people that I have a very, very low assessment of the possibility of happiness in that situation. I'm also finding as I move around America quite a bit that practically everyone I meet could be more open than they are. The greatest obstacle that gay people have is their fear of rejection on account of their homosexuality. I believe that the gay community here in San Francisco has a great deal more trouble dealing with power than they do with weakness. All of our strategies as children are based on weakness and trying to accommodate ourselves to a stronger society, stronger but morally superior and healthier and better in every way. To move as an adult to strategies based on personal strength requires an extraordinary adjustment. When Harvey Milk was killed, it seemed very natural for gay people to whom he had represented strength and assertiveness to return to the fearfulness and the insecurity that he had called them away from. I feel that in San Francisco we went through a real emotional regression when Harvey was killed that doesn't seem justified by the facts but was very, very clear. It's extremely hard for us to accept the power that we have; it's probably easier here than anywhere else because we've won a number of very gratifying victories. The fear is very close to the surface in most of us.

LEYLAND: What were the circumstances of your leaving the structure of the Methodist Church? Was it a crisis of conscience?

BRITT: So much of my life has been self-analytical that I've developed something of a skepticism, or at least humility, about my ability to analyze my motives. The more I analyze the more it seems that most of my life has been a matter of dealing with homosexuality, and people who say that's something peripheral or accidental to a person's existence are either dishonest or badly misinformed. There's a level on which I have to say I left the church because I was gay. But people who knew me then would not say that that was the case. They would say that I was a misfit, intellectually and in terms of my commitments within the church as I knew it. There's a level on which I can say that the loss of faith in that terrible year of 1968. when two assassinations took place, and I had reached the age of thirty, was a logical point in my life for a change of direction. I felt I had gone as far as I could go to be what other people wanted me to be; it had not produced personal effectiveness; it had not given me any real happiness; and it had not, as far as I could tell, done much good for other people either. The break was rather sudden: I was married for seven years; my marriage ended in 1967. I don't want to say it was a sexless marriage but it was not a gratifying marriage sexually. It suffered from the defects of every other part of my life in that I was not honest about who I was. It's not that I was having homosexual affairs on the side; I wasn't at all. Again I was not aware that there were other gay people in Chicago. So, as far as leaving the structure of the church I'll have to leave that to others to analyze for right now; it just wasn't working for me. The whole direction of my life reached a dead end: I was thirty years old, I didn't respect myself, I didn't believe that the work I was doing was important, relevant.

LEYLAND: What kind of work were you doing at that time?

BRITT: I was pastor of a congregation in the southwest side of Chicago, essentially an Eastern European section of the city with very few Protestants, which was undergoing a racial change. I worked with teenage gangs a lot which was gratifying but frustrating. Chicago was an exciting place in the sixties. I left Chicago the summer of the Democratic convention in 1968. Had I stayed there I would have been a part of the young ministers who were trying to separate the demonstrators from the police in Lincoln Park.

The next three years of my life were a period of real withdrawal and an attempt to create a new person, a new self. I dealt with all the problems I could deal with alone: I gave up smoking, lost a hundred pounds, got myself financially on my feet—did all of the things that people can do without dealing with the rest of the world. Then when I finished that process (this was in Dallas) I decided to come to California, not to "come out" but because I was aware of some things that were going on out here, particularly in the areas of psychology that I thought might offer me some personal help and also create a career possibility for me. I was still very much interested in working with the dynamics of human change, and I didn't want to do it again in a religious context. And that was not an unsuccessful attempt.

I had a transitional periood during the years after I left the ministry: What was really going on with me during that time was internal, and I think that's true of a lot of gay people still growing up. You create an internal life as a substitute for honest interaction with the world, and there's value in that. You develop all kinds of resources and, as an observer, you develop some skills. There is a book by Colin Wilson, *The Misfits*, which talks about various people in literature. I identified very much with that: the spectator role in life. You watch life passing by and form opinions and values without testing them out in action. Now that I've begun to test out in action the attitudes that I've learned during my life, I'm finding that they weren't bad; that it's quite possible to develop a fairly effective set of ways of relating to the world without acting on them for the first thirty years of your life. I'm glad that I got involved in the church, and I'm glad I undertook my explorations with existential psychology and philosophers like Heidegger; they've proven to be very valuable resources for me. Certainly the work I did in the personal and social behavior fields is now proving very useful to me in being able to grasp what people want and politically to be able to respond to their wants, not necessarily giving them what they want but being aware of what's really going on in a given political situation beyond the articulated desires of people. I'm fascinated by the different gay political styles: the difference between the prevailing political styles in San Francisco and the prevailing political styles in places like San Diego which have strong gay communities but which have not experienced the kind of success and victories that we have experienced here.

There was such a gap between the public perception of who I was and the internal struggle that I was going through. You have to overcome that gap, you have to bring your personal struggle out somehow into the public arena—I don't mean you have to bare your soul to people, but your actions have to bear some consonance with what's going on inside you, or you *are* schizophrenic. You need feedback from reality in terms of your real feelings and your real self, and I was not getting that during the first thirty years of my life. In California I reached on the personal level the ability to explore some things: I "came out." In October 1971 I came to San Francisco; it was still almost three years before I "came out," and when I say "come out" I don't mean publicly. I mean to begin practicing a homosexual life style. Prior to that time my serious sex life had been fantasies. There's nothing wrong with fantasies: they seem to be the only thing available to large numbers of young gay people still, I'm sure. But to reach out to another person honestly and to ask them for something is really the beginning for gay people. So I "came out" and not very long after I "came out" I became involved in Harvey Milk's political life.

LEYLAND: What were your initial impressions of Harvey Milk?

BRITT: That he was quite mad. Harvey was an absurd figure. He was totally aware that to be gay in this society is to be despised. I don't know anyone who has a lower opinion of the attitudes that people have towards gay people than Harvey Milk had. He assumed that the most liberal people in our society despise gay people. But he always acted as though that were not true. I have to think back to the old Christian paradox: even though you are the least of sinners you should act as though you were justified in the eyes of God. Because that's what Harvey Milk did. He started from an assumption that to be gay was the worst possible thing you could be in the eyes of society, and lived his whole life as though it were the best possible thing to be in this society. As he did that he found out that indeed it is and that the power of living on that belief changes people's lives. And he changed my life in the sense of giving me a focus, enabling me to choose between all of the different attitudes towards life and all the different philosophical rationalizations and to focus on the serious problem of living as an honest, openly gay human being in society. The decision to do that took care of ninety percent of my problems.

We should never underestimate the impact that Harvey had on the consciousnesses of the gay community in San Francisco and, I think, other places too. He was a unique embodiment of gay self-respect who really understood that to be gay in the 1970s was the most exciting possible thing you could be. This was the moment in history in which gay people could move right into American society everywhere and have an impact. Harvey used to insist that America is not moving to the right, that what is happening is unprecedentedly rapid change, not just in terms of politics but in terms of basic institutional patterns in our country. It was a very contagious feeling. He was also a very difficult person to deal with if you didn't share his goals; he loved being a problem to people, he loved going to the Chamber of Commerce and making socialist speeches. He teased homophobes because he had a quiet confidence that *we were going to win;* we could afford to make enemies partly because he assumed everyone was our enemy already, and partly because he knew in a relatively short period of time history would vindicate us.

LEYLAND: Do you think he might have overemphasized this aspect of *everyone* being our enemy? Obviously there are some progressive straights who are in favor of gay liberation, of gay rights...

BRITT: A lot of people made that point to Mr. Milk and none of them persuaded him. He always insisted that we had one foot in the White House and one foot in the concentration camp. We would never be secure relying on the goodwill of liberal politicians. Our only ultimate strength was having openly gay people in positions of leadership, and that was always his big political priority. He did feel a great deal of resentment toward gay people who found reasons not to support him and could not see the singular importance of having openly gay people in positions of leadership. I've learned a little more what that's all about by being in City Hall and seeing the kind of veto power that gives us over a whole set of bad possible courses of action. To be in the place where decisions are made as an equal partner in those decisions every day produces benefits for the community that are very hard for a person outside to recognize.

LEYLAND: What was your role in Harvey Milk's various campaigns?

BRITT: I was a foot-soldier mostly. It was after Harvey's election that I really began to take on a leadership role: I became involved heavily in Harvey's 1977 campaign—the successful one. I had a sense that it wasn't going well because his message was not getting out to the gay community. So I got involved doing work to be done that I felt wasn't being done. I went to an organization called the San Francisco Gay Democratic Club which was a very small group of left gay activists who had endorsed Harvey (the larger gay Democratic club, Alice B. Toklas, did *not* support Harvey).

LEYLAND: Why didn't the Alice B. Toklas Club support Harvey?

BRITT: There was another gay person, Rick Stokes, running against Harvey.

Rick was a founder of Alice B. Toklas, and it was understandable that he'd have a lot of support there. One of the first political things I did for Harvey was to help deny the Alice B. Toklas endorsement to Rick Stokes. We weren't able to get it for Harvey, but we were able to deny it by one vote to Rick who now is a good friend of mine. But at that point of history we were on opposite sides of the fence. That was one of the first exciting victories of the Milk campaign. Had Rick gotten that endorsement his campaign would have had a great deal more credibility in the gay community than it had.

I think Harvey's style was much more what the gay community needed to identify with at that point in history. He was charismatic, if I may say so, in the biblical sense of charisma, not the *New York Times* sense. So, as I said, I went to the S.F. Gay Democratic Club and said: Let's do what has to be done for Harvey. We got out some literature and hit the streets and I really think we contributed in a significant way to his victory. After he was elected I became president of that organization, which I had not even been a member of before. It was a very natural thing that we would become his gay political base. The club grew very rapidly with Harvey in office. We had some extraordinary people in the club, and the "No on 6" campaign was run locally by people from our club; it brought in a lot of new people. My role with Harvey as president of that club was first of all to bring in and develop new leadership to deal with the new strength our community had; and secondly to develop coalitions with other political forces in the city. As president of the club I went to a lot of meetings and became a member of the executive committee of a group called "Action for Accountable Government" which was a coalition of progressive political forces in the city and established very valuable relationships within labor, the Asian community, the black community. So when the appointment issue came up after Harvey's death I was known and had credibility. Since Harvey's death those relationships have grown extraordinarily until at this point it's clear to me that the progressive gay political community is the most effective member of a partnership of progressive political forces in the city who are in position now to make a serious bid for control of the city. Don't hear that as saying "Gays control San Francisco"; we don't, we never will, we should not aspire to. But we are ready to do more than our share of the work with other progressive communities to make this city the kind of city where not only gay people but other people who have been disadvantaged in the system can live the kinds of lives they want to live.

LEYLAND: In 1980 CBS aired a show on gay politics in San Francisco and the supposed influence gay people have over city politicians. Most gay people, myself included, felt that the program was biased, edited in such a way that the sensationalistic was emphasized. For example, they never even mentioned Harvey Milk.

BRITT: Most of the time I feel very strong because the people I do politics with are in a position of great strength. But when the national network takes you on, you feel weak. We do not have an immediate, effective way of dealing with the power of CBS. We need to move to a position where we have an input into one of the major networks. The appropriate requests have been issued. The mayor has asked for equal time, the Board of Supervisors of San Francisco has sent a letter protesting the show. We were given a great deal of time locally to respond, but it's not a San Francisco problem; it's a national problem. Gay people in other communities are going to have to take responsibility for responding. It was an abominable piece of journalism; those two journalists came to San Francisco to do an "exposé" of the excesses of homosexuality in the Sodom and Gomorrah of America. They had not the faintest interest in gay politics, and their program showed no understanding of gay politics. Not only did they not mention my campaign which they filmed almost in its entirety, they gave no indication of any reason why gay people would need to be political. There was no mention of any of the gay political organizations, or any information in the show about politics in San Francisco, who has power and what the nature of that power is. It was simply a taking of the rhetoric of gay rights and filling it in with the content of fear and hate and sensationalism. The only positive thing I can say is: Don't assume we had that much to lose. The assumption should be that most people look at the gay community through those stereotyped eyes now, and by getting that out in the open I'm not clear it does that much harm in the long run. Of course, there's personal pain involved for parents and kids, and I hate that. But one thing we cannot afford is to be invisible and to have our issue taken away from the public consciousness. My sense is that there are little old ladies in Wichita who saw that show and sat around afterwards and discussed it, and one of them said to the other, "But I have a cousin who's that way and he doesn't do that sort of thing." I think the emergence of the gay lifestyle into the consciousness of America is proceeding rather rapidly. With all of the distortion that was in the show the sense is out there that we're here, that we're diverse, that we're strong. When that message got out about black people, it changed the willingness of non-black people to accept blacks as a part of our society. If somewhere that program makes some young Harvey Milk mad, it may have been worthwhile.

Even within our own community you can predict the reactions that people are going to have to certain events like the riots or the CBS documentary or other political events, in terms of the extent to which people are leading from strength and to the extent to which people are still trying to accommodate themselves and are still fearful, still worried fundamentally about "what other people will think of me" rather than trying to carve out a personal statement about who I am and letting the world deal with that however it will. I come down very strongly on the side that to the extent you're trying to accommodate yourself to other people's expectations and values, you're not an effective human being. Politically to the extent that our community is still asking first the question "what will people think of us?" we are limiting our effectiveness rather dramatically. I really believe that right now if we make the statement that seems right to us, then the rest of the world will have to deal with that and we'll be better off.

LEYLAND: This is, in fact, one of the main points of gay liberation: not to be overly concerned with what people think or to seek after the approval of straight society as a main goal, but rather to assert ourselves and live our lives in a truly human way.

BRITT: To be gay is to be overwhelmed with the attitudes of other people, and in order to free ourselves from that we have to put those aside and develop our own sense of what is right. When Dianne Feinstein [mayor of San Francisco—ed.] said that gay people must respect community standards, it offended us very, very deeply because too much of our lives was necessarily spent satisfying other people's ideas of what's right and wrong—ideas which were not shaped with an appreciation for what it means to be gay, with any kind of objective, honest, adult attitudes around sexuality. You mention gay liberation. We are in the process not just of liberating ourselves but of liberating a total society from some very inappropriate attitudes about human relationships. We are not going to be able to liberate the larger society unless we deal with them honestly and call them to a higher sense of what's right and wrong than they've laid on us all of our lives. Particularly around sexism. In terms of my learning of what the gay movement is all about, I keep going back to the fundamental political situation in the home in which little boys and girls learn that they are dealing with powerful parent figures upon whose good will their economic and affectional well-being depends. In that situation we learn everything we learn in life about power relationships. I have a very strong sense that power relationships in our society are fucked up. We are not going to address politically any of the basic problems of our country including energy, inflation, foreign policy without addressing those fundamentally fucked-up power relationships that are taught in the home and, in a single word, are sexist. I see racism as a function of sexism. I believe that what the gay movement and the women's movement are at heart about is not creating gay rights, or women's rights, within an essentially sexist society, because that is not possible. The passage of the ERA is an urgent priority, but it doesn't achieve that much unless we attack the fundamentally sexist power structure in our society. The gaining of equal rights for black people under the law has been an important struggle for a long time but it doesn't begin to deal with racism as long as the power relationships that support racism are still there. On a psychological level black people for the first number of years of their modern movement saw themselves as a civil rights struggle, just as gay people have talked about "gay rights." I think that black people learned there's no such thing as black rights in a racist society and there's no such thing as gay rights in a sexist society. What we're really about is attacking and replacing power relationships that are unnatural and perverted with power relationships built on naturalness and humanness, whether it's around race, sex, sexual orientation or anything else. At this moment in history we who have been oppressed by sexism are, I think, the most vital and alive political force in this whole country and have a lot to say to our sisters and brothers who are fighting nuclear power and other forms of unnatural use of human energy.

LEYLAND: Gay people who I've talked to in San Francisco believe that you now have a much deeper perspective on sexism and women's rights than you did when you came into office a year ago, that you have evolved into taking a very firm commitment. Do you agree with this assessment?

BRITT: I certainly hope so, and I hope I'll evolve more. I know it's true I've always given lip service to women's rights, as it's true with most political gay people. But I think my personal experience over the past year and a half has brought home to me in a gut way the utter futility of a gay rights movement that doesn't challenge sexism. Women's rights are important but that's not the problem. I'm constantly impressed with the attitudes that we learn as children about the fundamental inferiority of women, the fundamental childishness of women and the urgency that little boys not associate with any of that at all, that we not be sissies, that we not in any way do anything that might cause us to take on any of the inferior attributes of females. That is so very basic to the way that we grow up; gay men need to listen particularly seriously to lesbians, and beyond that we need to insist that our straight sisters and brothers listen to our experience around sexism. Politically, as you know, I do a lot of stuff: I'm for Kennedy and against the draft, for marijuana law liberalization and a whole set of causes. And I'm angered that my progressive friends won't deal with gay rights until the end and that people on the left do not yet seem to see the pervasiveness of sexism in all the economic improper relationships in our society. I've recently been reading Michael Harrington's new book. I feel very close politically to Michael Harrington, but he's able to write his whole book about some badly needed economic changes in our society without mentioning the family patterns, the sexism in church, school, home and the media that to me move toward improper power relationships in our whole society. Wilhelm Reich was, I think, homophobic, but he did understand that fascism begins at home, that you are not going to have a just society, a society in which human rights are taken seriously as long as you have a sexually uptight society.

LEYLAND: It's now a year and a half since the assassination of your predecessor, Harvey Milk, and one can have more perspective on it. What are your basic reactions, attitudes at this moment towards the tragedy. Are they different from what they were at the actual time?

BRITT: I've never really had the luxury of looking back. My response to the assassination was: what do we do next? It had to be because a lot of us who were close to Harvey were called upon instantly to develop strategies for the future and we had to put aside our human desire to go away and feel something bad had happened to us. Because the community did come together with so much love and so much determination to take up Harvey's work, I personally received a great deal of strength from that. I suppose if there's a dominant change in the way I feel now from the way I felt then it's this: then I had a great deal of uncertainty and fear about the future, now I feel very strong. At this point there's no question that locally the gay political community has risen to the challenge of moving beyond Harvey Milk; my forays into the rest of the country convince me that that's true in other places too. So there's a basic movement from fear to confidence. And as far as the events of November 27, 1978 — they still have an unreal quality for me. But then most everything about the events of the last two years of my life have an unreal quality about them. People should never underestimate what their lives can be if they will respond to the opportunities that are out there. November 27, 1978 forced me and a whole bunch of other people who had been basically letting other people live our lives for us to get involved and to make some real personal statements.

LEYLAND: To what extent was homophobia an important element in Dan White's psyche and a motivating factor in his decision to murder Mayor Moscone and Supervisor Harvey Milk?

BRITT: Homophobia is connected with just about everything that happens in our society. Dan White was (and probably still is) an almost pure case of unadulterated homophobia. I would assume that in a situation of personal crisis it's to be expected that he would strike out in a homophobic way. I did not know Dan White except in a most superficial way. I don't think Dan White knows Dan White except in a most superficial way. But it's very clear that he was profoundly threatened by Harvey Milk, mostly because Harvey was gay but also because Harvey was a real, live, feeling, caring human being and obviously that was tough for Dan White to deal with. I have noticed in politics a very clear distinction between those in politics for their own personal ego needs and those in politics because they're part of some movement or have some desire to make some social change. Harvey Milk was a pure case of someone who was willing to take great personal risk, great personal abuse, in order to achieve social goals. He exemplified the kind of personal freedom that comes from the personal detachment that that sort of person has. Dan White quite clearly had no values outside himself, and certainly saw his own personal life as a matter of his personal acceptance or rejection by the larger world. I think he struck out at George [Moscone] and Harvey partly because they were what he could never be in terms of their personal freedom and character.

LEYLAND: When considering her appointment of a successor to Harvey Milk, Mayor Feinstein interviewed many people. What were your thoughts and feelings when you accepted the position?

BRITT: It was clear to me that Harvey Milk had an urgent concern that should he be killed (and he always assumed he would be) what he achieved must not end there. The tapes that he made show that he had a preoccupation with carrying on his work beyond his death. He told me that he made those tapes right after he was elected because so few people clearly understood what he was about. All of us who were close to Harvey shared that feeling and were concerned that this particular position of power that Harvey had won, not just for the gay community but for a gay consciousness that he had presented and a political set of commitments (not all of which were gay), not be lost. That was my concern on November 27, 1978, and it was my concern when I was sworn in on January 10, 1979. My behavior between those two dates was based on that commitment.

LEYLAND: It's obviously your responsibility to represent all the people in your District whether gay or straight, young or elderly, white, black, Asian, or whatever. Do you sometimes experience conflicts in that regard?

BRITT: As a general rule I have trouble thinking of a case where I've had to choose between my gay constituents and my straight constituents. The fundamental objective of the gay community in San Francisco has to be preserving San Francisco as a viable place for people to live and that's also the number one agenda of the kind of non-gay people that I do politics with. If the gay community had some agenda that was inconsistent with the general well-being of the people of San Francisco, then there'd be a conflict.

I would hope that any gay person who is aware of what it means to be alienated would have a special kind of concern that every community, like the disabled community, which has been set aside by the political process, be supported in their efforts for social change. In San Francisco that means I spend a lot of time working with communities like the disabled and senior citizens who essentially are defined as weak, powerless people, and trying to support them in their efforts to see themselves as strong communities of human beings with legitimate claims to make on the political system.

LEYLAND: What is your position, Harry, on the use of Buena Vista Park and Land's End as places of sexual contact for gay men? This was one of the things sensationalized in the CBS program.

BRITT: Gay people do not need to apologize to anybody for what goes on at Buena Vista Park or Land's End or in any Greyhound bus station restroom anywhere in this country. Gay people growing up are not allowed the kind of natural meetings in their homes and in their schools, churches that straight people are allowed. It is understandable that our community has looked other places. Given that history there's every reason to suspect that gay people will come together for sexual meetings in places like Buena Vista Park. At the very least we don't need to say anything about that until such time as we are allowed the kind of natural places to meet that the rest of the world has. More importantly, gay people mustn't apologize for Buena Vista Park. I feel that the gay community's general standards of sexual behavior are superior to the general population; we're much freer, we're much more loving, we're much more resourceful than the general population. It really angers me that an uptight America says to the gay community: do what you want to as long as you do it in private and don't offend us. I am profoundly offended by the anti-gay attitudes and practices of the larger society, and I haven't heard any apologies forthcoming from them. What goes on in Buena Vista Park is a part of our community's efforts to discover ways of loving one another.

LEYLAND: What is your opinion of Dianne Feinstein's current stands on gay issues? Recently some gays have charged that she is opportunistic.

BRITT: Dianne Feinstein has not the faintest inkling of an understanding of what the gay community is all about. It may be that seven or eight years ago the gay community should have been grateful for any acknowledgment that we received from any establishment politican. But at this point in time it's insulting when we are asked to support people because seven or eight years ago they threw us some fish or other.

LEYLAND: What conflict do you find between your socialist views and your involvement in Democratic politics?

BRITT: There's a tension between having socialist views and participating in the United States of America. It's not just the Democratic Party. It's clear to me that the problems we're having with inflation, for instance, reflect structural problems of the American economy that are not going to be dealt with without challenging the veto power that Big Business has over America's economic decisions. We must democratize the economic process in this country, or I think the economy is just going to collapse. To articulate that position within the Democratic Party is a matter of great importance. We cannot let the Democratic Party go by default to the right. Under Jimmy Carter we had a Herbert Hoover view of economics and that's disastrous. Whatever credibility we have (and the gay community has a lot of credibility left now within the Democratic Party), we must use that to insist on radical changes in the economic system. As you try to articulate these radical changes, you get a lot of flack, whether you're within the Democratic Party or whether you're in a non-partisan situation like the San Francisco Board of Supervisors. I do not see, at this time, outside the Democratic Party a viable socialist force. I work with the Campaign for Economic Democracy which is within the Democratic Party, and I work with the Democratic Socialist Organizing Committee, which is within the Democratic Party; and I work with the New American Movement and other groups which are trying to define the political debate in this country around serious economic change.

LEYLAND: What is your opinion of David Goodstein, editor of the *Advocate*, and his est-inspired "Advocate Experience"? I know that Goodstein was originally an opponent of Harvey Milk and didn't support you.

BRITT: My views on Goodstein were published in an article I wrote for the February 1978 issue of *Gay Vote*, the newsletter published by the San Francisco Gay Democratic Club, under the title "Being Gay: A Lifestyle, Or Just Something We Do in Bed?" Here is the text:

"According to the March 8 [1978] issue of the *Advocate*, gay people are just like everybody else—only more so. Based on a survey of the *Advocate* readership, which is presumed to represent all of us, publisher David Goodstein points with pride to our remarkable success in acquiring the rewards held out by straight society. It seems forty-nine percent of us work out or lift weights, one-third own income-producing real estate, and seventy-eight percent have either an electric comb or hair dryer.

"Undeterred by the admittedly white, middle-class character of his sample (why *would* a woman read the *Advocate*?) Goodstein is 'flabbergasted' that some of us think life in the closet is unhealthy, and he deplores suggestions that gay people are oppressed outsiders.

"California's Lt. Gov. Mervyn Dymally, on the other hand, recently spoke of gay people as 'perhaps the most misunderstood and the most mistreated of all groups.' According to Dymally, the fact that we have become identifiable as a minority group within the political process has meant that 'the Gay Liberation Movement represents the advance guard of the human rights movement.'

"The conflict between these two points of view may be the most important issue facing our community. At its roots, it's a psychological division: Do we accept our gayness as defining who we are or do we mask it in order to be more acceptable to society? Is gayness something that otherwise 'normal' people do in bed or a lifestyle based on rejection with our very bodies of oppressive cultural values? All of us have tried hard not to be different; that struggle is at the heart of our particular suffering. But if we are to discover our special power as gay men and lesbians we must move beyond that struggle to affirm that which makes us different.

"The natural allies of David Goodstein are those who want a society based on everyone's conformity with affluent white male values. The natural allies of gay people are other minority groups, with whom we can build a freer, more just society based on respect for differences between people."

Goodstein and I come out of a different set of experiences and still have some work to do to look at life the same way. Politically I would say we represent different positions. I don't regard him as an enemy, but it's clear there are some things he would like for me to do that I'm not going to do. When Harvey was alive, he represented a certain political style; it seemed to me very urgent that he be supported against other political styles. I think I've carried on that political style, but I'm increasingly impressed that gay people who are more conservative than I am work within conservative areas. We (Goodstein and I) have a fundamental disagreement about several issues; I believe that the gay sense of alienation is a very fundamental, psychological and political fact that we are not ready to move beyond yet. I hear coming out of the "Advocate Experience" less of a sense of alienation and more of a sense that we're not different from heterosexuals except for the relatively unimportant fact of our sexual orientation. I do not sense in David Goodstein the same commitment to make serious changes in the system that I think gay people should want to have. He has more faith than I in the ability of gay people to find a place within society without changing society.

LEYLAND: What do you see as the main areas in which gay consciousness needs to be raised in San Francisco and the United States in general. In attitudes towards women's rights?

BRITT: Well, you know, the great thing about being gay is that you do not have the option of accepting a comfortable definition of sexuality and male/female relationships. Every gay person is involved from birth in the process of creating a special personality, a special personal answer to all the questions you're faced with in life. That's what alienation means, as the black community learned—to create a "soul." The gay community has produced a lot of different alternative self-understandings. I'm not interested in gay strategies to accommodate. People who are alienated around sexual orientation or because of sexism in society begin to develop alternative ways of existing, natural ways of relating to each other. It's more than consciousness-raising; it's a matter of building a future and inviting the people who are presently trapped in historically outmoded ways of relating to join us in that future. We get back to that essential difference, not between gay and straight, but between people who are comfortable in the inappropriate sexual modeling that goes on in this society and people who are not. And that should include all women who define themselves as women, and all gay people who are willing to define themselves in terms of their history as gay people. All of us have a responsibility, I think, for shaping a future free from sexism which will be a viable alternative for America in the twenty-first century. I don't think the models that are out there now, daddy on top and mommy on bottom, are going to be viable in the future. I really believe that the fundamental thing we have to do is to move away from personal and political strategies based on the sense of powerlessness and to develop personal and political strategies based on a sense of strength. If we will do that, we can really take the lead in freeing our society to be more natural and more loving—in its economic policies, foreign policy and everything else we do.

LEYLAND: What do you see as immediate priorities for gay people?

BRITT: It's still true that most gay people live in situations where it's illegal to be gay, and that needs to be changed. But I am more concerned with developing gay political power and coalitions with other political groups. We are not going to have gay civil rights for our people without challenging the anti-gay attitudes and sexism in our society: that should be the priority for people at the forefront of the gay movement. To eradicate sexism is the prerequisite of effective social change in this country, and I think we're doing it.

PHOTO BY JOEL SINGER, 1982

JAMES
BROUGHTON

JAMES BROUGHTON (born 1913) is a San Francisco poet and teacher, an author of many books and plays, and a widely known pioneer in the realm of avant-garde cinema and poetry. He remains, in fact, the only established American poet consistently engaged in filmmaking. In 1975 he received Film Culture's Twelfth Independent Film Award for his outstanding work of thirty years and was cited as "the grand classic master of Independent Cinema."

Broughton was an original member of the Art in Cinema group who exhibited at the San Francisco Museum of Art in the late forties. His collaboration with Sidney Peterson in 1946, *The Potted Psalm*, helped launch the postwar experimental film movement in the USA. His first solo film in 1948, *Mother's Day*, now considered a classic of poetic cinema, is included in the collections of all major film museums. Other early films include *Loony Tom, Four in the Afternoon*, and *Adventures of Jimmy*. Under the sponsorship of the British Film Institute in 1953 he created a comic fantasy in London, *The Pleasure Garden*, which was awarded a special jury prize at the Cannes Film Festival of 1954.

During this same period Broughton was active in writing, reciting, and printing poetry. He started the Centaur Press with Kermit Sheets, he launched a forum for poetry readings with Robert Duncan and Madeline Gleason, he wrote for the Interplayers theater. His first book, *The Playground* (1949), was a verse play. Since then he has published seventeen other books, the most recent of which are: *Seeing the Light* (1977), *The Androgyne Journal* (1977), *Hymns to Hermes* (1979), and *Graffiti for the Johns of Heaven* (1982).

From 1958 to 1964 Broughton was resident playwright with the Playhouse Repertory Theater in San Francisco where six of his plays were first performed, notably *The Last Word, Where Helen Lies*, and *The Rites of Women*. During 1969 he was Playwright Fellow at the Eugene O'Neill Theater Foundation in Waterford, Connecticut, where his concurrent play, *Bedlam*, was produced.

Broughton resumed active filmmaking in 1968 with *The Bed*, a work commissioned by the Royal Film Archive of Belgium. Since that time he has produced a new film every year for the past ten years. These include such distinguished works as *The Golden Positions, This Is It, Dreamwood, Testament*, and *Erogeny*, which have won prizes at film festivals throughout the world and received wide critical acclaim. Retrospectives of his work have been held at the Museum of Modern Art in New York, the National Film Theatre in London, the Danish Filmmuseum, the Centre Beaubourg in Paris, and the Conservatoire d'Art Cinématographique in Montreal.

For many years Broughton taught in the School of Creative Arts at San Francisco State University. He is at present on the faculty of the San Francisco Art Institute. Twice he has been awarded Guggenheim Fellowships (in 1971 and again in 1973), as well as receiving an individual grant in 1976 from the National Endowment for the Arts.

THE PRESENT INTERVIEW, which appeared originally in *Gay Sunshine* no. 44/45 (tenth anniversary issue), 1980, was taped at Broughton's home in Marin County in October 1979 by Robert Peters. Also present was Broughton's lover and collaborator, the Canadian-born filmmaker Joel Singer. Peters (b. 1924), who currently teaches Victorian literature and poetry writing workshops at the University of California, Irvine, is known as a poet and has published more than ten books. See the in-depth interview with him elsewhere in this book.

Robert Peters interviews
JAMES BROUGHTON

PETERS: Is it true that you were once kissed by Cocteau?

BROUGHTON: And I kissed him back. I am rather known for liking to kiss men whenever possible.

PETERS: Where did this encounter take place?

BROUGHTON: In France, at the Cannes Film Festival of 1954. Cocteau was chairman of the Jury of Awards, which also included Luis Buñuel. The jury awarded my film, *The Pleasure Garden,* a special prize for poetic fantasy. The fact that Cocteau liked my movie thrilled me greatly because he had been for years a particular inspiration to me in pursuing my own form of film poetry. Though there is no apparent connection, my first solo film, *Mother's Day,* was invigorated by my repeated viewings of *Beauty and the Beast* in San Francisco in 1947. That opened for me the whole possibility of a cinema of poetic imagination.

PETERS: Did this exchange of kisses lead to any intimacy between you and Cocteau?

BROUGHTON: If you have read in Ned Rorem's *Paris Diary* of his first visit to Cocteau, you will know how the famous man protected himself from casual intimacy. Rather than communicating he put on a diverting performance. But he was aware that *The Pleasure Garden* was an homage to his own magic world, in its setting, its transformations, and its triumph of the romantic. Even though its tone is more comic than anything Cocteau would ever have written, I accepted his embrace as an approval of my own role as a poet in film. He said mine was a very French film for an American to make in England.

PETERS: What do you think he meant by that?

BROUGHTON: That I had obviously been influenced by the films of Méliès, Vigo, René Clair and Buñuel, as well as by the esprit of French music and painting. Years later, in 1972, I produced a film much closer to Cocteau's measured style in *Blood of a Poet:* a journey to the interior of the soul, not through a mirror but through a primeval forest, to the "bed of the ultimate rapture." This is my work called *Dreamwood,* which was made on a Guggenheim Fellowship and which featured Margo St. James. It is my major homage to Cocteau.

PETERS: Like so much of your work *The Pleasure Garden* is a celebration of life rather than a denunciation of people who would turn the world into a cemetery. In dealing with strictures put upon our sexual and creative freedoms, how is it that you seem always to find much humor and delight in such confrontations?

BROUGHTON: Apparently I was born cheerful. They told me I came in smiling and never cried as a baby. Sunny Jim was my first nickname. I seemed to approve of the world, and for a while the world seemed to approve of me. However, not many years later when my individual personality began to develop my mother took a much dimmer view of me. To her eye I was plainly developing into that dreaded creature, a sissy who preferred ballet and poetry to football and business. My mother had very stern ideas of how *he* a man óught to be.

PETERS: Whenever you refer to your mother, it sounds as if she was always peeking in to see whether you were playing with yourself. Like your poem that begins, "What a big nose Mrs Mother has."

BROUGHTON: I suffered greatly from her disapprovals. I was berated and beaten for manifesting my true enthusiasms and enjoyments. In fact, the heavy Puritan morality that surrounded me as a child was oppressive and its wounds still haunt me. But as I described in my Foreword to *A Long Undressing* and in my film *Testament:* "One night when I was three years old I was awakened by a glittering stranger who told me I was a poet and never to fear being alone or being laughed at. That was my first meeting with my angel who is the most interesting poet I have ever met."

PETERS: Have you ever met this angel again?

BROUGHTON: He has always appeared to me whenever I was bamboozled or heavy-laden. He carried me through the agonies of childhood. What desecrated shambles might I be if it had not been for him? And now, wonder of wonders, he has come to live with me in the flesh, and permanently. In the person of Joel here—this beautiful thirty-year-old angel.

PETERS: When you first saw Joel did you recognize who he was?

BROUGHTON: No. But I did when we first went to bed together. All the trumpets in heaven started tooting. The sound of wings was deafening. That, and the applause of the gods.

PETERS: In your film *Testament* was that Joel who acted the role of your phallic muse?

BROUGHTON: Doesn't it look like him? It's amazing. That sequence was filmed two years before Joel ever came to San Francisco. So I must have had an image of Joel in my soul when I chose the Greek student in my Art Institute class to act the part, and directed him to fertilize the huge egg of my life which Aphrodite finds in the grass. Certainly I wanted such a Mercurius angel to participate benevolently in my creative life. I had regularly invoked an erotic image of a god, but I never really expected him to manifest as an actual human being that I would fall in love with. After all, I was married and living in suburbia with two children, ten and twelve years of age.

PETERS: What about you, Joel? Did you also invoke an image?

SINGER: When I was about thirteen I became conscious of a powerful attraction to older men and from that time on all my masturbation fantasies and longings involved men much older than myself. And they were always poets. Then some thirteen years later when I first encountered James at the San Francisco Art Institute, I immediately recognized in him my idealized lover.

PETERS: How did you get together with this amazing mad person?

SINGER: James was my graduate adviser at the school. He was the only faculty person who genuinely responded to my film work, so I arranged as many meetings with him as I could. I was madly in love with him but then he took a leave of absence for a semester and I didn't see him for three months, which was devastating. But one night I bumped into him at the Berkeley Museum where a four-hour-long experimental film was being screened. He had just returned from Philadelphia. We sat next to each other and held hands throughout the entire film. I arranged to meet him later that week to show him the film I had been working on during his absence. It was called *Perisphere* and was dedicated to him. After watching it we suddenly found ourselves locked in a passionate embrace, I think he was sitting on my lap. I remember then walking with him to his car and just as he was about to drive away I leaned in and asked him if he wanted to get it on. He said yes.

BROUGHTON: And with some amazement. I had never before had such a direct proposition from a student. I was as confused as I was dazzled. Joel's entrance into my life had the effect of an earthquake. I went to consult a famous psychic in Sacramento. She told me that Joel and I had been soulmates for centuries, that we had experienced various lives together during the past two thousand years, having been father and daughter, husband and wife, fellow nuns, and other combinations of sex and relationship. All this confirmed what we ourselves had felt: the shock of recognition of having belonged together since the beginning of time.

PETERS: Do you believe in reincarnation?

BROUGHTON: We have both experienced some of our former existences through past-life recall with Dr. Helen Wambach. What fascinated me was to learn that everyone has been as often a woman as a man in his sequence of lives on earth. This confirmed my vision of the androgynous nature of man. And Joel has made my own androgyny much more real to me. What is most wondrous: he has reconnected me to my "original nature," to the freedom of the beautiful and potent first love I experienced in my early teens. And he is himself the great love I had been, unknowingly, searching for ever since.

PETERS: How did that first love happen?

BROUGHTON: When I was sent away to boys' school at the age of nine. You see, my father had died when I was five, in the influenza epidemic after the First World War. My mother, still a young woman, set about capturing a new and richer husband. She dragged my brother and myself to respectable resorts where we were dressed in sailor suits and told to be polite when we were exhibited to men in golf knickers. The man she finally chose was a self-made Republican bigot. He was horrified by my desire to be a ballerina. He refused to marry my mother until I was sent away to military academy where they would "make a man" of me.

PETERS: What was military school like for someone as sensitive as you?

BROUGHTON: Actually it turned out to be quite unpunitive, once I got used to it. And in time became a kind of Eden, although I didn't realize that until later. At first it was astonishing and exhilarating to find myself in a dormitory of boys playing with themselves and with one another. Eventually I formed passionate friendships, hero-worships and love affairs. By the time I was eleven years old I had completed my initiation into the erotic camaraderie of males, ranging from the playful to the fiercely loyal. Having been raised, like most boys, largely by women—governesses, babysitters, gradeschool teachers, sturdy aunts, and a widowed mother—I found it exciting to be living exclusively among men and boys. I was happy for the first time since the days when my father was alive. I had discovered the enchantment of the male body.

PETERS: Do you think this early experience among males prompted the themes that run throughout your work?

BROUGHTON: The first love of anyone's life is usually a powerful conditioning factor. In my case I was fortunate to experience at the school a remarkable, an ineffable love relationship which lasted until I was fifteen. He was not the first boy I had been to bed with, but he was certainly the most ravishing. He is the one called Littlejohn in *The Androgyne Journal* where I tell about his golden glories. He was captain of the baseball team, muscular, blond, with one of the most beautiful penises I have ever known intimately. Furthermore he possessed an absolutely intoxicating body odor.

PETERS: He sounds like something ideal.

BROUGHTON: Not only that, he was also one of the tenderest lovers I have ever had. Every morning, before the other boys were awake, he came to my bed and gave me love lessons. He taught me all the delicious pleasures of making love. He instructed my body in all its erogenous abilities. He taught me the raptures of sexuality. What a poetic way to begin the day!

PETERS: Were you already writing poetry at this time?

BROUGHTON: Constantly. I think the poetic impulse awoke in me in conjunction with my love for boys. Maybe that is why poetry has always been for me a kind of erotic turn-on. Writing poetry is almost as orgasmic as sex. I was also writing plays then because I was fascinated by theater forms and the possibilities of the stage.

PETERS: Did you and Littlejohn ever suffer any mockery or punishment from the other boys in the school? Or from the teachers?

BROUGHTON: No, the whole place was permissively loving. Many other boys had passionate attachments too. Some were even excessive in daily fucking. It was wonderfully innocent and natural. No, the axe fell upon my love from outside the school. From my own mother.

PETERS: How did that happen?

BROUGHTON: After the autumn when I had turned fifteen, Littlejohn went to New York with an uncle for the Christmas holidays. He wrote letters to me about the plays he was seeing, and in answering them I said how eagerly I looked forward to making love with him again, how I longed to kiss every inch of his body. I remember that was the exact phrase I used. Well, my mother must have been suspicious. She intercepted one of my letters before I could mail it. I was called on the carpet before her and my stepfather and denounced for having committed the most despicable sin possible to man. Such an evil relationship would have to cease immediately. I was abruptly removed from the school then and there and kept virtually a prisoner at home in San Francisco. I was sent to a big public high school nearby and made to report home right after school to be locked in my room for the night. I was shattered and bewildered. How could the most beautiful and natural thing that had ever come into my life be a disgusting crime? Why was loving someone the worst thing I could possibly do?

PETERS: Did you feel like a member of a persecuted minority?

BROUGHTON: I was struck forever by the absurd hypocrisy of the grownup world which preached love for one's fellowmen and then branded one a pariah for actually loving a fellowman. I was hurt, confused and resentful. But I had enjoyed five crucial years that bound me forever to the knowledge of the pleasure that males could enjoy together. I was cast out of my Eden but I would never forget the bliss of sweet adhesive comrades.

PETERS: Is that experience the source of the erotic affirmations which run throughout your work, from the boisterous Pan of *Loony Tom* to your latest celebration of the phallus in the *Hymns to Hermes*?

BROUGHTON: I guess it might be. I have often thought that a solution for the ills of the world would be to send all boys to a school that taught them to love one another. And I mean real loving, the way Littlejohn taught me. I don't mean rhetorical peptalks. I mean get them all into bed together to learn the ecstatic habit of male love.

PETERS: Would you seriously advocate such an educational system?

BROUGHTON: Why not? Why couldn't there be a world where people love rather than destroy? Governments provide millions for weapons and wars. Have they ever spent a dollar to finance national love training?

PETERS: Does Joel at all resemble your Littlejohn?

BROUGHTON: No. Littlejohn was a golden Greek god, Joel is a darkeyed angel of the Lord. Joel comes passionately out of Biblical song like a redeeming Eros disguised as Gabriel. You see how polytheistic I am. I am always personifying the powers of the universe because they take forms and speak to me.

PETERS: When I was writing my Shaker book, *The Gift to Be Simple,* I felt possessed by Ann the Shaker woman, I felt her speak through me. Do you feel possessed by your spirits?

BROUGHTON: They speak *through* me as much as they speak *to* me. They are my connections to the mysteries of life. For me poets are divine messengers who transmit the visions they receive from the invisible knowers of the words. They are priests in the service of the inexplicable. The more clearly they deliver their unclear messages the greater their work.

PETERS: I am reminded of Spicer's notion of the poet as a kind of radio set for some program out there in the universe. With Spicer it was like a funky old

Atwater-Kent radio trying to get through the static to reach the right channel. You, however, give it a more metaphysical dimension.

BROUGHTON: Whether funky or transcendental it is crucial to poetry. This is where you separate the true-born poets from the ones who take it up as useful academic business. Poetry as a commodity in the literary world is one kind of business, but the real thing, the authentic business, is in the direct service of the divine. I think poetry's purpose is to bring us closer to the divine ground of being. Insistently secular literature without any vision of the archetypal is for me only a provisional treat.

PETERS: Even if we don't give names to these archetypes, we still experience them, don't we? A cave, for example. We may not have any real idea of Plato's cave, but if we look into a hole in the ground we may have prehistoric responses to it.

BROUGHTON: Whenever I encounter a cave, I can't help expecting Hermes to emerge from it with a message from the souls in the underworld.

PETERS: Aren't there other possibilities in a cave? The anus, the vulva? A mouth, a womb?

BROUGHTON: I have been wanting to make a film of the caves of the body, of all the private orifices. I think they are direct gates to the soul.

PETERS: When Manson and his "family" got stoned they used a portable toilet in the stoning room because no one was allowed to leave the room. One girl was shy about shitting in public. Manson's response to this was to stretch himself out and make everyone look at his asshole, to show that this was the place where all males and females were exactly alike.

BROUGHTON: Oh, but they're not! There are enormous differences. I photographed a great many assholes in Pittsburgh and I was astonished at the variety of shapes and textures and colors. Look, you have just recently seen my own asshole close-up in the *Song of the Godbody* film that Joel made of my body. Did mine look like anyone else's you know?

PETERS: I thought maybe it was a black tulip coming into flower.

BROUGHTON: And you couldn't be sure whether it mas male or female? Straight or gay? So that is the metaphysical point, perhaps. Every cave is different but every cave is like a cave, and every cave is an opening to a chakra and a process.

PETERS: I grew up thinking that women didn't have assholes because they were too pure to shit. I never heard my mother fart and never smelled anything. We had an outdoor outhouse so there was no telling whose you were smelling. My mother led me to believe that men were dirty because they always wanted sex and that women were always clean and kept themselves washed all the time the way she did. As a result men became very interesting to me because they were dirty. Maybe that's why I'm so trashy today.

BROUGHTON: My mother was censorious only about sexual behavior. Other natural functions, like belching and farting, were cause for laughter in her life. I don't think one should, in any case, make an either/or out of trashy versus lofty. The two go together as do all opposites. For me sacred and profane dance hand in hand. I admire my beloved's turds as much as his big brown eyes.

PETERS: Your approach to religion seems very lighthearted. Were you raised in any particular denomination?

BROUGHTON: I was confirmed in the Anglican communion. Probably because my grandmother Broughton was a devoted pillar of the Episcopal Church. She often entertained the bishop, and I particularly enjoyed his constant quotations which always began, "As the poet says. . . ." That, and the fact that he regularly patted my head and squeezed my arm. I still love the ritual of high mass: the pageantry, the poetry of the gospel, the robes and candles and incense. I have always paid more attention to the music than to the doctrine. I have my own trinities: like Jesus, Dionysus and Shiva. And Pan, Krishna and Anubis. I pray also to the blue monkey who turns the Wheel of Fortune and to the Norns who put together the great jigsaw puzzles of our fates.

PETERS: Did your ancestors come from England?

BROUGHTON: My grandmother's family came to Massachusetts from Somerset in the seventeenth century while my grandfather's ancestors were settlers with Oglethorpe in the Carolinas. Their strains cross in the Mother Lode, for both my grandparents were born in California. You can understand why I feel rooted in American history and literature. For instance I have always felt at home with the Transcendentalists. My three closest literary gurus I call Willy, Waldo, and Walt. The second two I'm sure you can identify. The first one is that other transcendent poet so important and precious to me, William Blake.

PETERS: Did you have other lovers after Littlejohn?

BROUGHTON: It took a long time for me to recover from the castration of that first love. How much we all suffer from the righteousness of the wrongheaded! I had not even wanted to go to Stanford, that was a snobbism of my mother's. By the fourth year there I could stand it no longer and I ran away. I ran all the way to New York, hitchhiking, where I got a job in the merchant marine. The only book I took to sea with me was the Everyman edition of Emerson's *Essays*. I still have that book here. See, the binding has fallen off. And look how the essay on "Self-Reliance" is heavily underlined. Emerson was a great comfort to me on that adventure, particularly for his lofty vision of the function of the poet.

PETERS: Were you on the crew of a ship?

BROUGHTON: Yes I was, and I found it bracing to be living again among men, to be sleeping in a bunkroom with seven other males. One of them on that first voyage was Emil Oppfer who had been the beloved of Hart Crane. He introduced me to hot zabaglione one morning in Genoa and we became affectionate buddies. Later on he also introduced me to certain editors in New York when we were living there and he was writing for Danish newspapers. Thus began my years of hit-and-miss journalism from the *New Republic* to the *Herald-Tribune*. But these were also the Depression years that led to the war, times of disorientation and loneliness when the life of poetry was devalued by collective utility. "War effort" was never my kind of effort. I grieved for the doomed boys in the service and caressed as many of them as I could, in bars and baths and bushes. My creative life found no room to blossom until the end of the war.

PETERS: How old were you then?

BROUGHTON: I was thirty-two. In *Seeing the Light* the first sentence reads "When I was thirty my greatest consolation was the thought of suicide." But two years later I discovered what I call in that book The Brotherhood of Light, by which I mean the beautiful creative friendships that life offers us, "the love between fellow artists." These renewed my life after the miseries of wartime. Of course I continued my solitary writing. But now collaborations with other creative men provided a great source of stimulus anud affectionate involvement. These began with Sidney Peterson when he and I made a larky dada film called *The Potted Psalm* in 1946, and then a year later with Frank Stauffacher I began shooting *Mother's Day* and pouring my heart into it. During that project Kermit Sheets came into my life and helped me with directing and editing the film. Thus began a creative collaboration that was lastingly fertile. By 1948, the year that Joel was being born in Montreal, Kermit and I were settled in the flat on Baker Street which Pauline Kael and I had fixed up the year before. In the basement we established the Centaur Press to print books of poetry and upstairs in the parlor we set up the editing table for Farallone Films. Anaïs Nin gave us a font of type, Robert Duncan gave us a manuscript, Adrian Wilson gave us advice. Kermit not only helped me give birth to my films and plays, he himself brought forth handsome creations in the books of my poems that he printed. That was similar to what Joel is doing now, printing with his own loving intensity. Creative love relationships can produce remarkable offspring.

PETERS: Do you mean that in your collaborations you feel you are creating a child by another man? Or he is having one by you?

BROUGHTON: Yes, they are like love affairs that produce a mutual pregnancy. I have always sexualized my feeling for those I worked with, whether they were straight or gay, but only recently have I become aware of how strongly this has been an erotic element throughout my life. Don't all men who work together closely experience something of this? Maybe it should be made more conscious. Maybe all the partnerships, enterprises and expeditions that men engage in should be more overtly erotic.

PETERS: Would you try to sexualize all business?

BROUGHTON: Wouldn't that be more interesting? The first psychiatrist I ever went to, an Adlerian, condemned homosexuals for their tendency to sexualize all aspects of life. I on the other hand would consider this a great contribution to society. In fact, I am for sexualizing everything: education, religion, politics, institutions, science. I would like to see sexual love implicit in all acts of human interchange. Sexualize the schools! Sexualize the churches! Sexualize the armed forces, so that they will lay down their arms to lie in one another's arms!

PETERS: You sound like some kind of erotic mystic.

BROUGHTON: I am, I am! I want nothing less than to establish Holy Orders of Sexual Love throughout the world.

PETERS: Are you speaking of gay men?

BROUGHTON: No, of all men—straight and crooked, big and little, gay and glum, young and old. I envision the loving comradeship of all men even more literally than Walt Whitman did. My *Hymns to Hermes* celebrate the phallic power and creative energy which all men share, and which women delight in too. Gay men may acknowledge a more conscious sense of phallic pleasures, but all males relish them privately.

PETERS: How long did your relationship with Kermit Sheets last?

BROUGHTON: Many years. International interest in the films took us to Britain in 1951, and there we made *The Pleasure Garden* thanks to many generous English talents. It was the special devotion of Lindsay Anderson and Basil Wright that ensured the completion of that rather precarious project. Later, when we lived in Paris, Kermit nursed the printing of my *Almanac for Amorists* through Olympia Press. Our particular friends in Paris were Alfred Chester, Edouard Roditi, Christopher Logue, Eugene Walter, Kenneth Anger, and the boys of the *Paris Review*. I wrote *True & False Unicorn* in Paris and Princess Caetani published it in Rome. Our last summer in Europe we spent with Auden on Ischia. When we returned to San Francisco, the Beat Boys were gathering, led by that punchy trio who still perform together—Ginsberg, Orlovsky, and Corso. We were all scooped up into a new era in North Beach. Kermit decided to take on a fulltime job of theater management, so after a time we lived separately. But our collaborations in theater and cinema continued off and on until 1970.

PETERS: You have also been married and had children. Did you feel you were completing yourself in a different way when you slept with a woman as distinct from when you slept with a man?

BROUGHTON: Sex with a woman is simply a very different experience, and one that can be barrels of fun in its own way if love is truly involved. Marriage, however, requires a special aptitude. It becomes a game of opposites, a dance of life and death, a concern with priorities and procreation.

PETERS: In my own marriage I seemed always to be held in the same relationship to my wife, held in one kind of captured role, and I didn't understand why a woman would want me to be the same way all the time. What has been your experience?

BROUGHTON: It's true that in heterosexual marriage one is locked into the stereotypes of householder, breadwinner and, above all, parent. That becomes confining and inflexible. By contrast, in my life now with Joel I can enjoy living out all aspects of myself, including some I didn't know I had. I can also be son and father, bride and mother, old wiz and baby brother. And so can he. I can encompass an androgynous richness of soul that a wife would find discomfiting. I think it unfortunate that many a woman, for fear of losing her husband, cannot allow him freedom to pursue his masculine soul-adventures.

PETERS: How did you happen to get married?

BROUGHTON: I was in my forties, I was deeply into Oriental philosophy and Jungian analysis, and I was in love with Stan Brakhage. But he would have none of it, and I was weary of living alone and feeling myself an outsider. My friendship at this time with Alan Watts was a great joy and a real intimacy of the spirit. We were soulmates of a fine comradely sort: whenever we met we would burst into laughter as if we shared some delicious cosmic joke. Which we did. I loved him dearly, but he too was married. During this period Suzanna was a lively companion and confidante. Our friendship had arisen in the theater world, I enjoyed her warmth and outrageous wit, we grew very close. At our wedding Alan Watts was the officiating minister, Kermit Sheets was best man, and Stan Brakhage filmed the event. Within a year we had a baby girl and two years later a baby boy.

PETERS: Are you glad you've had children?

BROUGHTON: Of course, of course. I think they're fascinating. I enjoy watching them evolve, I'm very curious how their lives will develop.

PETERS: When they were babies did they bring out a special kind of androgyny in you? I know I enjoyed being a mother, changing pants, feeding them, burping them. It was like letting the female side of me come out.

BROUGHTON: Don't most fathers experience something of that? Almost every couple has to take turns with the diapers and with pushing the stroller around the park. The strongest empathy I felt with motherhood occurred in the delivery room. I was present, right alongside my wife, when each child was born. I really felt then that we both gave birth to them.

PETERS: Don't you feel that a gay father is capable of giving a different sort of love to a child than a straight father? I know with my own children the bond of affection was disrupted when I left the family to live out my gay needs. The kids have had to be much more open-minded and tolerant, they have had to love me in a different way than they would have had I not been gay.

BROUGHTON: Perhaps androgynous parents would be more likely to produce tolerant human beings. My children are still teenagers and have yet to find their individual forms of living and loving. My main concern is not to burden them with expectations and denunciations such as I suffered.

PETERS: Do they seem comfortable when they visit you and Joel?

SINGER: As far as we can tell they seem perfectly relaxed with us, and they accept our life together. James and I have been living together for four years, and we've traveled many places with the children. We include them in all our activities, from the Gay Freedom Day parades to Christmas dinner with their cousins.

PETERS: You have spoken about creating imaginative children with your collaborators. How do you compare them to your real children?

BROUGHTON: I don't feel that the human children belong to me in the same way. That is, I think of them as independent souls who will make their own lives their own way as I have made mine, contradictory to everything my family expected of me. On the other hand my figurative children, those I have given birth to from the fertilizations of male collaborators, belong to me in a very real sense. They are accurate expressions of me, perpetuations of my spirit and personality. Most parents mistakenly claim this of their natural children and are usually disappointed. My human children keep changing and surprise me, the imaginative ones never change but continue to surprise other people.

PETERS: Do you think of yourself as bisexual?

BROUGHTON: I prefer the term androgynous.

PETERS: I want to question that term. I know that you have written about your own experience of this in *The Androgyne Journal*. But doesn't it simply imply a freakish creature with breasts and male genitals?

BROUGHTON: Hermaphrodite is the term used for the anomaly of the two sex organs in one creature. Androgyne is the more symbolic word. It refers to the original unity of everything, the concept of a divine creature being both masculine and feminine and hence different from both of these. Unfortunately the word has decadent associations since it was used in nineteenth-century literature to denote the immature and the effete. Can you think up a better word to describe the mystery of the Two in the One that make a transcendent Other? Instead of Androgyne would you prefer a word invention like HeShe?

PETERS: Do you think it necessary to attach gender to feelings of sensitivity or toughness?

BROUGHTON: Only as metaphor. It's only a way, however awkward, of talking about things which are hard to express when our language is based on oppositions and dichotomies and makes no allowance for an Irrational Third. It is the Either/Or mentality which straitjackets our thinking, so that one is invariably asked to choose between—between him or her, gay or straight, right or wrong, good or evil. You are never allowed both. In my teaching I crusade for the beautiful Both/And, for the He & She in everybody. Men need to experience both thrust and surrender, receptivity as well as assertion, being fucked as well as fucking. I think this has to be fully experienced in the body. It's easy enough for people to give lip service to the idea of opposites living in dynamic harmony, but very few of them take the risk of living out the experience of their potential androgyny. I have been urging these themes in most of my films since 1967.

PETERS: How did you happen to make *The Bed* after not making any films for many years?

BROUGHTON: After five years of marriage devoted largely to babies I had a desire for fresh grownup adventures. I had published several books in those years and taught at San Francisco State—where Kermit produced my *Bedlam* play—but no film ideas had reached production. Then one day out of the blue a sturdy redhead from Stanford's film school appeared at my door. Brimming with racy energy and high spirits, he offered me his complete devotion to any project I might want to shoot. I had been given a commission from the Belgian Film Archive and here was the tough angel of a cameraman to make it real: his name was Bill Desloge. This was 1967, the "summer of love" time in San Francisco. With our mutual friends and acquaintances we made a lovefeast together, exploring the polymorphous possibilities of the life of a bed.

PETERS: Did you have trouble at that time showing the film because of the nudity in it?

BROUGHTON: I even had trouble finding a lab that would print it. Yet before long nudity became commonplace in films. *The Bed* was a bit ahead of its time just as *Mother's Day* and *The Pleasure Garden* had been. It is difficult to believe nowadays that these films were considered outrageous when first shown; they were prompted only by delight and the politics of pleasure.

PETERS: In *The Golden Positions* in 1970 you celebrated the nude human form in an utterly delightful way, parodying the history of art and literature in undressed living tableaux. And then at the end there is an extraordinary group of sculptural couplings: a man and a woman posing in a variety of tangled embraces. Were you trying there to personify erotically the concept of the two-in-one androgyne that we were talking about?

BROUGHTON: Yes, yes! There you have the He and She in HeShe positions of union which no couple would normally get into. I was trying to make iconic metaphors of how we might feel the experience of androgyny. It is a kind of western Tantra. I approached the subject another way in the final scenes of *Dreamwood* where the hero is shown after the orgasm of his quest with the princess of his soul revealed within his own body. Did you know that *Dreamwood* deals with the epiphany I described in *The Androgyne Journal:* my actual copulation with the Earth?

PETERS: Your very latest film, the one called *Hermes Bird,* where you show Joel's beautiful cock taking ten minutes to rise to its full erection, made me uncomfortable watching it. I've never before looked at a cock undistractedly for ten minutes. And your ecstatic Hermes poems on the soundtrack were like religious music accompanying the image. It challenged my furtiveness about sexual expression—you know, when you feel that a cock will disappear before you have done with it all that you want to do.

BROUGHTON: I intended *Hermes Bird* as a contemplative movie. I hope men will look at it and recognize with joy that this is the eternal phallic miracle which they all share. I want them to take pride in their genital splendor, not be ashamed of it. The film was shot in extreme slow motion with one of the official cameras used to photograph atomic tests at Bikini. This way you see the phallus as you never could in reality, every small pulse and throb of it as it slowly opens into flower, growing in thrust and assurance, elevating toward heaven. I think our cocks are much wiser than our minds. They keep us in touch with our divine instincts, they are the creative joysticks of the soul.

PETERS: Are you saying that fucking is a religious experience?

BROUGHTON: Sexual union is the most religious experience possible, it is the most thrilling form of meditation, it is direct contact with the divine. In the man that I embrace it is the god in the body that I salute. I want to go to bed with God, I want to fuck God, I want to be fucked by God. That's what I mean when I say "I believe in ecstasy for everyone."

PETERS: Do you think the sensation that one has being fucked by a man is anything at all like what a woman feels?

BROUGHTON: How can we tell? But why shouldn't the surrender to love be comparable for all human beings? One thing I do know is that my most profound visionary insights come to me at times of sexual surrender. This is when I am completely united with the gods.

PETERS: But this is utterly opposed to the teaching of all religions.

BROUGHTON: That is exactly what is wrong with all religions.

PETERS: Can promiscuity be a way to salvation?

BROUGHTON: Certainly. It is the search for the divine in one's fellow creatures. Cruising should be called The Quest for the Holy Male.

PETERS: Doesn't sex militate against productivity in creating?

BROUGHTON: On the contrary! Come forth, come forth, at least once every day!

PETERS: You mean, if you come every day, then you produce every day? Is that one of Broughton's laws?

BROUGHTON: I think it should be a law of the land.

PETERS: So now with Joel you have a full-time live-in collaborator? He is making films *with* you and films *of* you, he is inspiring your poems and printing them with his own hands, he is a great cook and a young father for your teenage children...

BROUGHTON: And he is the world's greatest lover! Yes, I have the ultimate in collaborations. Joel ties my whole life together back to its source and opens it anew. Isn't it extraordinary that the truest love of my life should come to me in my sixties? And make me thirty-two all over again. Our love defies all rational strictures. Which probably proves why it is valid.

PETERS: Was it difficult to disentangle from your wife? I remember my own wife saying, "If only it had been another woman, I would have known how to fight back."

BROUGHTON: Our intimacy had been waning for some time. But I expected, as I suppose most husbands do, that we would continue in some kind of reasonable truce. Suzanna knew my history with Kermit, she knew that I had been in love with Brakhage before I married her. Still this was humiliating for her and she resented the separation. I had qualms of my own at first, but resistance was futile. Joel did not create a mere sexual triangle. He came from another world, calling me to the fulfillment of my destiny as a poet.

PETERS: Do you think it important that gay couples consummate their devotion through an actual marriage ceremony, as you and Joel have done?

BROUGHTON: Only if they feel it necessary, as we did. We wanted a way of sanctifying on earth what we felt was already ordained in heaven. We felt the power of it privately and we wanted to objectify our faith that our sexual love was sacred.

PETERS: Where did your wedding take place?

SINGER: Actually we have had three weddings, in three consecutive years. The first one took place in Montreal at Christmastime and was rather like an impulsive elopement. We were staying in a funky old hotel in Vieux Montreal. I went out in the snow early one morning to get us some coffee and on a chance I phoned a gay priest I had been told about. He was a Marist father, very active for gay rights in Quebec. We met him later that day and he said it was quite obvious that we were meant for one another, so he arranged to marry us the following afternoon which was Christmas Eve. The ceremony took place in a storefront chapel on Blvd St.-Laurent with a pair of gay clergymen as our witnesses. It was a secret and special Christmas present to ourselves. Then, the following summer when we were again in Montreal—for the World Film Festival to which James had been invited—we were offered a more elaborate ceremony at a big house in the Quebec countryside. The same Marist father officiated, but in company with an Anglican priest in his full regalia also, which pleased James and probably his forefathers. My two sisters were present, my dearest old friend was best man, and twenty members of the Montreal Gay Community Church were handsome wedding guests.

BROUGHTON: A year later we had a third wedding in California. Legally I had been a bigamist till then since my divorce from Suzanna wasn't final. When the dissolution was granted, we had a long festive ceremony aboard the old ferryboat in Sausalito where Alan Watts used to live and where he gave me my first LSD experience. This time the priest was a Methodist from the Glide Memorial who makes films for the National Sex Forum. I wrote a poetic masque for the occasion celebrating the androgynous wonder of all such unions. I called it *Behold the Bridegrooms.* [Printed in 10th Anniversary Issue of *Gay Sunshine Journal,* 1980.]

PETERS: You two must feel fully wed to one another by this time. What do you look forward to now?

BROUGHTON: Going to heaven together. Until then I would like to devote myself to the bringing of erotic enlightenment to all sentient beings. As I wrote in *Hymns to Hermes:*

> *Let us be fireworking diamonds*
> *Let us become orgasmic goldsmiths*
> *Let us give birth to a new breed*
> > *Lovemen of the Godbody*
> > *Holymen of Fuckerie*

PHOTO BY RALPH SIMMONS

KIRBY
CONGDON

KIRBY CONGDON was born in 1924. His first publication was in *One, The Homosexual Magazine* in 1955, and two collections of poems, *Juggernaut* (1966) and *Dream-Work* (1970, reprinted as *Chain Drive* in Great Britain, 1976), are centered on the male image. A third collection, *The Academy*, is in progress. *Dream-Work* is called "an underground classic" in *The Male Homosexual in Literature: A Bibliography* by Ian Young, and representative work is included in the anthologies *The Male Muse, Angels of the Lyre*, and *Orgasms of Light*. His collection of prose poems on men, motorcycles, sex, and death, *Fantoccini*, appeared in 1981. He met his former partner, Jay Socin (1914–1968) at Cherry Grove and his present partner, Ralph Simmons, at a leather and motorcycle bar in Manhattan. They live in Brooklyn and spend as much time as they can at Fire Island Pines or in Key West. Ralph is office manager for Modernismo, a mail-order house for male art and erotica, and runs his own Cycle Press, an avant-garde publishing outfit. Congdon was a typist and typesetter for twenty-five years and took over Interim Books, another small-press operation, from Jay Socin. He is currently working on a bibliography for The Scarecrow Press, a reference-book house, as well as on other literary projects of his own. *Crank Letters* was published in 1982 by The Smith Press.

THIS INTERVIEW was conducted by Maurice Kenny, a Mohawk poet, who is very active in contemporary Indian writing and who owns the Strawberry Press. He also puts out *Contact II*, a poetry review, from Brooklyn Heights, where this interview (previously unpublished) took place in March 1977; Kenny has published Congdon's collection *Animals* (1977). His own chapbooks include: *Dead Letters Sent; With Love to Lesbia; I Am the Sun; North;* and *Dancing Back Strong the Nation*. His poems appear in the gay anthology *Orgasms of Light* (1977).

Maurice Kenny interviews

KIRBY CONGDON

Kenny: One thing that has always struck me oddly is how you manage to juxtapose your "machine" image and your "animal" image, perhaps not in the same poem or even in a collection of poems, but across the entire body of your work. Perhaps I shouldn't be but I am always amazed how you are equally at ease in using the mite or the gull, and the motorcycle or the Brooklyn Bridge. Is this because you came originally from rural New England into New York City and now Brooklyn?

Congdon: Well, I suppose that contrast of subject matter is a kind of fulcrum; I've always had difficulty balancing the two: nature and the machine. Yet that is a problem of the age, rather than with me. Eliot and Spender (in his "Pylons") and Crane tried to cope with it. First there was the approval of the machine, the proletarian poetry, as I guess they call it, poetry of the twenties—I'm thinking of Mayakovsky, and the Futurists and the Vorticists—or whatever—heralding the century of progress as they called it later at the 1933 World's Fair. I remember going to summer school in the third grade and the theme of the class was communications, the mechanics, the machines, of communications. We built a big train out of cardboard. And a few years later we were promised that the machine would take drudgery away from us. Do all our work. That was a fantasy: the reconciliation of the human with the mechanical, that Crane tried to express, and which Eliot, who apparently was more sophisticated, was already doubtful about. *The Waste Land* came out in 1922 and Crane's *The Bridge* dates nearer 1930, I think. So the conflict has always been a concern. And in all the arts, it's been a concern. I hadn't been aware of this, at least not with any conscious knowledge; I was never a good student; I absorb and regurgitate, in a creative way I hope, but I have no recall for facts. I came to the conflict, the machine/nature thing, by the back door. I was intimidated by the recent history of poetry. What could you do after Eliot's exposure of a mass, mechanized society? Repeat him? Argue with him? Take the idea a step further? I felt I couldn't go back to rural things, to Wordsworth or Whittier, and still be honest, still be a part of my own scene. Like most poets when they are young, I wanted to write more than I had anything to write about.

Even my own generation was intimidating: Karl Shapiro had the war sewn up; Richard Wilbur was writing his perfect lyrics; James Merrill was being elegant and so on. John Malcolm Brinnin, I remember, presented the problem—that we had no myth to draw from—in an introduction to an anthology. He was by the house at Fire Island one afternoon and I mentioned this introduction to him, but he didn't seem to be able to offer any suggestions about where to go from there. I was living in Manhattan then on Forty-ninth Street and First

Avenue. Lived alone there for seven years, till Jay, Jay Socin, my old partner, moved in, and I would write sitting on a stool by the oven (there wasn't any heat in tenements in those days) and I threw myself about, in the literary sense. I did write quite a few poems about love, but the gay thing was still taboo in the literary, in the publishing sense, and dangerous in the economic sense, because in those days you got fired if you didn't behave correctly in bed, if your employer got word of it. And I think I did get fired by a former classmate who was my boss in 1968 for being gay. At the Committee for Economic Development of all places! (I was a typist then. And nothing but a typist.) So that subject, gay life, was out as far as making a public commitment about it, although my first poems appeared in a gay magazine. But that was no step toward my own progress. I had to use a pseudonym. I dropped it though, because I was ashamed to hide. This was in the fifties, and no hardback publisher would touch a gay idea, and the hardbacks, the commercial houses, were the only thing you could look toward. There was no small press. LeRoi Jones and Diane di Prima were doing things but that amounted to an in-group in effect. And not gay, anyway. So, anyway, what else was there for me to write about?

Well, like any writer, you write about what you know, and what I was most aware of then was the upheaval New York was in with the postwar building boom. There was either a pit on this corner for a seven-story basement, or a framework of girders over your head on another corner, or the El was coming down, or the underground pipes and cables were torn up in the middle of the block. Wherever you went, there was all this activity. It was a rebirth, socially, too. The gay bars had started, the bird circuit it was called because they all had names like the Blue Parrot, the Swan, and the veterans were beginning to assert their right to their own life styles. Oh, not openly; it was all sub rosa, but among ourselves we knew the intolerance was wrong, and all our talk was about that sort of change going on.

But that was gossip. I couldn't use it for poetry. But I could use the stimulus of the change in the city itself. And I wasn't just grasping out at it, although I was nervous about how valid it was for poetry. But it came naturally. I loved the sight of these massive construction sites, and the machines that were involved. It was, in its effect, a new religion, but different from the machine-religion of the twenties because we were wiser and less gullible. And I tried to see it—the city machines—to show it with the benefit of hindsight, that it wasn't a millennium in itself, but it was still a natural, unforced, subject that was an exciting thing to anybody. At first I wrote about these machines just because they were there, but later I was able to select about twelve of the best ones and that's what my first book, *Iron Ark*, is. For me, it was my answer to T. S. Eliot, my own private solution. His distaste—I felt it didn't at all have to be distaste; it was also very exciting. It wasn't world-shaking but it sure was more exciting to accept New York as it was than lying etherized on a table, or growing old on the beach, or being snowbound, or talking about Pocahontas.

Construction work is a very sexual thing, for me, anyway. I love things made out of cast iron—toys, ornaments. Actually, I'm not mechanically minded at all. I like things like radiometers, and perpetual-motion machines and windmills, but I can't plug in a lamp without blowing a fuse. As for my bike, I always say I carry a dime on me for a telephone in case it breaks down since I'm so ignorant of how the damn thing runs! But, anyway, I gave the machines in

Iron Ark a kind of character. But not anthropomorphic beause that's so easy. I tried to see the machines as identities in themselves, as primitive forms of life, not talking to us, or imitating us, but being a kind of form of life just simply to the extent that they are able to be lifelike, sort of like the stem of a plant under a microscope—the juices moving, the cells operating and functioning, not doing much more than being mechanical performances, actions, but still suggestive of an identity, a will to exist, to be itself. When I grew up every tin lizzie was a family pet, each one had its own character, its flaws and idiosyncracies. And isn't that what defines much of life—being individual, having individuality? God knows, motorcycles are individual, the only machine I know, or have operated, except for tanks in the Army, but I only trained in one there. I didn't get to know them, the tanks, as—what?—as complexities, as individual systems with quirks that identified them as individual. I've seen a rider, a motorcyclist I mean, kick his machine in irritation. I think it's because he loved it, and it disappointed him because it didn't love him back. It wasn't grateful! You don't kick a car, or whatever. Maybe a trolley car! Trolley cars are lovable. I loved trolley cars. They were still around when I was a child. And trains.

How this relates to my affection for animals isn't, it can't be, very direct. In fact, I didn't get my first bike until I was thirty-nine or forty, and I had been writing about animals before then, years before. So there's probably no direct connection. If I write as easily about one as the other, as you seem to want to say I do, perhaps it's empathy. Instead of alpine vistas, like the Romantics were doing, as they did, it is just motorcycles instead for me. It, a motorcycle, is for me the twentieth century; it is having the twentieth century, all its technical power, between your legs, and being, for once, in complete control of it, to be in control of power without being oppressed or threatened by it, or intimidated. For Shelley it was a waterfall, or was it a glacier, in that "Mont Blanc"—the power in those things. I don't think a motorcycle replaces the beauty or the awe in a glacier or in a mountain, but it has an equal interest. And it certainly is more tangible. I mean you are on the bike; you can never really sit on a mountain except as someone lost in the vastness of its size. I hate to be lost, to be submerged. My worst nightmare is suffocation. That's why I'm really not good in bed. That is, in s and M. I like the titillation of restraints, of being held, which is like being wanted, but I can't stand claustrophobia. Jay said once I never slept without one foot sticking out of the covers, ready to run!

KENNY: In your collection *Dream-Work*, you pursue the use of the image of the motorcycle and its destructive powers, yet certainly you have regard for this machine as you own a cycle and obviously enjoy cycling. Why, then, do you impinge displeasure, joy, with death and destruction?

CONGDON: I don't see why you say the motorcycle has destructive powers. I don't know, either, why the motorcycle is associated with death. I think there's a step in thought missing. The motorcycle is sexual; it's phallic, it's movement, our age, it's a release from normal gravity; it's like sex, a flight, an escape, an involvement in an action that diminishes the importance of other distractions. Of course, I see what you mean, I think. You're asking why do I associate pleasure with pain, I mean as part of the s and M thing. Well, you know, the French call the climax a "petite mort." One dies voluntarily in sex, and it is voluntary and not just symbolism. It's cosmic. You become identified with, or a part of, all existence so that the human concern seems unimportant. I mean whether you get up and wind the clock and set the alarm and go to work and pay the bills. All personal concerns are abandoned in sex. You gain your identity, you lose your life, your ordinary life, by finding it's compatible, in tune with existence in general. I'm trying to think of the Bible—you gain your life by losing it. That seems to be what all this movement to the Far East, to the monasteries in Japan has been about. I don't like that though; here's where we should be spiritual, where we need it. In the United States. Emerson. You can burn yourself up, if you want that, right on Times Square. It's been done, you know. That's spiritual enough for me.

KENNY: When did you first start using machinery as a central image? Naturally, I see the cycle roaring across the Brooklyn Bridge or down the Long Island Expressway, as a bird might fly the sky or a fish swim the sea. Is this a juxtaposition that you envision?

CONGDON: No. I don't see motorcycles as poetic symbols. That's too much like dear old ladies romanticizing the vulgar to make it more palatable to themselves. It doesn't have to be romanticized. I don't think hang gliders or parachute jumpers have to rationalize these things in romantic or in poetical terms. You do it for its own sake. The romance is that you do do it just for its own sake. There are easier, more practical ways to travel! A plane is a plane. A bird is a bird. A motorcycle is a motorcycle. A rose is a rose. And so it's a rose. It would be more interesting, I think, to see a bird as being compared to a jet airplane. I mean there isn't any hierarchy of poetical values, of poetical references. I mean, why not say a flower is like a machine instead of saying a machine is like a flower or an animal or whatever?

KENNY: You have written poems to or about the various creatures of this planet and have been deeply concerned with fables. Is this not true? Do you equate the use of the real machine and the real creature with your writing of the fable (a kind of synthetic creature of another world)? Is it a fairy tale?

CONGDON: I got into the fables through my collecting of books. I collect first editions of important poetry. My earliest poets are Thomas Chatterton and George Crabbe who wrote "The Poor of the Borough—Peter Grimes." I don't know if they were gay, but it is a gay sensibility working in these poets. All artists are gay, I think, or are open in their attitudes toward the individual and what he may do. My collection isn't a gay collection. Mostly I just cover the twentieth century and whatever seems important. I stray away from it though, and I've tried to have a complete collection on motorcycles since this area only started recently. I plan to do a bibliography on it. And then I've wandered off into the hero, and the hero with the machine, like Lindbergh and his opposite, Tarzan, one accepting, one rejecting the machine. This begins to touch on the male image, but no pornography. Ralph, who I live with now and who has Cycle Press, Ralph Simmons, I guess I should explain, he has the largest collection of gay paperbacks in twenty-three counties.

But, anyway, in my own collection I have everything chronologically and it begins with Aesop up in the corner below the ceiling because he seems to be the earliest poet who is influential to the western world. And so, as I meant to say, this led me into a few bestiaries and fables. I wrote an essay on this, that Aesop was not emphasizing moral behavior, but rather he was, in his time, merely showing us the morals of the universe, and those morals, those codes, that history is very seldom kind or thoughtful. He was a realist. In fact, he was seeing the universe as a machine. Foxes eat chickens. Gas exploding moves the piston. The general idea is the same. No, I don't see any contradiction; only the subjects are contradictory, perhaps. Maybe my empathy, holding everything together, is the common ingredient. Life, our bodies, operate by themselves; we are machines for the most part, and as I said, the machine is a primitive form of life.

KENNY: Have the creature poems and fables developed from your rural background? One would imagine this.

CONGDON: Well, I suppose I was more aware of rural life than my friends. My first eight years were in a town atmosphere, West Chester, Pennsylvania, and because of the Depression we moved to my great uncle's house, which his father, my great-grandfather, had built with Gold Rush money. He went to California as a carpenter and built our house when he came back. Some of his work is in one of the houses preserved in the Mystic Seaport Museum, just by accident. Anyway, I was old enough to see the difference between a town and the country. We had only ten acres, a one-horse farm. The horse-drawn carriage was still in the barn when we moved there. I had pet chickens, and planted trees and had a garden, and when I got older I built stone walls and made some masonry repairs. And the walk to the one-room school was across a ledge and through a couple of fields and I would see woodchucks or a snake now and then. Interestingly enough, snakes put my mother into screaming hysterics. Her own mother said she hated men. She had eight children so you can't blame her.

My own mother once remarked that homosexuality was a kind of running "disease" in her family (she was Norwegian) but she never enlarged on it and she may have a more sophisticated view of it now. I've insisted on my family accepting my position but I think they all feel it's something I chose arbitrarily and could quit if I had a mind to. My brother had a copy of Karen Horney's *The Neurotic Personality of Our Time* and I asked my sister to read it too, but they were all oblivious to the fact that I could be one of the neurotic personalities of our time! They don't see the struggle. I think, for them, it's just some more poems which I either write or I don't write. I am an amateur artist and pianist and my writing is, to them, just another hobby. Yet when I was growing up my sister represented literary aspiration but now she says, "Books aren't my bag any more." My mother read to me as a child and responds to individual poems I have sent her, but I have never shown either of them *Dream-Work* and there's been no curiosity about it, although I mention it. My brother is some kind of business administrator, about twelve years older than me. In our lifetime, he's said about fifty words to me and I think forty-nine of those were involuntary! For Christmas and birthdays he used to give me things like a football, or a catcher's mitt! He had a boy scout group for a while but never mentioned it to me. So, in a roundabout way, my introversion, sexual as well as cultural, seems to play a part in my animal subjects since they represent another aspect of a basic emotional need I didn't find elsewhere. It's interesting that the emotionally cold English also devote themselves to their animals, loving dogs

and horses and caring not a whit for the fate of the fox! My mother loved animals, and had a dog and brought up birds in the house when they had fallen out
of a nest, but hated cats. Now she has lots of cats and ignores the birds!

I used to work around the place, too. It was real country since there wasn't
a house in sight to the west. My mother bought about ten acres next to us because she liked the landscape of it, and during my college days I'd spend
weekends and clean up the brush and the thickets. There's a natural waterhole
which disappears in July. I still love all that but it's painful to go home now as
it all seems uncertain. My sister auctioned off my grandparents' house in Mystic
with two floors of things that went back to my great-grandparents. I didn't
realize what was happening and this was a great shock. And so I worry now
about everything else that's left.

I inherited a bankrupt estate when Jay died and I have tried to re-establish my
emotions in it, but it's no substitute for one's real past. The sense of place and
the sense of continuity is very keen to me. My mother has used this need as a
weapon and was always selling the place to get a rise out of me and so I've tried
to divorce myself from being in such a vulnerable position. Especially as the
place, the physical thing of it, represented the stability I didn't get emotionally
from my family. So on that account, too, I gravitated toward life outdoors. I
never had any childhood boyfriends, and I was ignorant about sex, how it was
done, until I was in the Army. I had crushes on boys off and on since the age of
six or seven, and I kept wondering until I was twenty-six when it would switch
over to girls as it was supposed to do! It never did. There are still very few
women whom I like to hug in greeting, and even then I would not touch or hold
them in any more delicate way. Nor did I touch a man until I was twenty-six.
And neither of my parents would touch anyone at all. I can't imagine how they
had three children. It must have been horrid.

KENNY: To continue with the machine image, it's been said that you've been
influenced by Emerson. How does this poet's work and thought manifest
poems heavy into the machine image?

CONGDON: Oh, Emerson. I carried his *Essays* for three years during the war,
and never read it! It was a comfort, though, just to know it was there. He was
dismissed when I went to college, but we had an essay or two in high school,
and I love his pronouncements: everything is a circle; everything compensates,
or things like that. I love the neatness of it all. Loveless but neat! He's a
machine, too. A beautiful, spontaneous machine, spilling out all that uplifting
verbiage, a concrete mixer, pouring it out to grow into slabs of Truth with a
capital T.

I wanted to major in philosophy at Columbia. Of course, I know now I don't
have the capability to either read, understand or teach philosophy. As I said,
I absorb, but I can't recall; it all comes out all over again, in a mish-mash, as my
own ideas. This doesn't bother me; I prefer it, but it precludes any professional
involvement with philosophy as a subject. But I do expect ideas in poetry. If I
haven't learned something in some kind of philosophical way in a poem of my
own then I feel it's failed; it's just been a poem that's been invented, manufac-
tured, and that's not being creative. Creation is really not creating, but discovering, leaving yourself open to an idea you yourself really don't have any
control over. The world, like salvation, the inspiration, the meaning of it, it

comes to you, you don't go out to it and get it simply because you want it.

KENNY: And your "religious" poems?

CONGDON: I don't have any religious poems. Except all poems are religious poems, of course. Otherwise they aren't doing the work they're supposed to be doing. It's funny, isn't it, that the worst poems are in the collections of religious anthologies. Ladies who insist on having "Mrs." before their names, or the initials of religious orders. It's so shallow. They're afraid to be artists, the whole church thing. They are afraid of facing anything on their own feet. Religious art, I despise it; the whole motivation is wrong. Just terrible.

Still, true art is religious. The church is for the rite, the rite of marriage, or of the burial. Then, the history, the tradition, is a comfort; it's a ceremony, a dance, when you have to lean on something other than what you yourself know. Maybe that's art too, its purpose? To lean on something you yourself do not know. Maybe. The Pope got a collection together in the Vatican some years back, about three years ago. I'd feel very uncomfortable seeing it. Because if it's any good, it's good despite the fact that it's religious art, not because of it. It's pretending that our culture is still a church culture. It's the Pope, it's like him pretending he likes women and is male, and denying the gay thing outright. You would think he'd get a severe case of sciatica or some nervous disorder, being so shallow and false. His "love" is only an administrative thing; it's empty. As a result, I think the church culture no longer exists for us. If it did, the blacksmith would still be making hinges for the doors instead of the Putney and Sons Hardware Company in Schenectady or whatever. The church is just a business, which sociology and psychology has superseded. It should get back to the rite. Like the parade. A parade up Fifth Avenue is a thrilling thing, blatant and obvious but thrilling. But ministers and priests, I always feel embarrassed for them. They have to struggle so just to accept the existence of life and the love that goes with it. Catholics are always paving everything with concrete; they hate life. The Protestants would be as negative too, but they remain confused. Having overlooked the evils of Romanticism, it's hard to backtrack. But nature, the wilderness, the body, the cock are still negative artifacts to any religious group, or so it seems.

KENNY: How do you handle your homosexuality in your poetry? Or do you ignore it? How do you handle it in your life? Is it your complete life style?

CONGDON: I think in the earlier section of the first interview I did for *Gay Sunshine* a few years back that I said all my poetry is homosexual, and yet I don't intend for any of it to be. It's by me, and I like men, and so it's written always by a person with that predilection, that interest, but hardly ever with that subject as such. I do like to write, whenever, whatever I do write, with a feeling of sensual gratification, but it's a gratification that is mental or emotional, rather than in my cock. I get a hard-on when I write about sexual things but this is incidental; it's not the purpose of a poem.

Words, of course, since they are sensuous tend to become sexually affiliated. Their associations make them sexually affiliated. Words that can be just ordinary, like "sun" or "motorcycle" can be just names, but for me they are, when I'm writing creatively, sensuous and sexual too. I also see death as sexual, but I don't think I've written about death as such, ever. But the dying of things, the transiency of things, is something that is a constant sadness for me, and that is never either sensual or sexual. I feel that what is sad is something to cope with; it's an involuntary aspect to things. To bring sadness into a poem because it is sad, that would be false and cheap. Or if you write about motorcycles or leather because it's sensational, or because it's fashionable, or if you write about the sexual because it's taboo, then you're inventing and manufacturing. The poem has to have a larger purpose than just being a poem. So homosexuality I would hope is there in my poems but it's incidental to it.

And in my life? Is homosexuality my complete life style? I hadn't thought it was, but now that you mention it, I guess I never do let up on it. The leather gear and the bike is certainly it. I do go all out: the leather harness, jock straps, leather pants, the whole thing. That's why I got a bike originally, as I think I said in the first interview. I felt it was cheating to have all this lust for the leather image without having a bike. I try not to be swayed by public opinion, but I am swayed by my own opinion of myself. Actually, other people don't care, anyway, what you do as long as you don't pretend. They don't want morality; they only want consistency. Not even conformity so much as authenticity. They want it to be rational, for things to be done for a "reason." If you're from Texas that is a reason to wear cowboy boots and a ten-gallon hat to a cocktail party and these are adored because the wearing of them is legitimate. Not very much so, but still the excuse for wearing them is explicable and therefore justified. If I walk down the street with full leather, I have to prepare myself for criticism, direct or indirect. People want to know, "Where's the bike?" Even if I'm carrying my helmet. But if the bike is in immediate evidence, the attitude changes to unstinting approval, because I have a reason. Walking, I'm pretentious and people have a terrible strong need to put me down, but I can be as elaborately overdressed as I want if I'm with my machine. The more black leather and chrome, the more there is approval and the malice disappears. Unfortunately, the quality of authenticity gets confused with conformity along the way, and things get confused in other areas.

Cops are the most critical group I come across. They are true homosexuals in their mentality, wanting to be feared and loved at the same time for their overt masculinity. I sense that they resent me when they see the mirrored goggles and the rest of the gear. At the same time they are envious. I steal their thunder. Sometimes they've stopped me, if I'm walking, which is illegal. But when did that ever bother a policeman, since the whole philosophy of enforcement and restriction is based on the premise of expediency, any means to achieve the end, which is military conformity. They themselves, if you've heard one talk, are inhibited by their own fear of aberration. They spot you with their eyes immediately, and look hungry and they tear their eyes away in guilt. They love the leather, but they disguise it by their own respectable association with law and order. They love male authenticity, but conformity and approval more, since they don't have the nerve to operate as individuals outside of the group. The police are told not to think anyway, so what can you expect from them, except a shadow life. They are the ones who are the twilight men, not us! They want love with a gun. And what a funny occupation, to want to enforce something. To force anything is unnatural, and to want to do it as a way of life just seems strange.

KENNY: How did you get into S and M?

CONGDON: Oh, that was at Cherry Grove. I had the summer off one year. I was at the Pines but I used to walk down to the Grove to see friends, and somehow I was talking one afternoon on the deck at Pride House with an English teacher and he finally suggested we go inside. And I said, sure. And on the way in, there was a closet by the bedroom door and I saw a leather motorcycle jacket hanging there and wanted to try it on. He said later that he took the interest as a signal. Anyway, he saw a convert and told me about s and M, which I thought was absolutely ridiculous and as a kind of joke he showed me how it was done, and he tied my hands and wrists to my cock and balls, and I got a big hard-on, and I was amazed and I was fascinated. And I was hooked and delighted. He took a Polaroid shot of me in his own leather outfit, and I used that shot in a broadside with the poem "Dialogue with God," which was later included in my collection *Juggernaut*. But, anyway, that year the Harbor Bar opened, which was one of the first leather bars in New York. I was scared of it as being too rough, but of course I went. All the tough numbers only turned out to be accountants and junior executives.

But I got an outfit myself and we moved to Key West that year, and shocked the town. A local tabloid tried to drive us out of town and we were brought up at the Chamber of Commerce, and one voice spoke up for us, as I heard later, and suggested that the town wait until we did something wrong, and then act. All we had done was appear at the local beach with bikinis instead of baggy shorts. A friend of Jay's who was with us had gold rings in his tits and that caused a sensation. Anyway, as soon as the tabloid came out, we were immediately asked to come to a party that evening. And I met practically all my best friends at that party and Key West is my second home town. Jay and I had bought a house near the center of town, and so that made us look very respectable and it all worked out to our advantage. The tabloid went out of business and the publisher left town. We had a masquerade party that winter and the whole thing was stimulating for us as well as for the permanent people, most of whom had originally drifted into Key West a few years before as we had done. That was in 1965 or so. Now the town is booming and if we had done the same things this past winter as we did in 1965, we would have just disappeared. In the sixties people were hungry for the northern influx of one or two new faces to talk about, but now it's comparatively a metropolitan resort area. As most everyone who is involved in Key West comes from Fire Island Pines, it seems, I don't think the Chamber of Commerce is thinking of the gays as a liability these days.

KENNY: How political are you, or have you been, in the gay movement? Are you somewhat reclusive? To the entire political scene. You don't march and have not physically protested. Do you allow your political voice to emerge from your poems?

CONGDON: I'm not at all political, sexually or otherwise, in public. But I write crank letters at the drop of a typewriter key if I feel some straight person has maligned a homosexual idea or person. These people know better but they can't resist testing their superiority under the guise of humor or frankness. I hate them. They represent the bullies I had in childhood whom I couldn't retaliate against, for fear, or lack of courage, or whatever. I forgive them not. That's my own intolerance. I would go on a gay march if I could go as an individual, on my bike. That of course may defeat the purpose of the mass statement. The thing is I hate being submerged in any group. I hate teams. Group sports. Even having more guests in the house than I can talk with. I am never "with it" in any group. I'm a slow learner and am really only entirely comfortable when things are going at my own speed. As for protests, I think I do my share in the form of crank letters.

KENNY: What was your own involvement in the historic beat scene?

CONGDON: I was not involved in the beats at all. They were, at first, simply not my style. My background was still very much of a family one. Coming out of anonymity, so to speak, at the age of eight, from a town, and suddenly finding rural America, with relatives all over the landscape, and living in a house my great-grandfather built with his own hands, and finding more intellectual stimulation at home than I did in high school, there was nothing that I felt I wanted to reject or was disappointed in. We were poor but the insecurity we had was in itself an incentive to hold on. I grew a beard and worked in an art colony after the army and went to school on the G.I. bill at Columbia about the same time Allen Ginsberg and Jack Kerouac were there, but I saw no need to reject my values. I dutifully hitchhiked across the country and believed in bohemian things but the beats, while my age, were, in their sophistication, a generation older than me. I wanted, then, to go the other route, with my other contemporaries at Columbia, none of whom I knew until later, incidentally, and now only by name, such as John Hollander, Daniel G. Hoffman or Louis Simpson.

I reversed myself later, but, no, the first time I went to a coffee house open poetry reading on the East Side, I wore, as I recall, a necktie and sports jacket. Jay Socin had said to me afterwards, "I don't think that is your kind of place." But I thought to myself that somehow it was my kind of place. The next time we went, I left my collegiate clothes at home and wore the Levi's and so on that I preferred anyway. That was a surface change, but it was also a long-term mental one. I had originally written a put-down article on Jack Kerouac in the fifties because I saw the beat scene as so much bluster. I was writing an Englished version of Ovid's lines on Icarus, so you can see where I was at easily enough. But I had run across a limited edition pamphlet in the Brown University library and I wrote them, accusing them of probably neglecting if not ignoring the beats, just be challenging, and I ended up, as a result, in helping Brown put on the first public exhibition on the beats. Involvement with their work helped me to break away from Ovid and to commit myself to what concerned me in regard to ideas and emotions rather than to merely being literary. I also learned that the position of the artist is one of contributing and of giving, whereas that of the merely professional is one of exploiting and receiving. Of course this difference of values was much of what the beats were saying—one hopes!

As a consequence of working on the beat exhibition, Gregory Corso came and stayed with Jay and me for a couple of weeks. (Jay always said it was a couple of months!) It was a tumultuous time, I had never met a well-known poet before, and was terribly impressed to have him in the same room. He represented all that I had believed in in the way of being a poet; he had ideas, his own style, emotion, and pride. I had a beat-up grand piano and I played for him one afternoon as he sat motionless in a big easy chair. He was not only exhausting himself, but I think exhausted. I think he was on drugs, and asked Jay for a source, but Jay never even smoked cigarettes, let alone marijuana, let alone anything wilder. The two of them did a hectic movie together. I was left out of the project, but I tagged along just to be along as they made it. William Carlos Williams died at that time, and Gregory was phoned for comments. I think he said that Williams was the father of us all and I remember resenting the fact that any other poet should be my father figure. I felt I was father to myself. However, I did look up to Corso, even though he is ten years younger, but I disliked being overwhelmed by him, as he tends to do as a personality. I think this promulgated the quarrel we had. As a consequence of it, he said later, he thought better of me as an individual. But I thought less of him. I have always doubted the necessity some people tend to feel that one must show an aggressive nature in some way in order to gain their respect. I had thought it was the other way around, that one was innocent, and an individual has an inalienable right until proven otherwise, but this assumption is usually interpreted, especially among the straights, as a weakness in the same way courtesy is considered a weakness by the gross. But Gregory was generous to me and gave me gifts: a draft of *Bomb*, a handsome collage I've had framed, and a beautiful drawing in colored inks, and a little tin wind-up bird without a key which I think is poetical. His work seems the most satisfying of all the beats to me. Gregory was courting his wife-to-be when he was with us by long-distance telephone. Her parents were sticky about it apparently and she had put him off, and Gregory wept when he hung up. "I wish I was gay," he said, and told Jay and me that we didn't know what it was like to be rejected in love like that. While I felt this was a slur against the gays and while I feel the gays know more about love than a hundred straights put together, I do feel that the straights have a harder time of it in romance. The girls flirt and most of the time they cheat because they don't mean anything by it except to get attention. A gay who flirts without sincerity gets his ass chewed out. The gays are more casual but they're also more honest.

KENNY: What do you think of the publishing world?

CONGDON: The commercial and academic publishing world gets a lot of brickbats, insults and criticism, especially from me, and I think they are all pretty well deserved. The board of directors always seem to have this idea that poetry can be shoved onto the desk of the newest fiction editor since the subject is so fey and trivial. I got a brochure this week from Pittsburgh announcing new poetry books and the excerpts exhibited in the flyer were so weak in either emotion or idea that I could hardly believe it. If they would say, these publishers, say to themselves we're afraid of poetry, we don't know what it's about, we don't know how to evaluate it, you would think, okay, so correct the situation and good luck. But the damn fools are fools. They aren't interested in poetry. They can't talk about it. You never see an editor at a party, or a reading, or at a dinner. They have no curiosity. They don't think poetry, or talk poetry, or feel poetry. Poetry is an ornament because they had a poem intoned to them once in school.

My place in the established press is zilch. The small-press area on the other hand has kept my spirits going. It is a great relief to know that I am not throwing stones into a bottomless well but can have anything I turn out, which I feel is ready for publication, printed in one small-press magazine or another. I love working with the one-night-stand magazine editors. They're open to ideas. They write intelligent letters. There's a give and take that is stimulating. I know their sheet is going to fold in three months but the belief in poetry, the enthusiasm make me feel young. I feel a part of things. I have a very small following, if it's that big, but, as I conclude one of my fables, it is better to have one good friend and ninety-nine enemies that to be tolerated by a hundred. The small press, I think, has kept a lot of people alive, and I mean that in the literal sense, of staying alive and to be willing to live.

KENNY: How widely are you published in the gay press?

CONGDON: The gay press has been extremely receptive to me and my work. In other areas I find that your work is a commodity; it's used and you're forgotten until you're needed again. But in the gay press area a rapport and a warmth is set up that lasts beyond the exigencies of production problems. You are remembered and valued; you aren't just more of the competition, one more contributor. The commercial presses have more national prestige, but the man-to-man stimulation of being involved in literary activity exists only in the small press and in particular the gay press. This is my experience.

KENNY: I know you lived with Jay Socin as lovers. How much influence did this love have on your work?

CONGDON: Well, I lived alone for seven years and Jay, in effect, moved in on me, and so, while he provided a stable companionship, my own ambitions in poetry came first, and I valued the companionship because it served my poetry. Also, he was my family. We knew we would never leave each other. Sex was secondary with us. We both had what we called sub-lovers. He provided the equanimity I needed to write. He knew my relationship with my mother was upsetting and he could understand it in depth. As for the actual writing, well, I had been writing years before. I influenced him more than he influenced me at all. He knew Howard Moss, and Frank O'Hara and Julian Beck a little, and Jimmy Merrill and Kimon Friar through a poetry group I think. But these people were ones he had not seen too much of since we had been together and I met them but we never did more than meet. Howard Moss was a guest one weekend but I was so unknown, and he was so powerful, seemingly, I felt uncomfortable about it. We have been friends, but we've never cried together, as they say. Jay published *Iron Ark*, and started Interim Books originally, and so in that way he was influential. Otherwise, our loyalty to each other was the important thing, and as I said was like a family tie.

KENNY: Do you have a stable family now?

CONGDON: Ralph Simmons had taken a room with Jay and me a few months before Jay died (1968), and we are lovers in the full sense of the word. I have an ambitious and selfish nature and an impossible ego, which I subordinated to Jay because Jay was a hypochondriac; he was impulsive about decisions, and also he had the money and so I sort of tagged along more often than I liked to do. But I also knew then that I had never gotten along with anyone else before, and

I tended to be psychologically destructive toward lovers when their charm wore thin. So that relationship wasn't as well balanced as it should have been. But fortunately Ralph is someone who is not about to be put down, and his strong personality is a very good counterweight to my own. I can't think of a better partnership. My only anxiety is that something unexpected will disrupt it.

KENNY: How do you stand with your contemporaries?

CONGDON: I don't know. I come across statements like one in the *New York Times* I think it was that no great poet goes unpublished. That puts me into a self appraisal that isn't very encourageing. And then I think of the friends who have worked themselves into a lather to print me, and I wonder, is their judgment any good? And then I think, well my stuff is as innovative as William Burroughs, and, shit, after writing for twenty-five years I ought to know what I'm doing. And I think I'm ahead of my time. And then I think well maybe it's all old-hat after all. And then I think about the traditional lyrics I've done which are my most serious things. And I wonder, if they're so god-damned good why don't the commercial publishers snatch those up? And then I recall that I hate submitting things, and so I don't send them out, and that's why I don't get published by the commercial houses. So I don't know. As I said, the only people I feel comfortable with are the young kids who I know don't have prejudices as to what is publishable or hang-ups about what is or is not literary or poetical. And then I give myself the advice I tell everyone else: to write for its own sake, and not for other people's opinions. And I think, well, I'm still creating, and my contemporaries are just pushing out a re-hash of their early work. And so it goes. I have no idea what my position is. If anybody wants to discover me, I'm here, waving and screaming with one hand and writing deathless literature with the other.

KENNY: How are you handling aging as a poet and as a gay male?

CONGDON: Oh, golly. I'm buying a new motorcycle as soon as I can manage it, and I keep wondering, is this going to be my last one? I believe the mind gets younger as you get older simply because it knows more, and gets rid of old inhibitions. It isn't a cure, but I feel that how you feel about yourself often makes you attractive, even if your body has lost the sleek fit of the flesh it had earlier. I had thought, by my age, the sex drive would have tapered off, but I find there is no let-up. My only anxiety is about the time when riding my bike is impractical. I had trouble with a stiff arm some years ago when I got caught in the rain and couldn't take my arm off the handlebar, but I exercise to give me more stamina. Otherwise, I am improving rather than deteriorating in my piano playing, music composition, and writing.

About the only thing that has changed in regard to age is that where I would be willing to paint a room, or clean a window, I avoid doing anything that isn't going to be a permanent improvement or a finished accomplishment. I find it grueling to waste time looking for something, like a glove, or the top of my pen or a file. Otherwise, I am my usual, cranky self and not the least bit mellow.

In regard to aging, I'd like to finish with a poem about it, which will be part of a subscription broadside by the time Winston's book appears, but this will be the first book publication of it.

If the final winds were to come
and corrugate the dunes of dust,
like scars, on the wind-drift skins
of the winter land,
and if stars fell down
from the push-pin points
of their impossible size,
of if the sun erased
each blaze of grass
across the waste
of man's debris,
and the ocean's salty desert rose
to drown mountain chains,
I, in some heroic gesture,
would rise and so survive
as any man would stand
before his heaven
and for his kind
though he himself may die.

But death's tiny fingers nag
like little duties on its rock
where the hairs of ice split
   threads like thought
sewn across those fine lines that,
   criss-cross, crease
the seamy surface of that face
and make aeons crack,
or flowers rust in their decay
and wilt the glory of the day
and shadows bend their September
   bars
on a breaking summer's narrow back.
The fine hours of promise pass,
and, smiling, we are such fools
when, most smug, we feel most wise,
for the gaping ages, silent, come
and then, just as speechless,
   on they go
in cycles, circling, careless,
round each jaded eye
as our visions fade
with the ego's tedious demise.

But, and still, and yet, and now,
we press on through, though useless
and unused, to this enduring fact:

If clocks can sing in the freezing room,
and quick fish swim,
so free beneath the glaze
the cold has laid
between the banks
of frozen streams,
darting, as they do,
lest they be caught
in the long shades of strange dreams,
or windbells ring in a dry creek's bed
as cactus flowers in deserts bloom,
and the tiny lung of mites can bellow air
so those engines' fires thus are fueled
with such fine and earnest care
they work the mincing teeth
of such jaws as those
that mesh the smallest crumbs of time,
then I, too, persevere
through confusion, through travail
and let my tight heart's hope
live on air.

It is this breath that I inhale
that defies despair
though the senses fail.
It is this body's health I feel
in each stubborn heart's brazen beat.
It is this
on which our last defense depends
against such defeat
as death assumes,
in its presumption,
to be complete.
This is what it is:
the knuckles doubled up
threatening heaven;
that fist of the heart
knocks endless
against the end,
forever and ever.
Against the silence
the heart's
sound
says:
Forever and ever.
Forever and ever.
Forever and ever.

PHOTO BY BILL BLAND, 1976

MARTIN
DUBERMAN

MARTIN DUBERMAN is a critic, playwright, and social historian. He has taught at Yale, Harvard, and Princeton, and is currently Distinguished Professor of History at Lehman College, City University of New York. His first book, *Charles Francis Adams, 1807-1886*, won the Bancroft Prize in 1962. Another biography, *James Russell Lowell*, was a nominee for the National Book Award in 1966. A collection of his essays, *The Uncompleted Past*, appeared in 1969. His history of Black Mountain College, the experimental community that (from 1933 to 1956) pioneered many of the current innovations in art, education, and life style, was published in 1972. The National Academy of Arts and Letters awarded Duberman a special prize for his "contributions to literature" in 1971. His first and best-known play, *In White America*, won the Vernon Rice/Drama Desk Award for 1963/64. Others of his plays have received a variety of New York and foreign productions and seven of them were published in 1975 under the collective title *Male Armor*. His play *Visions of Kerouac* opened at Lion Theater Company in New York in December 1976, and was published in book form by Little, Brown & Co. in 1977. Duberman is continuing to research — between other projects — manuscript collections in archives all over the country for a long-range history of sexual behavior in the United States. Duberman is one of the founders of the Gay Academic Union, as well as serving as a member of the original Boards of such diverse gay organizations as Lambda Legal Defense Fund; NGTF; and The Glines Theater. Duberman has just (1982) completed an agreement with Knopf and the Paul Robeson Estate to write the definitive "life and times" biography of Paul Robeson (to appear in 1986).

In the six years since this interview was conducted, Duberman has in fact been publishing his research findings extensively. Among his most important articles on sexuality (mostly gay) have been the following: "The Therapy of C. M. Otis: 1911," *Christopher Street*, Nov. 1977; "The Anita Bryant Brigade," *Skeptic*, Nov./Dec. 1977; "Male Impotence in Colonial Pennsylvania," *SIGNS*, Winter 1978; "Documents in Hopi Indian Sexuality: Imperialism, Culture and Resistance," *Radical History Review*, Spring/Summer 1979 (plus follow-up exchange in Spring 1981 issue); "Masters and Johnson: Greeks Bearing Gifts," *New Republic*, Jan. 6, 1979; "I Am Not Contented: Female Masochism and Lesbianism in Early 20th Century New England," *SIGNS*, Summer 1980; and "Writhing Bedfellows: 1826. Two Young Men from Antebellum South Carolina's Ruling Elite Share 'Extravagant Delight,'" *Journal of Homosexuality*, Fall/Winter 1980/81. Duberman has also made public some of his research findings in various conferences on sexuality, e.g.: as a panelist at the Museum of Modern Art symposium on "Fascism and Gays" (1979) and the MARHO symposium on "Sex, Power and History" (1979); as chairperson of the panel on "The History of Sexual Behavior" at the annual convention of the American Historical Association in December 1976; and as the concluding speaker at the New York University conference on "Power and Sexuality" in March 1978. Finally, Duberman has been publishing an ongoing column on gay history since June 1981 in every issue of *New York Native*.

THIS INTERVIEW was taped in New York City in 1976 by George Whitmore, and originally appeared in *Gay Sunshine* no. 32 (Spring 1977). Whitmore is a free-lance writer, poet, and playwright.

George Whitmore interviews
MARTIN DUBERMAN

WHITMORE: You've been researching the history of sexuality in America for some time now. When are we going to see some of the results of that?

DUBERMAN: I may unwittingly have embarked on a lifetime project. I've spent much of the last three years simply catching up with the anthropological and biological literature. The historical material has been easier to master—so little has been published. This past year I've begun tracking down manuscript collections in archives all over the country. [See details of publication in biographical note.]

WHITMORE: Is it very hard to get at this material?

DUBERMAN: Very. Almost none of it is catalogued. The amount of material I find is usually in direct proportion to the amount of sympathy the archivist has for the project. As the *very* sympathetic archivist at the Lilly Library in Indiana told me, "There isn't a manuscript library in the country that doesn't have material on sexual behavior. And there isn't one that will volunteer it. The only way you're going to get it is to present yourself in person at each and every place; then the luck of the chemistry, the astrological signs or whatever, will determine how much they'll show you." So far I've been very lucky. I've turned up some extraordinary stuff—everything from suppressed portions of Hopi and Navaho homosexual rituals to unpublished legal opinions and medical cases to a *forty*-volume handwritten diary kept over several decades by a New England "gentleman" recounting his erotic (including gay) adventures—something like an American version of *My Secret Life*.

WHITMORE: You came out publicly for the first time in your 1972 book, *Black Mountain*. Have there been professional difficulties?

DUBERMAN: Only a few. But I wouldn't want others to generalize from my case, since I already had tenure and am, as they say, "heavily credentialed." Even so, there have been some repercussions. I used to be invited to do reviews and articles on a wide variety of social issues for a wide variety of publications. Now I get few invitations. Not that I care: my energy's going elsewhere—and happily. I did learn recently that even before I came out, a member of the appointments committee at City University tried to block my appointment as "Distinguished Professor" specifically and solely on the grounds that I was an "active homosexual." In 1976 I learned that the nominating committee of the Organization of American Historians first decided to recommend me for the presidency—and then reversed itself. The maneuvering, I've been told, was pretty heavy and devious. At one point the committee chairman announced he would resign rather than offer me the nomination. My chief antagonist, sad to say, was apparently a historian who I happen to know is a closet gay. Sadder still, the clinching argument was that no one of my sexual orientation should be allowed to "represent" all American historians. Frankly, I was more astonished that I'd been considered than that I was finally dropped. You never know these days: one minute they pat you on the head, the next they kick you in the ass.

WHITMORE: The fact that you have two disparate careers—scholarship and playwriting—running neck-and-neck is interesting. How did it come about?

DUBERMAN: As a teenager I wanted to be an actor. I toured in summer stock playing George in *Our Town* when I was seventeen. I wanted to go to college at Carnegie Tech and study acting. Somehow, I ended up at Yale, studying history. Don't ask me how. Clever family maneuvering, I think—though I can't recall any open discussion, let alone argument, about it. Anyway, I had wanted to be writer even before wanting to be an actor. I remember scribbling moralistic little tales when I was five or so about "Bad Bill" or "Naughty Nancy": many crimes (like talking back to Mommy), much punishment, final redemption. With that start, it's a wonder I didn't end up doing S and M floorshows at the Anvil.

WHITMORE: You had a particularly advantaged education, didn't you?

DUBERMAN: I went to a private school.

WHITMORE: Was it experimental?

DUBERMAN: No. Not at all. Sort of country club, upper middle class. Classic prep school—or the nouveau riche, Jewish version of it.

WHITMORE: The Horace Mann School?

DUBERMAN: Yes. In Riverdale. My family had been poor. My father grew up in Russia, a peasant on a beet plantation. He didn't come to this country until he was twenty—having fled from the army. Didn't know a word of English. He started working for seven dollars a week, learning to be a cutter in a dress factory. By World War II, we were middle class. By then, my father had his own dress factory, a small operation. But during the war, he got government contracts and started to make considerable money. The family moved from Seventy-Second Street and Broadway to Westchester, and I was sent to a private school.

WHITMORE: Were you "out" during your undergraduate years at Yale?

DUBERMAN: Not really. A few furtive experiences in my senior year. The last few months I've been trying to recall specifics—for that autobiography I mentioned. I've been reading over two diaries I kept, one in the late fifties, the other during the seventies. I had thought the two would show an enormous contrast—how one gay man's head had changed over a twenty-year period. But when I read the early parts of the seventies diary I was shocked at how *little* I had changed at that point. I was saying most of the things in 1970 I had been saying in the fifties. For example, I was scornful of the gay march that year. "What the hell is this? What are these imbecile people up to?" I wrote in my diary. My attitudes and self-image *had* begun to shift somewhere in the late sixties. The plays I wrote then did have explicit homoerotic material in them; I had been coming out, in a sense, behind my own back. But the conscious and significant changes didn't come until 1971 and 1972—after which I became politically active.

WHITMORE: Have you changed a great deal?

DUBERMAN: I think so. But only in some areas. The fifties—alas—molded me. I became—and remain—achievement oriented. I doubt if I'll ever be otherwise.

WHITMORE: You certainly did advance rapidly. You immediately wrote a prize-winning study. Two big books, as a matter of fact, early in your career. What led you to Charles Francis Adams, of all people?

DUBERMAN: The Adams book was almost an accident. In my first year of graduate school at Harvard I was put in a dorm room with a guy whose mother happened to be curator of the Adams House in Quincy, Massachusetts. She got me interested in the Adamses at the very time the Adams papers were first being opened up to scholars. So I fell into it. I decided to do my doctoral thesis on Charles Francis Adams, though as a person he hardly inspired me.

WHITMORE: If it wasn't his personality, what did attract you to him?

DUBERMAN: His involvment with the anti-slavery movement tied in with the kind of social protest I was then moving towards myself. A restrained, measured kind of protest. "Liberal" reform. Adams was active in the anti-slavery movement, but wasn't part of the radical Garrisonian wing. Also, I *was* attracted to him somewhat as a person. I think what grabbed me about him was that he was such a fucking *rock*. In a sense he didn't have an emotional life. At least he wasn't subject to the wild swings of mood that I then was. I think at the time I wanted to become that kind of man.

WHITMORE: Looking for the man you wanted to be/possess.

DUBERMAN: The invulnerable man. Seemingly invulnerable. Adams ended up senile at the age sixty. Like all the so-called invulnerable men. The first to crack under unexpected pressure.

WHITMORE: James Russell Lowell was quite different. A very sweet man. I was most impressed, when I read your biography, with how genuine and almost passionate his relationships were with his male friends.

DUBERMAN: Many nineteenth-century New England "Brahmins" were like him—despite their reputation to the contrary. With intimates, they were capable of surprising (to us) affection—and lack of self-consciousness about expressing it. Lowell had Adams' rocklike integrity, but was also impassioned. Unlike Adams, he had great warmth and a much greater capacity to take radical personal and political risks. He became a sort of model for me—the kind of person I hoped to become. In the fifties, I had wanted to be like Adams. Not that I could ever carry it off. I always felt like an outsider, even when at the center of things. In high school, or, going back much further [*Laughs.*], I was "All-Around Best Camper." A "star." Did all the right things. At the top of my class academically in high school and college, played on various athletic teams, dated girls. Never labeled a "sissy" or "Jew-boy." I was very busy denying what I sensed inside: that I wasn't really part of the "in" crowd, that I *was* different—and hated being different. I remember once seeing a photo essay in *Life* magazine: something like "representative criminal types." One was a picture of the "Standard Homosexual." I remember staring at it and thinking, "Oh my god—it looks just like me! I've been found out! Despite the fact that I'm the star of the tennis team! There it is—in *Life!*"

WHITMORE: The classic double life.

DUBERMAN: I wish it had been *more* double, on the sexual side. I didn't have my first sexual experience with a man—and there were only a few incomplete, unsatisfying ones with women—until age *twenty!* Well, a few earlier ones. At summer camp, as a kid, we did something called "fussing." We had a mattress at the bottom of the closet in our bunk [*Laughs*]. The closet, no less! We were pretty well organized. Don't know how old I was—about twelve, I think. The code question we'd ask each other was, "You feel like 'fussing'?" If yes, we'd go into the closet, two at a time. Body rubbing, essentially. There was a definite hierarchy, too. You know: who got to go into the closet with whom, who did the choosing. Just like a gay bar.

On one level, I knew early on I was gay. At seventeen, for instance, I went on a bike trip—old-fashioned bike—across the country. Camped out every night, went through the Rockies; all that. At one point we stopped in Calgary, Canada, for the big rodeo. I remember going to see a fortune teller. She told me to write on a piece of paper "the question closest to my heart," and to put it under the (literal) crystal ball sitting on the table between us. "Put it under the crystal ball, close your eyes, concentrate very hard and I will then be able to answer your question." What I wrote on the piece of paper was, "Will I always be a homosexual?" Fortunately—being rebellious by nature—I didn't follow her instructions to the letter. I peeked. I saw her take the piece of paper out through some opening in the bottom of the table, read it, then put it back. "Open your eyes now," she said. "You're a very troubled young man. I'm getting that very strongly. But your particular trouble can be cured. What you have to do is leave your old life and join our gypsy caravan."

WHITMORE: "And join our gypsy caravan"?

DUBERMAN: Even the gypsies were into "cures." I *was* tempted—though I'd seen her trick with the piece of paper. A measure, I guess, of my desperation. "Maybe she can cure you," I thought, "maybe you ought to go with her." I was terribly torn up about it, couldn't decide. In the end, I didn't show up at dawn with all my worldly goods.

WHITMORE: You must have wanted to be cured very badly.

DUBERMAN: The "sickness" model had been drummed into me. That's why I waited so long to have sex. I finally got up the courage to go to my first gay bar—the Napoleon, in Boston—when I was in graduate school at Harvard. Soon after, I met a man who I was with for five years. During most of my twenties. The relationship wasn't entirely monogamous, but nearly so for the first few years. I was very close to him. I'll call him "Larry." He was different from me in many ways. I'm usually attracted to opposites; not always, but usually. Larry was nineteen or twenty, working-class Irish Catholic, from a small town near Boston. Very attractive physically—to me, anyway. He was my somatic ideal, I was his intellectual one. That's the way to put it, I suppose. I was living in the graduate school dorm, he lived with his family. But he'd often stay with me. There was no way we could afford to live together on a regular basis. Neither of us had any money. He had a lousy job in a department store, I was trying to get by on my "tutor's" salary.

You know, sometimes when I think about the fifties, I think everything has changed—the culture, me, the community. Other times, I think very little has changed. A student of mine from my Princeton days recently came to see me. He's twenty-six now, but has only been out about a year. His big breakthrough to date has been meeting a guy in one of the johns at the porno movies he frequents who *actually talked to him!* This is a bright, politically sophisticated guy—active in SDS as an undergraduate. Yet here he is at age twenty-six not knowing where to go to meet other gay men, except for bathrooms.

WHITMORE: That's one of the failures of the movement. The information gap.

DUBERMAN: It made me think things are no easier for gay people now than they ever were. In other moods I know—or hope—that's wrong. But I'm not sure. Like take my relationship with Larry. We had a damn good thing. *And* a support group, a circle of friends. There were bars, too. The life was circumscribed and secretive, of course. And our self-image wasn't so hot. I remember long talks with my gay friends at Harvard about whether we could achieve *any* sort of satisfying life, "stunted" as we were. We accepted as given that as homosexuals we could never reach "full adult maturity"—whatever the fuck that means. *Then* it meant what everybody said it did: marrying, settling down, having a family. We knew we'd never qualify, and despised ourselves for it. But it's too simple to reduce "growing up gay in the fifties" to a one-dimensional horror story. We had lots of good times. And Larry and I had a good relationship. Plenty of ups and downs, sure. But plenty of warmth and affection, too. I don't know of many better relationships today. Or as good.

WHITMORE: Did you date women?

DUBERMAN: Yes. There have always been women in my life. Sometimes at the center of it. But strong as those relationships were—and are—they've never been sexual—I mean, genital. Until recent years, that would usually produce a crisis. After a time, the woman couldn't understand why I wasn't interested in sex. Then a confused sort of confessional would follow, during which I'd never really confess, leaving the woman far more bewildered than before. Very painful, unfair situations. But I didn't know what was fair. I kept thinking, "This relationship is my road to a 'cure'." And my therapist kept encouraging the relationships, insisting they would become sexual if only I was sufficiently patient. He advised me *not* to tell the woman I was homosexual—that was my device for scaring her off. I took me a long time to learn that intimacy—with men or women—doesn't hinge on, can't be measured by, the amount of sex involved.

When I started teaching at Yale in 1957, my five-year love affair with Larry ended. For a while I again had little or no sex life. I was terrified of going to the two gay bars in New Haven—Pierelli's and George and Harry's. I took a vow, in fact, that I wouldn't go near them. I was afraid I'd be seen, reported to the administration—and fired. That *did* happen to a friend at Yale, so I think my concern was realistic, not paranoid. But gradually my resolution weakened, especially if I got drunk. I'd go into one of the bars, look around nervously, get frightened, leave.

But then I started going to New York on weekends. I remember one place called the Grapevine, on Second or Third Avenue. Gay men *and* lesbian women. It had dancing, too. A lively, crowded place. There were other bars, of course. The Bon Soir on Eighth Street. That was mixed gay and straight. They had floor shows. The straight people sat at tables, the gay men stood at the bar, groping each other. [*Laughs.*] People didn't socialize, they groped. Everard's was open then. There was one period in my life—late fifties/early sixties—when I went to Everard's a lot. Usually I'd meet one guy and go to a room. A function of inhibition, I now think. If I was going to be gay, I was going to be gay in a way that was "seemly." In a way that approximated how straight people—sensible, adult, healthy straight people—behaved. You find one person and stick with them My sexual repertoire was limited in those days, too.

WHITMORE: Sexual fashions change.

DUBERMAN: With Larry I played the stereotypical dominant role: made the decisions, did the fucking.

WHITMORE: Was that very prevalent then?

DUBERMAN: Oh, I think so. Certainly in my experience. Much more than now. I even remember the terms "husband" and "wife" being used.

                    *   *   *

WHITMORE: How did you come to write *In White America*?

DUBERMAN: A producer—knowing I was a historian who also had some theatrical experience—approached me about doing a play on the American presidency. That sounded boring, banal. I presented a counterproposal: a documentary play on the history of being black in white America. I had just begun teaching courses on the Civil War period, had gotten interested in black history and, in a limited way, involved in the civil rights movement. I knew it was closer to my interests than the American presidency. The producer wouldn't buy it. My agent wasn't enthused. I finally decided, the hell with them, I'm going ahead with the idea.

WHITMORE: Was it mostly library work?

DUBERMAN: I knew the nineteenth-century material well already, from my teaching. The tough part was finding earlier and later stuff to surround it. But the script didn't take me long to write—two, three months. When it was done, my agent decided she liked it and sent it to Judy Marechal, then a well-known off-Broadway producer, though only in her twenties. From the day she got the script, it was only seven weeks before we opened. So I began theater on an up note, to put it mildly. "This is easy," I thought. "You write a play, and it immediately gets produced. Simple. Terrific." Ha!—what I've learned since!

WHITMORE: What about the casting? Were the actors well-known at the time?

DUBERMAN: No. Gloria Foster had made the film *Nothing But a Man,* but it hadn't been released yet. Moses Gunn was entirely unknown. He had just arrived in New York.

WHITMORE: How were the reviews?

DUBERMAN: The *Daily News* refused to review it; they said the play was "incendiary." The *Times* review was restrained, mostly a plot summary.

WHITMORE: Was it a popular success?

DUBERMAN: Not a commercial success. It ran more than five hundred performances—but closed $4000 in debt. We'd sell out on weekends, but have a few bad nights during the week. Especially in the beginning. If the producer hadn't been so good, we wouldn't have stayed open long enough to build the audience we eventually did. She juggled bank accounts, begged and borrowed, to keep us alive. The touring companies later made some money. And later still, amateur and stock productions. There were even—this was 1964-65—some productions in the Deep South. The Free Southern Theatre toured the play in Mississippi. I never saw that production, but Elizabeth Sutherland wrote a piece about it in the *Nation*. The audiences, she reported, were almost exclusively black, people who had never been to "theater"—and so weren't cued into "appropriate" responses. They'd simply join in with the cast. Often the performances took place in a black church in a small town. Hundred-degree heat, people hanging out of the windows, packed to the rafters. As Sutherland described it, each performance was like a joyous revival meeting. But one night, just before curtain, a group of cars pulled up. The local vigilante group. All they would say was, "We came to find out what was going on." Everyone was terrified. They came into the church, sat in a separate section, didn't react at all through the whole play. Later, Sutherland tried to interview them. Only one man would talk to her. "It was just what we thought," he said. "Communist propaganda."

WHITMORE: There was a hiatus in your playwriting after that.

DUBERMAN: I didn't write plays for a couple of years. I was finishing my biography of Lowell. Starting in '67 I tried my hand at some one-acters. The first full-length play I completed was *Payments,* in 1969.

WHITMORE: You hadn't come out publicly yet. But don't you think it was rather obvious, in a number of those plays, that they were written by a gay man?

DUBERMAN: It should have been. But when Barnes reviewed *Metaphors* in 1968, he talked about my "delightful little play," making no reference whatever to the homoerotic content. People looked right through it, not seeing, as always, what they didn't want to see. Actually I was surprised myself at how "gay" the plays were. In the mid/late sixties I was deeply involved in psychotherapy and deeply persuaded by the "sickness" model. Some of the plays reflect that. But also my growing rebellion against therapy and its "norms." In a sense, I was coming out behind my own back.

WHITMORE: Was *Payments* written from personal experience?

DUBERMAN: Bob, the central character, was based on someone I know—in fact was deeply involved with for a while. But few of the details or events in the play coincide with the real-life Bob. His wife, for example, never knew about his hustling—whereas in the play she initiates it. I think I put some of the self-hatred I felt for myself at the time into the character of the older man, Paul—untrustworthy, manipulative, greedy.

WHITMORE: It's an overwhelmingly ambitious play. How was it received.?

DUBERMAN: My agent sent the script out to producers we considered braver than most. They all turned it down. One man who had already produced a highly successful play with a gay theme, and who was himself gay, sent a wondrous letter to my agent: "This is the single most fascinating script I have ever read, and I've read many thousands of scripts. But I want absolutely nothing to do with it." Nor was his the most extreme reaction. Several producers denounced the play as disgusting, vile. One woman who had greatly admired a one-acter of mine when it had been done at Actor's Studio in 1968 told my agent that she "had an obligation to Martin's talent to see that all copies of the script were burned. If the play is ever performed, it will destroy him."

WHITMORE: All this was over a play about a call service. It's hardly shocking.

DUBERMAN: It was then. When we did the play as a workshop at New Dramatists in 1971, we lost almost half the audience every night at intermission. Even six months ago, when the play was done at the tiny Back Alley Theater in Washington, D.C., there was a lot of frenzy and resentment over it. The play may finally be done in New York this winter, but it's far from definite. [It wasn't.]

WHITMORE: How do you feel about *Payments* now?

DUBERMAN: I think it reflects the time in which it was written. I have mixed reactions to it now. It represents where my head was at in 1968-69—meaning parts of the play can legitimately be called homophobic. Of course, nobody in the play comes off well, gay or straight. Somebody long ago called it "an icepick in the heart of America." I wrote it when I was in the middle of a very destructive analysis, and the country in the middle of the Vietnam war. My attitude was "fuck everything and everybody." Besides all that, I think the play does accurately reflects how most gay people—in those "preliberation" years—viewed themselves: unloving and unlovable. Perhaps most gay people still do. Though fewer and fewer all the time, I like to think.

WHITMORE: Well, with gay plays or plays with gay characters we're always dealing with political categories, as well. Recently I sort of short-circuited the question by setting two plays in 1959 and 1969 because I'm interested in those problems, the problems those characters faced then in relation to homosexuality and being women. One is about secretaries in an office. They're mostly strong women, but I wouldn't say they had highly developed feminist consciousness. Do you worry about this problem?

DUBERMAN: Well, to take an example, when people carry on today about the "retrogressive" qualities of *Boys in the Band,* I think they're doing the play—and themselves—a disservice. They're denying the past, moralistically insisting that people *should* have felt and behaved differently in 1969 than they did—

WHITMORE: —that they never were like that anyway—

DUBERMAN: —demanding a false history, a Soviet-style rewrite palatable to current political tastes. When gay people say that *Boys in the Band* shouldn't be performed because it presents a bad image—

WHITMORE: Whereas I think it's a bad play as well—

DUBERMAN: —well, that is a whole other issue. Beyond what *Boys* says truly about the lives of gay people in that particular period, in my view it also continues to say something true about qualities that most of us, however liberated, still carry around within ourselves. And in many cases, not just qualities, but sizable chunks of personality and behavior. *That's* one reason we get angry when we see it: we don't like being put into contact with aspects of ourselves that we disapprove of. I don't believe it when gay people claim they "can't relate" to those characters in any way. Don't they *ever* fall into self-deprecation, disguise deep feelings with shallow banter, play stereotypic sex-role games? All that *is* still part of gay life, however reprehensible we may find those attitudes and however actively we may be working (within ourselves and through the movement) to change them. Wholly to deny *Boys*—or *Payments*—is to deny not only the reality of our past but real elements in our present. And I think that's what the "purists" are demanding. It reminds me of the tyranny of Socialist Art—sloganeering—in the thirties.

WHITMORE: Or almost. It hasn't been laid down for us in a systematic way. Is all this ideology leading us in new directions as writers, or do we have to step back a bit?

DUBERMAN: I think if you consciously impose a set of ideological standards on your writing—or write in order to exemplify them—your work will be lifeless.

WHITMORE: Well, I do try to apply them in the beginning. In my selection of what to write and who to write about. Certainly not in the midst of it.

DUBERMAN: I think all writers are—must be—deeply uncertain about why they write and what they write. I think most good writing comes out of tension, irresolution, conflict—trying to work through something, often again and again, that nags in the gut. I'm worried about political commissars passing judgment on what is "permissible" in the arts.

WHITMORE: The Arno Press version of *Coming Out* reprints your tangle in the *New York Times* with Al Carmines over *The Faggot*. Isn't a lot of what he was saying to defend himself similar to what we've been saying here?

DUBERMAN: Close but not quite. I was too hard on Carmines, insensitive to his particular style of doing things. But I still believe he miscalulated in defending the political ineptitude of *The Faggot* on the grounds that he was concerned only with Art. That defense might hold *if* what you produce is Art. *The Faggot*, unfortunately, isn't.

WHITMORE: These political categories we worry about. Don't they also get applied to people, not just characters? I notice a willingness, probably coming out of the sixties and the standoff then, to generalize people, and a sort of covert assumption that everyone can make themselves over, completely.

DUBERMAN: I doubt if we have as much choice about what we are as we like to think. I'm reminded of a screening I went to recently of the first half of the Adairs' film on gay life [*Word Is Out*]. One of the interviews was with a male transvestite. He said something like, "Look, we're all born naked and we all choose one form of drag or another." Violent groans and hissing from the people sitting behind me. Something politically intolerable had obviously been said. I asked one of the men behind me what he was hissing at. "Sexism," he said—as if that catchall somehow exonerated him from further explanation. He didn't hiss at the lesbian in the film who wore blue eye shadow and teased hair. Nor at the working-class drag worn by others in the film—male and female. Weren't they, too—like the male transvestite—trying to project or conceal a particular self-image, and stereotypic ones at that? The transvestite at least seemed to know what he was up to; *he* had made a conscious choice. The difference between him and most of the rest of us is not that he wears drag and we don't, but that he knows he does and decides what he wants to look like. Very few of us are that conscious in our choices. We fall into acceptable modes of speech and dress; what's acceptable to peers becomes more important than finding out what's intrinsic to ourselves. The men who booed the transvestite were proud of their "feminist consciousness." I wonder. Their reaction can just as easily be explained as fear—of being tarnished with the brush of effeminacy. That old terror at the taunt of "sissy." Better to embrace it. I think gay men have a great deal to learn from the radical feminists, but I think some of the message is getting mistranslated. What I admire most about the lesbian women I've worked with politically is how they manage to be forceful *and* supportive of each other. Their energy doesn't get channeled into competitive point-scoring to the same degree ours does. Maybe that's one reason lesbian women are miles ahead of gay men—at least so *I* think—in the sophistication of their political analysis and in their ability to work together cooperatively. Gay men are men first, gay second—most gay men, anyway; certainly me.

WHITMORE: And we as men, here in New York anyway, are in a rut as political activists. The Task Force, for example, working towards the rather limited ends of civil rights.

DUBERMAN: Well, let a thousand flowers bloom. If only they would. We're a long way from defining our needs, and a longer way from agreeing on how to rank them according to priority. Perhaps what has to precede is much more discussion than we've had in the gay community about the nature of "gayness." In what ways and to what extent *are* we "different," beyond the obvious difference of sexual orientation? And that's a corker. *Are* we a "subculture" to the degree that, say, Jews or blacks are? Not that they've had an easy time trying to define themselves, either. Though I know my Jewish background has molded my perceptions, it's hard to define *precisely* how. Yet I don't doubt that a "Jewish consciousness/personality" exists.

WHITMORE: One reason we have no doubt it exists is because society at large has decided it does. If there was something called the "School of Jewish Writers" in the fifties, it came about because it was called that. Not just because there were Jews who were writing. So why are we so underground?

DUBERMAN: I think critics have had an easier time defining the Jewish genre because those writing in it were writing more fully about the dimensions of their experience than we gay people have yet managed in terms of our experience. Most of us are uncertain what "gay consciousness" is, what "gay theater" would look like, what "gay poetry" consists of. Perhaps because we've just begun to accept and affirm ourselves.

WHITMORE: I think one problem is our constituency, limited as it is at present.

DUBERMAN: We haven't a *well-defined* culture with a history. Our history is only beginning to emerge.

WHITMORE: We do have a present, now.

DUBERMAN: Yes, but it's difficult to say *precisely* how the gay present differs from the straight present. Whether the differences are ones of degree or kind. Whether we're writers who happen to be gay or whether being gay informs and affects all aspects of our lives, gives us a special perspective on experience.

WHITMORE: Much of your work has been published in what I would call the general media. Of course, the straight media is often the gay media, too, since gay people are equally hooked into it. But do you have any conflicts about directing your work to the general media?

DUBERMAN: I've published in the gay and radical media—for example, *Metaphors* in the *Gay Alternative*, various pieces in WIN. But take that fifties diary I mentioned earlier. Part of me doesn't want to publish it *anywhere*, since I find the "me" of those years appalling in some ways. But maybe I have the obligation to publish it *because* it's appalling. If so, where would be the most valuable place? In *New York* magazine, say, with its huge straight readership in need of enlightenment about what it's like to grow up in a homophobic culture? Or in a small gay publication, whose readers might need or welcome the sharing of common experiences? I don't know the answer.

WHITMORE: We both know of a number of gay writers who aren't writing gay stuff. And the gay readership buys their stuff and reads it, probably in greater numbers than they buy the gay-press material. In poetry, for instance...

DUBERMAN: John Ashbery?

WHITMORE: I was thinking of him as a prominent example. Yet I wouldn't think of his writing anything other than what he does write and is best at. I suppose great talent makes its own rules more often than not. But I don't particularly blame—and I was getting at this—younger writers I know who make choices other than the choices I made, early in their careers. They do have fewer options than an established writer. The standards of "talent" and "excellence" applied to gay writers are often higher than those applied to others. You have to buck two things. First of all, the talent test, which means you're not given as much leeway as people who are writing general things. And second, there's the market. I'm not troubled by narrowing my focus, because as a writer that's a good thing—maybe the most necessary thing to do. There's a very vital movement of gay poetry in this country. What I do have a problem with, though, is accepting the fact that the audience is so extremely limited. Because I think that smacks of voluntarily silencing myself in some way, the way gay writers always have.

DUBERMAN: Let me come at that from a tangent. Some of the elements often singled out as distinctive of gay culture are the same ones sociologists bracket under "victim symptomology"—like self-deprecation, self-mockery, the send-up. Some activists feel those traits should be discouraged, and, in time, eradicated. "We need only act like victims," they say, "as long as we choose to be victims." It may be that as same-sex lust and love gain increased acceptance, to that degree the distinctiveness of the gay style will become diluted—the less we're victimized, the fewer traits of victimization. The movement's success could foster the very cultural homogenization we currently protest against. *If*, that is, the sociologists are right—*if* we're "different" only to the extent we've been oppressed. But is that true of other minorities—blacks, say? I don't believe it. I don't believe black culture can be reduced to "victim symptomology." And I don't believe gay culture can. But we have to explore and discuss more than we have what *other* qualities set us apart. Most gay people seem to feel we're "jes folks." It's what I call the "NAACP mentality": "Hey, mid-America, except for the difference in our skin color [read 'sexual orientation'], we're just like you—so why not open up to us all the privileges and opportunities of the society?"

But as Lorraine Hansberry and James Baldwin argued long ago, "Maybe we shouldn't be eager to rent a room in a house that's about to burn down." Maybe we—blacks, gay people, women, et al.—should be putting our energies toward building a new house, a better house. I think the gay movement today, perhaps especially on the East Coast, is dominated by the NAACP mentality—otherwise known as liberal reformism. That has its place; we *do* need our civil rights, and I've been active in reformist organizations. But that isn't enough. It could end in total co-optation. We badly need a resurgence of radical energy—and thought. We need to think about whether our special experience can lend itself to some *basic* redefinitions—of gender, sex roles, sexual behavior, interpersonal relations. Do we know something the straight world doesn't about how men and women *could* relate? About the enrichment that comes from discarding standardized sex roles—in and out of bed? About the joys—and problems—of living alone? About the pleasures—and risks—of sexual variety? About the multiplicity of sexual selves within each of us? About the connection (or lack of it) between erotic zest and companionate "marriage"? About the distinctions to be made between "love," "lust," "affection," "sex," "friendship"? I think we do. And I think we have to start saying so.

*   *   *

WHITMORE: Your play, *Visions of Kerouac*, was commissioned by the Kennedy Center but not produced there.

DUBERMAN: They didn't produce any of the six plays they commissioned.

WHITMORE: How did you decide to do a play on the Beats?

DUBERMAN: After they asked me to write a new play for them—free choice of subject—I floundered around for a long time. I thought of doing a documentary, a kind of panorama of American history as seen through the eyes of its radical "outsiders"—people like Garrison, Frederick Douglass, Emma Goldman. But the documentary form felt tired to me. The next idea I had was to do something about Wilhelm Reich in America—the last years of his life, when he was jailed by the government. I read Reich for six months, but that play wouldn't come out of me either. Then I got on to the Beats. I had read almost nothing by or about them before. *Howl, Kaddish, On the Road, Naked Lunch* — that was about it. I only gradually understood what had attracted me. It was the Kerouac-Cassady relationship — the story of two mythically macho men and their inability, despite deep passion for each other, to connect. Once I became conscious that that was my theme, it really grabbed me.

WHITMORE: What made you aware of that? Which book?

DUBERMAN: Their relationship? It must have been *Visions of Cody*, and Ginsberg's introduction to it.

WHITMORE: I think your play is an epic drama, not so much documentary as poetic, flashing back and forth from 1958 to 1942, forward to 1968. Twenty-three characters. My first impression was, "He's not going to pull this off." But you did. How did you research it?

DUBERMAN: What I did first was simply to sit down and read through all of Kerouac — which was a lot more than I expected. Some twenty volumes. A lot of it's garbage. I think most of his "spontaneous writing" comes across as just that — someone high on bennies, typing. I do admire parts of *On the Road, The Subterraneans*, and *The Dharma Bums* a lot. But my fascination is with the life, not the work.

WHITMORE: You transcribe most of Kerouac's main imagery, but the language of the play seems seamless to me — your own material and his. How did you approach that aspect of it?

DUBERMAN: I wish I could tell you, but I hardly understand it myself. Somehow I fell into the rhythm — not only Kerouac's, but the style of the group. As I read through Kerouac, I'd come upon a phrase, a line, even a word — something would reverberate. Usually I wouldn't know why. But I'd jot it down. When I finished reading all his books, I looked back at what I'd jotted down and at passages I'd marked. I read and reread them. Some sort of transmogrification took place. Actual lines from Kerouac are in the play — in some of Cassady's speeches, whole paragraphs. More often a sentence of his might spark off a page of dialogue from me, or a whole scene. Later, I might go back, discover some stuff I'd forgotten and insert additional lines directly from Kerouac. The amalgam became so complete, I'd now have trouble separating out the constituent parts. Sometimes within a single line there are three words that are Kerouac, five that are me, etc.

WHITMORE: It's not really a gay play, but I think it is a play about male love.

DUBERMAN: Definitely. The feeling between Kerouac and Cassady was powerful and passionate. They never found a way to express it, other than in "acceptable" male buddy-buddy bullshit terms — tough guy heroics, all-night benny sessions, screwing together in whorehouses, sharing women, treating women like shit. That's the tragedy. The destructive tragedy of growing up male in America. Those two men loved each other deeply, but couldn't accept the depth of their own feeling. If they had, both might be alive today. Ginsberg seems to think so too — at least that's how I read his introduction to *Visions of Cody*.

I don't mean (and my play doesn't say—though some people insist on reading it that way) that they felt physical lust for each other or that their feelings required sexual release. Who knows? I don't and don't pretend to. Besides, I see the tragedy as larger than sex or no sex, and larger than the Kerouac-Cassady relationship. My play's about the horrors of being "manly." Which most men—in diminishing numbers, I think—seem to believe accrues in direct proportion to the *absence* of tenderness.

WHITMORE: Your treatment of women in the play. It's quite obvious early on that they're merely appendages of the men.

DUBERMAN: I think the women in the play are like the women in Kerouac's life—belittled, peripheral. Except for his mother, who was central.

WHITMORE: You don't flinch from reproducing the way the men treated the women. When I saw it there were women in the audience flinching at it. How did you decide to maintain balance? So that the play didn't propagandize for what it was trying to depict? When you first told me you were going to do a play about Kerouac, that was the one thing I feared—that no matter what, it would end up glorifying some of those values. Glorifying Kerouac.

DUBERMAN: I hope the play does the opposite—shows how our culture's prescriptions for manliness cripple and kill. Still, I hope people who see the play feel for Kerouac, too. I do. I care about the sweet person inside of him who could never get out—or rather, stay out. Kerouac was a chameleon. He could be ingratiating, charming, lovable. And as a young man, he was extraordinarily handsome and charismatic. But with liquor in him, he could be a brute and a bully. And the older he got, the more he drank. The last few years of his life he did almost nothing but drink. His Catholic upbringing reasserted itself, too—along with its usual handmaiden, political conservatism. No, he wasn't attractive towards the end. But he was poignant, touching. So much wasted talent, unused capacity. And I mean human, not literary.

One other thing. When you say it's not a gay play—and I agree with you—it is a gay man, Ginsberg, who embodies the basic decency of the Beats. In that last scene, Ginsberg is settled, whole, knows who he is. And even though he's appalled at the drunken right-winger Kerouac has become, he still cares for him and is able to show it. I like the fact that the most openly gay man in the play is the man who comes out looking best—without any accompanying polemic.

*   *   *

WHITMORE: You said you had been in therapy—almost eight years, I think. Getting out of therapy had a great deal to do with your coming out politically?

DUBERMAN: It was a major milestone. There were others. Like when "old friends" in the Hamptons let me know my lover wasn't welcome to stay overnight in their home. The shock and anger of that gave me a big shove "out." Also important was the emergence of a support group—the gay movement. It gave me the fresh perspectives I needed to re-evaluate the negative attitude I had towards my own homosexuality—and to question the cultural definitions that had fostered it.

WHITMORE: When did you get into therapy?

DUBERMAN: When was I born? I was first sent at age fourteen or fifteen, sent by my parents because I was "introverted," uncommunicative at home. I knew even then that I was gay. I remember telling the psychiatrist a dream I'd had about being in a glass house. I was doing something sexual—homosexual. I suddenly realized in the dream that everybody in the adjoining apartment houses was staring at me. I was covered with shame. "What were you doing?" the psychiatrist asked. "What were you embarrassed about?" "Dunno," I said. I did know. But I wasn't about to say. At that age I hadn't had sex with any-one. Hell, I was so full of guilt I didn't have sex—give or take three or four fur-tive blow jobs—till I was twenty-two!

WHITMORE: Was therapy always about being gay? Was that what it boiled down to for you?

DUBERMAN: Mostly. When I was fifteen I only went for a couple of months. That therapist's solution to what was wrong at home was for me—literally—to put my arms around my mother and hug her. "Everything will then be fine," he said. I remember pacing my room that night in a panic. I could barely *talk* to my mother, let alone hug her. But I finally forced myself to go downstairs. I grabbed the startled woman, put my arms around her like a robot and hugged her. She promptly burst into tears and said something like, "I knew it was going to be fine... I knew it..." And of course one week later, everything was back to status quo. So that was my first "cure." Hug your mother.

There were others. Through the years therapy did a horrendous number on my head. And on most of my friends. But I should add that in 1973 I briefly went back into therapy after the breakup of a love affair. Even though I was skeptical—furious—at what therapy had earlier done to me, I felt desperate enough to give it another try. This time I was lucky. The therapist was a marvel-ous man. No moralisms or judgments. No suggestions of "cures"—in fact he was himself outraged when I described my previous experience in therapy. He helped me towards important clarifications of certain feelings and events, shook up some of the tired formulas I'd been using for explaining my behavior. The point is, I'm not anti-therapy per se. There are a few good people around—mostly, but not solely, among the younger therapists. Of course, there are only a few good people in any profession.

The men I was in therapy with before were not among them. In graduate school I had a therapist who insisted that I break off with Larry, my lover—who I talked about earlier. The therapist told me that our relationship—that all homosexuality—was simply "acting out." That was the standard phrase then. Homosexuality was "instead-of" behavior, "as-if" behavior—a device for avoiding deep-seated anxieties. Only by closing the "escape hatch," the therapist said, would I be able to face and overcome these anxieties. That meant not only giving up Larry but refraining from all homosexual activity. I put Larry through incredible hell. I told him we had to stop seeing each other if I was ever to "grow up," become an adult. But I couldn't stick to that. I'd stay away from him for a few weeks, remain celibate, but then would miss him so horribly that finally—usually drunk and crying—I'd call him, we'd see each other, go to bed, then I'd be full of remorse, guiltily report my fall from grace to the therapist, be sternly reprimanded, take the veil again. The cycle went on and on. Larry went through the fucking wringer. Me too. Finally I couldn't stand it. I quit therapy *and* gave up any hope of working out the relationship with Larry.

In 1964, when I moved to New York, I decided to try therapy again. For the same reason—upset at the end of a love affair. I stayed with that therapist from 1964 to 1971. And when I say "with him," I mean I had an individual session every week and I was also in two therapy groups, each of which met two nights a week. So a large chunk of my time and energy went into therapy.

WHITMORE: It was your social life.

DUBERMAN: Damn near. Earlier, in my twenties, I'd had two long-lasting affairs. But in my thirties, while in therapy with "Carl," I was alternately celibate and furtively promiscuous. I had become more and more convinced, through therapeutic brainwashing, that homosexuality was an illness, that I had to get myself cured, that the only way to get cured was to devote myself to therapy, to do what my therapist said I should do. And what he said I should do—surprise!—was to stop all homosexual activity. At one point in the mid-sixties I didn't have sex for fifteen months. And I see myself as a very sexual person. You can imagine the will power that took—and the depth of self-loathing.

The first few years in therapy with Carl, I fought back a lot. I had enough doubts about him as a human being—his arrogance and dogmatism—and about the slickness of his formulations, to be suspicious and resistant. But what did me in was group therapy. Because there were some wonderful human beings in my groups, two women in particular with whom I became very close. I did believe they, unlike Carl, cared about my welfare. The more they parroted Carl's line—which was almost invariably—the more my resistance crumbled. If I got in an argument with Carl, someone in the group would say—lovingly, which is why it was devastating—"Martin, *listen* to what Carl is trying to tell you. He's trying to make you well. But you—you keep defying him. It's your authority problem, Martin. It keeps you from getting on the side of your own health." I finally caved in. I remember saying one night, "Okay, if your're all telling me the same thing Carl is, and I know some of you love me, then it's got to be me. I must be as sick as hell. I give up. I'll do what you tell me from now on."

And then Carl socked it to me. "The first thing you do," he said, "is to cut out all homosexual contact of any kind. The second thing is, I never want to hear another word in this room about anything that relates to your homosexuality." At the time I was involved with someone and having a lot of trouble—I wonder why?! [*Laughs.*]—in the relationship. Carl was always impatient and curt when I tried to talk about it in the group. His attitude was very different when Sally, another group member, talked about the difficult relationship *she* was having with a man. One night I blew up—"It's okay for Sally to talk about the problems she's having in a relationship, but when I talk about mine, nobody responds." To which Carl said, "That's because Sally's involved in a *real* relationship. You just waste group time. Because all you want to do is focus on symptomatic, non-authentic behavior and try to get us to commiserate with you. You don't care about growing up and getting well."

But don't get the wrong idea. Carl's definition of what it meant to be a "healthy" woman was also insane. When Women's Liberation began, he denounced it as "castrating bitches and discontented Jewish princesses refusing to accept their adult responsibilities as wives and mothers." He was no less oppressive of women than he was of gay people. An interesting sidelight to that is that Carl was having sex with a number of his female patients. Once, a woman in our group was made to sit in a corner with a dunce cap on her head—literally. I forget what her "crime" had been. She was finally readmitted to the group circle after agreeing to fuck with Carl in the middle of the room. Other times, Carl would take a woman patient into his inner office, right during group session. No reticence or explanations. He would simply announce that he and "Jane" were going to retire to the inner office and fuck. Because Jane "needed" it. It was important for her transference—or some god-damn thing.

I was once physically beaten up in group. Literally beaten up. By a fellow patient, a borderline psychotic I now think. He was Eastern European, very disturbed, very strong physically. Later he almost killed one of the women—grabbed her by the throat and throttled her—when she accused him of treating women like shit. Anyway, he and I had been arguing about something. Suddenly he jumped out of his chair, hit me so hard on the side of the head that I landed on the other side of the room, then jumped on me and pummeled me some more. And wasn't stopped by the therapist. Nor anyone else. No one would have dared intervene without Carl's go-ahead. He damn near killed me. Carl later admitted that if any of the blows had landed two inches higher, on my temple, I would have been dead, given the guy's strength and fury. I finally struggled into the bathroom, washed the blood off me, sobbed my eyes out. As I was cleaning up I kept thinking, "My god, what madness!" I was sure that when I got back into the other room, I'd be comforted and the other guy held accountable. No way! The first thing Carl said—and all cues were taken from Carl, regardless of what anybody was feeling—was, "Well, Martin, you finally got what you've been asking for." And then added, "You made 'Paul' do that. You provoked him into it." I'm convinced Carl wanted me beaten up. He was full of hate towards me, at my periodic challenges to his authority.

After therapy ended in 1971—I'll explain why in a second—some of the group members saw each other now and then socially. (That had always been forbidden; in fact we had never known each other's last names.) It was only then that several admitted to me that they had often thought Carl had the worst of our arguments and that he had abused me mercilessly. That made me wild! "Why the hell didn't you say so at the time?!" "Well," they said, "we figured you had to be treated with special severity because you were such a difficult case." The truth, I think, is that Carl had everyone in a state of terror. One of the built-in horrors of therapy is that all conflict can be reduced to "the patient's problem." A therapist like Carl, with his monstrous ego, was incapable of being contradicted. I never once, in seven years in that office, heard him say, "I'm wrong" or "I'm sorry." It was always the patient's problem. I can remember leaving group sessions sometimes feeling so destroyed I couldn't function for a week.

Carl once told me that of the eight homosexual patients in his various groups, *all* had been "cured"—except me. The reason *I* hadn't been was because I was "the single most defiant human being he had ever met." To which I say in retrospect, "Thank god!" One of those eight "cured" homosexuals was in my group, though for years he didn't mention his past. Finally, after I had capitulated, agreed to give up homosexual "acting out," he said, "Martin, now I can tell you: I, too, have a homosexual history. Because of my therapy with Carl,

I've been cured." The man was married, had two daughters, was living in suburbia, had met all the going criteria, in short, for "mental health." When he told me I was overjoyed. "My god, it's true—you *can* be cured! Here's a living example!" It confirmed me in my determination to abide by Carl's dictates. Much later, the man confessed to me that he had never completely given up sex with men. Having found a woman with whom he was able to have intercourse, he had married her. But after the birth of their two children, they rarely had sex. He made a pact with himself that he would never *look* for homosexual contact, but if, when walking down the street, he "happened" to catch another man's eye, then he'd chalk it up to "fate" and let himself go off with the guy. So that turned out to be the actual—as opposed to the official—modus operandi of how he had been living his life. So much for the "cures" of psychotherapy.

WHITMORE: So what did he talk about in therapy?

DUBERMAN: Oh, his problems on the job, whether he should shift from the business department to the editorial department. That sort of thing. And he also gave me a lot of advice. Like "restrain the animal." I tried. But I kept going off the wagon. I'd confess tearfully in group, renew my vows, last another couple of weeks or months. I think what was finally critical in my "escape" was the changing social climate. I began to read and hear about other possibilities, other definitions of gayness.'This was late, 1970-71. But the new insights and options did slowly accumulate. In the summer of 1971, when the group recessed for a month's vacation, I debated whether I should go back. "What should I do?" I wrote in my diary, "I'm almost forty years old. Isn't time to accept the fact that even if Carl is right and I am a sick human being, the imprinting has been so deep I'll never make it into Adulthood?" Those, alas, were still the terms in which I debated the issue with myself: should I *settle* for the fact that I was this truncated human being known as a gay male, that therapy couldn't do anything more for me, that I was one of the incurables. The issue was taken out of my hands. Just before we were due to reconvene, everyone got identical letters from Carl. A weird letter, to put it mildly. He was "fatally ill" and the doctors had recommended that he spend his "last remaining days" in a tropical climate. Later news, from various sources, reported him as "recovering." You go figure it out. Anyway, the group—and therapy—was over.

WHITMORE: Saved by the bell.

DUBERMAN: Carl, mind you, was one of the acknowledged pioneers in the field of group therapy, had a considerable reputation in New York at the time, was an editor of one of the psychiatric journals. In other words, I haven't been describing some nut on the fringes of respectability—however nutty he now sounds.

WHITMORE: What did you ever do without therapy?

DUBERMAN: Very well, thank you.

READING IN AUSTRALIA, 1976

ROBERT
DUNCAN

BORN in OAKLAND in 1919, Robert Duncan lived for years in New York City where he edited *The Experimental Review* with Sanders Russell. He was part of the vigorous scene in the early 1950s at Black Mountain College, where he taught briefly, and became associated there with his contemporaries Charles Olson, Robert Creeley, and Denise Levertov. He returned to San Francisco in the later 1950s where he was instrumental in giving impetus to the Berkeley-San Francisco Renaissance of those years, along with Kenneth Rexroth and his friend Jack Spicer with whom, during a complex and challenging relationship, he helped begin the Poetry Center at San Francisco State. He has lived in San Francisco for most of the last thirty years with his close companion Jess Collins, the painter. Among Robert Duncan's more than twenty books are *Heavenly City, Earthly City* (1945), *Roots and Branches* (1964), *Bending the Bow* (1968), and *Caesar's Gate: Poems 1949-1950* (1973).

This interview took place during three day-long sessions in December 1978 and January 1979 at Aaron Shurin's house in San Francisco. There was a definite feeling of generosity in these discussions, a feeling that we were sharing experience, and in fact we all brought material to the interview; our own poems offered became part of the texts to be studied and were referred to in the course of our exploration.

Duncan's enthusiasm gives to his speech a head-over-heels impetus that often finds him interrupting himself to further his unfolding language. We tried to reflect this urgency in transcribing the tapes. To flesh out the picture, there is Duncan with his white tufted hair at either side of his commanding eaglelike face—one eye holding you down and one eye roving.

—S.A. and A.S.

INTERVIEWERS: Aaron Shurin (b. 1947) is a San Francisco poet, author of *The Night Sun* (1976). Steve Abbott (b. 1943) is a San Francisco poet, author of *Wrecked Hearts*. The interview appeared originally in *Gay Sunshine* no. 40/41.

Aaron Shurin and Steve Abbott interview
ROBERT DUNCAN

DUNCAN: The shattering experience when I was in love is why couldn't I say "I love you" and saying was impossible for me. I was struck dumb because the depth of feeling was so fundamental that if you advanced to the level of speech, the network of things drawn into that fundamental point was so complex you couldn't speak from it. It was felt throughout the entire body and you could not find within it any actual confidence of loving.

It was so intensely important that I be loved that I made situations absolutely painful to me. My lover N. was working on his thesis and if he wasn't back necking and fucking with me in a half hour I was in a sulk. I was like a monkey on his back, not really a creature capable of loving. You wouldn't do that to someone you loved, right? We don't have a word meaning two entirely different things. We've got a nexus called "loving" and we experience falling in love as a terrible necessity that be brought into the domain of loving. Otherwise you could fall into sex or something. But the fact that we experience this terrible fall, this wrenching out of ourselves, this self-preoccupation, we suddenly come to something we are to care about or take care of. And against all that is how much we need to be loved. How does a child love its parents? It does but it also recognizes that it does not love the parents the way they do it. But in a sense it can take care of the parents too.

ABBOTT: For me, the falling is like when Daddy throws you up in the air and then catches you. And when you're caught it's so wonderful.

DUNCAN: Exactly! I was always practicing that. Piaget sees that in the baby right away when he throws something out of the crib. So you make a toy by attaching a ball to a string. All those returns are delights. And he sees the first one as the hand which you don't first recognize as being yours and the delight in the movement which brings that hand around. Parents are always going and returning too. So those first (love) scenes I was describing were forcing returns for me. Not forcing but assuring that they would take place.

ABBOTT: But when you fall in love, don't you ask for a return that can't be returned? For instance I feel as if there were a hole in me, in my heart, where I don't feel I was ever loved enough. So I'm seeking a Daddy to fill this. But it can never really be returned and I'll have to live with this the rest of my life.

DUNCAN: Well, I see myself, at times it becomes a family joke, I say to Jess: "Here I wanted a Daddy and you're not any better than Daddy was at repairing these things." We've got a picture throughout our family life because it also reoccurs. I don't find any of this disappears. I'm no better off than when I was eighteen except I've learned to expand areas of this feeling. I still have a figure called "trembling." We have an area of exchanging endearments and there are times we also say how intensely we feel but *still* you can't speak for that level, when all of a sudden you're almost easier except that we're comfortable with each other and, in a way, some ground has been made.

The feeling of needing to do something cannot be immediately realized. First, you're not capable of love till you've found out how it's practiced and you find out how you love. You don't love straight out. Or you do, but it doesn't communicate to you or anybody else. It's like writing a poem. Just the feeling of writing the poem is terrific, to find out language is suddenly speaking for you as nothing has spoken before, including yourself. And all sorts of strange things prove to be you. But I never felt depressed because a poem was off although I certainly struggled with it trying to get it right. My feeling of its not being good was often how little it belonged to me. It was saying something and was exciting but was not yet what I really would feel. The same thing with falling in love when I go back to when I was eighteen.

I still feel my first lover is an eternal person for me. I was raised in terms of reincarnation and karma belief and falling in love was, and still is for me, experienced as an appointment. That first love relationship was absolutely painful. It must have been painful for him too, incidentally, because I could have an absolute scorn for his mind where he did not share my sense of things. He was not an artist in temperament; he was a school teacher and he was up against a kid who, when it came to modern art, Pound or Stravinsky, was demanding, absolute, very little willing to allow sharing unless sharing included the world of painting, writing, music I had come to believe so in. He thought of himself as the rational one and I was taken to be irrational, imaginative. The excitement was the union of opposite types.

The world of my mind and of my work was, even then, the most important. I sought a love where sexual needs and response and daily companionship would extend fully to include the central intent of an art. That's what I had to know fully in my heart about Jess before I went further with him, to recognize how much of an accord we were in our arts and responses. I had fixed in my account of falling in love that union of opposites, not here male and female, but of contending forces united in their contention by love; working out a karma struggle. But I broke through that fixation to admit that I was in love with him where the sense was of a deep accord, not of winning or losing, but of going on with him in a common life.

In my mid-twenties I had quit writing poetry and tried to settle down into the terms of one relationship. I tried to cease my driving concern for this mind and this work I had had because it seemed so much more important that the sexual love and the companionship be there. I was in love with him and I did not want to come to judge how he responded to art or poetry. My absolutism remained. I guess I only put it aside by staying away from the area of concern. He was an artist but a commercial artist. We could share fully our going to galleries to see art but whenever I got off about poetry and ideas of philosophy or structure, that look of the rational male barely countenancing the irrational flight of fancy would come over his face.

I stopped writing poetry until 1943 and '44. When Pound was finally captured by the American forces I was moved to write "Homage and Lament for

Ezra Pound in Captivity, May 12, 1944." The basic forces of my poetry had been stored awaiting that time, but if I think of the revelation of my sexual nature in its development, I think of how important loss was, and lament. Early poems in the loss of my first lover are eaten through by self-pity as I remember them. Then in the earliest poems, a poem like "Persephone," written in 1939, the theme of rape, rapture and dread. And the blood in those poems comes forward from actual initiations in blood.

I see through this, and through many passages of my poetry still, two violent events of my high-school period in which I was absolutely saturated with blood, just covered with blood. I got my first car when I was a high-school sophomore. My father was an architect and when Roosevelt started the building the money came back. So we were really in high style. Anyway, I'd just gotten my driver's license and was driving a group of friends between Taft and Bakersfield over a rolling desert road. We'd not been drinking which was fortunate as you will see. We went over the hill like a roller coaster and they said: "Duncan, Duncan" (it was "Sims, Sims" then). "Let's go back and do it again." So we did. Wow! The only trouble was the road turned. We weren't the first to go off there. We plunged into a ditch where only two weeks before a whole Mexican family had expired. I was the first to come to and the girl I'd taken to the football game and dance had her face split open by the rear view mirror. And I was absolutely saturated with blood. The steering wheel was coiled around me so how come I didn't have a broken bone, who knows. The girl next to me was also seriously injured. So I see that blood thing.

The next blood thing came after my father's death. I was about seventeen. My mother was having suitors and we'd gone to a Chinese restaurant in downtown Bakersfield. They wanted to do something so I said, "Well, I'll walk home." Now it was near the end of summer so we've got that valley heat sort of thing. For some time I'd already experienced the area of fascination and played with it as a child. I'd catch a man looking at me and I'd look into the gaze and suddenly they'd behave like I never made men behave before. I did it once when I was in a car and a man was in a barber shop. He got so upset he had to get up out of the barber chair. [Laughs.] I would catch a look and go deep into it. What was on my mind was I had discovered something I'd read about in Greek myth. It was really true like I thought it was true. My family believed in elementals, so satyrs were real to them and nymphs were real to them. I found out there was something satyr-like about me, something nymph-like about me. I could fascinate. And I was wise to in it in some way I didn't know at all. Also I was always in a context in which I was vaguely aware that I was doing it because they couldn't get at me. I'd be surrounded by people. I was in a family car and so forth. So they would be behaving in an odd enough way, usually getting angry, but I wouldn't possibly know what happens next. I thought I was a hypnotist.

Now we've got me, I'm sixteen or seventeen. I picked up one of those glances and it followed me. It was a boy of about eighteen or nineteen, a fairly husky road-boy as there still were in the late Depression. And my experience there was Oh! Here we've moved into an entirely different realm! I knew there were other realms so I experienced it as a new dimension. Everything's changed! I could see everything's changed! That's what this gaze means. Now I understand in a new way the heat of May. Now I can hear what the grass and the trees were saying. Now I'm in entirely the same dimension as birds and water. And in this poem of Persephone you have me back in a winter landscape where I used to cut out from my house, going to see a girl I had a crush on, and walked to her house some five or six miles, walking through the Kern River bed. And all the way I used to have fantasies about what kind of men lived in these houses and are that close to this landscape which seemed to me, when I was fourteen or fifteen or sixteen, almost *dizzyingly* sexual. And yet I had not yet admitted to any threshold that I could possibly masturbate although there was mutual masturbation going on. At school they talked about boys who went and jerked off in circles and I couldn't exactly understand what jerking off was but I knew it was some kind of rite. I pictured a rite that the boys who were in the know did. And yet when I went the river way, I waited for a river spirit or nature spirit. So with this exchange of glances, in a way we get right to the Persephone rape that underlies it.

The dusk was already coming and instead of stopping at our house—between our house and the park was fairly large field, about four or five blocks, that wasn't developed. Now I knew I had this power but I never connected this eyepower with playing sex games with kids in schools or necking in cars. I understood that in Bakersfield, in cars, necking, there wasn't that much distinction. Although it's interesting that no one went down on me when I was in high school. My experience when I saw, written on a john wall, something about sucking cock, I thought, "There's somebody crazy around here. Next I'll be reading about cannibals." I was just horrified! and when I went to college and came home, having read *Ulysses* where Molly has her fantasy—I remember saying earnestly to a lesbian friend of the family, "What's Molly thinking about? I would never think something like that." She roared with laughter and said: "Tell me that after next semester."

So it was all heavy necking. Even with mutual masturbation it was rubbing without taking your penis out of your trousers. Or you would sleep together and still in that little cognizant state where you're not actually recognizing what's going on. I would leave masturbating to when the hand now only becomes a sexual organ. The hand changes character, it gets sexual and then we're talking about masturbating. But this was cuming somehow as you hug and snuggle but you're not yet genitalized. You're polymorphous and the genitals are as significantly aroused, but not more so, than any other part of your body.

SHURIN: So you're cuming but not coming out.

DUNCAN: Well, in this particular one—by the way, this pick-up, I'm coming out into a different world remember. I'm coming out now into my Greek world, and yet, I would have been allied to it no matter what. It never disappears. It's constantly present. I was raised on these myths but more than that, my family believed they were true. And they, in their religion, had gone into that realm and I discovered it in poetry as possibly being there. I'd been there. But this is the first time I'd read about the rape of Persephone. The first time I'd encountered one of those people I was looking for in the river valley! And those people were always male! But then no wonder that I caught an absolutely lunatic glance. Probably by the time one of these glances got through to me, and I was taking them up, it was a very disturbed person, a tremendously repressed homosexual.

So we went to an area far enough from the tennis court that it was dark, though it was still quite visible. I had no dimension in which I thought we should not be public. The tennis courts, to me, looked as if we were already in the realm I'm talking about, the realm of my near hypnagogic self, the visionary realm. And right over there was the other realm. The people playing tennis were lit up. It made it more clear that the park where we were was in that other domain. I had no calculation that we might be seen or arrested, any of this.

But in this particular case now, the character that was following me was *also* that removed from reality. The excitement I felt, or the pitch of it, was felt with all the violence of the Greek scene. My mind was on the kind of power Ganymede had over Zeus, but you must remember, Zeus was not in the realm of the living. So I knew what Persephone felt but there was also no question in my mind that I was a male nymph.

How do I so much know and with *no*, again no words, or *maybe* just the most strangled sort of key words that admit you're present in a lunatic-like way? I mean we'd just followed each other to a place where there are no people and it was.... He had a *very* strange look in his eyes that matched the way I felt. His eyes looked like moonstars look—beautiful and exciting! And all the time I'm trying to look beautiful and exciting, trying to look like him, because I *feel* my face change. I'm entranced but so is he. That's what I caught. So I answer entrancement with being entranced. So I'm facing him and at sixty, I'm facing something I faced when I was sixteen.

He's taller than I am, more muscular than me. Then *trembling!* Both of us trembling! He embraced me very...he...we *move* to the ground! All what we're doing now physically was exactly what I'd been doing in cars, necking and so on with boyfriends, staying overnight with T. And *very,* very gentle! Now we come...and, and...we're rubbing but I really began to suddenly be afraid. But this is still where all the rest of us would get off like like when you've come to the rest of a wave and it's continuous to the whole body feeling and no one has taken out a penis in front of you. So you're *encased* in it, in this continuous feeling, and you get wet.

It's moving with a terrific rapture and I see "My God! but this rapture is not only moving somewhere I ain't never been before but it's actually *scary.*" So I move myself from it in a *very* weak tone of voice, very, and I say "I gotta go home. It's, it's kinda late and I...." Well, I *had* to go home because I knew, my god, that something appalling was going to happen. Now what's interesting about this threshold is that I'm not sure exactly what would have happened and at this time he says "I've gotta piss" and he turns away from me. And that's still logical except I'm shaking and know, instinctively, I'll get in trouble if I start walking away.

The he turns around and the face facing me, his face, is one of MANIACAL fury! He has brass knuckles on and says "You dirty little cock teaser, I'm really going to give it to you." He grabs me by the—suddenly the physical force is really very present—and starts hitting me on the chin first. You can still see the scars though I was on a plastic surgeon's table afterwards. And at this point I'm still in another dimension. I can see the people playing tennis. They're close and the court absolutely lighted that I can see their faces and their studied not hearing. I start *screaming* just as loud as I can. It's *inconceivable* to me! There's quite a lot of confusion because that was a magical realm as on a lighted stage and they almost look supernatural because they're so far away but not physically far away. What does happen is a woman four blocks away phones the police 'cause she can hear the screams and has no trouble reading that there's bloody murder going on. So the police are on their way.

He then gets me. Also I learned, of course, you don't suffer any pain. I wasn't aware of anything at all because when your chin is torn open, the nerves torn open, you don't have any sensation, brass knuckles or nothin'. They've gone too far already. So he's succeeded in grabbing me by my leather jacket and he starts hitting, repeatedly, on the back of my neck where he should, of course, have killed me. But my skull is an extreme barrier at this point.

I meanwhile had moved into still another dimension. Everything is absolutely clear. I realize I have only to wait a few seconds more, almost as if I had an interior timer, and my coat would be so bloodied that when I—I could wiggle out of my coat, I knew that. But this is how calculated it all was. My coat would be so bloody he wouldn't be able to hold onto me. So I slipped out of my coat, grabbed it, and started running. By this time there's police cars all around but I don't connect to them or they to me. They went to the park but there was nobody there except for the tennis players who said: "Well, we were so intent on our game here. . . ."

Now in the Depression years we had a Catholic school teacher renting a room from us. I used to talk about God with her and interesting theological things. So when I got home I went to the bathroom because, well, my first problem is I can't explain my bloody coat and bloody shirt. But when I went into the bathroom to clean up and saw the *bone* of my chin exposed and shreds of flesh around it, I mean, already I was a little sick at the idea. So I walk down the hall and tap at the door of the Catholic maiden teacher. She says: "Come in Robert," and I open the door. At that point she turns around and faints and I faint. [*Laughs.*]

Luckily my mother soon arrives home and when I come to, my mother and the chief of police are bending over me. I was in the hospital waiting to be rolled into the operating room and they're saying: "You've gotta describe him, he . . ." And, and I say "I was to blame. I was the one who led him on. I was to blame. I was the one who led him on." And my mother says: "No, no. You don't understand." And the chief of police says: "He's killed two boys already. We've got to get his description." And I refused. I would not give a description.

My family whisked me away soon afterwards but while I was in the hospital I talked, so certain levels of Bakersfield knew what had happened, not so much in my mother's circle but telephone operators and the like so that when I went to college, I met old friends there who knew what had happened. Even here I think we both, the attacker and I, belonged to what happened, hmm? But what I knew in the aftermath is that when I went back to T., my schoolboy crush, I was afraid of him. I was afraid something was going to happen that would go beyond what we had been talking about.

ABBOTT: If you'd not interrupted the road boy by saying you had to leave, do you think the violence still would have occurred?

DUNCAN: Well, we don't know those other boys left. And when they finally did catch him, he had the picture that he was eradicating evil. I mean I had no picture that he was just a disappointed male. After all, I'd seen a few like T. coming back from the bathroom when he'd just had to get it off himself. No, this violence wasn't violence *per se*. He was an actual paranoid schizophrenic who was killing these magic creatures who made him feel such horrible sexual compulsions.

SHURIN: Can I take this back a little bit, into the realm of imagination. We've got this figure of falling in love, and you have the landscape, the Persephone landscape in which...

DUNCAN: Rape. Rapture and rape. Now that wasn't the experience of falling in love.

SHURIN: Right, except that certainly Persephone fell. If anybody fell she fell all the way down.

DUNCAN: Oh, I see. Yah, right. But she makes the descent which is different. She's raped and drawn into the descent. My figures of falling are really figures of falling. I remember when I got involved with Marjorie in NY, and Manhattan has ruined *more* of my scenes than any other city, her psychiatrist told her she should stop seeing me. I remember we were around 34th and Madison when she told me this. And I *fell*. My legs literally gave way. Hesiod says "The primal eros loosens the limbs" and as I told Olsen: "I know what that means. You fall." But now Ekbert Faas, who is working on a biography of my early life, has found in interviewing Marjorie that I didn't actually fall. What was important to me in my account of myself was that I experienced the metaphor. I hallucinated the falling.

SHURIN: What I wanted to get at was the image that was propelling you toward these sexual encounters. What I was hitting off was your line "My other is not a woman but a man." And I wanted to know what sense of the other at that time.

DUNCAN: I think in this scene of the attack I described we'd be in that one because, remember, I said I looked at the face and became its mate. My face became its other. Now this is certainly an other that is of the same species, not a Narcissus, because I didn't dream my face would look like his. But of the order because I thought I was entering a realm and being drawn into it. That's the dangerous foyer, the primal eros. The tenderness in that world is all felt differently from affection but *is* tenderness. There was tenderness in my foyer experience and I still don't see that tenderness is manipulative. For me the tenderness and something terrifying were mixed.

SHURIN: Now were you writing poetry at this point?

DUNCAN: No. Well, yes I was writing some and I have some because my mother saved poetry from this period. When my high-school teacher, who started me writing, was asked: "What was his poetry like?" she replied: "I only remember darkness and blood." That's what it was. But really, writing poetry starts after this episode.

SHURIN: This field of sexuality where darkness and blood are somehow bound up was one of the earliest points which you were driven to write about?

DUNCAN: Early, very early. And it becomes dispersed throughout my poetry. And in Passages, one of the forms of Passages always was like a seizure with a

mounting terror and then a suspension within it and with a potentiality. So very
early I had initiations that I found profoundly important. They're blood initiations. I'll give you a third blood one. The book that the Venice poem belongs to
starts with three poems for J. In Nov. of '47 I was drawn into an immensely intoxicating sexual relationship and then, very swiftly, was living with J. This was
intense but wasn't exactly falling in love.

My ideal, my strong picture like with N., with whom I did fall in love, was
of someone ten years older than me. In that way I think I was replicating my
mother's and father's relationship in which I was my mother falling in love with
my father. I don't feel it so much physically but there was a lot, in falling in
love, with the actual identification with the woman's position for me. So I set
my cap for N. who was a wolf playing the scene. I hadn't met him but had
heard about him first and then snared him and so on. It was Jane Austen all over
again, getting my man like I saw it in the movies.

I met N. at this dance place, I could follow as well as lead in dancing, and
afterwards we went home together. Not that I was the *femme fatale*. I was the
good girl you'd fall in love with forever so I had to play it like the girl lost and
lonely and if you don't phone me, etc. I knew he'd asked a few questions so
I wasn't going on nothing. But it was a *very* exciting Romantic picture for me.
But J. is ten years younger than me and I don't have any picture of *falling* in
love with someone who's ten years younger. I was about twenty-nine 'cause
Spicer had just moved into a Co-op house since he'd fallen in love with a boy
there.

Anyway, I'd just hitchhiked across country on twenty dollars during which
time I'd developed this blinding pain in my head which was the result of four
impacted wisdom teeth. The pain was so severe I had to use my last dollar for a
room so I could sweat it out 'til the pain subsided enough for an operation. The
operation was successful except for a torn arterial connection not satisfactorily
cauterized so if my blood pressure went up at all, I was just choking with
blood. Well, J. turned me on and I remember staggering down the street to a
phone booth. I was just *streaming* blood, which leads me to this poem. You
see there's nothing in Duncan's poetry that is not solidly implanted in things
really going on.

SHURIN: In these early poems you're first beginning to find a language.

DUNCAN: I'm drawn to Pound because of the hypnagogic sort of thing. In
Pound I found those nymphs and maenads with the same charge as I felt them.
I found an identification with trees which is very strong for me. Trees are not
phallic for me. They're beings and that's very different. I see roots and branches
in trees. And a stream of water is a power or force and I wanted to become
water very much. I wanted to become tree and talk with trees and water with a
lot of confidence. They seem to be talking back to me.

SHURIN: When you began to find this language to express your sexuality, which
you did very early, *did* you have a sense or *what* was your sense?

DUNCAN: I was finding my sexuality through these figures. It wasn't as if I was
expressing it. I was realizing it, making it real through these things. Very early
my family read me these stories and myths which they believed revealed deep
secret mysteries about spiritual nature. And so I was told "You'll understand

this when you come into it." Even Cinderella wasn't viewed as just a fairytale. I was told there's a lot here, as in your dreams, which you'll eventually know.

SHURIN: What I was trying to get at in terms of language was what was the sense you had that it was a taboo area in language that you were entering in beginning to speak about your homosexuality. I know that you were one of the first people to publicly use cock in a poem.

DUNCAN: Yes. I was the first person ever to write publicly that I was homosexual, that essay "Homosexual and Society." Well, you couldn't miss that the area was taboo but in my family it was not excluded from their thought. The scoutmaster who was arrested — well, wasn't exactly arrested because my parents had recommended him and didn't want to be discredited. The leading people in Bakersfield met at our house so we little kids knew what was going on. Everyone was suddenly aroused because he'd been caught right out buggering little boys at the summer camp. My parents saw to it he went without bad reference but without good reference either. What they felt was not moral outrage but a concern for their own reputation.

Then there was a county official who'd been in remote circles of our family. He had a Correction Camp. He was charged and brought up because he was sexually, ritually whipping the boys there. That they didn't try to cover. But the anger of my family was *not* that he was doing something homosexual but that, again, it was a misuse of children. My father wouldn't let sex jokes be told that involved children.

SHURIN: So it was permission from your family rather than negation from society.

DUNCAN: They made it clear that other people thought otherwise. They had to in relation to their religion. It's just like money in our household. If money was out on the plate it was family money to pay the paper boy or take a streetcar. If it was in the purse it was mother's money. So if you needed money you'd take from the plate but you didn't do that if you were in somebody else's house. That was strongly emphasized. And the same held true as to how people should behave.

ABBOTT: You often have birds singing in your poems and songs in your poems. Is singing a part of the feminine in you that's coming out?

DUNCAN: Yes. Medea's song upon seeing Jason is at the point when I'm at Black Mountain. Medea is really seeing the way I saw N., seeing "the man." The feeling was so strong, by the way, that I don't have that feeling again. It's not that feeling I had when I met Jess. I was reading Lady Murasaki whan I was living with N., when it was breaking up.

Genji has a mistress and cannot fulfill the relationship so he makes a reincarnation promise to give her a life that he will consummate. With N. I very strongly felt — I was shattered really. I mean *I was* breaking up, but then intense as it was, during the last year I got engaged to marry Virginia Admiral. I was hitchhiking to New York all the time from Indianapolis. I had torrid affairs, I mean I was picking up people as frequently as any little nineteen- or twenty-year-old. I wasn't figuring the arithmetic of this at all. I'd demolish the whole place if the least straying came on his part but *I* wasn't straying. My diaries at Cal are in the aftermath of all this. Still, when I first met Marjorie I'm so wrapped up in the fact that I have been, that N. had to rescue himself and that I've been sexually disowned.

I'm circling around to your question of how come I had a sense of the social punishment that could come down. You couldn't miss it. In the thirties we had friends who at fifty were back on a scene they'd been off thirty years because they'd been in prison. You didn't miss *that* heavy ticket. Being in closets was serious business, not frivolous coppin' out in those days. And when I had no inner reserve about it, everybody was warning me over and over again about my outrageous behavior because there were not a lot of people who were gonna be visibly queer. Then we went to *Snow White and the Seven Dwarfs* and, in the balcony, he went down on me, that was the *most*. He had me more terrified than I'd dreamed. It wasn't like I had him out of his mind there. He was being wicked. He had me out of my mind and he knew it.

ABBOTT: So you liked to scare each other.

DUNCAN: Oh, I know one marvelous moment four or five years ago. [*Laughs.*] Jess said at the breakfast table: "But I was scared of you the first couple years." And I was *appalled*. I thought I could have given the account that at last I'd found somebody who wasn't scared of me and my intensity and my coming on like a local whirlwind when I got carried away. Somebody who took me *au naturel*. But he didn't go into some game with the scare. I didn't say "What do you mean?" I said "I've begun to realize when I meet young poets that they're scared of me and I can kind of see what it would be. I come on so heavy and there seems no way in which this thing is not just hitting you."

After my rape scene I was in a play and an Italian kid in the play gave me a ride home on his bike and stopped in the same park 'cause he'd heard the story of this thing. Now I was still in the context where you jump into bed yet you're still not registering eyes, hands, or even penis touching penis. I'm in dreamland where you swoon. You don't pass out, you swoon. So the next step was this kid I didn't like. I guess there was something going on. Well, we start necking, I'll go along with that, but he takes out his prick and says "Suck it, suck it." And I'm offended because for all the time I've been in bed naked with T. there's been no pricks in my world. Just like when my cousin pointed out my hard on. I worried, does it look like it ought to look? "Hello cock, what are you doing?"

There's a difference between sweet young cock and the "cock" cock. Yet also in high school I was just *dying* for the disclosure you've got to feel and see the cock. They were just separated for me. One of the great things in the gym locker room was were you going to get a grope. But the grope is not yet really — 'cause masturbation is where the hand and the cock is sexual. No wonder the Egyptians ritually masturbated. But I was unwilling to admit I masturbated. Probably I did what was masturbation by pressing and coming. And where I was in the Mount Hotel where they put me after the rape, I mean, I must have looked as queer as a kid could look at seventeen. There was a guy in the kitchen who got me to his room and then as soon as he shows me that he has a hard cock, that wasn't anything I wanted. But that was after this beating.

What I wanted was love, not lust. Lots had to be aroused, lots of romantic foreplay, before I was actually sucking a cock. I mean I've done lots of cocksucking but I remember coming to Sanders Russell where they had just picked up a soldier and he had one of those hard ones you couldn't get off no matter what. They were lined up in a row to suck it and I was just disgusted. The whole thing looked like a deformity. Not on your life. [*Laughs.*]

ABBOTT: It looks to me like the energies were coming from different chakras. The lower chakra is simply the physical sensation but your sexual fantasy was coming from a higher, more magical plane.

DUNCAN: We've got a struggle in which the two are uniting. Rightly it starts from the higher chakra if it's ever going to get there because the society doesn't ever want it to be there. It doesn't want a connection between the higher chakras and the lower chakras. It wants to believe the lower chakra is not a chakra at all.

SHURIN: Even in terms of homosexuality, they don't want connection between the imaginative and the actual. They like to keep that separation.

DUNCAN: You see me constantly going towards naturalization and the spirit of realization. You find me, over and over again, *real*izing things. One of the most important things for me in poems is realizing. If this poem will not be a root *back* to the place where the hand knows the cock, the mouth knows the cock. No matter what is in it (the poem), that it go there and know and find what it is. If that isn't what it is then what is language doing? And we can talk about that with everything.

Olson in *Maximus* has an imaginary body yet with his own body, he didn't exercise it. He misused it. To him it was a broken down automobile, the opposite of what he announces throughout the poem. Meanwhile he's galloping toward advanced emphysema and announcing the breath is the thing it's coming from. He does *not* say breath is holy or he wouldn't be smoking. Both of 'em did it which left them up in their heads. You're *never* gonna get past your lungs when you lungs are squeezed down to that.

If my poems are repeatedly making announcements about the blood and so forth, they're certainly not the foreground of a masochistic, sadistic actuality because that would be so redundant, what's vividly on my mind as an experience, but when we talk about higher chakras, they're announcing "recognize what all your fantasies are and what they say up here." [*Gestures to heart.*]

When I was living with the commercial artist in New York for two years, Lou Harrison [See interview with composer Lou Harrison in *Interviews* vol. 1] had a black boyfriend who was a preacher uptown. Lou had a great cult with blacks and they were great fun to be around. It was the original cast of Gertrude Stein's *Four Saints*. It was heaven really, being with such famous people. And he had 'em all up there and there was a time I read my poems aloud and I read my African Elegy aloud.

It was the first time it actually *dawned* on me that the African Elegy was simply a projection of certain things going on. And when I come to the "Negroes, negroes, all those princes" and I finish this whole thing and I'm in rapture, all those faces beaming at me, and then this great big *gorgeous* hunk of a black stud says "Do you have any par-ti-cu-lar black gentleman in mind" [*Laughs.*] and *I* thought, God! I *didn't* have any particular fellow in mind. I'd made it with slight black guys who were interesting because their skin coloring was different than mine but they didn't belong to the hairy, scary land of the

"Princes, princes." Again, we've got blood in that scene. It was Othello that was on my mind but it was a dream scene and I was moving it and going forward to what I was seeing. In fact, in that one, I find *I* am that figure. So I'm the one who has that jealousy and princely domination and I'm finding myself restricted by the way I dominate a scene.

ABBOTT: What was the homosexual scene like in your college years?

DUNCAN: I'd joined a frat house and during Rush I thought gee, I'm not going to have any trouble getting new boyfriends because by the time I'd gone through all the frat houses, when I'd finally pledged, I'm getting telephone calls from all the other frat houses. So I started going to the opera with a very attractive, intelligent substitute for T. and I thought, gee, that's nice. So your drawers were wet when you got home and all.

I remember the sophistication of the frat house 'cause they said: "Well, we know why that guy's taking you to the opera all the time and when he stops taking you to the opera we'll know ya came across so he better take ya to the opera for the whole season." [*Laughs.*] This was at the end of the Depression and I knew they needed my money. My family wanted me to pledge a frat house and I'd pledged the poorest lookin' one because I could see I'd have command of the situation. But also I could see they wouldn't care if I was queer or not. And I got to be a sort of pet 'cause I was out front whereas Boggs was just absolutely treated as, well, they took him to a whore house once and then had him describe—they knew he was queer but wouldn't come out of the closet so they just tortured him.

I began to see this wasn't like high school. There's a very busy circle of things going on. We'd go to a place where you could dance, where they'd drink quite a bit, and I began to be aware. All frat houses took their pledges to Finocchio's just to give 'em this shock of what they'd never seen before so I do remember another Wow. This was 1936. Finocchio's had imported from Japan this great youth, he was probably eighteen, and they also had another twenty-year-old gorgeous, bewildering male presence in women's clothes yet. Well, I saw there *were* pleasure boys. So that was hovering in my mind but I was also harried because I could see I was not going to make the scene that they had. First place, I couldn't imagine "where do they put it?" They did this strip down to the size of a postage stamp. They looked like Khalil Gibran, like there was nothing there. [*Laughter.*] But if I strip I'm going to be revealed as a hairy male right?

ABBOTT: You didn't think of shaving your body?

DUNCAN: Not at *all!* Let's go back to body images. I'd seen these Greek statues but of course they never had any hair on them. Which I didn't either then. And I already had a strong image I wanted hair on my body, not shaggy, but enough to define what was going on. And I was very worried...

ABBOTT: Would this be a compensation for coming out? I mean I used to have this feeling, growing up, of wanting hair to prove I was a man.

DUNCAN: My father wasn't hairy. But remember, this was a period when we did not *see* males. They wore uppers on their bathing suits and at no time did you see chest display, *ever*, in the thirties. You did see working men I guess but this was a middle-class world and you just did not see men who were not of your class. There were Chicanos, I guess, but you read them out. It wasn't polite to be looking at people who were working so all the people you were actually ripping off you didn't connect with.

ABBOTT: Gore Vidal did. He talked in an earlier *Gay Sunshine* interview about how randy the working-class men were.

DUNCAN: Well, once we *looked*, there they were. But avoidance must have been very common because it certainly was where I was at. So looking was first a breaking the barrier of the stranger. The whole homosexual community was fascinated by two things: youth, of course, bringing people out was a very important thing. But of all absurdities, bringing someone out when they've been out since they were six and ready to build mantraps. [*Laughing.*] At that age I would have jumped into a meat chopper. And yet bringing out was a very definite occupation. Did you bring him out, etc. But that's the male business of did you have the maidenhead. Remember, that's only the first time.

Then there was the great business about the one-night stand. Always you're talking about the disappointment, a wolf getting you for a one-night stand, okay? But it wasn't a wolf. We talked about a one-night stand when we knew they weren't going to be coming back, when you knew this wasn't the beginning of a sexual friendship.

This is something we ought to talk about when we come to *Gay Sunshine*. We've got lots of phrases about our disappointment in relationships but *nothing* in our society opens sexual friendships for us. When we come to Duncan's formula, it's so centered in having to have a household that it will sacrifice whole areas, because I experience falling in love and adultery and so forth. I've come to realize it's the ground of something more intense and more meaningful and in time you come to realize what it is. I don't think our eyes are wrong or our bodies are wrong. One feels hopeless because it's your whole life you share. So unless you're willing to move in with somebody for a week, whatever it is, that wholly, that sexuality—that's where I saw you, okay? But then I know also you mustn't share your whole life. When I'm sitting here talking to you I'm sharing my whole life with you. So you find the ground. But we don't provide sexual ground for a conversation. So let's make this sentence number one: We have never treated sexuality as language so we do not have sexual conversation and when we say "sexual intercourse" we think we are being horrible or clinical when actually intercourse is talking together, communicating. Our society *nowhere, nowhere* permits this information that we might have been talking when we were first playing because very soon we come to the place where "that kind of talk is for the one person."

What are we as writers and poets? When you bring the news to lives that are forming themselves, then they suddenly see, gee, we're not trying to be liberated or something. We're trying to find how do you have an actual parenting sexual communication. Not promiscuity. That was only a word for it. Everybody experienced me, by the way, as promiscuous. This was usually women around and they lectured me I was psychotic. Sanders Russell who had an absolute cult of the stranger; that meant only once and they had to be strangers. And I know the excitement. I had a kind of mystique of the stranger, very much since I was picking up my room every night. I was really rather afraid of the stranger. I'd pick up the Daddyman who'd let me sleep at night and also they were nice and cuddly sex and didn't *involve* anything. I guess that's a form of hustling isn't it. But the stranger was a very significant person. Remember I couldn't say "I love you." You could have sex providing it is *not* like communication.

ABBOTT: You can communicate fantasies sometimes easier with a stranger.

DUNCAN: Yes, but you're both fantasizing.

One thing about a stranger: you don't have to figure out when you're in phase 'cause you are in phase when you're out looking. When you come to a constant relationship you have to have a whole range of interchanges about phases, confidence that you'll return to the very specific thing you want. So your fantasies, if they're excluded—If I want to do something and the other person doesn't that's not in question. But if I began to exclude a sexual act, then I blow up, am absolutely unhandled, because no matter what I do you have a scrap present. If you have an exclusion of something, then you have something worse than the fantasy because all your fantasies are nervously surrounding this one thing that's on your mind.

Oh. In my marriage, the most important thing, because I didn't really have an image of cunt, I had to do a lot of cunt licking and smelling but especially seeing. So sexuality was very centered there. In relation to buggering it was never really centering until after that, with J., there was some anal licking and seeing. We're talking about organs really being present, present to the eye. Your chakras makes sense to me. I'm not going to worry if they're chakras or not. We're talking about is it present throughout. Do they have the imprint? Is it in your consciousness or not? You have one thing in reference to asshole and anus and returned with your interior feelings of it. And with your peristaltic feeling and emitting of turds, all this is your interior feeling. You can't look at your rectum. Of course now with movies, etc., you have a lot more pictures but could I hold it in place if I saw it, smelled it, tasted it. So in these early phases, the first thing when I sucked my first cock was I had to decide how did I *feel* about this *taste*. And there was no difficulty.

ABBOTT: You were quoted as saying, "We have yet to begin to create the psychological and mythological tradition to build the gay culture and gay arts movement that would be needed." Do you want to expand on that?

DUNCAN: Oh, yes, let's go first, did we ever have such a culture? I've written on this, when I discussed chapter three of *The H.D. Book* in *Tri-Quarterly* review, and it is the chapter specifically on the Eros. I traced through there how inadequate it seems to me are the tracings even in the few areas where our Homo-Eros appears.

"The Homosexual In Society" article of 1944 arose from my reaction to a fashionable gay party and seeing a young poet, seeing what I feared I might be too, in his affected voice. Hadn't he lost his own natured voice, having lost his manhood essentially. And if you think about the term manly today it's a very forceful and troublesome word, it's avoided a great deal, what are you if you're a man? So we're full into the center of what is my picture. I think we're discovering a homosexual manhood in a more solid ground than was provided in the Greek world. In the Greek world they were thought of as a very special cult; Plato doesn't propose anything other than that. Higher thought; by being removed from women they were removed in their minds from triviality, and among the trivialities were daily life, how you cook. We don't any longer believe that knowing the nature of food and nutrition is demeaning to a mind; it's the center of our idea of what mind properly is. So when you're talking about manly and manhood it goes along with our new ideas of nutrition, of food good versus food bad. We've got a charged politics today, Nader would represent that, that people are putting out false food as well as false fronts. So when we list the goods we're in the actual territory of manliness. When Plato lists the goods he knows nothing about the goods of food and the bads of food. We don't even find that data when we move back to the Greek world; it doesn't seem to be as complete a picture as ours. And your poem [Steve's "Night on Amoeba Mountain") for instance, addressing the green at the end and an alliance with the plant world and its natures and what is in it, this is also central to us in what the mind and the manhood is realized in. And Plato's day, the whole classical period is so far apart from it that when it attempts to give a description of the plant world it's got very little picture of it, very little observation.

So if we go back just to the place when we're talking about the homosexual world, first I can't separate that from finding our manhood. Women's Liberation and what it says today—I do not hear more than very clear evidence that they've been so deprived and closed away that they're giving expressions of acute pain that they can't locate what womanhood is. So that we're very far away from finding out what manhood is. Now we come to why and how I see the homosexual is closer to that. A man in love with a man not only finds himself in the presence of his manhood but also in the presence of the other's manhood, and so he cannot but know the agony and the separation from nature. And his formula can't be as simple—although it certainly is—we hear it on the stage, it's done over and over again—yes, the formula can be we both flunked out from manhood. A man can scream at a man like a woman can scream at a man that he's not a man. Or a man will scream at a woman that she's not a woman, the contempt goes two ways doesn't it. And a woman can scream at a man that he is a man, you can do both. The accusation can be that you're not a woman, and that's when you're angry. Or the accusation can be that you are a woman, that's when you're angry. It can be you are a man or you're not a man.

Just think of our social class, we all have got a thing of what this is. Now I'm not talking about role-playing, but about something very central to the field. Again like the one you talked about when you talked about a cult. The weak place in Marx is not at all in the economic description of the society, not at all in the sense of the things that are being made, but in psychological penetration—society not only consists of what we make. And he's pretty solid if we take him through about what the goods are of the society. This is a place where we begin to think about the actual goods of a society, it's the beginning of socialism, and in Marx they become fairly solid. Except of course he's so attracted by the fact that class division gives him a political lever, one class against the other, that he loses entirely that there's profoundly evil labor to be done, and the laborers who are working in profoundly evil labor are profoundly evil. And you get the present-day Marxists who can't account for the fact that the strongest thing in back of Nixon was the working class, not the labor bosses. There were millions of votes out there because they didn't want to end the war industries where they were making their rip-off. And they do not want socialism because all the people in unions have guaranteed medical benefits, for instance, and if all of us had it the unions wouldn't have even a lever anywhere. If we had socialized medicine and if we had guaranteed what any working-class person has who's in a union, the union wouldn't be able to charge them their dues. So this is something Marx didn't even look at. But he also didn't look at the most fundamental thing of all, and that is no matter where we put it in class, that's just tops and dressing to what you feel a man is and what is a woman. And that's the mystery, we come into the mystery then because it's always been there and I can't believe it isn't.

When I think of Jess [Duncan's lover] his reality is very like my own for me. It must be the nature of living together for years, the sense of manliness and womanliness is ongoing; the range of roles shared and exchanged — child and parent, and so on. Roles are so mere, you turn around and want Jess to fix your tinker-toy and discover he's not going to be Daddy that day and you've got to go and figure it out yourself, and you say "but I thought you were going to fix the whole mechanical thing for me." All of those dimensions we've got set in our minds are really trivial in relation to the underlying thing we're asking. But when we come to the level in which we don't get to choose — we really do or do not desire, and we don't do that all the time, and we also have attractions, we have to answer what do they mean finally. And that thing is total and social; we come up against it at every turn no matter how we define it. I talk in that NET television thing about how much space was earned for my generation by the next generation who actually comes out in public. I was never not out in that sense. Anybody who knew me at all couldn't even read me after "The Venice Poem" without knowing. And after I'd made the declaration in 1944. But that's nothing to demanding a way of living. Jess and I heave a great sigh of relief that we didn't take a place twelve years ago in the middle of the gay ghetto. Our neighborhood is happy, it doesn't plunge us into a very special environment. That's like would you like to check out on being Jewish by living in the Jewish ghetto. But remember they're not forced to live in this ghetto so it's not a ghetto like in Europe. We forget that the ghetto in Europe was a place where people were forced to live, consequently we've got a very different kind of Jewish experience than we do if we went — the freedom to be or not be in a synagogue for instance. Aaron can dwell upon his Jewish name and go voluntarily to a synagogue, but in a Jewish world he wouldn't. Actually I know contexts, Jewish contexts, in which Aaron would be called to order, could be a Jew no matter what. Now it's a different thing than when he's in the areas in which I go towards Jewish too, because it tells us something essential about our human nature that isn't anywhere else. Okay, now we're getting towards that manhood.

There's something essential about human nature. When I talk about god who certainly comes in my poetry, and I certainly talk about creation and about an intent in creation — every single individual in that creation is part of its revelation. This counter-culture erases how complex that is. When we've got appearing groups and continuous intent through human history, and there has been a continuous intent to formulate what man's sexuality is, the prohibition of it formulates it. And the cultivation, there's two things you do, all of which point to it, show it, this is significant, this is part of the dream, this is part of the revelation. If this part of the revelation were known we wouldn't just be Jews because we'd be like the Phoenicians.

Yet if you didn't have any purification and withdrawals you'd be back only having orgies; orgies seem to be the earliest form of a sexuality and we're talking about the development out of an orgiastic, an orgy space, into the place where it becomes united with ideas of love and united with long lifetime intent so they aren't sudden seizures. Sudden seizures will still remain, I don't mean they'll be erased. And in the new community I don't think we're going to have just one thing, clearly we're not going to be just one thing, to be homosexual any more than one thing is Jewish, or one thing is the black movement. But if you think about the Jewish religion—there *is* a kind of homosexual religion— so I've got your question plus your first question about cult. The place I went to dance and you meet—the lambs meet the wolves—this is ritualizing on a religious level of meeting, this is a folkway that has gone on for a long time, its terms were folkways some of them very traceable. I'm not going back to witch cults in this but going back to males, cults of males, cultivating what specific roles they're going to have when they meet. And they're already new to learn; you learn certain new things about a community that's already there. I think I mentioned how important it was for males of about thirty-forty or so to be bringing people out. With great pride that they could see that they were homosexual and then bring them out, show them that they were homosexual. This is what is usually not understood. Bringing someone out was not putting someone where they weren't but seeing that they were homosexual and bringing them out, so it was kind of missionary work. Remember our present missionary work was that you go in and bend the heads of a bunch of savages and convert them. But these were not conversions, they were seeing that they were members of a group and revealing to them that they were. So they have a very different missionary role. And they would be like Paul and the early Christians where you say—I think in a moment not having to do with sexuality, what this same power was when at the Ross in Washington I said "This dinner, I've got to go thank the cook" and I go to the door of the kitchen and a black woman comes towards me and says "You are a lover of Jesus too, aren't you?" and I swallow and as painfully as I ever couldn't say I love you say "Yes." She said "There are not many of us." Now that is the power that has to do with bringing people out.

Today there are mass persuasions and you don't know, I mean maybe they're bringing out, there's nothing about this yea or nay. But we moved into a period in which bringing out—yeah, what is falling in love but bringing something out, now we're getting around to it, falling in love is bringing something out at a deeper and deeper level. So that scoring is bringing out who's there. Scoring— when you're just checking-in, are you going to make it—even that brings something out. But scoring is where actually you've caught just the eye and each becomes the initiator of the other into what, for an amazing percentage is proper to both. Remember I only once got caught in something not proper. Even it was a terrible revelation. And when I fall in love each one must—not only does it enter my nature and shape it, like I spoke scorn of E. but I don't dream that he wasn't a revelation. You don't hang around someone for years, no, you like argue yourself out of it, you can be embarrassed—all sorts of other layers, but you can be embarrassed by how silly the preacher is at church when you have to go to church. So there is a level in which I think we can identify a kind of religion in the homosexual and the homoerotic. Also in art, that somebody can be a poet —it was so important to Robin [Blaser] and Spicer and me that we find poets;

we didn't succeed—the grain of a poet, that there could be a poet—because actually when I speak of poetry it's exactly like this. And I don't always understand why it's a poet, but in my terms as a poet it's very rare. It's amusing, some kind of absolute, and it's being in love with language and not knowing it all the way through, but the only ones who knew it all the way through were poets.

SHURIN: Falling in love with a man is bringing the man out, and bringing into hu-man-ness a hidden nature of man.

DUNCAN: As a matter of fact love is a primary intent, now, not just a nature. Nature's ahead now and we're talking about intent. Up to Darwin God's design and intent would be presumed to be like making men out of little clay things and a model—like we take the Bible saying we were made in his image. It's like over in Plato-land, I've got a little model here and I make a little man. As a matter of fact there is such an image but now we know it's really fundamental, it's through the whole universe, the DNA. The chemical works lawful throughout are the image, if there's an image at all, but there's not an image it's a process, and it's got laws consequently, an image doesn't have laws. But image is ahead all the time because once you have Darwin you see My god there's a mysterious intent that no one can see. Now it looks like god looks in the most grand gnostic pictures of god; the whole universe must take place in order for him to find himself. Because he doesn't exist except through the universe and the universe is absolutely the field in which he is taking place. As a matter of fact, when we look at Jewish history, we see that it has to take place in order for something to happen. That must be god happening, so we can show its intent in the same way, but the Jews don't know what it is that has happened. They know when they go through terrible experiences in this, in mystic Jewry, then Belsen-Buchenwald are not meaningless they're revelations, and they're appalling revelations no matter what they are, of greater and greater more and more appalling nature of god. So you either fall out, not want it at all, or you're going to hold it together in your head.

But the intent I see is really the largest intent, so my poetry becomes more and more confidently filled with the fact that there's a creation as I get deeper and deeper into Darwin, which is absolute material creation. I do not accept at all ideas as anything other than the flowers, the fluvia, odors and everything else of the world of material—the material world—back there when I called things, because things can be anything in Plato-land; it's materialism, utter natural materialism all the way through. And spirit is material, unless you think you're breathing anything other than material as you're breathing in and out, oxygen and so forth. And the whole material world is spiritual, that plant over there is as—do we want more spirit than that is. I mean that Matisse draws heaven out of taking one deep look for about five weeks at that plant, so we're all feeding, language all the way through. And the ideas of manhood then, you're right, we fall in love with man, really we're reaching toward the manhood we see possible in that person. And the answer goes: and that manhood is not something that's there but is only there the way we then make love. So our phrase making love is the same as making poems. [*Applause.*] And some people just make poems. And we're talking about no, that's not what you do with a poem, not only do you feel a shapeliness the requirement with a poem, but you can't anymore make that poem without—any further than you are that deeply in love with it.

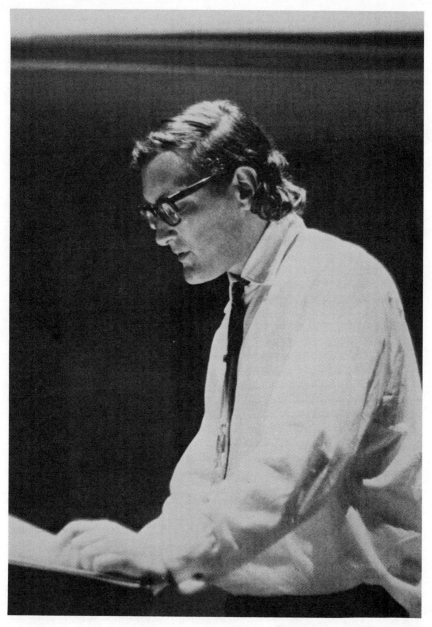

PHOTO BY SIDNEY B. ZAMOCHNICK

KENWARD
ELMSLIE

KENWARD ELMSLIE was born in New York City in 1929, grew up in Colorado Springs, Colorado, and now lives most of the year in Calais, Vermont. The son of a rancher, he graduated from Harvard College in 1950. He began his literary career with ventures in several forms of theatrical writing—including nightclub comedy material (for Dody Goodman and Lisa Kirk) and sketches for off-Broadway revues (Ben Bagley's *Shoestring '57* and *The Littlest Revue*) as well as a jukebox hit song, "Love-wise," made popular by Nat King Cole, Nancy Wilson, and Mabel Mercer. By 1960, his literary focus had shifted to poetry, and five collections of his poetry have been published: *Album* (Kulchur Press), *The Champ* and *Circus Nerves* (Black Sparrow), *Motor Disturbance* (Columbia University Press), which won the 1971 Frank O'Hara Award for Poetry, and *Tropicalism* (Z Press). He has also written a novel, *The Orchid Stories* (Double-day), and the books and lyrics of a musical play, *The Grass Harp* (Samuel French), composed by Claibe Richardson, produced on Broadway, and subsequently recorded—the album was chosen "The Best Show Album of the Year" by *Show* magazine. The first opera libretto he wrote was *The Sweet Bye and Bye*, set to music by Jack Beeson. Its professional première was given by the Kansas City Lyric Theatre in 1973, and it has been recorded by Desto Records. A second collaboration with Beeson, *Lizzie Borden*, was produced by the New York City Opera, televised by NET, and recorded by Desto, and was revived in April 1976 at Lincoln Center. His next libretto, *Miss Julie* (based on the Strindberg play), with music by Ned Rorem, was premièred by the New York City Opera. The librettos and scores of *The Sweet Bye and Bye*, *Lizzie Borden*, and *Miss Julie* are all published by Boosey & Hawkes. He has also written two librettos for Thomas Pasatieri: *The Seagull* (based on the play by Anton Chekhov), which was premièred by the Houston Grand Opera in 1973, published by Belwin-Mills, and subsequently revived by the Seattle Opera in January 1976; and *Washington Square* (1976), based on the novel by Henry James, and first produced by the Michigan Opera Theatre. He has also collaborated with the artist-writer Joe Brainard on two visual books, *The Baby Book* and *The 1967 Gamebook Calendar*, published by Boke Press. His poems have appeared in eight anthologies, and he has written one full-length play, *City Junket*.

Kenward Elmslie can be heard singing on *Rare Meat* (Poets Audio Center), a cassette retrospective of his poems and songs, and also on *Big Ego* (Giorno Poetry Systems Records) and *The World Record*, produced by the St. Marks Poetry Project, New York City. In 1982, Ben Bagley's Painted Smiles Records released *Kenward Elmslie Visited*, an anthology of his sung works, ranging from cabaret numbers and Broadway show tunes to opera scenes and poem songs. In March 1982, *Lola*, a musical for which he wrote the book and lyrics, composed by Claibe Richardson, was produced off-Broadway by the York Theatre Company. His most recent publications include *Communications Equipment* (Burning Deck Press); *Moving Right Along* (Z Press), a collection of poems and theater works; *Topiary Trek* (Topia Press), illustrated by Karl Torok; and *Bimbo Dirt* (Z Press) and *Palais Bimbo Snapshots* (The Alternative Press), both illustrated by Ken Tisa.

THIS INTERVIEW was taped in San Francisco in early 1975 at the apartment of *Gay Sunshine* editor Winston Leyland. It originally appeared in *Gay Sunshine* no. 29/30 (Summer/Fall 1976).

Winston Leyland interviews
KENWARD ELMSLIE

LEYLAND: Maybe we could start by talking about your most recent opera libretto.

ELMSLIE: I've just finished *Washington Square*, based on the Henry James novel. It was commissioned by Michigan Opera Theatre, and will première on October 1st, '76, starring Giorgio Tozzi, Catherine Malfitano, and Brent Ellis—an ideal writing situation, to know where your work is going to wind up, and to collaborate with a terrific composer, Thomas Pasatieri. He sets my words with caressing clarity, and he also has a fantastic sense of what makes effective lyric theater. Plus which he's fun to be with on the road, humpy looking, and a good friend in a crisis. I adore him. The project took a while to get off the ground. Tom first came to see me in '66, and broached the idea. I'd only seen the movie *The Heiress*, so I told him I couldn't face doing another long-dress opera about a spinster who closes the door on life in the last scene, which is how *Lizzie Borden* ended—an opera I'd written the libretto for which was first produced around then by the New York City Opera. The critics and the audience tended to grumble about the music by Jack Beeson, but the theatricality of the story and the production carried the day, and *Lizzie* has subsequently done herself proud—she's been televised by NET, recorded, and even revived, and seems to have escaped the graveyard almost all contemporary American operas justifiably get dumped into, post-première. People find the music more accessible now, for some reason, and can hear past the gnarled dissonance and enjoy Jack's lyricism, tight-assed WASP lyricism, but lyricism nonetheless. Anyway, when Tom phoned me up last fall, how about *Washington Square*, this time I said yes right off, because we'd written an opera which had proved itself the year before in Houston—*The Seagull*, based on the Chekhov play. It was a very happy collaboration—really for the first time, I felt my words had been given a fair shake, an enormous problem in opera, where the music thrust sometimes goes one way, and the word thrust goes another way, and ends up being emasculated. It's very hard to get a proper mix. When I finally read *Washington Square*, I found out to my delight that it's quite different from *The Heiress*, which is a tale of revenge. The novel is a story of fulfillment—a repressed girl, totally mind-fucked by her father and suitor, survives and becomes a person, on her own. Somewhat to my surprise, challenging and pertinent.

LEYLAND: Which of your previous librettos has been most successful? You did one with Ned Rorem, *Miss Julie*.

ELMSLIE: A disaster! Strindberg's dialogue is made up of endless bickering, which reveals subtle psychological shifts of class-and-sex warfare. Small detail work on a verbal level is fatal for opera, which moves in a lumbering way, on a grand scale, like a big battleship. Bickering, *sung* bickering for long stretches might be fine, for a twelve-tone man, but not for Ned. And while I shaped the dialogue into chunks of text as best I could to provide Ned with some sort of take-off point, Strindberg pinned me down as a poet: it was my least favorite writing experience, and the show was a New York Opera dud production-wise. I respect the music, and two superstar performers might make it all work, but who knows—hindsight evaluations, phooey! In some ways, I know very little about my own work. The first time I saw *Lizzie Borden* on television, it scared me shitless! I felt divorced from it as "writer," and I watched it as I would anything on TV. It was the same cast I'd seen onstage, pretty much the same direction, same everything—but one character in particular, the stepmother Abbey, I'd always thought of as a figure of fun. On TV she turned into a frightening, really vicious monster.

LEYLAND: Which you hadn't intended.

ELMSLIE: I enjoyed writing her part, so I was fond of her, felt chummy. But on TV, she was a monster! I'd written a monster!

LEYLAND: How did you become a librettist?

ELMSLIE: Totally by accident. When I first came to New York, in '52, I wanted to write Broadway musicals. I was living with John Latouche, who, as lyricist, was my culture hero. Long before I met him, I sleuthed out his shows, sometimes seeing them again and again, particularly *Beggar's Holiday*, music by Duke Ellington, and *Ballet Ballads*, composed by Jerome Moross. The texture of his lyrics (like Brecht's) hit a different opened-up level of language I responded to more intensely than to the marvelous show-biz expertise of Cole Porter or Ira Gershwin or Lorenz Hart. At that time, John was writing an opera with Douglas Moore, *The Ballad of Baby Doe*. Douglas had a protégé in the music department at Columbia, Jack Beeson, who needed a librettist. John sort of turned me loose. I had an awful time thinking up a subject, so Douglas Moore suggested The Life and Times of Aimée Semple McPherson, the Billy Graham of the twenties. A great idea! Jack thought he was Richard Strauss, and I was his Hugo von Hoffmansthal. I had a different view of things. I was secretly trying to write a musical that would be Great Art, an all-sung musical.

LEYLAND: Was this in the early fifties?

ELMSLIE: Yeah, around '55. *The Sweet Bye and Bye*, as we called it, was first done at Juilliard, and the *Times* called it an "achievement," but it didn't really come off. The audience was baffled by its semi-pop collage of bathing beauties, big religious choral numbers, romantic duets, a jazz ballet, a melodramatic shooting, and an ironic ending. It bounced around in tone too jauntily for the opera buffs: they get off on high notes, and to hell with the laughs. Two years ago, *The Sweet Bye and Bye* surfaced in Kansas City, its first "pro" production. Again, no dice. The director turned the stage into a womb, no kidding. But a topnotch album was made. I listened to it stoned once, and at last it coalesced in my head into a huge super-musical, constructed with a high-energy surface, like a good regular musical, but with layers of finesse packed in underneath—it seemed incredibly *evolved*. It could have been the grass.

LEYLAND: You've written a musical, haven't you? *The Grass Harp.*

ELMSLIE: The hardest thing I've ever had to do including poetry! To try to fulfill a lifelong ambition: to write a Broadway Musical, a form jampacked with zany demands, and to keep afloat myself as a poet, and also deal with Truman Capote's highly personal vision of his boyhood—wow! I worked on it for years, slaved.

LEYLAND: With Truman Capote himself?

ELMSLIE: No. Claibe Richardson, the composer, and I wrote four or five test songs, to see if we could cut the mustard. We invited Truman over, and performed them. He was great! He told us to make it our own, and literally gave us the rights, no strings attached, which was very trusting of him, as we were unknowns. After a tryout in Providence, and another tryout in Ann Arbor, on to Broadway! It lasted two weeks, got some raves and some pans, lost a quarter of a million. Claibe and I turned mean as snakes and out of sheer perversity, produced a show album of it ourselves, in Cologne of all places, an album which helped metamorphose *The Grass Harp* from Broadway flop to Cult Musical.

LEYLAND: Would you like to talk about the writing of a libretto in terms of collaborating with the composer?

ELMSLIE: In writing *The Grass Harp*, Claibe and I worked close to each other, literally, at the piano, in fact. I'd bring in a bit of a lyric, which might inspire a melody fragment, which might help me expand the lyric, which might lead to an extension of the melody—back and forth, it's hard to say which comes first sometimes. Claibe has set lyrics, as is, and I've written words to his music— but generally it's back and forth. With my librettos, the words come first, totally; I mail the stuff off, act by act, and the composer sets it. Sometimes I make up melodies in my head just to keep me on the track, to give me a stanza shape and a beat. Happily, the composer never hears my music. Except once. I brought a lyric called "Love-wise" to Marvin Fisher, a real Tin Pan Alley composer I was working with, and I sang my "dummy" melody to him, hamming it up brazenly, as a gag. He actually used my melody, shaped it up, helped me with the end of the lyric, and after two weeks of polishing this one little song, we abandoned it. Some time after, a friend of mine, Gerrit Lansing, phoned me up and said "Your song is on the jukebox!" I'd always wanted to write a jukebox hit, and sure enough, I rushed to some gay bar, and there it was: Nat King Cole.

LEYLAND: How long have you known Gerrit Lansing? I admire his poetry immensely, and included some of it in my recent anthology *Angels of the Lyre.*

ELMSLIE: I used to stay with his family in Chagrin Falls, Ohio. We knew each other from childhood. We both moved to New York around the same time— and for a while we set each other writing exercises—which was quite liberating for me. The bent of his interests was different from mine: alchemy, tarot cards, magic, Aleister Crowley—esoterica, in those days. Poetry was a central interest of his, while for me at that point it was peripheral. I remember meeting John Ashbery through him, at Dunster House, at Harvard. I was terrified by John's blazing eyes—they cut right through me. Later on, I began to write poems, but I was a closet poet. I didn't know what to make of them because they didn't fit my idea of who I was, as a writer. That was after I'd moved to New York.

LEYLAND: This was when you first started to write poetry?

ELMSLIE: Well, I would write all sorts of odd things, but I didn't quite trust them. They didn't seem to relate to anything I was reading. I didn't know where they came from, what to do with them. I enjoyed writing them, while I was writing, but they were just sort of a puzzle to me. At some point in the fifties, I showed them to Gerrit—they'd become a habit. I would write these things instead of working on songs; they offered me freedom. Gerrit said, "You're a poet." I thought he was putting me on, so I sent a batch off to *Poetry* magazine in Chicago to check them out, and they accepted them. Beginner's luck, but I went around thinking, "I am a poet. I am a poet." So, I kept on writing and sending them out.

LEYLAND: Gerrit Lansing was a friend of Steve Jonas in Boston. Did you know Steve Jonas also?

ELMSLIE: Once Gerrit took me to see him, without telling me who he was. He lay there, on a mattress on the floor, and I wondered why on earth Gerrit had brought me to see this Puerto Rican drag queen. Then Steve Jonas began a non-stop discourse which freaked me out—a paranoid fantasy about money and power and the Kennedy family. He rigged up a harebrained theory that the Kennedys were manipulating all the banks and controlling the gold in Fort Knox.

LEYLAND: So you began to write poetry in the fifties?

ELMSLIE: Yeah, in New York. John Latouche was my mentor, and my main interest was writing musicals. Poetry was a guilty sideline. It was odd how we met. I was in Cleveland, fresh out of Harvard, and I'd written a one-act ballet ballad inspired by John's *Ballet Ballads*. I brainwashed the German stage director of a black-white settlement house to couple my piece with *Willie the Weeper*, one of John's ballet ballads. It was a dream work—Willie lights up a joint, a dancing alter ego appears, and the piece is made up of various hallucinatory ups and downs. I don't think I even knew what marijuana was. So John Latouche came out to see his work, and I was appointed his driver-arounder. He asked me to stay with him if I came to New York. It seemed unbelievable! My writer hero! So I went to New York, spent a night with him, and several months later moved into his penthouse for good. It was an incredible environment for a pimply shy sheltered kid to be thrust into! I'd mainly led a kind of quiet life, full of limitations and barriers, full of good manners. Quarrels were out in my family, scenes taboo. No sex talk. No money talk. Not much touching. Suddenly I was propelled into a wild world of alcohol binges, rages, all-night arguments, volatile gatherings of egomaniacs, Myra Deren, Keisler, Ruth Yorck, Jane Bowles, Paul Bowles, Oliver Smith, Lena Horne, Josephine Premice, Alice Bouverie, Ellsworth Kelly, Gore Vidal, Valerie Bettis, Virgil Thomson, Ned Rorem, Libby Holman, Jack Kerouac, and it was very dynamic, very complicated, very high energy. John could get to people fast, on a visceral level, and he was filled with a violent emotional intensity. When he was angry, his angers were unbelievable. I was silent, impassive, secretive about my emotions—a perfect foil. John was making an animated cartoon at that point, so at nine, the cartoonists would arrive, and our bed was in the living room for some reason. I just accepted the lack of privacy. And then the day would unfold, with waves of people, and parties at night. I was very priggish, and I remember getting angry at Tennessee Williams because he wasn't interested that I was a writer—instead he said I had nice legs, which I thought was very Rotarian sexism.

LEYLAND: How long did you live with John?

ELMSLIE: He died in '56; four years. Because of the turbulence of his life, I sort of pulled him away from New York, which I think he wanted too. We went up to Vermont and found a house together and started a life together up there. I still go there—the house is near Calais.

LEYLAND: This has been a retreat from the hectic tempo of New York?

ELMSLIE: Yeah. I keep spending more and more time up there—I go in May, plant my vegetable garden, and stay put till December. When it really snows, the road is impassable. It's too rough for me, so I come back to the city.

LEYLAND: What kind of poetry were you writing at that time?

ELMSLIE: I thought I was taking off on my own, but there was magazine called *Semi-colon* published by John Myers who was the first publisher to print a book of my poetry: *Pavilions*. In this magazine there was a short play by James Schuyler called *Shopping and Waiting*. When I came upon it, I couldn't believe it because it was very close to these odd things I would write and stick in a drawer because they seemed so strange. I felt so at home with this one work of his. Later on I got to know him. John Latouche's interests were way ahead of their time—the *Book of Changes*, mescaline, magic, and he also moved with ease out of the Broadway arena into the world of the avant-garde, so it seemed natural for there to be a poetry reading in John's penthouse one night, featuring two young unknowns—John Ashbery and Frank O'Hara. I didn't know them at all, and I didn't know what to make of Frank. He read an incredible poem, "Easter," full of "fucks" and fecal rage. I hated it—the violence of the language scared me to death. Ashbery read a witty poem called "He" which could have evolved out of a Cole Porter "list" lyric, so I could understand *him*. It took me a while to pick up on their language. At a certain point, writing show lyrics just gave out for me. It was too constricting. I happened to go to a jazz joint called the Five Spot around this time, and heard Kenneth Koch read his plays, with Larry Rivers providing a jazz background. I found this event very inspiring— a kind of hilarious energy which I savored was generated by these plays. What I feared about poets and poetry at that point was that they were in some dark stifling corner that reeked of cultism, that very few people could understand. And I felt a writer had an obligation to be accessible, understandable to a big public. I began seeing a great deal of Kenneth—we were tennis partners, and sometimes shared houses in the summer. His epic masterpiece "Ko" was published around then, and I admired its comic sweep. I began to stop worrying about the size of the audience, or cultism. I was hooked by poetry. I got to know Frank O'Hara better subsequently. I don't think I was tempted to try to write like him, but I was drawn to him as a person.

LEYLAND: In all these interviews, people have seen Frank in different ways. How did you find him as a person?

ELMSLIE: I went through a series of phases. If we were at a party with a lot of other people, it seemed safe to flirt with him, but I didn't dare flirt when we were alone. It was really fun flirting with him, and he flirted back. Then I had this idea of a Great Romance, more than a mere infatuation. He had the knack of making people feel they were really part of his life, and they *were*.

LEYLAND: Evidently this didn't extend to everyone. John Giorno says in his interview that he felt excluded by Frank, hostility by the New York School of Poets towards poets of a different tradition. Strong antipathy toward what William Burroughs was doing for instance. Even towards Andy Warhol's work.

ELMSLIE: That's true. But hostility doesn't quite ring true to me. Frank was hardly doctrinaire; one reason I liked him was because of his fantastic openness. He liked movies. He liked musicals. He took them seriously. He liked TV junk—his likes went out in all directions. He was totally unstuffy about different kinds of poetry, and very generous about other people's work.

LEYLAND: Different people have said these contradictory things. Isn't it possible that in his character these contradictions were there, this generosity, an instant ability to communicate and to make people feel at home, but also some of these negative aspects?

ELMSLIE: Sure. He could be very imposing, the Pope of Poetry. People would come to *him* to say hello, at a party. He could be very snooty, very arrogant, cold, and I once heard him hiss the word "hate" as I've never heard it hissed.

LEYLAND: I think that's what John was saying, that if he liked your work, or liked you, he could be very outgoing, but if there was antipathy for some reason, he could be very cold.

ELMSLIE: Towards me he was very—gallant. He was a veteran compared to me, he'd paid his dues, but he never let me feel that. He was very, very supportive. That's why I mention his generosity of spirit—he wasn't bound up in his own work, as poets can be.

LEYLAND: You were saying you felt a warm attraction for him. What happened to this?

ELMSLIE: It was comic. He asked me to stay one night, and *nothing* happened. We were both very drunk, and fell asleep in mid-embrace. Then he came over to stay with me one night and we started to make out, then I suddenly thought, I'm not at the baths or something—it freaked me out that he was Frank. I had a romantic notion of grandeur between us, two poets taking off into an emotional atmosphere, and the sex part didn't fit into that, so, dumbbell that I was, I pulled back. It's awfully hard to extend sex into friendship. I wasn't able to cross that line with Frank.

LEYLAND: What happened in your personal life after your relationship with John Latouche?

ELMSLIE: Well, nothing all that exciting. I lived with a would-be actor for a few years, and then lived alone. I got into the habit of writing poems about my rapid-fire crushes. Sometimes I'd see one of these ex-crushes walking around. They'd have changed, and I'd have changed, and the poem was still there: a memory device to put me in touch with feelings I'd have otherwise forgotten about.

LEYLAND: You've been somewhat influenced by John Ashbery's work?

ELMSLIE: I think his work is more exciting, at this point, than anyone's. His book *Three Poems* is a fantastic masterpiece. His poetry keeps on developing. I'm struck by his work, and we're good friends, but at this late date, I have the feeling I'm stuck with my own style pretty much.

LEYLAND: You met him when you first moved to New York?

ELMSLIE: Yeah, but we weren't friends, particularly. He was away in Paris for most of that fifties period. But I remember one summer in the Hamptons — John Latouche was making a short movie of a play written by Jimmy Schuyler called *Presenting Jane Freilicher*. Frank and John and Jane played themselves, and Jimmy hovered, voyeuring. I got to know them a bit while this film was being made, but I was painfully shy — and they were unbelievably articulate, but not all that interested in outsiders. I used to get bug-eyed at Frank's sex adventure stories. He'd regale mixed company about his black postman, who'd climb up five flights of stairs to make out with Frank. Or the time he was blowing the guy in the subway who makes change — at which point the subway train arrived, and there were tons of people pouring past the booth, with Frank both trying to keep a low profile *and* give head. He'd tell these stories in front of Janice, Kenneth Koch's wife, and other women and straights, spelling out everything so it wasn't just shocking, it was hilarious. From my English father, I'd absorbed the notion that it doesn't matter what one does, as long as one is discreet about it, so as not to offend other people. Frank would have none of this.

LEYLAND: Would you like to talk about poetry you've written over the past several years? You have five books —

ELMSLIE: Let's see. *The Champ* came first. Then *Album, Circus Nerves, Motor Disturbance*: four, not counting privately printed books — *Pavilions* and *The Power Plant Poems* which Ted Berrigan brought out. *Circus Nerves* was a light collection of for the most part diary poems. *Motor Disturbance* was a gathering of ten years of work, heavier I'd say, and with a wilder range. *Album* was an informal jumble of short stories, playlets, song lyrics, some poems, some comic strips, whatever I had lying around at the time. Joe Brainard visuals weave through it, and the same holds true for *The Champ* — a long poem inspired by a Raymond Roussel text which I deliberately mis-translated, and in place took off completely on my own — one longish section is devoted to made-up ballet titles. Joe's drawings alternate with my text.

LEYLAND: When did you first meet Joe?

ELMSLIE: It was over ten years ago. I was giving a reading for peace which Julian Beck of the Living Theater organized. Early in the morning, I went down to the Staten Island ferry, and read a poem or two. That's where I met Joe, and Ted Berrigan. There was a sudden invasion from Tulsa, of Joe, Ted, and Ron

Padgett—which came just at the right time as far as I was concerned, because they enlivened the poetry scene considerably. Ted put out a magazine called *C*—it was terrific, you could write works and wham, they'd come out. I've always loathed sending works out, and then one waits and waits and by the time the poems come out, one has lost interest in them. It took me a long while to begin to know Joe. We began seeing each other by doing comic-strip collaborations. Then one day I touched his hand! Instant sizzle. I fell totally in love with him, asked him to marry me. Out of niceness, he said yes. He was twenty-three, and I was thirty-six. He cherished his independence, nights off, while I was after the whole works—not realistic on my part. The first time I undressed him, I was scandalized by his undershirt—loops of rags, like a costume. And his skinny body. So *skinny*. And fucking was out. It bewildered me why I'd fallen for him, but it was a passionate involvement. So the way our life worked out was this: summers together under one roof in Vermont, and a more independent relationship in the big city: sometimes together a lot, sometimes not.

LEYLAND: Have you done other collaborations with him?

ELMSLIE: We had a press for a while called Boke Press which served to bring out our collaborations. The first one, heh-heh, was called *The Baby Book*, a take-off on baby books, you know—first saying, et cetera. Then *The Champ* which Black Sparrow Press brought out. Then *Album*. He's a hard worker, keeps at it all day, and this was inspiring to me in many ways. At one point he was making orchid drawings. So I decided to write a series of stories in which orchids would figure in some way, one orchid per story. It was a kind of game. I had read somewhere that Thomas Mann worked on *Buddenbrooks* every day, and would read his harvest at night, to entertain the folks. So that was the goal I set myself, to write something every day, and then read it at night. I quickly bogged down, though I did dash off three or four orchid stories. They seemed crazy to me. I hadn't seen anything quite like them. I *had* read *Hebdomeros*, a novel by the painter de Chirico. The whole work floats, waves of images carry one along— very strong language. I tried, in these orchid stories of mine, to write them in such a way they'd tap into this level of hypnotically floating fantasy, but that the fantasy would have the true-seeming texture of carefully observed real life. It's a mix of found texts, autobiographical material swirled about, poems, visual word-cubes with word beginnings and endings snipped off. The stories are interconnected, so, in effect, it's a novel—a sort of life story recounted by a nameless narrator. Doubleday published it as a Paris Review edition.

LEYLAND: Did you first move into a gay milieu when you came to New York?

ELMSLIE: I moved into John Latouche's milieu, which was extremely mixed, as you may have gathered. And that's the way I prefer it. I love being with women, socially, all the more so because I don't live with one. The same goes for men who are on a different wavelength, straights, if you will. Any milieu based on sexual rapport tends to be consciousness-lowering, in my experience, after the initial boost of finding others like oneself, in the same boat, as it were. Anyway, I tend to be a loner who likes to mix, not a "belonger." Mostly I see a small number of close friends and survivors who happen to be poets or composers or painters, people I feel comfortable with and/or inspired by. Their sexual proclivities aren't that big a factor, unless I want to go to bed with them, which has nothing to do with "milieu." I was once asked to an uptown gay party, and saw a hundred men in business suits through the open door, and scooted away fast. A hundred poets? A hundred ASCAP members? A hundred Scotch-Irish-German-Jewish-Hungarian-English myopic six-foot-twoers, which I happen to be? I'd have run just as fast. I once spent a weekend in the gay sector of Fire Island, and I hated it! Endless talk about big cocks and doings at the Meat Rack. Sex ghettos are not my idea of fun. Counterproductive elitism is all it is, he sobbed.

If I sound snooty, I don't mean to—at thirteen I was packed off to an elitist boarding school—St. Mark's—and perhaps it's left its mark. Fool that I was, I kept a diary filled with lovelorn mush about a football player, Carleton Rand. My diary was discovered by some snoop in my bureau, and it provided my classmates with spicy reading matter. They picked a nickname for me fast— "Homo." I also subscribed to *PM*, a leftist newspaper, and I thought of myself as a socialist, leaning towards Communism Russia-style, this in a school for plutocrat brats who applauded the news FDR was dead—a day of wild rejoicing. So I was a pariah on two counts, and fooled around much much less than some of the jocks did, which was somehow normal. I was miserable. When I was seventeen, I actually fell in love with a girl, a devout Catholic—and even proposed to her. We necked, period. Then I switched back, Harvard, senior year— except for a couple of brief escapades in later years, the result of one being pregnancy. I said, fine, I'll take care of baby, I've always wanted to be a father. She thought about it, but it was aborted. I felt sad about that.

Anyway, back to adolescence. I thought of homosexuality as a disease, a curse, and I was convinced I'd come to a bad end, even go insane. I had loads of family fears. My grandfather and two uncles had gone blind, so I was worried about that. And the suicide rate of cousins kept mounting—another worry. And both my sisters had nervous breakdowns. I felt I had to be careful, and homosexuality was definitely in the high-risk category.

Being with John Latouche was like crossing some sort of frontier. I was proud of our relationship, but it had its problems. He spent money like there was no tomorrow, so at one point I gave him one-fourth of my inheritance. He deserved time to write, and I didn't need the money for survival purposes myself. My sister Cynthia came to New York unbeknownst to me to take action, I suppose fearing that this older man fairy was exploiting a naïve innocent kid. I later found out my father told her not to meddle: it was my life, I was over twenty-one. While I never confided in my father, I knew he knew about me, and thought of me as a rarefied exotic with enough gumption to follow my own bent, a son to be proud of. He served in Africa in World War .., and I remember him talking with considerable emotion about how beautiful the Arab boys were, right at the dinner table. I was very proud of him that day. He came to this country from England, hired to be a tutor to the youngest son of Joseph Pulitzer, the newspaper publisher and founder of the Pulitzer Prizes. My father fell in love with J.P.'s daughter, Constance. The Pulitzers were filthy rich, so my father went off to make *his* millions in Canada. He never made his millions, but when my mother came down with TB, they married, and that's why I grew up in Colorado Springs—it was a TB health resort. I liked growing up there. My mother died of cancer when I was ten, and I turned troublesome—inexplicable tantrums. I was sent to a shrink. Do you masturbate, he asked. I said yes, not knowing the meaning of the word, ashamed to ask. *With* anyone, he asked. I replied, yes, with Billy Silvers, he being my best friend—a total lie, as we did nothing sexually together. In subsequent sessions, I figured out if I tapered off on the times I masturbated, the doc would let me go. And so he did. I was a slow sex learner, and my first affair happened when I was twenty-two, in Cleveland—with a fifteen-year-old black dancer who played Toby in *The Medium* at the black-white settlement house where I worked. I don't think I was rebelling for the sake of rebelling, or anything dumb like that. I loved his looks, he was so sweet and elegant, and fun to fuck. I worried a bit abut being sent to jail, but then my sex fantasies were full of jail scenes, so...and I was terrified my Cleveland sister would find out, but I rather enjoyed living a double life. I don't think kids would bother with all this secrecy now.

LEYLAND: Young people in small towns still have to move to the big cities.

ELMSLIE: It must have been apparent what the situation was in Vermont, when John Latouche and I lived there. Vermonters used to call us "partners," a very precise, mature way of putting it, a better word than "lovers" somehow. In the backwoods of Vermont, there's a basic tolerance of people who are "different." Vermont didn't evolve out of a theocracy, as Massachusetts did—it grew, like the West, out of land claims. It had a long history of frontier life, frugal and hard, but given to riotous living. I find it congenial, particularly as a lot of young people have opened things up by coming in as homesteaders. Visiting Bolinas, I was reminded of Vermonters—the same awareness and preoccupation with water and land, the basic basics. In the city, I feel cut off from the basic basics. It's a major pleasure to go out and pick fresh peas, to grow what you want, hard-to-find items like celtuce and fava beans and great herbs. Jimmy Schuyler is knowledgeable about plants, and during our Vermont walks, he'd name the plants—I owe my interest in gardening to him.

LEYLAND: When did you first meet him?

ELMSLIE: Around '53, I'd say. But I got to know him better when he was re-covering from a breakdown, and used to stop off in New York on his way to Southampton where he was living with the Fairfield Porter family. He has written some incredibly beautiful Vermont poems which help *me* see the land-scape. He's such an honest poet, absolutely solid, puts down what he sees—no tricks, no showing off. Kenneth Koch and I love to take off in different direc-tions—I'm drawn to put certain words in a poem and sometimes people think it's a real-life happening, but it isn't—the word is in there for its shape or its sound. I put a St. Bernard in one poem, and someone asked me, do you have a St. Bernard. Well, no! I construct my poems so real-life happenings are mixed up with invented phrases, found phrases, inside thoughts, so that there's a kind of fluid going back and forth between a series of interior states and a hardnosed outside reality. I try to catch the fast shifts of consciousness that constantly go on, and to arrange them with grace in each poem. My work is dense, packed with a lot going on at once, and I think this gives some readers trouble on the page. One recurrent reaction I get to my poetry is that it makes much more sense to people after they've heard me read it. My voice clarifies a music in the words they don't tune in to at first, so that the poems don't seem to be "all there"—but my voice leads them through the words, and after they've heard the poems, they have no more problems. Attending rehearsals has helped me, I think, know how to give fair value to my poems when reading them. I feel lucky that I'm both a poet and a librettist. Rehearsals get me out of the house, and out of the loneliness of hours at the typewriter, the solitude of writing, the boredom of waiting, in between poems. And it's a reward to see what a libretto changes into, set to music. At first hearing, with the composer at the piano, it sounds insane! Tom Pasatieri is great—he sings all the voices, plays piano, and somehow conveys a sense of the opera, single-handed. When it goes into production, the first orchestra rehearsal breaks me up. Total fulfillment! It's like a sex charge, my entire body succumbs to flashes and waves of pleasure.

LEYLAND: Have you ever written any music yourself?

ELMSLIE: Not exactly. Sometimes I improvise music, so-called, to my own poetry, and a couple have been written down by friend musicians. But I don't know much about music, technically. Tom once asked me, "Do you read music?" and was really shocked when I said no. He couldn't believe I was a librettist and couldn't read music. Another confession: I know very little about opera. I can't stand most of the operas in the standard rep. I'm forced to start each libretto on my own, without falling back on precedents. It's so hard to know what will make a good opera. I thought Chekhov's *The Seagull* was a dreadful idea when Tom first approached me. Too much talk about books and art, talk talk talk. I was resolved not to do it, and he got me drunk on margaritas, and I felt this whammo need coming from him. He got himself a librettist, me, and it worked out just beautifully, made a very solid opera.

LEYLAND: Have you ever sung?

ELMSLIE: Occasionally, at a reading. And I was in a drag show with Anne Waldman once. Anne wanted to sing "The Woolworth Song," a silly thing I'd made up, from a play that is set in Alaska, *Furtive Edna*. We started off in Eskimo costumes, and really laid an egg. With all these marvelous female impersonators coming out, we didn't have a chance. So we switched to evening clothes the second week. But I was bored in a tux, and Anne was bored in her evening dress, so I insisted on wearing drag, and Anne would wear a tux as her drag. The producer refused us, "There are enough guys in drag, you are poets, I don't want you in drag!" I was furious, very hurt. There was a revolution backstage. All the drag stars surrounded the producer, and said, "If he wants to, let him." Right on. They found a bugle-bead dress for me, sack, and I bought an Afro wig, and put on nail-polish, toes too. And they helped me with my make-up. So the final week we sang "The Woolworth Song" in full drag to much applause. The show was off-off-Broadway, on the Bowery, and Anne and I went bonkers, became helplessly stagestruck, rushed to the back of the theater after our number to watch Jackie Curtis, our idol. Sometimes the show lasted three hours. The audience seemed to be in total ecstasy! We'd be up to all hours, stagger home, then two more shows the next night. After the show closed, as a treat, I invited Jackie Curtis to come see Mabel Mercer at the St. Regis, to hear her sing "If There's Love Enough," a song from *The Grass Harp*. I'd never been out with anyone in drag before, and it was an eye-opener. Waiters flipped, women did elongated double-takes, some people were really upset. So after dinner, we got to the posh supper club and heard Mabel. I began worrying, what if Jackie has to pee? At the end of the set, Anne Waldman and Jackie went off, to the ladies' room. I was left to fret at the table with Joe Brainard. Hours passed, so it seemed. Finally they came back, and Jackie explained there were five security men waiting when they came out of the ladies' room, to grill them with questions. Surrounded by ornate uptown gilt and elegant guests staring, this terrible scene took place, and of course Jackie and Anne carried it off in high style and returned to the table, truly unruffled ladies.

LEYLAND: Disconcerting the staid can be great fun. When John Wieners was in San Francisco, I had lunch with him downtown. As we left, a well-dressed matron coming from the opposite direction passed us, and John turned to her and said, "Oh, how are you? I'm John Wieners and I'd like to spend the afternoon with you." She was sort of taken aback and said, "No, I don't think so..." Maybe you should read your poetry in drag.

ELMSLIE: I've wanted to read the first part in a suit, and then reappear in drag, and save the songs for part two, do a total switch. It's very freeing, I found, performing in drag, and for me has nothing to do with camp. It's a re-creation of one's self. I think poets are experts at that anyway. It's an occupational pleasure. I've noticed that some poets, not all, can change their appearance radically.

LEYLAND: John Wieners was in semi-drag when he read here in San Francisco.

ELMSLIE: Aside from what John wears, his face changes totally. Several times I haven't been sure it was really he. For a while, he looked like a young Ezra Pound. A couple of years went by and he looked different, like a character actor playing a floorwalker in a department store. John Ashbery keeps changing, too, not as radically, but every so often he has a new look.

LEYLAND: Maybe that happens more with gay people.

ELMSLIE: Maybe. I do think some straight poets are so heavy and limited, and you feel an oppressively heavy male kind of idea pressing down. It's so dreary. For gays, there's no point in stifling themselves with that kind of self-image. But then I've met a lot of gay drips, caught in an equally dreary gay self-image, harping on sex obsessively.

LEYLAND: Homosexuality hasn't yet been explored in a wider sense, erotically, spiritually, then communicated to large numbers of people.

ELMSLIE: In Greece and Rome, there was writing that dealt with homosexual love realistically, openly, writing about people switching back and forth, women complaining about gay men, true-to-life situations.

I agree, there is a long way to go. I don't think writers have begun to exhaust gay subject matter. But it still seems to me that a desirable society would be one where one wasn't really sure of anyone's sexual status, a society where no one feels obligated to be "different" to show their sexual identity.

LEYLAND: I think we're a long way from that.

ELMSLIE: I'm afraid so.

PHOTO BY JULIA FAHEY

TAYLOR
MEAD

TAYLOR MEAD has been involved in more than 80 films since 1960, often in Gay camp roles. He started out as a child-man-hero in Ron Rice's Beat Generation film, *The Flower Thief*. During the sixties he starred in several Andy Warhol films, most notably *Nude Restaurant* and *Lonesome Cowboys* (1969); also in films by John Chamberlain, Wyn Chamberlain and Michel Auder. He was seen briefly in Jean-Luc Godard's *One Plus One* and John Schlesinger's *Midnight Cowboy*. He won an Obie Award for playing the General in Frank O'Hara's play, *The General Returns from One Place to Another*. He has acted in a Brecht play. He has written three volumes of a diary, a mixture of aphorisms and poetry: *Anonymous Diary of a New York Youth*, vol. 1, 1961; vol. 2, 1962; and vol. 3, 1968, entitled *On Amphetamine and in Europe*. His poems appear in the gay anthology *Angels of the Lyre* (1975).

THIS INTERVIEW was taped in New York City in February 1975 by poet John Giorno (see the interview with Giorno in *Gay Sunshine Interviews* vol. 1). It was revised and edited by Winston Leyland in May 1975 and originally appeared in *Gay Sunshine* no. 25 (Summer 1975). Giorno's most recent LP albums are: *You're The Guy I Want To Share My Money With*, with Laurie Anderson and William Burroughs, and *Stretching It Wider*, with Glenn Branca.

John Giorno interviews
TAYLOR MEAD

GIORNO: What is your part in the Brecht play you're doing now [1975]?

MEAD: I play the son of Old Dogsborough, a political boss, from whom the Chicago gangster played by Pacino tries to—*does* take over; it's a parallel between Hitler and Hindenburg. Since my father *was* a political boss in Michigan, the role is very real-life. And I brought a new candor to the role. [*Laughter.*]

GIORNO: Would you describe your father to us?

MEAD: My father was called the Silver Eagle of Michigan, because he had broken his nose playing football for the University of Michigan. And he was a boss; he was chairman of the Democratic Party, and all kinds of other things. His roommate at the University of Michigan was a very honest and eloquent speaker—so from the very beginning my father thought that the man would do well in politics and everything, although the man wanted to become a Jesuit priest. His name was Frank Murphy, and my father became his campaign manager. Murphy became mayor of Detroit and governor of Michigan, and high commissioner of the Philippine Islands, attorney general of the United States, and then he wound up in the United States Supreme Court. But he was a great favorite of Roosevelt, and he refused to call out the troops when the workers occupied the automobile factories in Detroit. For his nerve and everything, he became a favorite of Roosevelt, and they felt that he was presidential timber. But even in my father's obituary they said that when he went to Washington he left my father behind in Michigan; and that he was the worse off for it, because he didn't know his way around Washington politics. Murphy was very honest, but he needed an opportunist crook like my father to give away—I shouldn't say crook because my father was just simply playing the old political game, of you know giving away jobs, and playing footsie with the Mafia and everybody else, to get out votes.

GIORNO: He must have ripped off a lot of money then.

MEAD: I know that when my father came to New York he went to visit the gangster Frank Costello out on Long Island, and Costello gave him an envelope; my father had been head of the Liquor Control Commission of Michigan.

In a high-level meeting in Palm Beach my father forgot that I was there, because he was afraid that my mother wouldn't approve of the way he conducted his politics. But she did approve of his being to the left of center. Anyway, when he got to talking and wasn't aware I was there, it was some of the most interesting stuff I've ever heard in my life—it's how a country is run, was run at that time; or still is, I'm sure. And that's why the Watergate hearings leave me a little bit cool: all those noble senators on one side, and the crooks on the other side is a *crock* of *shit*. And the most noble senator daring to say that they got their vote out respectably—impossible, unless they've got some manager like my father.

GIORNO: What was your adolescence like in boarding school?

MEAD: Well, there's a subculture that goes on in boarding school. Like the first day I arrived at Loomis, the football captain—the *handsomest*... oh, really attractive—said "Can I have a date?" Just like that. And I said, what's this guy saying. I couldn't believe it. So I said, "What are you going to do, pick me up in a taxi?" He didn't like that at all, and that put me outside the whole thing that was going on there, the whole first year at Loomis. I goofed from the word go and then I was too shy with the other people sometimes. It lasted the whole first year. Then the school work was so difficult. Like the midyear exam in English was like 500 lines of poetry from memory. And that was given to us by a sadist genius named John Horne Burnes, who wrote a book called *The Gallery*. Quite a good book about World War II. And he had the finest class I've ever been to, but his exams were sadistic and I really hated poetry for the next ten or fifteen years. I just couldn't read Shakespeare. I couldn't read anything and now my eyesight is getting worse and I feel like going back to reading. I only read big print.

GIORNO: How old were you when you left Detroit?

MEAD: I was thirteen when my mother died, and my father moved me out of Grosse Pointe; he hated Grosse Pointe, but I had all my friends there and everything, it was very traumatic. And at that time I also had just discovered my first lover, two lovers. I was in a movie at the Punch and Judy moviehouse in Grosse Pointe, and this boy put his hand in my lap—he was the handsomest boy in the school, but he really wasn't the most attractive, he was the toughest—and I immediately knew the whole score, the moment he made that gesture; and that was at twelve or thirteen years old. And we went out under a full moon and I said "Let's wrestle, and no holds above the belt"... and [*Laughter.*] I was even too witty for sex. And so we wrestled away under a full moon in a beautiful field, which of course is now all overgrown with buildings. And then I got on a bicycle and started to ride home, and had this strange exotic feeling and I had to walk my bicycle home. I had a terrible conscience thing about it, and I thought, "Something is very wrong, I must have done something very wrong." Or that's too good to experience, or something like that. And I swore "Never again," and I would think all day long "I must not do that," but it only got me more excited.

And this went on until I was fifteen, and I practiced committing suicide, and everything. And I would have done it too, but I found a very handsome twenty-one-year-old friend hanging in his room. It was on Sixty-ninth Street, and I had been with him before that evening. He was talking about a lover, a new lover, a young doctor, and he said "Oh, it's going to be forever isn't it Taylor, and we're going to get an apartment together and he's coming to see me in the evening and everything." And I said "Listen, this is New York City, you're lucky if it lasts two months." He said "No no, it's forever," And in the morning when I came down the hall I saw his door partly open, and I thought he was standing in the corner of the room. He was hanging, he had hung himself in the corner of the room and left a bulb burning like he expected his lover to come find him there. He had a distinct aura all around him. I took about four steps into the room, and my hair stood on end, and here's this beautiful guy hanging like a huge Chinese doll, with a sort of funny kind of smile.

GIORNO: What did you do?

MEAD: I couldn't go another step, and when the police came even the police were shocked. They said, "Jesus, why doesn't somebody cut him down—why didn't somebody cut him down." But neither I nor the superintendent who I had called could approach the body; it was just too grotesque. It was too much for either of us. Too much for the policemen. He hung himself on one of those covered-over gas pipes that used to be on the walls of old brownstones. And he was from a rich family; he was heir to a lot of money. His grandmother had given him a trip to the Caribbean for his Christmas vacation. I hear that at the funeral, his mother threw herself on the coffin and began yelling his brother's name, and it turned out his brother had shot himself two years before. And that was the end of that family. And so I left Sixty-ninth Street.

That night he came to me in a dream and just began talking to me. Suddenly I said "But Wayne you're *dead!*" And I started screaming and I came wide awake. Then I moved several times, because I couldn't go out, if anyone left a door partway open I couldn't go through it. That went on for months and months. But I moved several times and I kept seeing him all the time—terribly spooked by the whole thing—so I moved back to the place where I had lived next door to him, after a couple of months of trying to get away from it. It probably saved my life, really.

GIORNO: How many times have you tried to commit suicide?

MEAD: Almost every day, since about eight or nine [*Laughter.*]. I've practiced hanging myself in a closet, or jumping, or razor blades, and it was getting awfully close—getting quite serious where I was doing downers—and that stopped it. Boy, that stopped it dead.

GIORNO: When did you start making movies, Taylor?

MEAD: At the Sixty-third Street YMCA somebody asked me to be in a movie. I played a deaf-mute dope addict/dope pusher in a movie called *Too Young, Too Immoral* which broke all the records in Times Square. It ran for four months at the Tivoli Theater, on the corner of Forty-second. It was a corny little movie but it was quiet interesting and fun. One day the manager of the theater came out and began talking to me in sign language, and saying would you like to go see the film, and I answered in my ordinary voice not thinking and he nearly fell off the curb. I thought gee, what a compliment, he's seen the picture fifty times, he thinks I'm a deaf mute. And people would sort of look at me like I was a junkie. At one point in the movie I started to push someone off a subway platform and I missed, and *I* fell in front of the subway—we really filmed it in the subway. And one time someone came up and said "But you're supposed to be dead, I saw you run over by a subway train." And I thought, "Gee, these are the kind of people I would like to perform for 'cause they really are the ordinary people; they really believe, they're really naïve and quite beautiful; they really can be sold anything. And of course whenever they go to the polls, they're sold whoever has the TV channels.

GIORNO: What was your first talkie?

MEAD: Well that was a talkie movie in which I was silent, but then in San Francisco Ron Rice started filming me wandering around San Francisco—the film was called *The Flower Thief.*

GIORNO: You have a print of that?

MEAD: I had a print which I left at my friend's house in France, and his butler took it to Marseilles and sold it or something. The print disappeared and the butler died, you know? Someone got hold of the other print and just re-edited it, and things are lost forever, some of the best scenes.

GIORNO: So what does that mean? The movie has vanished? There are no prints?

MEAD: When we showed it I would do the music and stuff, and Ron was quite willing—I really am good at that. I love to do the soundtrack. But it's been showing now in a badly edited version without sound and people have been complaining to me, because we didn't make the movie for a coterie of superintellectual moviegoers; we made it as a rotgut thing for our friends to enjoy anyway, in San Francisco. Most of them were pretty hip, but I mean they were from all economic strata and everything else. But I would say it's like it was made for at least the equivalent of the foreign movie audience. So now I'm in the process of restoring the print here in the United States, putting sound on it.

GIORNO: How many movies have you made altogether?

MEAD: About eighty, ninety, at least. I'm extremely shy so I wouldn't make the theater rounds although my teachers in Pasadena and New York said that I could easily make a million or should be the highest-paid actor on Broadway. But ten or fifteen years ago I went around, and I could tell by the look on the receptionist's face that they couldn't place me, you know? They couldn't categorize me. I've simply gotten movies or plays by being stopped on the street. I was stopped on the street by Jerry Benjamin once and he said "I want you to do a Frank O'Hara play and a LeRoi Jones." And I said "Okay"—'cause that's the only way. I did *The General Returns from One Place to Another* by Frank O'Hara and won an Obie; we only showed it six times.

GIORNO: What was your first Warhol film?

MEAD: That was *Tarzan and Naomi,* made in California. The Beverly Hills Swimming Pool was my shark-infested lagoon. We used Simon Rodia's watchtowers as part of a jungle native village, and Dennis Hopper was my stand-in. Whenever I was supposed to climb a tree I'd hand Dennis some money on camera and tell him to go climb the tree, and Dennis thought it was all a big joke. I swear that film relaxed him—because he'd been so stiff in his movie roles—and really helped give him a new philosophy.

GIORNO: What was he doing at that time?

MEAD: He was working as an actor. He was in *Rebel without a Cause* and was a very close friend of James Dean.

GIORNO: How was it playing opposite Naomi Levine?

MEAD: Andy [Warhol] at that time was afraid of riding in an airplane, so we drove out—Wyn Chamberlain and I could drive. We kept stopping at Carte Blanche places, knotty pine places—and finally I said "I'm leaving this trip unless I can pick the next place we stop for lunchbreak." So I picked, of course, a truckstop, a magnificent truckstop in the middle of Kansas or something, and when we walked in everyone was fascinated by Andy Warhol; they'd never heard of him, they've never heard of him now, you know? But they thought he was just a phenomenon. And he had a great deal of fun, but I think he was a little unnerved by it too, so we went back to eating at knotty pine restaurants. Naomi followed us out in an airplane; she flew out, she thought "Oh well they're going to make a picture, I'm going to be in it. And I said, "Jesus, she's pushy." And I thought, "How pushy of her," and I thought, "Jesus, this is really odious." And we shot a couple of feet of her as Jane, and she was great. She was marvelous, so she was in. She knew what she was doing. But then she tried to edit out some of the nude scenes and I had a knock-down drag-out battle with her up at Jonas Mekas' film co-op. She tried to rip the film; she tried to rip things out of the film that she thought her father, Dr. Levine, wouldn't approve of.

GIORNO: Taylor, have you ever made a giant Hollywood movie?

MEAD: Yes, I was in *Midnight Cowboy.* I had a tremendous scene which was cut out. I showed in the final print for a second, or something, passing camera in the big party scene. I had a drag number, singing "I'm Flying" from Peter Pan. I did a version of it on the Johnny Carson Show.

GIORNO: How many movies have you made with Andy that he has not released?

MEAD: I went to Europe when he was really doing some of his very best work. I really went to Europe after a disappointment with this boy. I stayed till '67 when I saw *Chelsea Girls* in Paris, and half the French audience walked out. I thought it was a great movie, although it's great if it's shown with one soundtrack going at a time, because the people in it are very brilliant. So many projections of it are both soundtracks going at once, and the audience just leaves.

In Paris they couldn't believe it, they couldn't believe Brigid shoving a spike through her bluejeans. And I thought "Jesus, what am I doing in Europe, it's really La Dolce Vita-land, you know?" And the United States really has the best and the worst, and I'm going back. And Andy was there showing it and he asked me to come back, and when I got off the plane I immediately started doing: did a scene first with Patrick for *Imitation of Christ,* which you're probably in too, aren't you? In the next day or two I did *Nude Restaurant* with Viva. And then *Lonesome Cowboys* was probably six months later, and that was one of the happiest movie sets I've ever been on in my life.

We went out to Tucson, Arizona for *Lonesome Cowboys.* Also we had a lot of separate cottages, so we could all get away from each other, and that was Joe Dallesandro's first big movie. He was terribly nervous about doing *Lonesome*

Cowboys and I simply said all they want is whatever you are. And he says I said something that relaxed him tremendously — not enough for me to make him at that particular point in time. [*Laughter.*] But he wasn't the star of that. The star was a beauty that Viva had spotted in the balcony of the University of Southern California in San Diego, Tom Hompertz. And that's who Viva makes love to throughout. And then at the end of the movie I came along, and said "Viva what are you doing, why you're giving him a hard-on." So I started doing a tongue job all over, and I swear that's the first time he was excited during the entire film. And just as I was going below the belly button for the big finale, or the beginning, whatever, Andy said "Oh I ran out of film, Taylor." [*Laughter.*] Well, I swear he had more film in the camera, the bitch. He was puking in jealousy deep down or something.

And then we came back to New York and two days later Andy was shot right where we are sitting now practically. Andy refused to press charges against her and we had another shooting on Forty-seventh Street. Andy again refused to press charges although the guy played Russian roulette with our heads and everything. That was '63 or '64. The guy came in and said someone owed him a lot of money. Fired a shot into the factory and had about six of us kneeling, time to take all of the bullets out of the gun except one. Actually, I think he took them all out and he went up and down clicking, holding the gun to our heads. And then he handed the gun to Paul, and I think he wanted Paul to do something, because he had a guy waiting outside the door and they were going to take one of us hostage, Andy or somebody in the car. But he gave Paul the gun and then he started to take the gun back from Paul, and I thought, "Gee, you aren't going to load another gun, are you?" But, before the guy could get the gun, I jumped, and it was like jumping the Rock of Gibraltar. None of these six people sitting there helped me. They sat there like it was a movie, they were so brainwashed on the movie world on reality, ; it was unreality sitting there, and if I had run out the door I would have run right into the other guy and I would have had it. Instead, the other guy had put a woman's rain hat on my head while he was playing contemptible games with us, and I took that hat and put it on my fist and went over to a window and punched out the window and the window exploded, and the YMCA across the street just emptied of people; and then I took the frame of the window and went to the door. The guy really started to split and I saw both he and his confrère going down the stairs, and I let them have the frame, which rattled back and forth. They had to run down four flights, and then I went to the window. All the time these people sitting there yelling out, "Get the license number!" But Andy wouldn't pursue the matter or anything.

Andy should be better organized all the way up and down by now. I mean, he pays famous people to be in his movies and the unknowns that helped to make his movies in the first place have mostly gone, are dead or poverty stricken. But he does nothing but a society trip now. He's done nothing since he was shot, you might say.

GIORNO: Andy stopped taking speed with that shot. Even before he was shot he was just doing handfuls of dexedrine and then he got shot and then he got better. And his system was so fucked up the doctor said, "If you take one more speed pill you will kill yourself" because his liver was fucked up. So without speed it was a different world to him. . . . When did you first start reading your poetry, Taylor?

MEAD: The first time I read publicly was at the café run by Larry Poons on Bleecker Street. It was probably one of the best so-called beat or hip cafés I've ever seen in my life. It was called, I think, the Epitomy. Larry used to read with a toilet seat around his neck. And Tiny Tim first performed there. There was such a warm atmosphere. It was the first time I had been there to read in public, and the tremendous responsiveness . . .

GIORNO: When was that?

MEAD: About 1959—Bob Dylan was playing. When Bob Dylan would come in I would stop reading immediately. I don't think I'd even had marijuana by 1961, and I thought Bob Dylan was just drunk. I'd give him the stage because I thought he was really fantastic. Sometimes he would play to a wall and the audience, the customers, would be behind him, and that was before he had made a record or anything. I said something about "You're not just a musician, you're fantastic, all the right things at the right time," before it had all been proven or exploited.

GIORNO: How gay was that scene?

MEAD: Well, we were gay mostly, out front, some of us. But the gay scene, the swishes, the coy, generally evil gay scene wasn't so much among the poetry people, although they were evil to each other. [*Laughter.*] But I think there were a lot of frauds among the poets of the fifties and sixties.

GIORNO: Externally it was this totally heterosexual scene. Actually, everybody was gay: Frank O'Hara, John Ashbery, Bob Rauschenberg, Jasper Johns, Andy Warhol, even if they operated in a commodity world that was heterosexual.

MEAD: Of course it was Allen Ginsberg that really laid it on the line. Then he went to India. He should never have gone to India, never should have stayed more than a year.

GIORNO: Allen has just gotten back to the U.S., though, so there's possibilities of hope. It was a long trip.

MEAD: Actually he doesn't even like people when they get excited or raise their voices. He still writes beautiful poetry. He's a beautiful person. But *Howl* made me think, "Why, here's the new leader of the revolution."

GIORNO: Well, he just did this thing, he mirrored everyone's emotions of the time, for an instant, which is a totally miraculous thing to do.

MEAD: I've always found that if I've appeared somewhere or a movie came out or something, it almost made me avoid the opportunities offered. But at the time I didn't want to take advantage. But discovering how difficult sex is and complicated and dangerous, I think I should take whatever opportunities . . . I think Allen is much more a man of the world than I am. I'm still just in crinoline sheets compared to him. I've had sex about six times a year. It's never varied. I'm terribly fearful too about getting stabbed. In a bar someone put their beautiful hulk right between my legs while I was sitting on a table and going erotic. All I had to do was reach out and grab, and I didn't do it, but I did it the other night somehow at the Eagles Nest. There was a person who obviously only wanted to make love in public, and was rather attractive. I just felt him up for a while, then I gave him to my friend, and he became bored with him too and said, "He obviously just wants to do a public number or fifteen-minute-long kisses and things like that at the bar. . . ." Andy Warhol used to say that when he would travel around—in a one-year period he went to thirty colleges—the contingent that met him was always a bunch of hairdressers, and he was always rather disappointed about the sexual advantages of being famous.

GIORNO: Was he very much of a bon vivant sexually?

MEAD: Oh, I think he blows like crazy, or wherever he can get it.

GIORNO: What was gay life in New York like when you first came here?

MEAD: I didn't know. I was nineteen before I really came out. I had been playing around with schoolmates before, just mutual hand jobs, into kissing all over by the time I was fourteen. But someone picked me up on the road in Lynchburg, Virginia, and he took me home and blew me three or four times. The bed creaked so much every time we moved that I kept giving in, he was a monster. I thought he was going to die from sucking all that, and his mother was in the next room and it was a nightmare of embarrassment. But I saw him a few days later and he wasn't dead so I thought, gee, maybe there's all kinds of possibilities. So I think I plunged right in.

I used to live for years up on Central Park West and then I cruised Washington Square. I was still terribly shy and my affairs were very infrequent and half the time dangerous, somebody wanting to rip me off, and then I was a whore for one day. The first two guys I sold myself to gave me money. I would only sell to the people I really dug, so I wasn't making that much money. The third guy took me up to the Bronx and took me to a house and robbed me. So I gave it up. In the first place he had me in a room with spotlights all over it, and he had a spider web tattooed on his ass. After we'd gone through all kinds of movements and walked out in the hall of his house I heard some laughter from upstairs, people talking. I said, oh oh, we've been photographed or observed, the whole thing, and he took me out into the dark and he says, "You know why I brought you here?" And I say, "To kill me." [*Laughter.*] And he laughed but he laughed just about like that was what he had in mind and he said, "Now give me the money." So I said, never again.

I just went around starving, and begging, literally begging on the streets of New York. Then I went to work at the Public Library. Then I got arrested by a detective in a Washington Square subway urinal, someone who I refused to, but he wanted to make an arrest and simply arrested me. Then that was in the Tombs which is the worst jail I've ever been in in my life. And within a few hours I wanted to kill myself. And that's the only place that could drive me to do that.

GIORNO: Bill Burroughs had a friend who hanged himself in the Tombs.

MEAD: I believe it. I believe the suicides and murders they have there are so beyond anything they say. I was within minutes of killing myself.

GIORNO: When I was in the Tombs the guy in the cell next to me was a junkie, was freaking out. He somehow had a coat hanger and he shoved it up a vein in his arm until he died. He bled to death.... You have been in other jails too, Taylor?

MEAD: Jails? I was in jails all over the country. Just hitchhiking around. I think Columbia, South Carolina, was the first time in jail. I was playing the piano in a dormitory at the university there and they arrested me for trespassing. I'd first gone to a girl's dormitory, playing the piano there and I wouldn't tell them who I was waiting for. So they thought I was a friend or something waiting to get even with some girl. They were searching the university grounds for me and I'd gone over to a chapel to play the piano, and they came and trapped me like I was some escaped fiend. Put me in a common jail in Columbia, South Carolina, with blacks and whites and everyone sleeping on the floor. And it was actually quite a marvelous experience. It was the first time I'd been with a large group of people from all kinds of backgrounds, colors and everything, and with a common goal, like to get out, or a common feeling of being caught in a big number up there.

And then I was in jail in Las Vegas. I was walking down the main strip of Las Vegas which is so fantastic and these policemen threw me in jail, which happens to anyone going through Vegas with no obvious means of support. Then they get you to get your parents, fifty bucks bail and then they tell you to leave town and they take the bail. Las Vegas cops were into beating up cripples, and it's sick. Terrible western scene. It's supposed to be different now. They probably still have those laws. There was one kid put in from San Francisco in the state of Oregon or Washington. He'd made it with the son of a city councilman or something. They threw the key away on him for three or four years of solitary confinement. And he ended up making chess sets out of orange peels.

And then in New Orleans. Some female cop had accused me of stealing clothes from a department store. And I said, "Why you *liar!*" And I yelled it out and some big cop came up behind me and hit me right around the jaw. And they threw me into a truck and charged me with loud talking in a bus station, and vagrancy, no money, but I happened to have fifty bucks on me. They hadn't even bothered to find out if I had money. They just wrote the charge down. And loitering in a bus station. They had grabbed me on Canal Street and taken me into the bus station. So I went to the judge and I knew he was going to have at least one of the three charges. So I said, "In the first place, I have the money. In the second place, I was taken off the street and into the bus station." I said maybe I did raise my voice. So he said ten dollars for raising your voice. For loud talking in the bus station, that was the charge. But then I discovered that the other jail that they sent you to was the meeting place of New Orleans. And I always regretted not doing a few weeks in there. You found out about everything that was going on in New Orleans. But I panicked and paid the fine.

Then there was Ashtabula, Ohio. I went and demanded to be put in jail there. As a matter of fact I asked to be put in jail in Virginia and Ohio because it was freezing. Well, they were furious. But they did it anyway. But I think they took the mattress off the bed and gave me a jelly sandwich and an orange. Then kicked me out. Once I stole a car in New England. I had been working in Provincetown. I suddenly quit my job without getting paid. And I was freezing that night and starving in a barn stable near Hyannis. And there was a guy read-ing in bed up in the window. And he had an old car there and a big house and I said well he has this big house and he won't miss that little old car. Then I tried to sell it. Finally, when I ran out of gas I just abandoned it halfway to New York. I came to New York and I was still starving. I went to the police station uptown on Ninetieth or something and I said, "Please, I just stole a car, you've got to arrest me." They said I had to know the mayor of the city to get arrested. At the time it wasn't funny at all. Really I needed just to sleep in a cell or some-thing. So I walked through Central Park until I just fell somewhere and passed out. I fell down in the middle of a path and just fell asleep. All summer people would sleep in Central Park, but I was too hot. I used to wander all over New York until dawn. All the way up to 150th, up to the George Washington Bridge.

GIORNO: Did you ever get attacked on the streets here?

MEAD: Yeah, I've been stabbed with an icepick and shot with a gun. A guy pulled a gun on me in Central Park. I just ran but ran right into a police barrier and tore my leg muscles.

GIORNO: And nobody came over?

MEAD: I don't know. He was just standing there holding up people as they came along. He only held up the ones that chickened out and said yes, yes. Sort of a Peter Pan gunman. But then a whole atmosphere seized New York.

GIORNO: What parts of Manhattan have you lived in?

MEAD: From Greenwich Village to the Upper West Side. I once tried to move into Harlem and they were so shocked that I couldn't get a room. I kept knock-ing on doors and they couldn't believe their eyes. I was desperate for a room. Half the time I was driven from my room by child beating. And I called all these agencies and they'd say they couldn't do anything like that. And then I'd go to the police station. Sometimes they would simply go and break in the door and say, "Leave that kid alone." Then of course the people would go back to doing it or move or something. So I ended up on Fourteenth Street for five or six years. And I was only one flight above the traffic. But the traffic was kind of nice.

GIORNO: Taylor's bed was sort of in the middle and radiating out from it was a garbage mirage of colors and space and form, news clippings and the junk.... Who's living in Fourteenth Street now?

MEAD: My old place? Some girl and her boyfriend. They have the same prob-lem I did which is no soundproof, only a partition between my little loft and the one next door. There are two guys in there who play the TV all day long. I lived next door to a great Frenchwoman for three or four years, and I didn't realize how good I had it. And then I bought the woman upstairs a rug. And I had it made for three or four years. The Frenchwoman's private life was influenced by the fact that her parents worked for this duchess, who was the lover of the Negress of Josephine Baker. So she was kind of very interesting. One didn't feel at all self-conscious about living next to her. Then these guys moved in with their TV. And even putting carpet on the walls, I couldn't keep out the noise and as much as I love TV I can't listen to somebody else's TV. George Bernard Shaw says that the first requirement of humanity is a soundproof room for everybody to escape from everybody else. First requirement of the Socialists for anything viable is separate rooms.

GIORNO: You never lived downtown on the East Side?

MEAD: Yeah, got ripped off immediately. I remember I once went looking for apartments with Allen [Ginsberg] and I warned him about the ripping off. He'd just come back from India but he took this apartment and it was so vulnerable. He lost all of his Indian instruments. I kind of admired Allen for going back, but I said, "Allen, it's not the same. It's worse than ever; you can afford to live in a much better neighborhood and not be ripped off or anything."

GIORNO: He's still living there as of now. You knew he was mugged?

MEAD: Oh he was mugged? Oh my god, that's like mugging the Buddha! What happened?

GIORNO: These guys pulled a knife and made him go into an abandoned building. He had just come from a reading, so he dropped, as he says, about $10,000 worth of manuscripts. They just took the money, and didn't know what the manuscripts were. About four years ago he was mugged on Tenth Street. He was going down with the garbage and he gets almost to the bottom of the stairs and this guy pulls him out and says, "This is a stickup." And he says aach! and he throws the garbage at this guy and says take my money, take my life, you can have it, and the guy wouldn't believe it.

MEAD: He says, "I'm tired of being bothered by you fans." [*Laughter.*] Well, I'll now comment on the new kinky scene. One other reason why I don't go home with strangers. Fist fucking. I was once fascinated by all the kinkiness, but after being horribly stabbed, after hearing descriptions of people who have come through a fist fuck. A friend has a couple of dudes waiting for me now with magnificent bodies who claim they can do the greatest job in the world. But I've curtailed my visits even along a social basis. Two guys tried to strap me to the wall and beat me. They started describing the people they had murdered and chopped up and left in cans. This is supposed to turn me on. So I started dancing and said, "Oh, how wonderful!" And I danced right out their front door.

GIORNO: Do you still get royalties for any of the Warhol films?

MEAD: For twenty films, I'd say I got $1000. There was a trip to California, but Andy didn't pay for that. He ended up suing Carte Blanche. He didn't lose a dime—he gets other people to back him. Even though he's worth over 100 million. He's got as many movies as he wants to chop up into sausages. Andy Warhol's pork sausage. That's where Pork comes from. [*Laughter.*] Oh, they're being shown, *Lonesome Cowboys* made hundreds of grand. It didn't make millions like *Trash*. And we each got $200 for that.

I need a quick Quaalude. Go into total recall. I get thirty Quaaludes a month from the state narcotics commission. Triple prescriptions by Dr. ——. I thought immediately that I'd lose my credit, be hassled. But I've been on it for ten months now and no one's knocking on my door except some rehab program. Quaaludes, there's no particular withdrawal from them. There's the calmness of life. If I had had Quaaludes when I was four or five or nine, it would have been the best possible thing for me, because it's a muscle relaxant, antianxiety. It makes me function tremendously, though I wouldn't recommend them to anybody. Many people it just makes them sit there jerking off. It's an aphrodisiac too, but with me it gets me really doing things and my third book was all done on a French Quaalude. Has to be supervised. I gave a Quaalude to somebody in Mexico and he proceeded to drive off a cliff. The vw bus was totally demolished. The guy who was driving and his friend were perfectly all right. I was thrown out against the cliff. The bus actually went off against the cliff, went completely around, destroying every window, motor, everything, landed on its four tires. They thought I was dead, broken pelvis or something. But I got that stitched up and I thought I was all right and then I got muscular spasms and had to go to the hospital in Mexico City. I told the doctor to give me Quaaludes and of everything they gave me in that hospital, nothing worked but Quaaludes for relieving muscle spasms, kept me from going right through the ceiling. But I perform on them sometimes. Sometimes when I'm onstage, it's really great, every time you say a line it's like you're saying it for the first time. 'Cause it's such a memory eliminator. You just remember the line.

GIORNO: You have a story about your experience with the Living Theater.

MEAD: I've attacked the Living Theater doing a première performance in the South of France. They have been attacked before, of course, many times, but many of the people in the company were frozen.

GIORNO: What did you do? How did you attack them?

MEAD: They were doing *Mysteries* and other pieces. They kept talking about the war in Vietnam, and Julian Beck was saying, "We must end the war in Vietnam, we must end the war in Vietnam, we must end the war in Vietnam." You know if you repeat anything long enough it becomes its opposite. I thought he was creating a torture scene there. Also I watched some of their rehearsals, and they would get into sort of an S & M mental number. But then they began doing everyone dying of the plague, and I thought everyone in the company was dying exactly the same way, and it was very stylized and kind of corny. And after all this stuff I suddenly got up and said, "Vive la plague—vive la guerre de Vietnam—à bas les intellectuels." And I said that about eight times, sort of screaming and yelling it. And they stopped, they did stop the performance while I did all that—everyone froze, death spasms and all that. "Any other messages?" Then there was a festival later where Jean-Jacques Lebel gave a happening in a little French town, and the Living Theater and I were all dancing together. And Judith Malina insisted it was just what they wanted to do, but I don't believe, I don't buy that.

GIORNO: Was that before *Paradise Now*?

MEAD: Yeah. *Paradise Now*—I'll give Al Pacino's critique on that: he was watching it, and he was getting pretty bored and everything, and he went out—or went away for a half hour, or fifteen minutes, and he said he came back and it was one of the few times—you know, with all the plays he's in—he said it was one of the few times he felt the whole theater throbbing. And he thought that was really something quite marvelous. And I think that's what they're trying to do maybe. But I've yet to see it happen.

PHOTO BY KOTARO MASUDA, 1977

ROBERT
PETERS

ROBERT PETERS was born on a farm in Wisconsin in 1924. Ph.D. in Victorian literature, University of Wisconsin. He has published books on A. C. Swinburne and John Addington Symonds. He was a trustee for the American Society for Aesthetics, assistant editor of *Criticism,* and is a contributing editor of *The American Book Review.* He was a Guggenheim Fellow, 1966–1967. His *The Great American Poetry Bake-Off: First Series* (Scarecrow Press, 1979) is in a second printing. A *Second Series* of his iconoclastic essays appeared in 1982. He is also editing a *Poets Now* series for Scarecrow: six titles per year will be published, each volume devoted to the selected poems of an important American poet. Peters is best known as a poet, though, and has published *Songs for a Son* (1967), *The Sow's Head and Other Poems* (1969), *Cool Zebras of Light* (1973), *Holy Cow: Parable Poems* (1974), *The Poet as Ice-Skater* (1975), *Gauguin's Chair: Selected Poems* (1976), *The Gift to be Simple: A Garland for Ann Lee, Founder of the Shakers* (1975), *Hawthorne* (1977), *Ikagnak: With Dr. Kane in the Arctic* (1978), *The Drowned Man to the Fish* (1978), *Celebrities: Poems in Memory of Margaret Dumont* (1981), *The Picnic in the Snow: Ludwig II of Bavaria* (1982), and *What John Dillinger Meant to Me* (1982). He won the Poetry Society of America's Alice Faye Di Castagnola award for his manuscript *Hawker.* His poems have appeared in several anthologies, including the two published by Gay Sunshine Press: *Angels of the Lyre* and *Orgasms of Light.* He currently teaches Victorian literature, contemporary poetry, and writing workshops in the Writing Program at the University of California, Irvine. He reads frequently throughout the country, guesting workshops and appearing before university and gay groups.

THE PRESENT INTERVIEW was taped in San Francisco in March 1976 by Don Mark, an Asian-American writer. It originally appeared in *Gay Sunshine* no. 36/37 (Spring/Summer 1978).

Don Mark interviews
ROBERT PETERS

MARK: Where were you born?

PETERS: In northern Wisconsin, Eagle River, a town of fourteen hundred people in the resort area of the state. We lived on forty acres of scrub farmland. Sand. My dad was almost illiterate; he could write and read only a little. He was born on the prairies of North Dakota. His mother died when he was two, so he was orphaned early. His dad would leave him alone in a sod house for weeks at a time, with sourdough pancakes to live on. So he had to roustabout early, and worked on threshing crews and with carnivals. He finally went to Wisconsin where his brother was a lumberjack. My dad always had a special gift for language, a natural gift. He invented similes all the time. He also taught himself to play musical instruments — four or five of them. He was like a big splendid happy child, and my own mother was like a mother more than a wife to him — or so it seemed. He had the spirit in the family, showed us the most physical affection. I was the eldest of five kids. And we were really poor. I deal with some of this background in poems in my *Bronchial Tangle, Heart System*. The interior walls of our log house were never finished — bare boards over the logs with cardboard cartons smashed flat and nailed up to keep out the cold. Nail-ends came through the boards. I recall numerous winter mornings lying in bed with nail-ends a few inches from my face covered with frost. My dad would usually get up first and start up a fire in the pot-bellied stove in the living room. Then the frost nipples would melt and drip down into my face. And, obviously, we had no electricity — I did most of my studying by a single-wick kerosene lamp. And there was the proverbial outhouse — in thirty-below weather it could be pretty cold sitting there. Every spring my dad would shovel out all the ordure the family deposited in the winter and spread it around on the potato and vegetable fields. Good European practice, right, much frowned on in this country.

MARK: What were morals like there?

PETERS: My mother always stressed being clean, mentally and physically. She had a sense of a different world out there which she (and my dad) were too shy and self-conscious to make their way into and through. This was a world of education and plumbing and electricity. Someday, perhaps. In the meantime, struggle. No member of my family on either side had completed more than a year of high school. And yet both parents knew that if their kids were to escape into that other world they feared it would have to happen through education. But, you asked about morals. Strange there, because we were lower than middle class, what Oscar Lewis calls subculture poverty, and hence freed of those middle-class taboos. In rural northern Wisconsin girls had illegitimate kids and nobody really thought the worse of them. You sort of made up your morals as you went along.

MARK: Would you say something about your early education?

PETERS: I was precocious, I guess. I had taught myself to read and to print words by the time I was four. I learned from ABC cards inserted between layers of Shredded Wheat. You bought these Nabisco boxes of cereal, and there were these splendid cards. I saved them and copied them out on scraps of wrapping paper, grocery bags, etc. Soon I was filling tablets with them; and my mother helped me form words. She walked to the country school a mile off one day and returned with all the books they read in the first grade. By the time I was four I had finished all these books and was allowed to enter first grade. The academic side of school was always possible for me—I worked hard; but emotionally I was always behind the other kids. And there were difficulties when I went to high school. I was twelve and emotionally immature—self-conscious, afraid of having fights, etc.

MARK: Did you have fixations on boys and men early?

PETERS: Yes, as early as five or six. There was a cousin in his early twenties. Eventually he, my dad, and I formed a country-western band and played at dance halls and taverns. I played guitar. A few essential chords. Nothing flashy. Picked up some extra money this way while I was in high school. I was then something of a religious prig and found it hard to deal with the drunks, etc., I was "entertaining."

MARK: Did you read much when you were a boy?

PETERS: No, not really. We didn't have many books at home. Those I read I brought home from school. Since the school was one of those old one-room affairs the library was little more than a set of shelves with a few books on it. My mother did subscribe to *True Story* magazine. I always read those. Actually, we owned only two books: *A Child's Garden of Verses,* by Robert Louis Stevenson, and *Tom Swift and His Skytrain.* The Tom Swift bored me, so I never read it. I was never really interested in activities most boys are. And the Stevenson—my mother considered it such a special book and fancy (an aunt had given it to me for my birthday) that she didn't want me to wear it out by reading it. And she had named me after Stevenson: my middle name, like his, is Louis.

I've come to appreciate my dad in many ways, but particularly for not teasing me for my indifference to his way of life: hunting, farming, fixing cars. He was a superb mechanic, and much of our meat supply came from what he managed to shoot in the woods. He never teased me because I preferred to lie in the hammock and read *True Story* while he built a machine to saw our winter's wood. I liked to pretend I was all the women in those magazines being loved, fucked, and abandoned by those splendid romantic dream men. I hardly knew what I was up to.

MARK: Did you have notions of being a writer then?

PETERS: Yes. But first I wanted to be an actor. Clark Gable was my hero. Once my mother came up to me when I was standing nude on the rim of a gravel pit being Clark Gable. My hands were busy with my groin, too. She didn't say anything, and we've never talked about the incident. Mucho embarrassment. My shyness prevented my pursuing an acting career seriously, although I did manage to do a couple of character parts in high school plays. I was tall, about 6′ 2″ then, aged 13. Hard to find a girl to play romantic lead to, right?

I tried writing poems early, but never got very far. When I was in third grade my teacher wrote a poem and submitted it to the county fair as mine. We won seventy-five cents for first prize. That wasn't really ethical. And she actually did a drawing to go along with the poem. I was in love with her. In high school I tried my first novel: a grim long thing about that Czech village Lidice Hitler's SS troops destroyed, shooting all the men as hostages, and deporting the women and children. I was even then something of an esthete; I wrote the novel (I never finished it) in a wallpaper sample book, as a way of making the novel "beautiful," apart from the writing. I was quite proud of it. I memorized a lot when I was in school: one Christmas the teacher had me memorize about twenty pages from an encyclopedia on Christmas in Other Lands for recitation to parents at our school program. What a boring thing this was to listen to!

MARK: How did you get along with other boys in high school?

PETERS: Well, I had crushes on a number of them, and like them, played heavy macho girl-talk. I was tremendously self-conscious of my body, and found it absolutely painful to be seen naked dressing for gym or showering. And I figured out ways of diverting threats of fights. I've never had a fight in my life—except verbally. Perhaps if I had had a couple early life would have been easier. I don't know. I concealed my fears behind pacifism, a pacifism based on Christianity. Hadn't Christ said "turn the other cheek"? My ploy with threateners was this: I was generally smarter than they were and sensed their hostility. To divert them I'd cook up some question to ask, to make it appear that I trusted them to give me information. That always turned off the violence. So, I paid for the disparity between my mental and emotional growth. And living in the sticks made it difficult to have friends. You just couldn't run over to somebody's house. The nearest boys lived a mile and a half away.

MARK: What were they like?

PETERS: They were called the "Dirty Family." By comparison, my family was rich. There were ten kids; and the father when he worked worked in the town sawmill. Three or four people slept in a single bed. There were few dishes and almost no cutlery. A common meal was a huge roaster pan of baked beans, plus fresh bread. The roaster was put in the middle of the table, and the whole family dug in with their fingers. The boys (two of them were my age) liked to play dirty—and I loved it. I found out about masturbation from them, and a few other things. They used to invite me fishing with them too, doing the things finally that boys do. We'd spend whole long wonderful days wading out into a lake to fish, and would hike miles through virgin forests and swamps to reach a good fishing spot.

MARK: There's a lot of northern Wisconsin nature imagery in your work.

PETERS: True.

MARK: Can you say more about your early gay feelings?

PETERS: I always had them, but thought all boys did, so wasn't concerned until high school, when I found my urgings to touch other boys almost overpowering. Perhaps I turned intensely religious to find strength to divert my sexual energy into more acceptable channels. I started reading the Bible, grooving on the pictures of semi-nude males. You wouldn't believe the fantasies I had over Daniel in the lion's den! Although the word had gotten to me that masturbation would rot either your mind or your penis, I, as they say, took the loathsome matter in hand and whipped off, never failing to pray afterwards, promising God I'd never do it again. But, when morning came...the same old thing. Much of my hunger for men to love was usurped by anxieties about the future. I wanted to be an actor, writer, preacher, to go to college, to do something with my life. Those imense stirrings. Probably every adolescent has them. And I fell in love with girls, too. Even proposed to a couple, who, fortunately, turned me down. I was a hopeless romantic. I even took a girl to the junior prom, not realizing that she simply wanted to use me as a way to get there so that she could spend the evening dancing with other boys. I was tremendously hurt.

MARK: What was your relationship like with your mother?

PETERS: Extremely close. I was the oldest, and her favorite of the five kids. She had grown up on a North Dakota farm and had a heavy Puritan ethos. She believed men were "dirty"—that was her word. My dad wouldn't bathe often enough to please her. We didn't have plumbing, or an indoor bathroom. So baths had to be taken at best once a week in a tub in the living room, one of those metal galvanized tubs for washing clothes. Water was heated in pans on the kitchen wood cookstove, a long process. And all the water had to be pumped from the outside well, by hand, rain or shine, snow or sun. I shared her views about compulsive cleanliness (I'm not as bad about it as I used to be), and saw sex as dirty. The dirtier it seemed to me the more it appealed. And since men were the dirty ones men intrigued me. I had placed Woman on a pedestal, with my mother on the topmost one. [*Laughter.*] Sort of fits the clichéd pattern, doesn't it? She was ill a lot then, goiter, too many kids, various miscarriages. So, as oldest kid, it was up to me to take over the housework. I was a pretty good cook. Became a housewife early.

Of course I milked the cow my share, cleaned the henhouse, fed the animals, planted and tilled fields. But my preference always was to be indoors. Dad sensed that I might escape the poverty, drudgery life he'd always known, and the way was through education. He urged me to go to school.

MARK: Did you go directly to college from high school?

PETERS: No. I was drafted into the Army when I was eighteen. And on graduation from high school managed to find a job with an insurance company. I took a couple of university extension classes. But it seemed that my college career, for lack of money, would never happen.

MARK: What would you have done with your life if you hadn't gone to school?

PETERS: Possibly been an insurance claims adjuster. My fantasy was that I would someday be a minister. I was very religious then. When I was twelve I had my whole family baptized. I was sure the Apocalypse was due, and none of us was ready. Sects near Chicago were putting on sheets and sitting on rooftops waiting to be assumed directly into Heaven. I was frightened. So one Sunday I decided to walk in to town and join a church. I intended to go to Catholic Mass, because I was impressed with a harelipped girl in the neighborhood who walked there every Sunday, without fail. Once I reached the church, though, Mass was over. But across the street the Lutheran services were beginning. I knew that a girl I had a crush on went there, so as she was going in, asked if I could go along. I liked it, and soon, as I said, had the whole family baptized. Eventually I was teaching Sunday school. At thirteen I was superintendent, leading prayers, collecting pennies, singing, teaching a class.

MARK: What happened to your faith?

PETERS: That's a big one. Lost most of it in the Army. Went in tears to the training camp chaplain, a Reverend Crutchfield, saying I couldn't correlate Christ's commandment "Thou shalt not kill" with killing Germans. He patted my hand and unctuously said: "Well, don't be bothered about it. All you must do is follow the orders of your officers and NCO's. They'll bear the responsibilty for any people you may kill." I was horrified. And from that moment I mark the wearing away of my faith. Also, the minister at home, Missouri Synod Lutheran, a Reverend Joseph Krubsack, had said that before I took Communion in the Army I should write to him for permission; otherwise, I'd drink eternal damnation. I did this for a while—wrote him; but one day I took a plunge and had Communion on base (Fort Jackson, South Carolina) and nothing happened. And I liked the Army preacher. So, I began to modify my views.

MARK: Did you think less of Jesus?

PETERS: No. He was fantasy person numero uno. At church there was a sweet statue of Jesus crucified above the altar—the usual one, of Jesus wearing only a loincloth. I'd spend hours grooving on him. I'd even go into the church during the week (it was only a couple of blocks from the high school) and pray and carry on—all reverently, of course. I idealized him—as I had idealized women. And yet his physical reality was a tremendous turn-on to me.

MARK: Was it the G.I. Bill that enabled you to enter college?

PETERS: Yes. I wouldn't have gone otherwise. Wouldn't be at the university, or writing the work I've written today. I was discharged from the Army (I'd served in Europe) in 1966, after a three-year hitch. At the University of Wisconsin, Madison, I completed all my work including the Ph.D. in just six calendar years. I don't know of anyone who managed to do it so fast. And it wasn't that I was brighter than anybody else: I was a compulsive worker, and wanted to use the G.I. Bill for all the education I could get. I took huge programs... twenty hours a term, full terms in the summers, every shortcut I could.

MARK: Your own genesis as a writer has been self-generated; that is, you didn't want to become a writer to evaluate certain idols.

PETERS: I went through a period just prior to the military of reading Gertrude Stein. Although, here again, I never finished anything. I bought *Ida*, her novel, and memorized chunks of it, went around boring people by reciting it, and then tried to write three- or four-page sketches in imitation. I still, even to-day, hear her rhythms clearer than I hear anyone except Roethke's, Whitman's, Tennyson's, and Swinburne's.

MARK: Did you ever have an inkling that Gertrude was gay?

PETERS: No, I wasn't up on those things. And it didn't dawn on me that women loved women and actually went to bed. I was so naïve. I never had any sex in the Army, kept myself virgin until I married at age 25. I had tremendous crushes (less and less on girls as I grew older), but would never touch any-body. Afraid. To be known as gay in the late forties was an immense disgrace. I couldn't have handled it. So, young man, force yourself into the hetero pat-tern. A phase. You're just passing through it. Not only did I fear sex with women; I feared sex with anybody! Sad? It was a relief to say you were saving yourself for marriage. But we did things like that forty years ago. I was sure that if I had sex with anybody I'd automatically fail.

MARK: Did anybody ever try to have sex with you?

PETERS: Yes, and I didn't even realize what was happening! There was a friend I saw a lot of when I was seventeen. We hung around this older woman, stayed up late nights (I was working in Wausau, Wisconsin, for the Employers Mutual Insurance Company), danced to such marvelous people as the Andrews Sisters and the Ink Spots. Roy—that was his name—and I danced wonderfully to-gether, practicing all sorts of great dips. Then, you know, we held one another when we danced. We even went to the Wausau High Junior Prom: Roy was in drag, sure nobody would recognize him. But they did, almost at once. I was still so naïve, I had no idea what was happening. And I wasn't turned on to him. He visited my family up north that summer—which meant we slept in the same bed. He tried to do things, but I pushed him away and stupidly main-tained my virginity.

Well, three years later, once out of the Army, practically the first thing I did was to seek him out and start the friendship anew. We had a couple of evenings—the first sex I'd had with anybody. I was passive all the way. Had no concept, for example, that sodomy (I'd seen the word in the Bible and thought it had to do with sheep and heifers) was even possible. How would you get that *thing* in there? I've often wondered where Roy is, and what he's doing. He decided to go from small-town Wisconsin to Chicago, where he could, he said, be anonymous, and live out his gay life. At the time I last saw him, he was drinking heavily.

MARK: Some people who form romantic idealizations find it hard to connect any physical contact with that ideal, distant form. Did you have crushes on people in a Platonic sense and crushes on people in a physical sense?

PETERS: I don't think I could ever dissociate the two. All these fixations were Platonic in the sense I never did anything. But there were super-physical crushes. I had them firmly in my fantasy-mind whenever I beat off. Or I'd have wet dreams over them. I was afraid to make the initial contact, and yet I'd hunger for someone to appear to carry me off. I guess I still suffer from that anxiety... afraid to make that initial crossing-over, craving for the person I want to make an unmistakable sign that he wants me too. Most gays go through this, I'd guess. I've always envied the younger gays, for they don't seem hung up in the same way.

MARK: These were crushes on both men and women?

PETERS: At first, but then exclusively on men.

MARK: Do you think that part of the energy that sped you through college so quickly was unspent sexual energy?

PETERS: No doubt. And I still divert a lot of sexual energy into my work. The illusion is that I get three times as much work done as most people do. For a period of a few months after coming out, I let myself go—went through a promiscuous period trying to see how many people I could get it on with. One month there were thirty, which for me was a record. I was beginning to drink (I'm practically a teetotaler now). Soon I realized that this was all heading down rather than up, so I called a halt and returned my energies to writing, teaching, giving readings around the country. Therapy helped me see this reality, too. When I come up here (San Francisco), which I do often, I seldom have sex. I see poets, editors, plays. I do some readings. And, too, I have a huge correspondence. I'm compulsive about answering people who write to me. My letters aren't masterpieces of writing, wit, etc.; but there are hundreds of them. Also, I had a regular book-review commentary program on Pacifica Radio Los Angeles, called *In Print.*

MARK: Can you tell me about Paul, the friend you've lived with for the past few years?

PETERS: He's a very private young man. He's published some poetry in *Poetry Now, The Midatlantic Review, Dodeca*. He is a homebody, interested in mystical things like spiritual healing. He's given me great security over these years. I was a mess when I met him. Good things have happened to both of us. A heavy private, personal friendship, with very little sex. My guess is that if we were rabidly into sex with one another we'd have been apart long before this. He is a beautiful force. His book *Loretta* will be out soon.

MARK: When did you get married?

PETERS: In 1950, while working on my Ph.D. Jean was another student and a writer. She'd just sold a short story to *Harper's Magazine*. She was neat. From the outset we never pretended we were romantically in love. Both assumed we'd have a long marriage (which we did—twenty years), and that our love would grow. We went through struggles: lack of money, illness, and finally the death of Richard. And the children came along too fast for her to continue her own writing. I've always felt guilty about that.

MARK: Can you talk about Richard's death?

PETERS: Yes. My first book *Songs for a Son* exorcises much for me. He was four and a half and had gone to nursery school in the morning, came home (I went to get him) complaining of a stomach ache. We both spent the afternoon in bed, both reading books. I was reading, of all things, Thomas Mann's *The Magic Mountain*—a grim work to read while somebody beside you is dying. Finally, he said he was tired and was going to sleep. The last thing he said was "I love you, daddy." I went downstairs, and shortly after heard this gurgling sound. Ran up to find him already in a coma. By the time he was at the hospital, he was dead. Meningitis. This death was for me the ultimate absurdity. I couldn't deal with it. Finally, therapy helped. And writing the poems—I started on them the day after he died. Before then I hadn't written poems to speak of: I'd tried some novels, and had written, edited, and published books on Swinburne's theories on literature and art, three immense volumes of John Addington Symonds' letters, and a source book on Victorian art. I had also published a raft of articles. I managed even to be elected to the Board of Trustees of the American Society for Aesthetics. In other words, I was a thoroughgoing academic.

MARK: Richard's death was the occasion of the beginnings of your poetic awareness. Is there a tie-in between death and poetry?

PETERS: Yes. What experience is more profound, and disturbing, than death? And I think that poetry is a—is *the* major way of dealing with it. But we needn't be grim about it, right? There is an absurd side to death. Grim humor, if you will. There is pathos in how a dead body looks. Absurdity. So rigid and fragile. So the fragile part... maybe humor isn't the right word, but the sense of the absurd appears, implying that there's an edge of humor in the event. Irony.

MARK: The way you describe a corpse is the way you could describe a poem: rigid, yet delicate.

PETERS: I get the feeling now that a lot of free long-line verse really isn't rigid: it isn't frozen. Maybe that's one of the faults. To me, if it's frozen it means it's got some strong sense of form going for it, which I like. I like formal poetry. It's a way of shaping something into a tiny form in a life that is probably full of chaos, personal feelings and all that. If a poem is going to be as chaotic as your life, it seems to me that you're missing out on a whole dimension of art. That's why I suppose the Ginsberg line—the long projective verse line—is often boring to me. I respect his achievements as a liberating social force.

MARK: There's a quote from Roethke at the beginning of *Songs for a Son.*

PETERS: His book *The Lost Son* was helpful and influential for me. Roethke helped me develop my line, because in the 1960s, early, I hadn't read any projective verse. What I tried to do in *Songs for a Son* was to keep the lyrics simple, so simple a child could understand them. There was a popular song at the time called "Waterloo"—Stonewall Jackson recorded it. "Waterloo, Waterloo, everybody has to meet his Waterloo. Everybody has to pay, everybody has his day. everybody has to meet his Waterloo." That's pretty much how it goes. It had a very strong Salvation Army drum rhythm in it. That immense beat! I would play it at full volume in my study. This was in Ferndale, Michigan, outside Detroit. I was teaching at Wayne State University. I would turn the volume up so loud it hurt my ears, and that *boom, boom, boom* was a way of getting some kind of pattern or metronomic stress into the grief. It made the pain less, simply to have that. It was like beating on the walls. Those rhythms I tried to get into those poems, which helped, I think, to explain my short line; I wanted the lines to be equivalent to what I heard in Stonewall Jackson's music. So I wrote about fifteen of these poems, and put them away for three years, not thinking they were publishable. They were secret, and wounds were healing.

Eventually, I took them out and sent one off to the Canadian magazine *The Fiddlehead*. The poem was called "Kittens," the longest poem in the sequence. They took it. That made me think I might be on to something. I sent another poem to the *Western Humanities Review*, the poem called "The Burial of the Ashes" ("Ceremony" in the book). They took that one, so I set out then to organize the whole, to see it as a patterned work, as a single poem. I happened to notice in an issue of *Poetry* that Denise Levertov was editing a series for W. W. Norton, of poetry books. I sent the manuscript in. She wasn't sure whether the poems had the quality she was after, or whether she was intensely moved by the experience itself—so she thought it over, for about five weeks, while I waited and waited. Then the contract came. A super break, indeed. I shall always be grateful to her for helping me launch a fairly busy career. That Denise liked my work enough to publish it meant a great deal.

MARK: Were you hiding your homosexuality in your poetry then?

PETERS: Yes. And in what was my second published book, *The Sow's Head and Other Poems*, much of the violence I felt, the butchering of pigs, the surrealist images of threat, John Dillinger—always a fantasy figure for me, sexual, as Jesus had been—much of the violence has my own incredible tension desperate to be out of the closet and terrified of taking the responsibility. Hardly a day in my life had I been alone... in the military... at college... twenty years of marriage. How terrifying to face up to the risk that there may never again be anyone to share a life with. And once the step towards self-declaration happens, there is rarely any return.

MARK: Did you send messages in those poems?

PETERS: Unabashedly. I hungered, hoping that some attractive reader might sense that he was needed by me and appear. He would pick up the book and say, "Oh, poet-man wants me." And he'd come to my door and say, "Here I am."

MARK: Who helped you? Anybody?

PETERS: Well, yes. Yes. A former student, who is the figure in my *Cool Zebras of Light*, my most thoroughly gay book. I call him "Lee." He's dead now. Shot himself a couple of years ago, after many wrist-slashings and attempts to O.D.

MARK: How did you meet him?

PETERS: My marriage at the time was pretty much gone, although neither my wife nor I were admitting it. During the European trip, on the Guggenheim Fellowship, I had endured a real mental crisis over a young Welsh poet. He was a superb muscular man who wore nothing but old Levi's and a blue t-shirt. And that was it. He'd been a teddy-boy, gangs, etc.

MARK: That's a very Marlon Brando image.

PETERS: Yes, and he was built like young Brando. We'd go out walking along the river Cam and lie down. I'd have my head on his stomach, looking up at the stars and talking. Never really able to do anything. Afraid. He was married, although his wife was in a severe series of shock treatments. I hungered for him as I had no one before. We had a falling out because of some confusion over a camping trip we were to take together. The experience is still painful.

MARK: Tell me something more about Lee, of *Zebras*.

PETERS: He'd been in one of my classes, but was no longer a student. He was telling me one afternoon that he'd answered a sex ad in the *L.A. Free Press*. I said, "Why do you need to do that? I'm sure there are students around here who think as you do." He said he was either going to do something about his homosexuality, or crack up. And I said, "If you know someone who turns you on, tell him; all he can do is say *no*." He replied: "I am in love..." "Well, who is it? Why don't you let him know." He said, "He's in this room." I looked around, and there was nobody there but the two of us! That is when and how our affair started. My wife had gone back to England, so Lee moved in with me until her return. The friendship was crazy and intense. But it's pretty much all there in *Cool Zebras of Light*. I have a lot of his poems, too, I hope to get around to editing some day.

MARK: So *Zebras* sounds like a gay man's *Fear of Flying*.

PETERS: [*Laughter.*] I hope it's better. I'm not sure I like the comparison. I smothered Lee. I couldn't bear him out of my sight for ten minutes. And he was always trying to make it with a surfer. He was hung up on them. But he had trouble relating to people—they sensed him as weird and wouldn't respond. He had the most superb brown eyes. And his body was lithe and taut.

MARK: You imply that if the affair wasn't turbulent, violent, and pressured it wasn't worth anything?

PETERS: Right, right. I suppose we were arrogant enough, or stuck on ourselves, to feel ours was going to be one of the literary liaisons of the age. Rimbaud and Verlaine! Lee was keeping his journal. I was keeping a journal. No scrap would be lost.

MARK: Sounds rather self-conscious.

PETERS: Well, it was. Pathetic too, I think now. It was a sick period I couldn't avoid going through. and Lee was always suicidal, schizophrenic. I thought that reason could always win over irrationality, so I tried to convince him that his talent would be heard, that life was worth living. After two years, I realized that I had to break off the friendship. I was taking too many risks emotionally—he could never settle down and be content to build on our relationship.

MARK: Did you play psychiatrist to his patient?

PETERS: No, no. When we were home from Europe I continued to see him often. He had to live fifty miles from me to go to school. I was largely supporting him financially—a difficult feat, since I was also paying a huge sum in alimony and child support. I could never say "no" to him...

MARK: The poems in *Cool Zebras of Light* have such an immediacy to them. They seem to have been almost written "on the run."

PETERS: They were. Most were written in Europe. Lee was off wandering Berlin, hoping to get picked up. I knew that I had to let him go, to find breathing space. Yet I believed he was out to betray me. The only way I could keep from screaming, of passing the interval until he returned, was to write. Modify the pain. Later I wanted the poems to transcend the tackiness of my self-pity. They should be universal somehow, larger than the limitations of the actual experience behind them. I don't think of the poems as "homosexual." They are love poems; they happen to reflect an experience between two men.

MARK: Could you say something about your involvement with the Shaker movement and how it's related to your poetry.

PETERS: It's the first time I've consciously tried to break from my own life and write about something remote from it. And yet, the connections are there, because Ann Lee, the founder of the Shakers, lost four children in infancy. So, considering the grief I experienced in the one dead child, how did she manage to survive the deaths of four? That was a connection. Then, I was also writing in a woman's voice, with, I suppose, whatever feelings I have that could be called female. One of my favorite poems in *Gift* is one in which Ann sleeps with her husband. Becoming the woman Ann Lee was a letting go of feelings I've always had as a woman. I recall a game I used to play with my sister. We would take the kitchen chairs out on the lawn and arrange them in a circle and play "pig family." It seems absurd now. But I was always the sow. I would lie down and pretend I had huge dugs and that all these little pigs were sucking away like mad. Maybe the Ann Lee persona is a way of letting more of that out again.

MARK: What do you think about the tie-in between poetry and performance? Do you think poetry is more valid if it's performed? There seems to be a movement among younger poets now that whatever one *writes* one must *speak out*.

PETERS: I don't see it that way, quite. Because for me the experience is still primarily on the page. I've done some thinking about this, because I've heard poets put down because "Oh, well, he's a *performer!*" As though somehow that was bad. There's a feeling that if he stood up and mumbled words into his beard (or into her purse) that is somehow better and less charlatanesque than giving a performance. I think if you're going to be invited to read poems aloud you are expected to keep the audience (assuming there is one) awake. I'm tired of readings where every fourth word gets mumbled down into the page. If I go to a poetry reading I want to be moderately stimulated. No matter how dramatic, well-delivered the poems are, that's not going to violate my experience of them on the page afterwards. In fact, it may enrich, enrich. I strongly believe then that a reading has to be a performance. Poets should go to school to become actors.

MARK: During our conversation you brought up poetry and personality. When one thinks, say, of a poet like T. S. Eliot, one doesn't think of an autobiographical "I" coming to the forefront. But with many contemporary poets their poems are unabashedly autobiographical.

PETERS: I hope we're moving away from that intensely emotional, confessional work. That's what I've tried to do with the Shaker poems—move out and away from my immediate self-concerns. And my current book (I wrote it at Yaddo) is a long work in the voice of Mad King Ludwig of Bavaria. I feel connections with him. If I believed in reincarnation or karma or setting back time, I'd love to have built those fantastic castles, loved all those handsome grooms, and sponsored Richard Wagner. Ludwig is an archetypal esthete, one whose nerves were so attenuated he'd orgasm listening to Wagner's music. He had whole operas staged just for himself, sitting in his immense Residenz Palais in Munich. And he had his horse to dinner, dined alone on a gilt table elevated through the floor, built a grotto arranged with machines to change the lighting according to his moods, had his hair curled every day so that he could better enjoy his food, etc. He was a great eccentric homosexual.

MARK: Is there such a thing as "gay writing"?

PETERS: Yes, but I don't want to be seen exclusively as a gay poet. My poems are all part of a larger whole. There is a splendid amount of good gay writing around. I suppose that a spate of bad poems has to occur when any minority is being heard. There is a place for jackoff poems, and there are some good ones; but they don't do much as literature, except stir the groin a couple of times. And that's not bad. Most poems are expendable, right? Poems you read along with the morning newspaper and forget. I guess there has to be a whole subcontinent of these for the sake of the few peaks emerging from the water.

MARK: Sounds snobbish.

PETERS: I don't mean it that way. And the tremendous amount of gay writing published over the past two or three years, no matter how ephemeral much of it is, is crucial to an emergent gay consciousness.

MARK: So you think it's important to publish all this gay work?

PETERS: Definitely. We're still a persecuted minority. The more vocal we are and proud of our subculture the more the bigotry quiets down. Our art is as legitimate as any around, and we should feel good about it. There's more to gay life than the Continental Baths and alcoholism and whacking people with purses. We must demand respect from the straight world, more than their tolerance, that is.

MARK: Do you behave differently as part of a minority than you might otherwise behave, or think?

PETERS: Yes. I know that in my teaching and in my personal relationships I try to excel. I feel a real pressure, since it is generally known that I am gay, to allow the straight world no room for complaint. What I mean is that if what I do is tops they'll have to acknowledge it. They can't say: "Oh, he fucked up because he's gay." Look at the tremendous record culturally of the Jews, who've been persecuted and suppressed for centuries. Their contributions to art and science are unparalleled. Drive comes from threat, unfortunately. But the drive to excel is part of our very tissue. Obviously, if you don't believe in your culture you aren't going to shake up the majority culture. I've never felt that the Jews ever believed their culture inferior to any other; and in the face of vast injustices they persisted, producing some of the finest minds in history. Our record should and can parallel theirs. The tradition of gay artists, as most gays know, is old and extensive. We need to move more vigorously than ever, demonstrating first to ourselves that we are a homogeneous culture and second that we are among the most gifted folks in the universe.

MARK: Do you feel more alienated from the straight culture since you've come out?

PETERS: Oh, certainly. But it doesn't bother me because my life is rich with people and professional doings. I do have a few deep straight friendships: Carolyn Stoloff, Carol and Max Yeh, Bill Collins, Arthur and Judy Lane, etc.

MARK: How gay do you feel the literary world is—people who write plays, novels, poems?

PETERS: Quite gay. In drama you think of Williams and Albee, the two biggest ones. And William Inge, who apparently couldn't handle it. In prose, there's Vidal, Isherwood. Tons of poets: Ashbery, Ginsberg, Wieners, Logan, Jonathan Williams, etc. It's assumed that artists and hairdressers and interior decorators are gay—that's the cliché. Right? But not politicians and businessmen. How long would the president of Continental Can or AT&T survive if they came out gay? How long would a senator, like Hayakawa, say, survive if he declared he was gay? Of course, this is California, and one never knows. And preachers: old Hargis swinging both ways. A couple he married compared notes and found he'd slept with both of them. Well, Sin has always been part of Christianity; the bigger the sin the more you can be forgiven and hence can walk away as the superior Christian. Sick. Sick.

MARK: Do you think that intellectuals and particularly those who are gay are living in a kind of *Garden of the Finzi-Continis*?

PETERS: No. We are creating our own vanguard for social and cultural change. There's more going for us in the straight world. The recent spate of movies and TV programs (even Bob Newhart the other night got into the act) show this. The gays on *Mary Hartman, Mary Hartman* were not at all the clichéd gays. And *The Family*, the new series, presents the gay youth as the most attractive person on the show. How deep the tolerance is, of course, remains doubtful. There may be a growing tolerance in the sense that the straight world says: Do your thing, but don't let us know too much about it. And don't expect us to rub up to you—we'll keep as much distance as we ever have. You might contaminate our kids, German shepherds, and poodles.

When I was a student at the University of Wisconsin (1946-1952) I knew I was gay, but was afraid to come out. The poets I liked, or the novelists, were ones with homosexual trends in their work: Christopher Marlowe, Truman Capote, Isherwood, Auden, Oscar Wilde, Thomas Wolfe, to name a few. I used to fantasize throwing myself between the knifer and Marlowe's body, and sparing him. I probably confused him with Leander in his poem, that super stud who swam the choppy waters to visit Hero. Marlowe real was probably very grubby. I also read and grooved on Whitman, had a special illustrated edition, with a couple of naked men being mystical. I sought in literature resolutions of my own sexual tensions, obviously. And I fell in love with Thomas Wolfe because I thought that anyone with that much sensitivity had to be gay. When I was in graduate school and had to decide on a dissertation, I was attracted to the English writers of the eighteen-nineties, Wilde's decade. I was also something of an aesthete who wore Levi's before Levi's were in, as they are now. I was playing "Northern Wisconsin Farmboy" in the face of what I thought was a slick university decadence.

MARK: What was your dissertation subject?

PETERS: "The English Poetry of the 1890s and the Several Arts." I was interested in inter-relationships, the ways in which poems crossed over to or borrowed effects from the other arts. Sort of esoteric. But it took me into the murky people of the eighteen-nineties: J. A. Symonds, Ernest Dowson, Arthur Symons, John Gray, Simeon Solomon, Aubrey Beardsley, etc.

MARK: Could you say something about your work on Swinburne and Symonds?

PETERS: Well, Swinburne intrigued me because of his algolagnia—he craved being whipped. I loved his eccentricity. And once I mastered his poetry I was amazed by the beauty and skill I found there. The idea was to write a book on the poetry to guide younger readers into it. Instead, as a prelude, I was fascinated by the criticisms he wrote—tons of them—and produced a study of that instead: *The Crowns of Apollo: Swinburne's Principles of Literature and Art.* It was well received by the academic world. I wrote a lot of it on diet pills, not knowing then that I was taking speed; a doctor had prescribed them. I'd come to a block writing, pop a couple of pills, *rev* for two days, write like crazy, then stay in bed for a day to recover. Swinburne probably would have approved.

MARK: What of Symonds? It took you eight years, didn't it, to bring out those three fat volumes?

PETERS: Yes, and because of my compulsiveness I nearly had a breakdown working on that one too. Wasn't into diet pills then, but simply pushed. Both Herbert Schueller, my co-editor, and I found it hard to trust anyone else with the drudgery, so we wound up doing nearly all of the project ourselves. I typed nearly all of the 2,000 letters from the originals—photostats. We both made trips to England and Europe following Symonds' tracks and meeting people who either collected his letters or who knew something about him. Schueller, a superbly gifted man—musician, theorist on the arts, editor—had written his dissertation on Symonds as critic. The whole project was his idea. I was a young professor, excited by the invitation—a real professional break. We advertised here and in England for letters. They came in from all places, but the largest collections came from the University of Leeds and the Dakyns family.

MARK: You seem to have a knack for getting into people's psyches. Did that happen with Symonds?

PETERS: It sure did. I began to think I was Symonds, and I am sure that the intensive work I did on him hastened my coming out. Symonds was also a married homosexual, with four children (I had four). He was an enthusiast of Whitman's Uranian poems. He had a couple of mental crises over his homosexuality. He was in love with art, and particularly with Greek male-love. He led a double life, in his own home in Davos, Switzerland. His wife hated sex, so Johnnie simply had his handsome Italian gondolier imported into his household as his servant. There was also a Swiss lad in Davos—Symonds helped his family buy a hotel to accommodate the English tuberculars who swamped

Davos for the cure. During this period my own marriage was shot, and gay fantasies became increasingly dominant. I admired Symonds' courage, wanted my own Swiss lad, my own gondolier.

I found a couple of portions of a gay epic Symonds spent a good number of years writing and never published. He called it "John Mordan," the name of a London newsboy. Either his wife or his friend Henry Graham Dakyns destroyed most of the poems. But two remain: "Eudiades: An Athenian Love-Tale" and "Gabriel." I published "Gabriel," with Timothy d'Arch Smith of London, two years ago, in a special, expensive limited edition. A blank-verse poem about Apollo who comes in the guise of a beautiful youth to stay with a group of monks. The year is A.D. 1000. He by this time has converted the whole monastery to gay love. It's Easter, and the monks are about to make their yearly procession up a mountain to venerate a statue of Christ on the cross erected there. But an old hermit races in from the shrubbery and rocks, pulls off Apollo's magic belt, and denounces the monks. Apollo (or at least the youth) dies. In grief, the monks take up the beautiful body and carry it up the mountain. As they reach the statue of Christ, Christ bows.

Symonds' letters are full of his stresses and strains. That's what makes them valuable. He was pretty much a second-rate writer, although his multi-volume history of the Italian Renaissance has currency with historians. And his translation of Cellini is the one you're apt to read. He also published good critical studies of Shelley and Whitman. The book on Whitman, almost symbolically, was published on the very day Symonds died. He also wrote three books of poems, none of them very good, but interesting because he had to pretend that his love poems (comprising most of the books) were all written to women, when in fact they were written to male lovers. His autobiography, which should be published soon, clarifies a lot.

MARK: What is the reaction to you in the university? You are a full professor, right? Does the subject of your being gay ever come up?

PETERS: Not really. I've had tenure for a long time. I've been teaching since 1950, so have a certain immunity a young beginning professor would not have. And I had proved myself academically and professionally before I came out. I am at a terrific school, the University of California at Irvine; the department is first-rate; everybody seems to do his work, respecting what everybody else is doing. I've been in some truly shitty departments—brutal infighting: the worst was when I was at the University of California Riverside and the critic Frederick Hoffman was in his final paranoid years. He brutalized students, and he tried brutalizing colleagues he thought disliked him. That was vicious. Academic bitchery par excellence. And the University of Idaho in 1953 was grim: the chairman had wiped out all courses in poetry without consulting anybody, and all courses in literature in foreign languages. I would have been fired had I not moved. Ohio Wesleyan University was another grim spot in the late fifties. There were so many old bloody feuds there, it mattered, if you were a young instructor, by which of the oldies you sat at department meetings. I was axed there by the one woman I thought was befriending me. I even was green enough to ask her for advice. Years later I found that she was the villain. And at Boston University, a similar problem. But Riverside was worse than all of the other schools lumped together.

All of this is a long way of saying that my current department is splendid. They respect what I am doing and even read my books. They also allow me to further my professional life by arranging the numerous readings I do. I am lucky, really lucky. And the matter of my being gay never comes up, at least overtly. Most departments would, I think, fail to give a young gay professor tenure, if he made much noise about his being gay. There's still a built-in thing. I suppose the argument is that if you are heterosexual you don't go around the department advertising the details of your bed behavior and your tastes, kinky and otherwise. Who knows how many crotch-sniffers and bicycle-seat sniffers one may be teaching with? So, it seems an academic law that the more you advertise your sexual interests the less your chances are of being hired permanently. For better or worse, it's in the nature of the beast. Perhaps a gay instructor would fare better in the social sciences than in humanities or science. The latter are apt to be rednecks in their thinking; the former threatened because so many English professors are closet cases.

MARK: Do your students know you are gay?

PETERS: I'm sure some of them do. But, again, I never push the matter. I try to keep a professional distance between myself and my students, at least while they are in my classes. Occasionally a gay student will come up and say, "I read your *Cool Zebras of Light* and really dug it." But that's rare. I usually respond by thanking him. Again, I teach at a very special university, and am grateful, so hope always to be above reproach. My sexuality has nothing to do with my students, it seems to me.

MARK: Do you suppose though that there are advantages to not entirely revealing yourself in your writing?

PETERS: There's a complexity if you can keep your reader guessing. A lot of Duncan's earlier poems are this way. You can read a poem like "Returning to the Rhetoric of an Early Mode" as a moving, beautiful apology for male love— or you can read it as a metaphor for the spirit working through earth and earthiness. I prefer subtlety and complexity in my art, whenever I can have it. So, why not play the chameleon? Be straight. Be gay. Widen the range of possibilities for yourself as a writer. Why stay locked into your own gritty psyche—the sterility of much American writing today is because poets confine themselves too much. Hide behind the cosmic eye, as Whitman did, once in a while. Maybe you produce better art if you do some concealing.

MARK: Can you say something of the poet as a center of mystique rather than as center for poetry? It seems that some poets draw a mystique around themselves—groupies, acolytes—while others don't. Self-publicity and advertisement.

PETERS: We are a celebrity-conscious culture. We demand celebrities on every corner to gaze at and cheer. The celebrity figure is the one who makes it, like Charles Bukowski who holds forth in rock palaces and packs them in at $3 or $3.50 a head. Last Halloween Bukowski sold out the Golden Bear in Huntington Beach. Followers don't know what he'll do up there on stage, but they're sure there'll be a show. They ask him non-literary questions like "What color was your shit this morning?" "When will you vomit again?" "Do you drink women's piss?" etc. I guess that results in a celebrity mystique. *Rolling*

Stone featured him a few months back, giving him more space than they did to George Harrison. And there are lesser figures. One is Ann Waldman who does her thing with *Fast-Speaking Woman*. I've had my critical say on her and the celebrity problem (and on Gerard Malanga too) in *Margins*. People flock to see the poet-celebrities. Those people, I'm convinced, don't read the books. They like a show.

MARK: Well, you seem to be contradicting yourself. Earlier you said that a poetry reading must be an entertainment, or something like that.

PETERS: True. But what I meant was that a poet should rehearse his reading, for maximum effectiveness. I didn't mean that he should strip naked on stage, throw grapes at the audience, slink about for effect. There's a difference. So much of the public aspect of poetry today is diseased by the celebrity thing.

MARK: You wrote a poem to Bukowski in your recent book *The Poet as Ice-Skater.*

PETERS: I like Buk's early poetry very much. I still remember reading it for the first time; I felt as if all the windows in town opened up. There was an empathy for the underdog I admired; now, I feel, he is apt to be cruel where earlier he was sympathetic. But, more on that celebrity problem. Gary Snyder is another figure who as a celebrity drags semi-literates in after him who believe in the virtues of building your own sauna and drinking manzanita-berry tea. Mindless kickers. Ginsberg draws similar people. I am not knocking the quality work both of these men have done—do understand that. But a critic has to sort out finally what matters in the poetry from the personality hype. Maybe Ginsberg's penis or Snyder's beard are poetry to some people.

MARK: In ancient cultures and today's so-called primitive cultures the shaman or witch doctor is a poet. The curative powers come from magical words. Do you think poets have a greater ability to drop their everyday personas and to don other masks?

PETERS: It's tough. My complaint is that not enough poets are willing to try moving outside themselves. Go back to old John Milton. Blake said he was of the Devil's party without knowing it. And Satan is the most interesting character in *Paradise Lost*. Blake was saying that Milton in order to write convincingly as the fallen angel had to assume the identity of that fallen angel. And Keats's notion of the poet as chameleon. Writing is then a kind of acting: I've always seen it that way. It's great stimulation to try to be someone completely foreign to yourself. I'm hoping next to be the Norwegian explorer Nansen who in 1895 walked across Greenland. Isn't all this shifting of identities what good art is all about? The reader too absorbed in a work shifts his identity. That's the play behind art, an exchange of identities on various levels.

MARK: You have scope in finding subject matters. You don't seem to feel any limitations of time, place or cultural barriers.

PETERS: Yes, I feel at the top of my writing powers. For me the clue is energy. I hope to keep vibrant, moving, even impulsive until the end. Loving life is most of it, and that includes caring healthily about the people you love and about yourself.

PHOTO BY JEAN LOUVEL

ROGER PEYREFITTE

ROGER PEYREFITTE, French novelist and chronicler of contemporary mores, was born in 1907 in Castres in the department of Tarn. He was educated, partly in Catholic schools, in southern France and took his advanced degree at the Free School of Political Science in Paris. In 1931 he embarked upon a diplomatic career which took him to Greece, 1933-1938. Recalled to Paris because of several homosexual incidents he had in Athens, his open life style finally led him to have to choose between resigning and being fired from the Vichy government.

To explain his development as a homosexual he turned to writing. His first novel, *Les Amitiés particulières*, 1945 (*Special Friendships*, 1950), was a critical and financial success, as was the 1964 movie based on it. The book brought him to the attention of poet and playwright Jean Cocteau (1889-1963), and the two began a close frienship. Peyrefitte had already been a friend for a long time with novelist and playwright Henry de Montherlant (1896-1972). But both these writers more or less hid their homosexuality from the world's view whereas Peyrefitte became a leader of the gay movement in Paris. Together with André Baudry he founded one of the longest-existing gay organizations in the world, Arcadie, which celebrated its twenty-fifth anniversary in 1978.

Among the books that followed were two autobiographical *romans à clef* about his diplomatic life, *Les Ambassades*, 1951 (*Diplomatic Diversions*, 1953), and *La Fin des ambassades*, 1953 (*Diplomatic Conclusions*, 1954); two novels about the Catholic Church, *Les Clés de Saint Pierre*, 1955 (*The Keys of St. Peter*, 1957), and *Les Chevaliers de Malte*, 1957 (*The Knights of Malta*, 1959); and his fictionalized biography of a minor French poet, Jacques d'Adelsward-Fersen (1879-1923), *L'Exilé de Capri*, 1959 (*The Exile of Capri*, 1961), which is virtually a who's who of the gay European world around the turn of the century.

Later works continued to mingle fiction and history: *La Nature du prince*, 1963 (*The Prince's Person*, 1964), set in Renaissance Italy; *Les Juifs*, 1965 (*The Jews*, 1967); *Les Américains*, 1968; *Des Français*, 1970; and a biography of Fernand Legros, *Tableaux de chasse*, 1976; two extraordinarily candid memoirs— *Notre amour*, 1967; *Propos secrets*, 1977; and *L'Enfant de cœur*, 1978. More recent books include the novel *Roy*, 1979, and a trilogy on the life of Alexander the Great.

In 1976 Peyrefitte electrified the Christian world by his statement that Pope Paul VI had been a practicing homosexual while he was Archbishop of Milan.

THE PRESENT INTERVIEW, in mixed English and French, took place on July 11, 1978. The setting was the author's combination salon and dining room at his home in Paris facing on the Bois de Boulogne. Scattered around the room were innumerable examples of erotic art, both homosexual and heterosexual in nature, collected throughout the world (many of these were photographed for a 1972 book called *Un musée de l'amour*). The interviewer, Dr. D. W. Gunn, had been an associate professor of English at the Université de Metz for a number of years and had returned to France for the summer. Transcription of the tapes and translation of the French parts were made by him and Michel Murat, a professional translator living in Paris. The interview appeared originally in *Gay Sunshine* no. 42/43.

D. W. Gunn interviews
ROGER PEYREFITTE

GUNN: In your letter to me you wrote, "Everything gay is mine." Would you like to explain what you meant by this?

PEYREFITTE: In order to do so, let me recount a little of my life. I was awakened to the meaning of tender and romantic feelings in my childhood when I was enrolled in a religious school [in Ardouane, Hérault]. And at the dawn of my life I found myself a nonconformist in love. I congratulate myself that I began not with an impure love but that for years I cultivated what I have called *les amitiés particulières*, special friendships — that is, a pure kind of pre-sexuality. I use this idea of pure and impure love only in order to render an image of my religious education, because you must not doubt that since everything that is gay is good, there's nothing gay that is impure for me. But I speak of an education which was at base a moral one. Living thus to the maximum and having seen this life lived to maximum, ending when my partner killed himself, became the subject of my first book, *Special Friendships*. That's the story which I think everyone who belongs to the "gay cooperation" has read, no? — I was marked then by two things: first, by nonconformity in love and, afterwards, with the realization that this nonconformity was in a battle with society. Society is the born enemy of people who are born gay — homosexual, pederastic, whatever term you like. There are nuances [even though the French use the terms interchangeably]. I know lots of homosexuals who didn't discover their homosexuality until an advanced age. (I remember some who said it was during military service, others who said it was when they were in the university, others much older. There was one case I knew of, a marquis who only discovered he was gay at age forty-five. With fright! Then he realized that he had lost forty years of his life. [*Laughter.*] One should never lose hope. Homosexuality can strike any straight man at any age.) But as for me, I was born thus. — Notice one thing; my particularity is to be too sensitive to feminine charms also, for before being a lover of sex I am a lover of beauty. And how can one not recognize beauty in women, especially young women, as well as in young boys? So in my first memoirs, which are in a book (I don't know whether it has been translated yet in English) recognized as a masterpiece of the same order as *Special Friendships* by even my worst detractors, *La Mort d'une mère*, a book which I wrote in 1949 after my mother's death, I spoke without shame of my attitude toward my mother. She adored me, and her love was very dear to me. Through my mother I came to understand women, and this led me to understand other things than physical love. As she was very devout, I remain quite influenced by my religious education even though I am what you would call a libertine of the spirit, an agnostic. I still think it's good to have guardrails in life. — I said in that book, *La Mort d'une mère,* that my first physical, as opposed to sentimental, encounter was with a young girl. I was then nine years old. I said that in a veiled way because the subject of the book was sacred and didn't lend itself to confidences about physical affairs, especially indecent ones. But in *Propoos secrets,* which is my naked confessions published just a year ago, which has had an enormous success in France, I spoke of everybody, beginning with myself. Since I recounted the morals of many well-known personages openly, I could not conceal intimate details of my own life.... *"Propos"* is "conversation." *"Secret"*—what is a good translation for that?

GUNN: "Confidential"?

PEYREFITTE: Yes, that would be a good translation.... Let me give you a detail from it which shows well that I was in the gay direction even when I was a young boy. That girl: I played with her, but I didn't try anything. I made her get down on her hands and knees, I pulled up her dress, and I contemplated her bottom. It's very curious. Because even then I ignored the difference of the sex. I never even looked at her sex! It's very curious. Just at that moment my nurse surprised me in this act and frightened my parents, who put me in the religious school. Only boys. As I said in *La Mort d'une mère,* that was putting me in the wolf's mouth! But my *amitiés particulières* were without similar incidents. I contemplated the beauty of a young boy exactly in the manner (I learned afterwards) of platonic love. With admiration I contemplated his face—not his *fesses,* his bottom. It was only after many, many meetings that I dared to kiss him. Thus a completely chaste relationship, though of a special kind. I am glad that I thus began. But still I was blocked by my religious education. Then when I was sixteen or seventeen, I was no longer in a religious school but in a high school in the town of Foix, in Ariège in the south of France. There I renewed my *amitiés particulières* but pushed further on. Once I was with this boy, and we both had erections, to speak plainly. But I never touched him, nor he me. But it was a step. It was only at eighteen that I was finally liberated sexually. My way always was only with boys. With them I discovered the full delights of sex. A year later I went to Paris to prepare for my diplomatic career. (People traveled less in those days; it was my first trip to Paris.) But the first year I didn't put my foot once in the École Libre des Sciènces Politiques. I was only interested in Parisian life—and only a Parisian life with homosexuals. I had several adventures. Not many, but several. But then I came to understand that I must cut this kind of relationship completely if I were to become a diplomat, because an inquiry was made not only into the family of the candidates in order to learn that they were honorable or at least with some means (in this time they wanted them to have a little money)—

GUNN: This would have been in the late 1920s?

PEYREFITTE: Exactly. I was a brilliant student and finished my studies in first place. I have my medal yet. [He goes to get it.] There, you see: "School of Political Science, Diplomatic Section, 1930; First Place, Roger Peyrefitte." That has nothing to do with the gay question.

GUNN: Yes, but it is very interesting because often in the States the gays are represented as men who—

PEYREFITTE: Yes, who are outlaws in studies! I was first in my high school in French, Latin, Greek, history. The last one in mathematics. I am closed to math. I was scarcely interested in natural history either. Very bad in geography because it was dry and uninteresting, at least as it was presented then. But very interested in history. I was fascinated by living questions.

GUNN: Why did you choose a diplomatic career?

PEYREFITTE: It was a way to escape my family. My father was a bourgeois with a certain fortune. He made it himself; he was a self-made man. Sometimes he told me: "Had I gone to the States, I would have been a multi-millionaire today." But he was a millionaire with many large holdings, a chain of shops, and so on. My mother was from a family of middle-class landlords. My father gave me complete freedom to choose my life. I was an only child, so naturally he was a bit sad that I was not interested in becoming a gentleman farmer. But he let me choose my own career. When I was sixteen or so, I had met a famous ambassador of this period, Jules Cambon, who was president of the Conference of Ambassadors charged with overseeing the application of the Treaty of Versailles. He was a member of the Académie Française. An important person. He had told me, "You are very curious. You would make good diplomat." So, with this word and the prospect of his introduction (because in this time, almost fifty years ago, before things became more democratic, the diplomatic corps was an awful little aristocracy, and it was necessary that someone introduce you if you didn't come from a family of diplomats), I decided to pursue this career. He gave me his name, and it was a sort of visa.

GUNN: When you found that your homosexuality presented a problem in following a diplomatic career—

PEYREFITTE: It would be absolutely impossible to go into a diplomatic career if you were only suspected of being gay. But fortunately I was totally unknown in Paris. My family was not Parisian, so when I had this year of pederasty there, no one at the Quai d'Orsay [i.e., the Ministry of Foreign Affairs] knew me. I had no scandal; I was not known to the police. And then I cut out this life immediately and completely and put myself into a sort of uniform.

GUNN: That wasn't difficult for you?

PEYREFITTE: Very difficult. I was dedicated to masturbation! Then after I received my appointment I went to deluxe brothels and possessed the beauties of brothel bottoms. Only bottoms! [Laughter.] It was a mixed life, accommodation only. I stayed two years in Paris in order to choose my diplomatic post. When you first pass the French diplomatic examination, you are rarely sent to a post of your own choosing. You are, of course, a beginner. So older colleagues had counseled me to stay in Paris; then I could request my post. I managed to be appointed to Athens. You see, I had already turned in the right direction! When I was in Athens—I told all this candidly in *Propos secrets* [and in a disguised way in *Diplomatic Diversions*]—I began the same pattern again. I went to the great brothel there, I asked the patron discreetly for a girl who could let me take her in a masculine way, and so on. But one night I had an adventure on the slopes of Lycabettus, the hill in the center of Athens in front of the

Acropolis. I was provided with a car and a chauffeur, but I was on foot, returning from a restaurant to my apartment near the top of the hill. At the corner of a street I passed an outside urinal. I saw a very beautiful young boy, perhaps eighteen years old. When he saw me, he went inside. I followed—and my life was changed. Naturally I never returned to the brothel, not even to possess a girl like a boy! [*Laughter.*] I began in this way, and I had many adventures, good and evil. I stayed five years in Athens. I was delighted by the discovery not only of pederasty but of ancient Greece. I dreamed already of Alexander the Great and imagined writing a book about him some day. (So I did: fifty years later, beginning last year. The first of three volumes, on the youth of Alexander, appeared. It will be the foremost work on Alexander. No one has ever written the definitive study, not even your dear Mary Renault.) I was fond of the country. I did have two or three little incidents there. I was robbed in my house, so I was obliged to lodge a complaint with the Greek Ministry of Foreign Affairs. Naturally they sent a discreet note to my chief, the ambassador. I did not know it at the time, but I learned it later. A second incident occurred while I was chargé d'affaires. My ambassador, the first secretary, and the consul general had all left, so I was given the post because I had been in Athens for more than four years, and knew all the affairs. It was during these three months that I had this incident: in the First Circle of Athens (a kind of Jockey Club then) with a young page to whom I gave my hat and a cane which I carried at the time. I had several times attempted to get the page to come to my apartment; each time I was there I would say discreetly, "I am expecting you to come." But he refused. That day he was reluctant to come near me, and when I gave him my hat and cane, he let them drop. I slapped him, twice. But the reason this boy had refused to come to my house was because he was the special boy of an admiral, who was president of the Circle! So he felt that he was forced to refuse me. It was not the reluctance of virtue.

GUNN: You were undoubtedly putting him in a difficult economic position.

PEYREFITTE: He complained to the admiral, who was furious. Now certain Greeks considered me to be pretentious. I had many friends in the ambience of Athens high society who adored me. They were on my side. But others detested me. I was known absolutely as a militant homosexual, completely liberated. I held my head high and couldn't have cared less about the world's opinion. Each Sunday I would traverse all of Athens in my chauffeured car with a youth on the seat beside me in order to visit the ruins and other monuments. I was naturally detested—then as now—by all the hypocritical homosexuals who were in the closet. All the old admirals and generals were pederasts and hated me because I was an open man living the life of a homosexual. Now I felt very strong after four years in Athens: I was the only one who knew all the affairs; and even with my little scandals, I didn't think they could get rid of me easily. Too I was protected by my chief of personnel in Paris, the Comte de Robien. But this admiral, protector of the Circle, immediately complained to the new French ambassador when he arrived in Athens. The new ambassador, who met me for the first time, was afraid to have as a secretary a scandalous man. He decided to send me back to Paris. So after almost five years there I returned to France. It was near the beginning of the War, in 1938. Thus, I was known at the Quai d'Orsay as a homosexual. In the report the new ambassador had sent in he had said: "Roger Peyrefitte has had, first, a scandal with a boy who robbed him; afterwards, he has been known in all Athens as a homosexual; thirdly, he has had a scandal in the First Circle of Athens, slapping a boy who said he received the slap not because he had dropped M. Peyrefitte's hat but because he had refused to go to his home; and so on; and so on." I was judged! M. de Robien gave me a little lecture; he said, "Naturally, you were imprudent. But we'll forget it, and you will go in a new direction." In reality I continued the same thing in Paris. As I have confessed in my notorious *Propos secrets* [and in *Diplomatic Conclusions*] I had two incidents with police at the time. I was found only with young boys. Now it's nothing in France to be found with adults, youths of eighteen or older. But because I was with young boys of thirteen or fourteen, I had to go twice to a member of the Quai d'Orsay to ask for immunity from the police. I was then evacuated with the Quai d'Orsay to a place in Touraine near Tours in order to save the archives of my nation. I displayed great courage, staying under battle conditions, and I had a letter of praise from the Minister of Foreign Affairs in the Vichy government. Afterwards I went to Vichy, and some days after my arrival I had another bad meeting with police because I had been found with a boy. I was called to my Ministry and told: "Either you resign, or you are fired." After the Resistance and all that the mentality of the French changed with the years. But, let me tell you, in 1940 *all* France was for Marshal Pétain. Everybody knows that. So when someone was run out of the government, one thought he was a Freemason, a Jew—some category which at this time, for very bad reasons in my eyes, was considered not honorable. So I resigned in order not to be put on the list of people boycotted by the Vichy government, and I returned to my family in the little town of Alet in the département of Aude, near Carcassonne. I am a Southerner, a Languedocien. My parents had a chateau there. I had to revenge myself and to forget all the ugly things that had happened to me: the police, the administration, and so on. So I wrote *Special Friendships*. In order to show these people with whom I had had so many problems—in Greece, in Paris, in Vichy; and with sharp words hurled by policemen (in Vichy a policeman had said, "It's because of men of your sort that we lost the war!" Ahhh. Stupid peasant!)—to show these people exactly what kind of man I was and the beginning of the whole thing, I wrote this book. I wrote a masterpiece. —Yes, I think I can say that.

GUNN: Had you already begun to write before this time?

PEYREFITTE: No, no. I had never written anything really. When I was eighteen I had known another member of the Académie Française, Henri de Régnier, who was a very great poet of that era (and who is still known as a poet). I had written a short story called *Les Petits Soupers de l'amour*, "The Little Suppers of Love." It was a sort of pastiche of eighteenth-century novels, because I was very fond of the spirit and style of that century.

GUNN: Voltaire, Marivaux, Prévost...

PEYREFITTE: Exactly. I read this tale to M. de Régnier, and when I was finished, he said: "Yes, yes. It's good. But—" I understood at once that I did not yet have the wings I needed on my shoulders to fly to Parnassus' summit. So I renounced my first idea for a career, which had been to be a writer. I had been the first in my school in French studies, I had been a member of the school academy, and so forth—all the preparations, you see, for a boy who has literary aims. But I understood that I was not able to realize myself with my pen. So I prepared instead for a diplomatic career.

GUNN: Do you think the diplomatic career helped you as a writer?

PEYREFITTE: Ah! It was a formidable preparation for the knowledge of society. When I came to Paris I was only a boy, a provincial who had hardly any knowledge of society. And there in my first year I fled from any contact with society into exclusively a homosexual ambience. Afterwards I knew only my fellow students. I began at the youngest age possible in the diplomatic corps. (You could present yourself three times at the examination, and many who passed did so only the second or even the third time. But I passed the first go, just at the age limit of twenty-three.) Immediately you are in contact with ambassadors, with ministers; you are a delegate on ministerial commissions. And immediately you become acquainted with the upper levels of society. At first I naturally hid my homosexuality, but I recognized at once others who were like me—and who were also in the closet. It was a very good preparation for my future literary career. In Athens it was the same thing. I knew Mr. Venizelos, who was president of the Republic; later, I met with the King of Greece, George II. It was extraordinary for a boy of twenty-five or twenty-six to have these meetings, which obliged one to have a certain preparation in conversation, even in manners. —As everyone knows, there are two kinds of people. I don't say those who are aristocrats and those who are democrats; that would be ridiculous. But there are people who have aristocratic aspirations, and others who have a popular attitude. M. [Jean] Genet is an example of the latter. All that is a question of education, of one's first relations in life. If you are a boy on public welfare and educated in jails like M. Genet, naturally you cannot know certain kinds of manners. But when you are introduced into society, you have an edge on others. A boy who prepares a diplomatic career naturally can claim to know a certain class and its purpose. —I am a son of the eighteenth century. But note: it was an aristocratic century with very revolutionary advances. I am not of the Court of Versailles. I am interested in the philosophers, such as Voltaire, Rousseau, Montesquieu. They are my people. They're no triumvir of the aristocratic system. But—What was the question? Ah yes, if the diplomatic career taught me something. I learned a lot with respect to that society I desired to enter. If I knew the other kind of society, it was through pederasty. I knew young masons, workers. I was very attracted to the lower classes.

GUNN: So you knew the two extremes of society.

PEYREFITTE: Exactly. And I owe my knowledge of the lower classes to pederasty.

GUNN: In your autobiography, *Propos secrets,* you wrote that you had never been attracted to the outlaw, unlike Genet and that large part of society which now seems to idolize the outlaw.

PEYREFITTE: To admire the outlaw. No, no, no.

GUNN: Yet in a sense you were always an outlaw yourself.

PEYREFITTE: That's right. It's very curious, because I am an outlaw, but in the bosom of society. Because I like society; I am not its enemy. I am a little like Pietro Aretino [Italian satirist and literary blackmailer, 1492–1556], *flagellum principorum*, the "scourge of princes," as he was called. A rather pretty expression, no? I'm a little like that. I live in society, and I like it. I would be very unhappy not to be surrounded by people of the world, for they please me. Not from snobbism. But because you perhaps meet among them better manners, a certain refinement, a certain breadth of mind, if you know how to present the matter.

GUNN: Have you ever had doors closed to you because you are a homosexual?

PEYREFITTE: Absolutely. But the doors which remain open for me are sufficient.

GUNN: Just last week, I think, you were at Monaco for the marriage [of Princess Caroline].

PEYREFITTE: Yes, it was very funny that I was invited to Monaco, and at the very moment I was publishing *Enfant de cœur*, an open homosexual confession. It's fantastic. You see that I am a man who sometimes manages to consociate contraries. *L'Enfant de cœur* is a memoir, the continuation of a book which I published ten years ago called *Notre amour*, the confessions about a relationship I had with a young boy. After it was published I had a hearing with justice; the Juge d'Instruction asked me if were true. Naturally I told him it was a work of fiction. They could not prove it one way or the other. But the father of a girl mixed in the story knew the whole affair, and he tried his best to cause trouble for me. He even went to see my cousin, Alain Peyrefitte [French statesman and member of the Académie Française, born 1925], who was at that time the Minister of National Education, and said to him: "You must see the Minister of Justice and demand legal sanctions. Because it is a true story; it is not a work of fiction!" My cousin dropped the matter. —I owe to this boy [Alain-Philippe Malagnac], whom I knew when he was twelve-and-a-half and who is yet at twenty-and-seven my friend, all my experience with homosexuality. As I said, I had been only a pederast. Like the ancient Greeks I could not have a physical relationship with a boy who had pubic hair. And certainly not [laughing and looking at the interviewer's beard] with someone who had facial hair. When I knew this boy, he was playing the part of—How do you translate "*enfant de chœur*?" The boy who serves mass at the altar in the Catholic church?

GUNN: Altar-boy.

PEYREFITTE: He was playing the part of an altar-boy in the film made from *Special Friendships*. At twelve his mother had made him read the book, and he was struck as if by lightning, as I should have been had I been in his place. For him I was a god. Later he read in the newspapers that boys were being asked to play roles in the crowd scenes for the movie, and, in the hopes of meeting me, he applied for a part. As he was very pretty, he was taken. I met him the first day I went into a dormitory of the Abbey of Royaumont near Paris, where the film was so marvelously made. His eyes caught mine at once. Later I had a secret relationship with him through the intermediacy of a friend of mine taking part in the production of the film. I said to the boy; "I risk all my life this day: If you are able to attach yourself to me, you will be my friend for life." It was fantastic to say that to a young boy. I said to myself, "But perhaps after some years he may not please me. He will be hairy and all that." But in the seconds I pronounced these words I guessed that the possibility of love, even of pederastic love, could transcend a question of hairs and become a homosexual love for life! But it was very, very, very dangerous, and a show of great confidence in the future.

GUNN: But it has lasted?

PEYREFITTE: Exactly. I recounted the whole story in *Notre amour.* It's really incredible that such a book has not been translated for two such pederastic countries as England and the United States. It's considered by all French readers as *the* book on the question. The story ended when the boy was eighteen. Because we met in Italy, in Capri, and we had a—He escaped me, and I thought it was finished. In order to console myself for this lost love, I wrote the book. And just as I finished it, I met him again; and the story began again. He is still alive, and it is still alive. When at nineteen he finished his studies, he became my secretary. More than a secretary. He was my friend. It's grotesque to use such a word [as "secretary"] with the main collaborator in my life. We worked together on three books. And together we followed the travels of Alexander the Great. When he was a boy, I had promised him that we would make the trip. And when in 1972 I finally decided to write the book, we went by car and airplane all the way from Athens to New Delhi. It was a fantastic time. But when we returned, I was closed up for a year and a half writing the first draft. He was lost, because he had nothing to give me. So he had the idea of creating a bar, rue Ste. Anne.

GUNN: This was the Bronx?

PEYREFITTE: The Bronx and the Colony. Naturally I furnished the money. Later, he bought another near Paris. He did other things. He was Sylvie Vartan's producer. His photograph was in the newspapers, and it was said they were going to be married because Miss Vartan [a French singer] was so in love with him. Naturally it was all imaginary.

GUNN: I heard that the Bronx was closed by the police for a while. What's the real story there?

PEYREFITTE: Yes, I described the whole thing in *L'Enfant de cœur.* It was closed one summer while we weren't here. The police arrived at two in the morning and surprised an American, who was masturbating in front of three or four clients, and it was considered an attack on the law. The law is grotesque. Grotesque! In a closed place before consenting adults, no minors. The stupidity of the law! It was closed for a month. Naturally all these affairs are dropped now, and they are in the terrible hands of justice, which enacts the ruin of someone when it takes over his affairs. There's at the Bronx now an awful, horrible little crook who was the ex-secretary of a friend of Alain's, kicked out for robbery. And he was named the temporary manager! We ignore the whole thing. I think in some months all those affairs will be cleared up. But now it is confused. And for me it was a tremendous loss of money. But what followed was worse. Alain was occupied in a myriad of activities. All that drops. And he tried to commit suicide. It was for me a horrible, awful experience. I felt the need to take up my pen again; for the writer consoles himself with his pen as the painter does with his brush and the composer with his violin or piano. So I wrote the story entitled *L'Enfant de cœur*. (There's a word play there. When it is pronounced one can understand either "*cœur*" or "*chœur*." So in French the title can be understood as either "The Child of My Heart" or as "The Altar-boy.") People have told me it's a masterpiece. I put all the strength of my love into it, this story no longer that of a young boy but of a man. Really, it's a hymn to homosexual love. The women in it have only walk-on roles. It's a very strong book. It should be appreciated very much. —So, you see, from my first book published in 1945, *Special Friendships*, to my last one, published last week, *L'Enfant de cœur*—and there are twenty-five books—there is not a one in which there is not at least an allusion to pederasty or to homosexuality. Even when I have written books like *The Knights of Malta;* even my book of travel, *South from Naples;* in my famous book *The Jews*—every one of them has a chapter or an allusion to pederasty or homosexuality, because I cannot leave out that ambience. So I can really say, I think, "Everything gay is mine."

GUNN: Almost every time you are introduced it is as the author of *Special Friendships*. Is it irritating to be always remembered for one book and the first one at that?

PEYREFITTE: No, not at all. Never had a writer published a book which had such a success. That narrowed the horizon a bit, but all is relative. In any case, I am still proud that a book which was published in 1945 has always the same large number of readers. Thats extraordinary. For thirty years young boys, young girls, of fifteen years have always written me thanking me as they discover the book. That is a grand foundation.

GUNN: The film also had a great success, no?

PEYREFITTE: Even in the United States. Apparently when it was shown at New York, the entire audience cried at the end.

GUNN: Would you like to say something about the situation of your books in America?

PEYREFITTE: In America it's curious. Because I have friends. I have fans. But I am ignored by the majority of the people there as you know. I am somewhat known through some translations of my books, but principally by French readers in the States, and they are very scarce.

GUNN: How many of your books are available in translation?

PEYREFITTE: Perhaps half. I think ten: *Special Friendships; The Exile of Capri; The Prince's Person*, a story of the sixteenth century, very funny, very bawdy, which I discovered in the Italian archives; six or seven others. But it's strange that a book like the *Tableaux de chasse, ou la vie extraordinaire de Fernand Legros*, who is an American citizen, has not been translated. My publisher, however, has told me that the States are more and more *un*interested in French literary productions. It's very curious. I was blocked at the beginning, of course, by an obvious reason. All the so-called American intelligentsia had two signs, two recommendations to follow: First, you had to be a Gallimard writer. Secondly, you had to be a leftist. I am neither one nor the other. Before the war Gallimard was the biggest publisher in all France (now he is only second), publisher of the *Nouvelle Révue Française* and possessor of all the literary world. In my book *Des Français*, published in 1970, I satirized this despotic review, which admitted to its pages only those whom Gallimard had invented. Never did the editors write the name of an author who was not of Gallimard.

GUNN: A sort of literary mafia.

PEYREFITTE: Exactly. The president of Gallimard was— What was his name? I don't remember. Very, very well known. A man who was professor at Princeton or Yale. We met. He admired my work greatly on a personal level, but not enough to promote my name.

GUNN: This wasn't Faulkner's translator? Maurice Coindreau?

PEYREFITTE: Yes. Nobody was known in the States if he had not been introduced by Coindreau. He said, "You must not read that. You must translate this." And it was done. He was the dictator for Americans of the French literary scene. I wonder how I had any books at all translated in the States. And when my 1964 book *The Jews* was translated (with a certain success) a number of years later, the *New York Times* ran this review: "Roger Peyrefitte, right wing homosexual, etc., etc." I said: "I am judged! No one will be interested in me." Still, it's fantastic that one of the few books published by a French writer since World War II which is favorable to Americans, my *Américains*, has not yet found a translator. I pressed my editor; I said, "It's not possible." At last we found the reason. American publishers refused to touch the book because "Roger Peyrefitte is very unsympathetic with two of America's idols: John Kennedy and the Reverend Martin Luther King. Therefore, we can't consider him." It's fantastic that this country of freedom has such an aspect of mediocrity, of deficiency, of prejudice.

GUNN: I've always thought that France was more free than America.

PEYREFITTE: You think so, yes? I think so too. Well, among all the postwar writers who were homosexual, all the celebrity in the States was concentrated on Genet. For two reasons: First, he was a Gallimard writer, so he was part of the arsenal. And secondly, because his very broad and very aggressive literature perhaps corresponded to the mood of a certain part of American readers. It is worth noting that Genet's glory is greater in the States than in France. Naturally, in France he had the fortune to be supported by Sartre, but he never had a real following among readers. I remember when I was at Berkeley, I saw Genet's books on the paperback stands under the heading "Sex and Crime." The reader buys the book. I was very amused when I saw in the *Who's Who in America*, among whose names the French are few, that Genet's has long been admitted. He was admitted to the French *Who's Who* only in the last edition! In 1976. He was ignored until then, but you found him in the American *Who's Who* at least ten years before that. It's very funny. I'll permit myself to say that I have been in the *Who's Who in England* from a very old time, twenty or thirty years ago, but I have never been listed in the *Who's Who in America*. I'm in the one for writers, but that is natural; it's not an honor. But the honor of being considered a man rather important in the world, as perhaps I am, is denied to me by the States. In the French, Italian, German newspapers I am very often quoted as one of the greater, more important living writers. But absolutely not in the States.

GUNN: You did make all the newpapers there a year or two ago.

PEYREFITTE: The pope.

GUNN: Yes. Would you like to comment on that incident?

PEYREFITTE: It was very funny. I am the most well-known defender of homosexual rights in France. That is certain. Often they call me "The Pope of Homosexuality." That's because I am the author of *The Keys of St. Peter* and *the Knights of Malta,* the most important books by a contemporary writer on the Catholic Church. When the pope, Paul VI, in February 1976 published a condemnation of three things — homosexuality, masturbation, and premarital sex — a review, *Lui,* came here to ask me my impressions. I was really indignant. Because I knew that the pope (not while he was pope, of course, because he is a very old man with no private life of a certain kind, but when he was archbishop of Milan) had had a relationship with a young movie actor, whose name I knew. I did not learn this from communists or doormen. In spite of the boldness of my characteristic homosexuality for many years, in a society like the Italian one, as in France, I knew people who were really at the top of the state. So, when I was in Milan years and years ago, I knew many representatives of what is called *l'aristocratie noire,* the Black Aristocracy because of the color of church robes. It was originally of the Vatican. And they told me the story, because they knew I wouldn't make capital of the fact. I knew this man who would go to a discreet house to meet boys. (All the Italians are bisexual; they have a wife, daughters, but—) And Archbishop Montini went there. I asked about it again when I was in Rome in those years, and other people told me: "Yes, that is a political secret in a certain circle. The boy is very well known and is protected by the pope." So I was indignant. And I gave this information, without saying the last name of the boy. [In *Propos secrets* Mr. Peyrefitte does say the boy's first name was Paul, and that it was for this reason the pope took his name instead of more naturally using his own given name, John.] The weekly Italian newsmagazine *Tempo* republished the article with a caricature of the pope, and it was like a nuclear bomb in Rome. Fantastic. The Vicar of Rome asking for prayers in all Italy for this injury done to the Holy Father. And on Palm Sunday one saw the pope on his balcony at the Vatican reading his "*Delle cose orribili e calunniose . . . ,*" alluding to my statement. That was like a bomb in all the world. I had a friend who was living in Colombia, South America; he told me it was an entire page in Colombian papers. Everywhere in the world: "Peyrefitte and the Pope." I was moved because I had never imagined such a reaction. But I was also very proud, because it was the most fantastic consecration ever made to a writer for many years for some lines of his.

GUNN: What is *Les Américains* about exactly?

PEYREFITTE: I took for my hero a student at Berkeley in the years of the famous revolt there, 1965 or so, in order to show clearly what happened as a result in France in 1968. Naturally I didn't make him a homosexual, but he has a friend who is an unrestrained gay. So we do have a picture of the homosexual question as it was a decade ago in the States; gay problems are important to the novel. — Naturally I had visited Turkish baths in San Francisco and other places with friends. Ah! I am glad to pay homage through *Gay Sunshine* to one of my dearest American friends, whom I have lost sight of now for years but whom I met in Paris when he was living here: the underground filmmaker, Kenneth Anger. He is a very clever and bright man. Beautiful work. He introduced me to all San Francisco, even including the Devil's Church. His name is cited many times in my book. — My hero was the lover of a young girl who was also a student — but a black. Already it was an antiracist book too. I say this because my book *The Jews* has been presented as a completely racist work. If a man from the right writes about the Jewish people, it's because "he's anti-Semitic." It's incredible. I am not leftist. I am not rightist. I'm an independent man, and I think the freest in all France. — Let me make a parenthesis about M. Genet. I consider him to be a very good writer, but you understand he's my opposite. "Sex and Crime." I don't like it. Sex is good. Crime is too much. I am against crime. I am above all against violence. I hate violence! I love violence in love, in spirit, in beauty, but not in action. Such people are poor people; they are primitives. You must impose your ideas by the strength of spirit and not by arms and revolution. I am against that, even though I am a son of the century of the Revolution. So I deplore a man like Genet. I accept that he was a thief, a prisoner. but I cannot accept that he should befriend the Baader-Meinhof, the Red Brigade, Palestinians, Black Panthers. Everywhere there is a handful of madmen (who perhaps had generous ideas but have such reprehensible means of imposing them), there you find Genet, like some pope. It's really a pity. Naturally he lived in misery when he was young, but he must thank the society which admitted him, which gave him glory and the money to overcome this perpetual struggle. He's yet an outlaw only because he wants to remain one; he would be accepted. I don't want to give an interview against somebody, but I was very shocked when I saw in the *Gay Sunshine* interview that he refused to acknowledge Cocteau's poetic gift. Cocteau was only a poet; his poetry is admirable. Genet could be grateful to Cocteau, because without him he would still be in jail. It was he, after the War, who got up the petition with Sartre and other writers to free Genet. Genet had been sentenced nineteen times to prison; a twentieth sentence would have committed him for life. So they intervened. Rightfully. Had they asked me, I would have said the same. But there's no reason to forget this extraordinary service Cocteau rendered him.

GUNN: Especially famous as he is now, he can afford to be generous.

PEYREFITTE: I couldn't believe it! I would have thought he would have said, "I can't forget what Cocteau did for me." He seems to have forgotten it. He seems to be the enemy of everybody, apart from Sartre and the Baader-Meinhof.

GUNN: I believe you were very warm friends with Cocteau.

PEYREFITTE: When I wrote *Special Friendships,* I sent him a copy. I wrote, "With homage to the author of *Les Enfants terribles.*" He wrote me a letter thanking me for the book, saying it was "admirable and resembled nothing which had come before it." So we met. Naturally I deplored his entry into the Académie Française [in 1955] because it was a diminution. When I wrote to him, I said, "I congratulate you because you wanted to enter." He responded in a playful way, "As they don't have what we have, it's amusing for us to have what they have." Oh! [*Laughter.*] It didn't satisfy me sufficiently, and so our relationship became cooler. But it was very like Cocteau. He was a bourgeois like me, but I am less bourgeois than he was. The proof is that I'm not an Academician.

GUNN: You never knew Gide?

PEYREFITTE: Yes, I met him twice. Immediately after the War, when he returned from Africa, a young friend of his made him read *Special Friendships*. He told me that Gide would like to meet me, so I went to his house. I felt no point of contact. I was surprised by his home. I am sensitive to my surroundings, and there was no taste, no décor: only books, as in a professor's office. You understand that I mean no insult. It's another thing, however, to be an artist. You can be a professor and an artist, of course. But Gide was only a professor. Only his books, a bust of him with a hat on it, an upright piano. I said, "This is no artist's place." I thought it was because it was after the War, but my friends said: "No, he was always like that." Because he was indifferent to his surroundings. Another time he came to my house to see my art objects and even photographs of the boys of Taormina, the photographs taken by the Baron von Gloeden, whom I discovered. — Yes! In my book, not translated into English, *Les Amours singulières* I have two tales, and one of them is "Le Baron de Gloeden." I was the first man in the world to study this man! A Harvard professor sent me his thesis on the Baron, and at the head of the bibliography he put *Les Amours singulières*. Now his photographs are reproduced everywhere. — Gide wanted to see those photographs. I said, "But M. Gide, you went to Taormina fifty years before I did." He answered, "Yes, but never should I have dared to pass the door of Baron von Gloeden." There you have Gide, with all his complexes of the Protestant conscience. When Baron von Gloeden was alive, he didn't dare to visit him, but fifty years later he comes to my house to ask to see the photos! No, I had no point of contact with Gide. I considered him an august puppet. Of course, he was recognized; the Nobel Prize and all was reassuring. And he has become the image of the homosexual writer, but actually he hardly wrote on the subject: *Corydon, If It Die..., The Immoralist*.

GUNN: Did you know the writer Julian Green [b. 1900]?

PEYREFITTE: I met him one time. I cannot like this kind of people with complexes. I am without complexes. All these Catholics who are always struggling with themselves, looking through the keyhole to see what is happening in the next room.

GUNN: Yet you were for many years the friend of Henry de Montherlant.

PEYREFITTE: Ah, that is another story. Montherlant was openly living a pederastic life. True, he never confessed it in words. That was another kind of hypocrisy. But he was a very important step in my life. When I returned from Greece, kicked out for pederasty, I was very glad to meet M. Montherlant. He was perhaps one of the greatest French writers of his time, and he had exactly the same tastes as I did. Years afterwards, when I had obtained full liberty with my pen, he too, like Cocteau, became an Academician [in 1960]. I felt obliged to separate from him, because I am a free man.

GUNN: Just now the struggle for gay liberation is very important in the States. Does that exist in France?

PEYREFITTE: I was one of the founders of the review *Arcadie*. I published a number of articles in it. Then I interrupted my collaboration perhaps ten years ago, but now I have given them an article, a very comic, pederastic story which occurred in Palermo in the seventeenth century. I discovered it while I was in Italy. It's for their three-hundredth issue celebrating their twenty-fifth year of existence. In France that's fantastic. *Arcadie* merits the gratitude of each homosexual. In this struggle for freedom I was the first fighter after the War with my unattackable book, *Special Friendships*, and I have continued for thirty years. It has come now to an extraordinary conclusion. By decree in 1962 homosexuality was declared by Gaullist deputies one of the social plagues. The law was not applied. I attacked it in many books. We asked Arcadians to apply pressure. And now a radical senator from Toulouse, a city in which I studied briefly in the south of France, M. Caivallet, has very recently asked that the age of consent for sexual matters be dropped to fifteen years. It's fantastic. It was adoped unanimously by the Senate two weeks ago. By chance the press said nothing. Had it written up the bill, there would have been protests, moral leagues, leagues of mothers and fathers. It passed. Naturally it will be presented to the National Assembly when it reconvenes. Then we shall see. It is obvious that I am one of the authors of this openmindedness on the subject in my country, and I am very proud of that. It is a greater glory for me than to be in the Académie Française like my cousin, the Keeper of Seals [i.e., Minister of Justice].

GUNN: In all your books which I have read I have noted one theme common to them all. It's not the theme of homosexuality. It's the presence of an open and very honest nature, whether one likes that nature or not. It strikes me how much you are against hypocrisy in all your works.

PEYREFITTE: I am very pleased that you recognize this. It is my ideal to be a man who follows a right path, against hypocrisy. That is the idea in my *Propos*, not secret but public. I had another well known occasion to demonstrate this idiosyncrasy of mine when I published my open letter in 1964 to François Mauriac, the famous French Academician. It was during De Gaulle's time, and Mauriac was one of his men. Then he read the truth when I denounced Mauriac for covering up his earlier homosexual life when he had been a friend of a certain count, well known in French homosexual circles, who had presented him to society when he was twenty. It created a sensation in all France. I must stay a free man. It's the reason I cancelled my application to the Académie Française. I am characterized by a desperate taste for freedom, the complete love of love, and the hatred of hypocrisy. I say, and nobody denies it, that I am the freest man in France. Perhaps in the world. It would, maybe, be another reason to be at least a little known in the States, because your country is the defender of freedom. Perhaps the customs there are not so free as we imagine, but we are obliged to consider, free from political prejudice, that if we didn't have the States in the world, we would all have been occupied by the Russians. Naturally no more possibility of being oneself, of writing, of loving. I would have long ago been put in a psychiatric hospital.

PHOTO BY KEN O'BRIEN, 1981

EDOUARD
RODITI

BORN IN PARIS in 1910 of an American father, Edouard Roditi has always been an American citizen, but attended schools in France and England, then Oxford University, before coming to the United States for the first time in 1929. By then, he had already published poems and prose in English and in French in *transition* and a number of other American, English, French and expatriate periodicals. These publications included, in 1929, the first Surrealist Manifesto to be written and published in English.

Until 1937, he continued to live in Europe, then attended the University of Chicago and the University of California at Berkeley. From 1937 until 1946 he lived in the United States after which he returned to Europe as an interpreter for the Nuremberg war crimes trials. Since 1946 he has lived in Europe, at first in Berlin and now in Paris. He was a free-lance multilingual simultaneous interpreter for UNESCO, the European Common Market, and other international agencies, and often returns to the United States to teach or lecture.

He has now published extensively in American, English, French and German periodicals, especially in the fields of literary criticism and art history, and has been a guest professor of English or French literature or of art history at the University of California, at Brown University, and elsewhere. His published books include: *Oscar Wilde* (in the "Makers of Modern Literature" series, New Directions, 1947), *Poems 1928–1948* (New Directions, 1949), *Dialogues on Art* (Horizon Books, 1961 and Ross Erikson Publishers, 1981), *Prose Poems: New Hieroglyphics* (1968), *Magellan of the Pacific* (1973), *The Disorderly Poet* (Capra Press), *Emperor of Midnight* (poems, Black Sparrow Press, 1974), *Thrice Chosen* (poems, Black Sparrow Press, 1981), and a collection of short stories, *The Delights of Turkey* (New Directions, 1977), as well as a number of translations from French, German, Dutch, and Turkish.

THE PRESENT INTERVIEW was taped in San Francisco in early 1975 by Winston Leyland and originally appeared in *Gay Sunshine* no. 29/30 (Summer-Fall 1976).

Winston Leyland interviews
EDOUARD RODITI

LEYLAND: You've lived in France most of your life?

RODITI: Yes. I was born in Paris of an American father and British mother and I spent all my childhood in France and in England, mainly because during the first World War they couldn't send me to school in America. Since I'd started my schooling over there I continued it up till the age of going to college and then I came to America for the first time at the age of nineteen. I've lived in America only during the war years, from 1937 to 1945, apart from a couple of brief visits before that. And then after the war I went back to live in Europe because I was working for the U.S. government there. I happen to be trilingual, and have made my profession that of a simultaneous interpreter, working first with the government and then with the United Nations. Then during the McCarthy era I got into some kind of trouble in that the authorities began to suspect that I wasn't all they'd expected a good civil servant to be. I lost my job, and in those days it was almost impossible to find a job in America if one had the reputation of being what was called a security risk. So instead of going to court about it, which would have been very expensive, I made my home in Paris and have been able to make a living, a relatively good one, ever since. A few years later the government approached me again offering to take me back, but I felt that the American government had proven once it was a bad employer and I didn't want to go back and work for them. I said to them, "You fired me once for trumped-up, dubious reasons and I have no guarantee that you won't do it, let's say three years before I am due for retirement and a pension simply to save having to pay me a pension, so let's forget about it." So I've never worked for the government again.

At the time I was fired it was rather a shock for me because I'd been a civil servant for nine years and the occasion was very nasty. They first accused me of being a Communist, which I obviously wasn't, and it was only after a lot of hemming and hawing that they came out with the story about my being a homosexual. Then it turned out that they had no evidence of it — I've never been in any trouble — it was just a lot of backchat and unproven gossip and the opinion of people who'd worked in offices with me, knew that I didn't have a girlfriend, that kind of thing. You can't go to court on that kind of thing, so I dropped the whole matter, forgot about it. Besides I was on not too easy grounds because I happen to belong to another minority which has an even more difficult time than homosexuals. I happen to be epileptic, and very few people know what the disabilities of that are. For instance, anyone who wants to immigrate to the United States is asked certain questions: Are you polygamous? Are you an anarchist? Are you epileptic? And if he answers yes to any one of these three, he's denied immigration.

I've been always very much concerned with the question of the civil liberties of those who have the ailment, or "blessing," of epilepsy. In other civilizations it is considered to be a blessing. You are considered to be a shaman or priest who is possessed by a god. That has concerned me almost more than the disability or the minority problem of being homosexual. In Europe I find that I have much more freedom, people are much less concerned with these matters which are basically matters of the individual's private life, not things which must necessarily be public knowledge.

So I've made my life there, and I'm very glad I have. Occasionally I feel homesick for America; I feel homesick for the English language, living most of the time in a community which is speaking French or Spanish. But I also have many American and English friends living in France and I speak English every day. I've never felt anything but American, which is sort of odd. But now I may come and live in America because when one reaches the age of retirement one feels like taking some precautions. There are such things as Medicare and what have you which would make it a bit wiser perhaps for me to move back.

I've also written a couple of books in French. When I go back now I'm going to see whether I can get some sort of coverage as a French author. One of the books as a matter of fact is a book on homosexuality which I published in French about 1961. I wrote it in French mainly because I couldn't get an American publisher interested in it. It's a book on homosexuality from a scientific point of view. I posed myself a couple of questions, and then sought the answers. The first question was: In what living species has homosexuality been observed? I went through all the range from insects up and discovered that it's been observed almost exclusively in vertebrates, in nearly all species of vertebrates and in very few species of invertebrates. You may laugh when I tell you in what species of invertebrates it's been observed—dragonflies and bedbugs. And then the second question was: Under what conditions does the frequency increase or decrease in the species where it had been observed? The answer to that was: Under conditions of stress or anxiety the incidence, the frequency increases. Now this is true of nearly all vertebrates. If you increase the anxiety of a colony of rats or mice or even sticklebacks you observe that more of them practice homosexual behavior. The case of sticklebacks is very interesting...

LEYLAND: What is a stickleback?

RODITI: A little fish, where the male has a red belly, and the female does not. Before the males become homosexual they start losing the red color of their belly. So I came to the conclusion that anxiety produces a certain stress which reduces the secretion of hormones of the secondary sexual glands, the hormones which affect color, or odor in the case of mice or rats. Mice and rats recognize each other's sex by their odor. And in conditions of overcrowding, overpopulation, the anxiety increases and they lose the specific odor of the female or the male and then the homosexual behavior becomes more frequent. In the case of sticklebacks it doesn't affect the smell since they recognize sex by color. Of course I wasn't able to conduct any experiments on overcrowding with elephants because they take up too much space. I was able to do the experiments only with very small animals, like sticklebacks and mice and rats, and certain types of insects.

LEYLAND: Did you do this through observation in nature?

RODITI: No, but under laboratory conditions created artificially. The causes for anxiety can be overcrowding, difficulty about food, noise and so on. Now all this does not apply to humans. Humans are by nature an anxious species, because they have something which theologians call a soul and which other species don't have. In addition there are cultural elements. You have certain tribes in the Pacific where homosexuality among men is a recognized practice. For instance certain New Guinea tribes will have heterosexual relations only when they want children. It's a form of family planning there. So my rule about vertebrates does not apply to humans, but it does give us some insight into the phenomenon. This book was finally published in France, about 1961, and caused a certain amount of sensation there, mainly among psychoanalysts and doctors who were very annoyed to see an outsider handling a subject which they felt should be reserved for them.

LEYLAND: Your book seems to be parallel to André Gide's *Corydon*.

RODITI: Yes, except that mine was much more concerned with biology or zoology and much less literary and psychological. It's a non-Freudian book in that it's really concerned with the incidence of homosexuality as due to social, cultural or biological factors. I'd come to this conclusion about anxiety affecting the secretion of hormones without being able to test that because I didn't have the biological lab facilities. And a couple of years later I got a most astounding report that someone at the Pavlov Institute in Moscow had read my book and had gone ahead doing the research on hormone secretions and proved that my hunch was right, that anxiety or stress conditions affect these hormone secretions of the secondary sexual glands, not the primary ones, and therefore bring about these changes of behavior. This whole science is now developed into a new science which is known as "ethology," so in a way I was a pioneer of this new science without knowing it. I want now to rewrite this book in English with new facts.

LEYLAND: Did you ever meet André Gide?

RODITI: I knew Gide a long time ago, before the war.

LEYLAND: Had you talked about this particular area with him?

RODITI: No, because my interest in biology developed much later. When I met Gide I was exclusively interested in poetry, literature, poetics, but not in any of the natural sciences. Besides, Gide's approach was quite different. Gide was a difficult man. I didn't know him very well. Of course I was very young at the time. When I met him I must have been nineteen or twenty and in a way I was a punk. I happened to be rather an attractive young man and I felt that this rather unattractive elderly gentleman was trying to make me and my reaction was not the most tactful one. That led to a rather difficult situation. I didn't see him again for a couple of years. Then I saw him again at a time when he was advising a publication, a magazine, to which I was a contributor. I was asked to do some particularly difficult translations, to translate poems of Gerard Manley Hopkins into French. It was almost impossible, and Gide didn't think it was possible, but he did agree that my translations were about as good as one could expect and they did go into press. Then I saw him and we'd overcome this little basic tension in that maybe I was no longer as pretty or maybe he could take me seriously as a writer. Our relationship then was quite different, and shortly after that I came to complete my college education in America and didn't see him again.

LEYLAND: Did you see him when you went back to France?

RODITI: No. In addition, there was another problem in my relations with Gide, and that is that I belonged to the fringe of the surrealist movement. The surrealists were none too friendly to Gide. I belonged only to the fringe again because of this question of homosexuality, because André Breton was very prudish. In the original surrealist group there was only one of the major French surrealist writers who was known to be homosexual and that was René Crevel. And Breton was so blunt in his condemnation of poor René Crevel's homosexual relationships that it hurt Crevel very much. That was one of the elements which finally led to Crevel's suicide. It was a minor element, and the real reason was that Crevel had TB and had already had a pneumothorax operation and was managing to carry on mainly on morphine. One day he discovered that TB had developed in his kidneys. It was very painful. Then Breton condemned his Stalinist beliefs. In those days there was a period when the surrealists shifted from official Communism to Trotskyism, and Crevel didn't shift fast enough. Breton, whom Crevel considered almost like a father (he was a close friend), became rather offensive. This on top of Breton's constant bickering about his homosexuality and on top of the physical disability led to his suicide.

LEYLAND: What was behind Breton's homophobia?

RODITI: Well there's a book on surrealism published recently in French by a woman on the whole surrealist attitude towards women and sex. She's a very intelligent French woman, relatively active in the women's lib movement, and she's come to the conclusion that the official surrealists considered women as being just beautiful dolls. They had a very old-fashioned attitude towards their women and a very humiliating one for the woman. This sort of Don Juanesque attitude towards women excluded any tolerance of homosexuality. So there was very little actual overt homosexuality in the surrealist movement. I think the only examples I remember were Crevel, and in a very concealed way the poet Ribemont-Dessaignes. Then in the dissident group, known as Le Grand Jeu, there was the poet Roger Gilbert Lecoute. But his homosexuality was mixed up with drug addiction, and in any case he was a dissident surrealist on other ideological grounds. I think that this whole Don Juanesque attitude towards women was what made surrealism, French surrealism at least, basically rather retrograde politically. Their Trotskyism, their Communism was always ineffectual because they were basically late nineteenth-century aesthetes of a kind. All their talk about Freud and psychoanalysis was poppycock, since Breton himself could not read a word of German and most of Freud had not been translated into French. What kind of notion could he have had of psychoanalytical literature when there was practically none available to him in French?

LEYLAND: When one is so homophobic usually there are often fears and stirrings inside oneself.

RODITI: I have a funny story about Breton. One day in New York during the war I happened to be on Third Avenue with an American friend. I met Breton, who was in exile at that period and spent a great deal of time going around the junk stores on Third Avenue because he collected primitive sculptures, especially American Indian dolls and so on. I stopped and chatted with Breton and, as Breton spoke only French, I didn't introduce my American friend to him. After that my American friend said to me, "Who was that drag queen?" And the fact is that Breton very often looked like a kind of caricature, especially in his old age, of Queen Victoria in male drag, in the way he walked, in his expressions, and you could see that there was something extremely feminine in him of which he was unaware or that he repressed.

LEYLAND: You yourself were involved in surrealist writings beginning in the 1930s?

RODITI: Earlier than that. I started in 1927 when I was seventeen. I published mainly in *transition*, a magazine that published Joyce and Gertrude Stein, and in a few other little magazines. But as I progressed I became more and more interested in what I considered the more subversive, and not politically subversive, aspect of surrealism. I was less interested in what I would call the sublime and more and more interested in black humor and the absurd, which meant that my admiration shifted from people like Breton or the poet Éluard to writers like Benjamin Péret, who is not so well known in America because he's very difficult to translate. I developed a great interest in such things as Ambrose Bierce's *The Parenticide Club,* black humor, everything that handles a notion of the absurd. It seems to me that that aspect which tries to undermine our concept of reality, our concept of what is proper, our concept of order, is infinitely more subversive basically because it is not merely political. It's a questioning of everything, beginning with God the Father and in fact it's an attitude which is close to that of certain religious mystics of the past, closely related to the paintings of Hieronymus Bosch, to the poems of certain Moslem dervish mystics who question reality and even go as far as questioning God.

LEYLAND: Were you influenced at that time by your own readings in some of these areas?

RODITI: Yes, and I've had a sort of weird mystical streak in me which comes out in some of my poetry. I've always been interested in cabala and in certain oriental mystics; not so much in the Hindus, the Hindus actually bore me. The ones who interest me are the Sufis. Or else then the other end, Zen. In India, I spent time in ashrams. I found that there is an awful lot of phoniness in India and a lot of confused thinking. I heard a most marvelous story of an Arab philosopher who accompanied the Moghul emperors when they conquered India. He was a very broad-minded philosopher, and when he reached Delhi he thought, well this is a wonderful occasion to meet the philosophers of this strange place and to try and discuss philosophical problems with them. And he tried with the Hindu philosophers and after some time he wrote, "What's the use of trying to discuss philosophy with people who not only have no notion of logic but have never felt the need for logic?" I think it's a beautiful remark. I'm not a stickler for logic, but I do believe in some kind of organized dialectic or organized structure to one's thoughts. I find this organized structure in Zen, which is very much like pre-Socratic philosophy in that it believes in the identity of contraries like Heraclitus did.

LEYLAND: Would you talk about your writing, how it's progressed, your evolution from the twenties until now.

RODITI: Well I started with the surrealists, and then I met T. S. Eliot. I met him in the early thirties because I happened to be doing a translation of St. John Perse and I didn't know that he was doing a translation of the same poet. He heard that I was doing it and wanted to see my version. As he had the rights to publish his translation, I finally let him use interpretations borrowed from mine. About this period I saw T. S. Eliot relatively frequently and we became quite good friends in a sort of professional way, as translators of poetry. He developed an interest in my own poetry and finally published some of my poems in *The Criterion*. He criticized my poetry a great deal and I could see that he was certainly no believer in automatic writing and in surrealism and all that. And this sort of opened my eyes to an entirely different kind of poetry which is much more structured, much more conscious, and which doesn't spring so much from the unconscious.

Then I led a kind of schizophrenic life as a poet for about twenty years, writing some very conscious poetry on the one hand and every once in a while reverting to my old surrealist work. During the thirties, the depression years, I became increasingly distrustful of ever being able to make any headway as a writer. Those were the days when people like Kenneth Rexroth were lucky if they made five dollars a year, and I was even less known than Kenneth. There was no way of earning a living as a poet, and that's when I began to look for another profession, simply to be able to pay my rent and eat. I decided to become a teacher of French since I knew French well. And the war got me into being an interpreter and this took up a great deal of my time so that for a long while I didn't finish anything. I published a book of interviews of artists and a biography of Magellan, but these are things which I did on the side. It is only in the last three or four years that I've begun to find time to finish all the stuff that I have in old files and drawers and haven't published. So now I'm getting into my stride as a writer rather belatedly.

When I look back through all these old papers and old files, I find that there is a kind of consistency in that throughout I've always been concerned with this area of exploring the mind through surrealism or through philosophy and also I've always been concerned to some extent with the absurd, that is to say with a kind of black humor. But now, having done this book on homosexuality some years ago, I'm doing a very autobiographical book on epilepsy and on the phenomenon of the aura which precedes the actual fit and which is a very strange moment, a moment in which one suffers certain illusions, delusions, hallucinations, a great uncertainty about reality. The moment when one comes back is very strange because, at least in my case, immediately before I lose consciousness I'm absolutely convinced that I'm dying. It doesn't seem at all physically possible to survive it. When I come to it's a resurrection. It is a strange resurrection because very often I've totally forgotten where I am and when. There have been occasions when I've come to thinking that I was ten years back or five years back or in an entirely different place. This book which I'm writing now is a book about the uncertainty of reality, which has been something which has haunted me all of my life.

LEYLAND: How long does this disorientation last when you come back?

RODITI: Well, you never know. Once it lasted about twenty-four hours, and then everybody around me was very upset. They thought they would have to put me in a psychiatric ward. I just couldn't orient myself back where I had been. This was after one particularly grave, serious fit. Normally it takes me a few seconds, a few minutes, but it can be a lasting phenomenon and so I'm rather exploring what the meaning of it is, how it can affect one as a human being and one's general attitude towards life. I don't think it's going to be a very cheerful book. It's going to be a book of the kind, "cancer can also be fun." But I've had learn to live with it.

LEYLAND: Have you met much prejudice in your life because of your epilepsy?

RODITI: Well, not so much prejudice as total consternation. There have been occasions when as I've had this fit and come to I've found everyone around me in an absolute panic, much worse that mine, phoning for ambulances and so on. I was the first one to say "Well, don't get so worried. This is going to be all over in a few minutes. Don't worry." It is something which, in the Western world at least, is just considered a catastrophe. I remember when I was a child my parents would never admit that that was the trouble. For years I was brought up to believe that I had some curious heart ailment and that my fainting spells were actually some form of growing pain. Nobody in the family would ever admit this. It was considered to be an utter disgrace. People still get into a panic when they see it. I've seen unfortunates have fits in the streets—a complete panic. I've come by and said "It isn't so bad. He'll be okay in a few minutes. I know what it's all about." I stuff a handkerchief into his mouth and so on. But people don't know what to do with it. They just lose their heads.

LEYLAND: What approach are you taking in this book? Is it a series of essays?

RODITI: No, it's an autobiographical book of self-exploration and confession. There are also certain passages which discuss the relationship between my epilepsy and my homosexuality. A kind of attempt to see whether there's any relationship between the passivity of being victim of these spells and the masochistic passivity of being the kind of homosexual that I am.

LEYLAND: Do you feel there is a relationship between the two?

RODITI: There is probably in that there are certain aspects of epileptic fits which are very similar to sensations of the orgasm. All sorts of philosophers have already said that the orgasm is like a small death, and the epileptic fit is certainly a small death, a slightly bigger one. And as I experience the orgasm mainly as a kind of psychologically passive phenomenon, not an active one, there may be some relationship there which I'm trying to figure out in this book. But even then it can't be anything that can be generalized; it's an exploration of phenomena experienced as an individual which others may experience differently. In any case I don't agree with Dostoevski at all because every definition, every description of his experiences does not tie in with mine. Mine are quite different. But then we are also beginning to realize that there is a vast range of different epileptic phenomena since some can be accounted as psychosomatic epilepsy of course. But over and above that there are fits which can be caused by injury to the brain, and the symptoms will vary according to the area of the brain which has been injured. In my case they are temporal lobe seizures, which means that there's no foaming at the mouth. Grand mal, petit mal and temporal lobe seizures are very different, and temporal lobe seizures vary very much from one patient to another. So we're beginning to know much more of the structure of the brain and how and why these things occur. It's a very individualistic disease, and it's much more individualistic than whooping cough or syphilis or anything else.

Now I feel much more free to express myself, not only because we live in a more permissive society but also because I realize that I've reached an age when even if I write and publish something which could be compromising in the eyes of some people, I couldn't care less. If they don't like it it's their worry, not mine. I write what I feel I should write because I can't take it with me and because I want to leave it as testimony, as document, and it's a take it or leave it proposition. If the publishers ask me to change it I say "No. I want my things printed as they are. If you don't like it I'll have them printed at my own expense elsewhere. I couldn't care less."

LEYLAND: When you were in France in the thirties did you know Gertude Stein?

RODITI: Very slightly. I was a very shy young man in some respects, and Gertrude Stein was very dominating. I met her probably in the most unpropitious time for a young man to meet her. If you read Jim Mellow's biography of Gertrude Stein, which was published about a year ago, there's a whole chapter on her relationships with "the young men," with the painter Tchelitchew, with René Crevel, with Bravig Imbs the writer, and I knew most of these young men. I was a good friend of Tchelitchew's. I knew Bravig Imbs, and I met Gertrude during that period when she was quarreling with all of them, and was terribly withdrawn and bitter about the success of Hemingway and the success—the good reviews—Bravig Imbs had gotten for his book and the fact that she was totally ignored. It was shortly before her trip to Chicago when suddenly she became big news and that changed her. When I first met her she was so offensive and difficult with anybody as young as I was that it rather discouraged me, and I avoided seeing her again. She was making bitter, nasty remarks about all the young men, whether writers or painters, and sort of hinting that we were out for publicity, which we weren't at all. She was just very jealous of whatever attention we got as young men. She was also frightfully funny, without wanting to be, I think. She really looked like a sort of middle-aged American Jewish businessman, like some of my father's business friends in drag. And then I met her the second time at a poetry reading when Edith Sitwell came to Paris. She was seated in the front row at the poetry reading and there was something so funny about watching these two very odd, eccentric women being extremely polite to each other, bowing and curtseying to each other so to speak. It reminded me of a very manneristic painting which is in the Brussels museum called "A Visitation of Saints" where you see these two saints being extremely polite to each other. Edith Sitwell and Gertrude Stein were a vision, I assure you. But somehow I was never able to become very close, to open up much with writers who are older than myself. Neither with Gide nor with Stein nor with Joyce. A little bit with Eliot. I was at my ease only with my own contemporaries.

LEYLAND: Why didn't you get along with older writers?

RODITI: So many of them had become just incredibly fossilized. I get on very well with many younger men. My closest friend for many years was Paul Goodman, but he was younger than I too, not much. But my close friends in the writing world, in the art world, are those who are not fossilized, and very few are not fossilized.

LEYLAND: It seems to be a syndrome which happens to many artists and writers, for instance Dos Passos and Eliot. As they grew older, they became more and more conservative.

RODITI: Eliot had always been conservative. As a matter of fact as he grew older he became less conservative.

LEYLAND: What about his High Anglicanism and Toryism? Wasn't that a later development?

RODITI: That had existed as far back as the early thirties, but one of the things which I was able to observe with Eliot was that he moved away from the very peculiar anti-Semitism of some of his writings of the late twenties and the early thirties, the anti-Semitism which comes out in "Sweeney Agonistes" and other poems. This was because he was so shocked by Nazi anti-Semitism—by the violence, the inhumanity of it—that he just eradicated it out of his own writing. So he did become much more liberal in many ways, and after his wife's death he shared an apartment with a homosexual friend for a long while. He was much more liberal, much less conservative, though he remained a religious man. Though politically at times intolerant, he progressed very much. So he's an exception.

I think that the reason for which so many writers become fossilized is because of the peculiar structure of the literary world. Once you're a success you're expected to repeat your performance with as little variation as possible. You're expected to do again and again the same kind of trick rather than explore new fields. I see that with publishers. They're always disconcerted if I come along with a new project which has nothing to do with any project with which my name has ever been associated. If you're a novelist, you stick to novels and not only do you stick to novels, but you stick to the same kind of novel. You can see that even more in painting. Rothko was expected to go on doing nothing but the same kind of abstract typical Rothko, and never anything else. If Rothko had suddenly done a perfectly classical subject, "Europa and the Bull," why Marlborough Gallery and every critic would have been up in arms: "He's gone mad!"

LEYLAND: Another person who has gone out in new directions is Christopher Isherwood. I don't know if you saw his adaptation of *Frankenstein* on TV.

RODITI: I haven't seen it. But Christopher is a very free man. I've known Christopher; we were in Berlin together when he was writing the *Berlin Stories*. Christopher and Stephen Spender and I were in those days going around in the same queer bars. He's always been much more free than Stephen Spender and much more free in his way than Auden, only he was a great admirer of Auden. He's remained extremely young.

And Auden towards the end of his life had become terribly bitter. The other day in New York Marvin Cohen showed me an interview of Auden that he'd not yet published. He'd interviewed Auden about a year before his death, and Auden hadn't wanted to publish it because this interview was so bitter, so critical of everybody and everything; he can't stand the young, that kind of thing. When you get to that point, you might just as well stop writing. I heard the other day a very strange story about Auden. Shortly before his death he expressed regret for having chosen to live in America and become American. Why? "Well, if I'd remained in Britain I would now be poet laureate."

LEYLAND: That's rather sad, isn't it?

RODITI: Yes. I had an even weirder experience about Auden. A few years ago some friend of his or of mine came over to Paris. We were lunching together and I said, "Oh, and what does Wystan think?" "Oh, well Wystan has been assured that he's going to get the Nobel Prize and he's been very, very happy about it." Two days later I met in Paris someone who'd just come from Geneva and who knows Nabokov. "Oh, what is the news of Nabokov?" "Oh, Nabokov is very, very excited. He's been assured that he's going to get the Nobel Prize." Three days later I opened the newspaper; Beckett got it. Auden practically collapsed, totally demoralized for several weeks because he hadn't got it. Well I couldn't care less whether I get a Nobel Prize or not, and as for being poet laureate...

LEYLAND: Why did Auden have such a great antipathy, bitterness towards the young? Is it because he felt he wasn't getting enough honors?

RODITI: He was not getting the kind of honors that he wanted. He's not the only poet that I've known who wants that kind of honor. Paul Celan is a contemporary German poet who committed suicide in Paris. He expected red carpets to be unrolled wherever he set dainty foot and he was during the last years of his life like a raw egg, always offended, because he expected that poets should be met by brass bands. The only poet I've ever heard of who did that kind of thing was the Italian late-romantic poet Carducci. One day, when his train was passing through the station in Bologna, somebody recognized Carducci leaning out of the window of the train. Suddenly the news went around the whole station: "Carducci's here!" The train had to stop one hour while he made a speech to the crowd. Imagine having to make a rousing speech from the window of a train to a mass of Italians in a railroad station. That's scarcely the poet's life. D'Annunzio did that kind of thing too.

LEYLAND: Isn't this tied in to a cynicism and a loss of idealism that things can be changed? For instance, in the thirties Auden was a socialist, and then at the end of his life he was politically conservative.

RODITI: I wouldn't call it a loss of idealism. I would call it a sclerosis of idealism. The idealism remains but becomes more and more restricted and one might almost say stiff, like a sort of arthritic limb. I've always been, I won't say leftist, but I've never been conservative. At one time I very vaguely flirted with Communism, when I was about eighteen or nineteen. Who doesn't at that age? But I soon realized that the Communists can be the most dreadful squares in the world, the most conventional, totalitarian-minded people. So I soon realized that basically I'm a kind of socialist-anarchist-idealist without any political program, I'm not going to set about changing anything because I'm too much of a pessimist. I know that we live in "a vale of tears" and, whatever you do, there's always going to be squares coming up on top, who are going to make life as unpleasant for us as they can. And I'm not the kind of man who ever wants to be in the White House. God forbid that I should ever land there! I also know that the kind of man who wants to be there is always going to make life unpleasant for us. So my anarchism consists in not taking institutions too seriously and being more like Paul Goodman, trying to find what the cracks in the institutions are where I can live safely in the woodwork, so to speak.

LEYLAND: Yet isn't there a danger in that? If a reactionary government takes over, the artist who says "I am completely apolitical" still gets censored.

RODITI: Oh yes, but I'm not completely apolitical. I'm competely skeptical, which is a form of being very political. I'm questioning everything. I'm not withdrawing completely, I just question everything—that marvelous element of Socratic doubt.

LEYLAND: You were in France then over the past thirty years, and you visited the U.S. quite often during that time?

RODITI: On the whole I've been living in Europe since the beginning of 1946, at first in Germany, then in France and now part of the time in Morocco since I have a house there and spend my vacations there. But I come back to America nearly every year. Sometimes I spend only a month, like this time, sometimes I spend as much as six months, depending on whether I have teaching jobs or lecture tours or other reasons to stay here. This has given me the opportunity, this business of living on both sides of the Atlantic, and occasionally dipping into Asia and Africa too, to observe and to be aware of a most extraordinary evolution in morals and everything in the past fifty years. After all I can admit to having practiced homosexuality now for a good half-century, which sounds shocking in a way. I must say that I don't practice it with the same enthusiasm as fifty years ago because it's lost much of its novelty. But in those fifty years I've seen attitudes—my own, the attitudes of other homosexuals and also of the non-homosexual world—change so radically that I find it very interesting now to look back. I can remember a time when most homosexuals had to be very discreet. In a way there were great advantages to this discretion. Since most of us were discreet, most non-homosexuals simply didn't seem to be aware of our existence and never worried much about us. In a way we had much more freedom. There was a time when, unless you camped outrageously, most cops never spotted you as being a homosexual, and for instance in France there was only one particular branch of the police at all interested in this matter and the rest, traffic cops and so on, unless you were an absolutely outrageous faggot, never spotted you as such.

There's a couple of amusing anecdotes in this respect. The famous composer Saint-Saëns, the composer of the opera *Samson and Delilah*, was a notorious homosexual and at the same time a very famous man. Legend has it that plainclothes cops of the special branch were always posted outside his home in Paris to follow him wherever he went so that he shouldn't get into any trouble when he went cruising. Now the other cops would never notice that he was cruising or that he was queer, but he was fully protected as a famous man from getting into trouble because it would be too much of a scandal. This is very typical of a kind of Victorian or Edwardian attitude to the life we lead.

LEYLAND: At the same time in England people were going to jail—Oscar Wilde, for instance.

RODITI: Well, they were going to jail only when someone like the Marquess of Queensberry denounced them. Except for the Wilde scandal and a couple of other scandals which put this matter in the headlines, all through the Victorian era there was a great deal of homosexuality in England, totally undercover. One can read it in all sorts of books which are coming out now, which are being resurrected, that it existed all along, all through. Probably Beau Brummel was a practicing homosexual in his way, but it isn't recorded in the official history. And if one goes through the records of police courts in England in the nineteenth century one doesn't find so very much of it there. Yet it was there all the time. We know from sociologists that there was a great deal of homosexuality throughout the Industrial Revolution for the simple reason that the social conditions encouraged it. With child labor a great number of orphans, a great number of abandoned children were brought up in orphanages and in France a great number of abandoned foundlings were brought up by what is known as the "Assistance Publique." You have only to read nowadays such books as Genet's *Thief's Journal* to realize that this kind of education was bound to produce a maximum amount of homosexuals. This went on throughout the nineteenth century and yet we have very few records of actual cases coming up. But any psychoanalyst who knows anything about this kind of upbringing will know that there must have been a great deal of it.

We see it again now in developing nations and if you go to a city like Calcutta, where there are a tremendous number of abandoned children and of foundlings, you have a very high percentage of homosexuals among the adults. This is a result of the upbringing, the social and emotional conditions in which people are brought up. There you get back to what I was saying earlier about the frequency of the incidence of homosexuality increasing with anxiety. After all Auden wrote a poem, a book which is called *The Age of Anxiety* and which brings out how much we live in an anxious society. Our society here in America in my opinion is much less anxious than the society of Calcutta or of Cairo, where people are much more anxious about where their next meal is going to come from, where there is a far higher percentage of abandoned children and orphans. In fact, in my book on homosexuality I point out that many of the societies in which human beings have lived since the Industrial Revolution seem to be intentionally producing a maximum number of homosexuals, perhaps in order to persecute them. They must have a scapegoat on which to vent their guilt feeling about the disorders that they are creating. They blame it on us or they blame it, as the Nazis did, on the Jews and on the homosexuals. But they've got to find a scapegoat for the absolute malevolence of the society in which we live. Would you agree with that?

LEYLAND: Certainly gay people are often treated as scapegoats. Many other minorities are scapegoats too.

RODITI: Yes, but imagine the position of a society which is by nature anti-Semitic, the day that it no longer has any Jews, and it's much easier to create homosexuals than to create Jews.

LEYLAND: What do you mean "to create homosexuals"?

RODITI: By the way you bring up your children.

LEYLAND: Well, that is assuming a certain theory of the origins of homosexuality which is not proven, and which I personally don't believe in.

RODITI: No, I don't think it's important as such, but if you go back to the writings of Freud you see that the great mystery is the choice of the neurosis. One can know that a certain way of bringing up an individual is going to make that individual neurotic, but you cannot predict that the choice of the neurosis will be homosexuality. Still it seems to me that in the society in which we live, the choice of homosexuality is a neurosis that is more frequent than let's say the choice of shoe fetishism.

LEYLAND: I don't think homosexuality is a neurosis any more than heterosexuality is a neurosis.

RODITI: Oh, certainly not. I certainly believe that civilized man is basically neurotic and I keep on observing how much more unhappy and neurotic many of the so-called normal people that I know can be. When I was being analyzed many years ago and I was working in a government agency, I broke off my analysis one day after a very extraordinary scene which took place in the office where I worked. Several of my colleagues whom I knew to be heterosexual and married lost their tempers and were so thoroughly neurotic about it that it suddenly occurred to me that I was less neurotic than they were. I was much more at peace with my particular choice than they were with their choices. We live in a neurotic society, and homosexuality is only one of the choices. It's no more neurotic than the others. They're all equally neurotic. But in the eyes of the majority it is more neurotic. The majority is not necessarily right.

Probably the non-neurotic state would be to be bisexual and to want to have sexual intercourse only with persons who were loved and were worthy of that love, and not to care two hoots about the others whom one does not love or who are not worthy of love. And the neurotic chooses unworthy partners, like a friend of mine who recently fell in love with a boy who turned out to be a complete phony, a thief, someone who claimed to be somebody he wasn't, with a false name and all the rest. For this particular friend of mine he was an unworthy partner. It was a neurotic choice, and we see that again and again among heterosexuals: heterosexuals who choose unworthy partners and partners who are not worthy of the kind of affection and love that they try to shower on them. And it seems to me that in our society this is a very frequent thing, this drive to seek affection and love, almost at random, and not necessarily from wise choices, from judicious choices. One should be perfectly content in life with finding a very limited number of worthy partners with each one of whom in turn one can achieve a rather lasting relationship. This business of buzzing around, fucking around, with a different person every three or four days is not necessarily a happy solution. Promiscuity is meaningful certainly, but it is nearly always very self-destructive. Promiscuity, especially in an urban society, such as the one in which we live now with such a high frequency of venereal disease and so on, is hopelessly self-destructive. Now I'm not condemning it on principle. I have learned from my own experience, having been much more promiscuous at one time than I am today. Nowadays promiscuity is not something which would particularly attract me.

It may be viable for a time, as a kind of growing pain which helps you to decide what your choices should be. You try your luck with all sorts of different types and finally decide that one type is the one that really suits you and then drop the others. But I think that this business of being promiscuous throughout life in the end becomes very self-destructive. I went through it too for a while, and I don't regret it because it helped me very much to discover what kind of partner suits me best. I think the ideal is a lasting relationship with someone and a reasonable freedom for adventure on the side, when the adventure is obviously worthwhile and not likely to wreck the more important lasting relationship.

It's very difficult to find a partner for a lasting relationship, and very often one realizes that one had found a partner after having lost him or her. One doesn't realize always how important it is until one's bungled it. But all these choices that one makes depend to a great extent on one's age and on one's sexual drive. I admit quite frankly that I have reached an age and a level of experience where I can observe a considerable reduction in my own sexual drive, and have much more critical selectivity in my attitude towards these choices.

LEYLAND: What kinds of relationships have you had during your own life?

RODITI: Well I think that the most unhappy one, or the most disastrous one, was a relationship with an extremely gifted poet and it lasted eight years. And although I knew that he was basically homosexual, he would never admit it to himself or to me and throughout those eight years always had relationships with women on the side, and literally tormented and persecuted me. But I never had the courage to leave him, not out of any selfishness, because I knew that I could perfectly well live without him, but I knew that he couldn't live without me, that the moment I abandoned him he was totally incapable of earning a living and of organizing his life. The fact is that after eight years we parted and within two years he'd become an incurable alcoholic and a totally unproductive writer. I still see him on very rare occasions. I try to avoid seeing him because it always makes me so sad to see this extremely talented person gone completely to seed. But whenever I see him now I realize how lucky I was to have the courage to break off, because he would have destroyed me in the same way as he destroyed himself.

Now this led me to believe that there might be a streak of masochism in me, because it was not the first time nor the last time that I chose partners who could be very destructive as far as I am concerned. I don't want to go into all the details, but one of my partners, with whom I had a relationship which lasted four years, finally attempted to murder me and has been in a lunatic asylum ever since. And that was when I went back to an analyst and tried to find out why I chose people who were so destructive. Since then I have been less masochistic in my choices. But perhaps this masochism has something to do with my being epileptic, because my neurologists seem to think that there is some relationship between the two there. But anyhow the years go by and one way or another one achieves an equilibrium, however precarious, between creativity and self-destruction, between the fear of loneliness and the drive to seek partners rather at random, without being too wise in one's choices.

In the last couple of years, I seem to be able to live perfectly happily without any partner, without any fear of loneliness and with only very rare relationships, oddly enough most of them with very old friends who returned, with no particular desire for anything new. A kind of distrust of new experiences, a feeling that they will either be repetitious of what I've already experienced or that they might be disappointing. And I remain very deeply attached to one or two of my old loves from whom I parted or who parted from me for various reasons, without any drama, without any jealousy, without any bitterness. One of them is married and has two children. I'm the godfather of the first and I was the best man at the wedding because he had no family. And now fifteen years later we're so fond of each other that my sister, for instance, when she met him a year ago, said to me afterwards, "You are obviously both in love with each other." Well we are in a way, but in a perfectly platonic way. There's no desire to go to bed any longer, but we're very, very closely bound to each other and would find it very difficult if suddenly we were deprived of this relationship. Well I think that as time goes by one becomes more dependent on a certain kind of human relationship other than a sexual one. And it may be one of the faults of our age to attach too much importance to the sexual relationships and not enough to the human ones. Would you agree with that?

LEYLAND: Yes, I agree. But there doesn't always have to be dichotomy between the two. It's possible to have a lover/friend in one person.

RODITI: Well one can have the two certainly. But it's very difficult to find someone who is a perfect sexual partner and a perfect human partner. And very often the one who is a perfect human partner is not a satisfactory sexual partner and vice versa. The ideal total relationship is extremely difficult to find. But sometimes one begins with being simply a sexual partner and a very satisfactory one and with time you realize there's more to it than you thought. And when the sexual novelty is no longer there, then the human relationship remains and that is the most beautiful thing of all.

LEYLAND: Which do you think was the most successful relationship of all those that you've had?

RODITI: I think with this particular friend who's someone totally uneducated, who was an orphan and whom I met under rather ordinary circumstances, without either of us even having the vaguest idea that it would end up by being a sexual relationship. We met quite by chance. We were introduced to each other by a friend, in a café where we happened to meet. We never expected to meet again. But then a year later we met again quite by chance and one thing led to another. About a week later we were living together and we lived together for three years. During those three years I knew all along that he was bisexual, he had always some relationship with a girl on the side, and generally with rather pleasant girls whom I found pleasant too. Very often we'd have dinner together, the three of us, and as he was younger than I I'd say to him, "Well, go out dancing and have a good time" and I'd stay at home reading or writing. He'd come back the next morning—more often around noon—having spent the night somewhere else. He was very tactful: he didn't believe in bringing her back to our home. This too was something particularly pleasant, that he had enough respect for me to avoid doing that. And then one day I noticed that the second or third girl was pregnant. It turned out that she was a very nice girl with a very decent family. I talked it over with him and asked him what he planned to do. In the course of the conversation it became obvious that he would very much enjoy having children. I said, "Well why don't you marry her?" and he said, "I wouldn't dream of marrying without your consent." And I said, "Well in this case I will certainly consent because I have the greatest respect for her and I feel that sooner or later, since you do like children, you are destined to marry." And so the marriage took place and I was best man. Fifteen years later we're still extremely fond of each other though we never had sex again. And I think this has been the most beautiful relationship of my life, in addition to which he's probably the most beautiful man I've ever been to bed with. He's a really beautiful person in many respects. I taught him to read and write; I taught him all sorts of things that he'd never learned in the orphanages where he'd been brought up.

LEYLAND: This was in France?

RODITI: Yes. He's a Moroccan, married to a French woman, and I'm very fond of him; I'm very fond of his wife and I'm very fond of his children. I feel that this is the kind of relationship which is miraculous, which you can't expect to achieve in life. It just drops in your lap from heaven. It doesn't drop fully blown. For it to develop the way it did there had to be something in me and something in him which made it possible. I think that what made it possible is the fact that neither of us was compulsive, that we could both be objective and relaxed about the relationship although it was a relationship which was very important to both of us. Each one of us had enough respect for the other to realize that as the years go by certain changes occur, and that nothing is really lasting as it is and as it stands. There's always an evolution. Because we remained both of us open-minded as far as this evolution was concerned, neither of us suffered from it. There was no conflict when the change came about. Neither of us was possessive. Neither of us was jealous. I think that jealousy, possessiveness, and a certain kind of vanity, of pride, wanting to boast about how beautiful one's boyfriend is in front of others, this is what can destroy a relationship and is what destroys heterosexual relationships too. Relationships are very fragile, whether homosexual or heterosexual, and especially in the kind of society in which we live, in which we enjoy much greater freedom than in the past. Homosexual relationships, which have always tended to be less stable statistically than heterosexual relationships, are becoming nowadays even more unstable.

Thirty years go, for all sorts of reasons, I used to go a lot into the gay bars when I was living in New York. And I used to go to Turkish baths and what have you. Not constantly, but I saw no objection to going to them every once in a while and it was fun. Nowadays if I go to one of the Turkish baths, I find it rather unpleasant and sordid. Three years ago, when I was in New York, out of a kind of sheer sentimentality and curiosity, I went to the gay bath—the Everard, which was a famous one in its day. I remember going there in the past and meeting five or six other writers. We'd sit in the coffee shop, having a sort of literary *salon* there. It was too hilarious for words, because none of us had gone there for that purpose. Anyhow I went there again simply because I hadn't been there for twenty years and I happened to go by it during the afternoon. I had some errand to do in that section and it suddenly occurred to me that it might be amusing to go there again and see what it was like. I went there and

I was horrified by how sordid it is. They hadn't given a lick of paint to it in twenty years and the characters I saw there were rather sad drunks and deteriorated characters. I wouldn't have dreamt of having any sexual relationship with any one of the hundred or so men who were there. Well after spending about an hour there I went off again.

Very often now I go into gay bars and I find them so utterly depressing that I don't stay. The only ones that I like are a couple of rather elegant ones in Paris where they have good music and good dancing. But not the kind of place where you see people, like in most of those that I've been to in America, who just drink and stare at themselves in mirrors, which is one of the most extraordinary things about American queers, the number of narcissists among them who stare at themselves in the mirror until they find one dressed almost exactly as they are dressed, and then they fly at each other. If there's one wearing blue jeans he'll only go with another one who's wearing blue jeans; if there's one wearing a leather jacket he'll only go with another one wearing a leather jacket, a crew cut will only go with a crew cut, a beard will only go with a beard and so on. Unbelievable narcissism, which strikes me, coming from the outside, as being something peculiar to the American gay bars.

There's so much fetishism about homosexuality in America, and I find that the fetishism is a depressing thing. I'm not interested in a leather jacket. I'm not interested in boots and spurs. There can be all sorts of fetishism. I'm interested in the mind and the soul that's in all this and he may be physically quite different, he may be dressed quite differently. He may be black, Far Eastern, white, I couldn't care less. What I'm interested in is the heart and the mind.

Many years ago there was in Europe a great fetishism about sailors and I remember once being with Cocteau and several of his friends. They were all talking about the charm of French sailors with their caps and so on, and I rather shocked them by saying I was no more interested in sailors' uniforms than in French Catholic priests' robes. I was not a wardrobe queen, so to speak. It's too easy to disguise anybody in a uniform and give yourself the illusion that you're going to bed with a sailor. I mean you can rent uniforms, it's too goddam easy. Supposing I suddenly became queer for Indian braves with all their feathers, well I could go to any costume agency and get all the feathers and just keep them at home and dress people in them. Pick them up at random and disguise them as Indian braves and paint them up to look like Indian braves. When you go in for that kind of fetishism, there's no end to the amount of disguises that will facilitate it. And if you're interested in individuals, in the mind and the heart and the human relationship, that is perhaps not as easy to find.

LEYLAND: You mentioned Cocteau. Did you know him well?

RODITI: Well I knew him quite well at one time, but in a rather impersonal relationship because I worked for the publishing firm in France, in Paris in the early thirties, which had some dealings with him. Since I was the young assistant to the chief editor there, I used to have to go and see Cocteau to bring him proofs to correct. As we were in a hurry I'd sit around while he corrected these proofs and wait till he had finished and bring them back to the printer. So that I had lunch with him and spoke to him and so on, helped him correct the proofs. It was a sort of professional relationship but a professional relationship which in view of his character and his manner of treating me (after all I have said several times that I was not too bad looking in those days) led to a certain intimacy though he didn't attract me at all. And I never went to bed with him. God forbid! In addition in those days he was so high on opium on some occasions that I had to do all the proof correcting myself, because I couldn't rouse him to the point of correcting the proofs, and if I'd left them with him they never would have gotten back to the printer in time. So I'd just tell my boss that he'd corrected them, but I did it. I never had much respect for him.

I think I've told you before that I've always been extremely distrustful of reputations of artists and writers older than myself. I've always been very much opposed to what subsequently in political circles became known as the cult of personality. When Khrushchev demolished or tried to demolish the cult of Stalin it was termed "cult of personality. " I personally have been extremely distrustful of the kind of buildup which gossip columnists and so on have given to writers and artists in the last twenty or thirty years. I was extremely distrustful when I first met Gertrude Stein, when I first met Cocteau. I've always felt that far too many of these celebrated people, these sacred monsters, were playing a part and were no longer really being themselves. They were living up to the image which had been foisted on them or which they'd managed to foist on their public and had become sort of like Lot's wife—pillars of salt. T. S. Eliot is perhaps one of the only ones whom I have admired and felt was a human being. Kokoschka the painter is also a human being, a couple of other painters whom I've known have given me that impression, but with most of the famous writers, older ones, I had the impression of meeting a kind of statue of them rather than the original.

LEYLAND: You mentioned over dinner tonight that you wrote a book on Oscar Wilde. When was it published?

RODITI: It was published by New Directions in 1947, but it was not a biography. It was an analysis of his ideas, mainly from the point of view of the nineteenth-century philosophy of the dandy. What I felt were the three more important chapters were a chapter on the aesthetics, the ethics and the politics of the dandy. It was really a book on the ideas of Oscar Wilde as they were derived from Baudelaire, from Beau Brummel and from the whole tradition of the dandy. The book has had its little success and every once in a while a chapter from it gets reprinted in an anthology of contemporary criticism. I would like to reprint it now because I'd like to bring it up to date from the point of view of the bibliography and so on, and also because when I wrote it I didn't have access to Wilde's unpublished letters. There were still copyright problems involved. Although I was able to read many of them in the William Andrews Clark Memorial Library in Los Angeles, I couldn't get the authorization to quote from them. Certain hunches of mine at the time could now be justified in terms of quotations from his writings. There's a great deal in these letters which clarifies. For instance, I had the impression that the English text of *De Profundis,* as it was known at the time, had been very much tampered with. My main reason for having this impression was that a German version of it had been published which was much more detailed, which had passages which didn't exist in the English text. Well now we have the complete English text which is published and which contains some passages which were in the German text and which are very uncomplimentary or very compromising for Lord Alfred Douglas and for Lord Alfred Douglas's mother. From this complete English text one can now come to the conclusion that Wilde was being an extremely honorable and brave man in his trials in that he was assuming the responsibility for some acts which were not his but those of Alfred Douglas. It would seem that many of the more unsavory homosexual relationships which came up in the trial with male prostitutes and procurers and so on were not necessarily Wilde's relationships. Wilde was paying for them but it was Lord Alfred Douglas who was dragging him into it.

LEYLAND: Did you correspond with "Bosie" Douglas at all at the time you were writing the book?

RODITI: Oh, no. God forbid! I had met Douglas some years earlier and I knew that one could never rely on anything that he said, because what he'd say one day he'd deny another day.

LEYLAND: His autobiographical writings are very contradictory.

RODITI: Yes, his whole attitude towards Wilde remained extremely ambivalent. Sometimes he would boast of his relationships with Wilde and a few years later he'd deny it. So that one couldn't really rely on anything much he said. And in addition he was perfectly capable of denying later what he'd told you and attacking you for having printed it. So I was rather careful not to use him as a source, because in any case I was not interested so much in the scandal as in Wilde's ideas as expressed previous to the scandal and in *De Profundis* afterwards. I still believe that *De Profundis* is an extraordinary text, in its way as revealing a text, in fact that's what I wrote in the book, as Scott Fitzgerald's *The Crack-Up*. It's an analysis of a complete crack-up in a man's life and beliefs, and a very courageous and perceptive one. Very few writers are capable of writing that kind of thing. DeQuincey wrote about it in his *Confessions of an Opium-Eater*. Wilde wrote it in *De Profundis;* Fitzgerald wrote it in his very extraordinary *The Crack-Up*. But we have very few examples of that kind of confession.

In my book I was much more concerned with showing that Wilde was a serious thinker, pointing out that a longish essay like *The Soul of Man under Socialism* is a very important political text. His critical dialogues are very important texts from the point of view of history, criticism, and aesthetics. You see this was written and published at a time when Wilde was not considered at all seriously by so-called serious writers, whether in England or in America. One of the most extraordinary proofs of this is that one of the critics of the *Partisan Review,* a man called Dupee, published a book of what the major contemporaries of Henry James had written about Henry James and he completely neglected to include in it what Wilde had written about James. Now there are some very perceptive passages in one of Wilde's critical dialogues about James and there'ss also some reviews of Henry James's books published by Wilde in periodicals. Really quite secondary writers were included in this book of Dupee's, but it never occurred to an intellectual of the *Partisan Review* to take Wilde seriously in the forties. The only two people in the intellectual avant-garde who took him seriously then were George Woodcock, a Canadian poet and anarchist interested in Wilde's political ideas, and I. And then Paul Goodman, but Paul Goodman didn't write about him. Paul read him and took him as seriously as I did. But otherwise in all our world of so-called avant-garde criticism, nobody took Wilde seriously. Nobody would dream of reading him and nobody like Delmore Schwartz or any of the "advanced" poets in those days would have dreamt of reading Wilde's "The Sphinx" or "The Ballad of Reading Gaol." They were dismissed as kitsch, and I took them seriously. Nowadays there's been a complete change. They are taken seriously again.

But that Wilde book was, as far as I was concerned, for me an important book. It led to a most extraordinary quarrel with a strange character called Edward Dahlberg, who's quite a well-known writer. It so happens that Dahlberg was not at all homosexual. God forbid that he should ever become homosexual and be let loose on our unfortunate community, nutty as he is. Anyhow he wrote a book of essays which was published by New Directions called *The Flea of Sodom*, of all things. And this book somehow managed to have a preposterous quantity of misprints in it, and a copy of it was sent to me to review. I pointed out that it had a hilarious number of misprints in it, and that in my opinion it was not a particularly good book. I didn't sail right into him, I wasn't vicious. Anyhow Dahlberg was wildly angry at this review of his book and then wrote a violent attack on me arguing (*a*) that I was a Marxist and (*b*) that I was a homosexual because I had written on Wilde. This was such a violent attack that all sort of friends of mine said that I must answer it in print. First I am not a communist as is suggested, nor even really a Marxist. I'm a leftist in an entirely different tradition. Anyhow, my answer was that Bernard Shaw had written about Joan of Arc and that didn't prove that he was a female saint and that identifying a writer with the subject of his books is really a bit childish. Dahlberg is now a well-known writer and the object of a cult in certain circles, but I still find him difficult to swallow as a writer. But that's my taste in writing, and everyone of us has his own tastes. I've never been particularly attracted to that kind of violently pseudo-apocalyptic writing. I've always preferred a certain more studied profundity. And as the years go by I find my tastes in American writing, among my contemporaries, boil down to a very limited number of writers, not necessarily homosexual writers. I still have a great deal of respect for Henry Miller, an immense admiration for Paul Goodman, not necessarily because he was a homosexual but because he was an extremely truthful and frank, and modest writer. I admire a limited number of poets, such as Cummings.

Very often there's a certain quality of truth. And by truth I mean to oneself, according to the Socratic dictum, "know thyself." The writer sincerely tries to know himself and to communicate that perfectly unique, individual quality. Now that perfectly unique individual quality may be homosexual . . . not necessarily. Many a homosexual writer does not necessarily communicate that. He may be just going through some form of *camp* and not knowing himself at all. I suppose that there are now a few homosexual writers whose works I respect. I have an immense respect for Ned Rorem's diaries.

I also respect Paul Bowles who is a very old friend of mine. I'm a little bit anxious and disappointed in his present literary activity. I wish he would do more creative writing. I have a feeling that since Jane's death he doesn't feel the urge to write creatively very much. I feel that he's getting very withdrawn, but on the basis of his past achievement I have considerable respect for him.

When I first knew Paul, he was primarily a composer, who also wrote some extremely witty, colorful surrealist poetry, very surprising. As far as I know he was not interested in writing any fiction. After his meeting Jane and marrying her, he developed this taste and gift for writing fiction. He stopped writing poetry, and at one time he wrote more than he composed. Since Jane's illness and death, he's written less and less fiction and as far as I know, has not composed anything. His no longer composing may be due to his increasing deafness. In any case, he was a writer of fiction, and pretty good fiction at that, during the period of his living with Jane. Now Jane was a very difficult person to live with. The *odd* person. She can be recognized in a great number of the characters in her own fiction and drama, also in some of the characters of Paul's fiction, transposed but quite recognizable.

There's something very autobiographical about Paul's fiction. Something very autobiographical, too, about a whole section of American literature of that generation. Read the early plays of Tennessee Williams. There are so many autobiographical characters in those plays. In *Streetcar* for instance, the heroine is Tennessee in drag, and it's also Tennessee's sister who can be identified to a great extent. And in some of his filmscripts, too. *Suddenly Last Summer,* a film of a man who gets murdered by kids, was a fantasy of his own sex life. Tennessee is another person (as I at one time, and many of our friends) who has tended to be very self-destructive in his choices, and choose partners who were dangerous. Now this is a fantasy about the partners that he tended to choose during a certain time of his life. Tennessee was aware, as I am, of the self-destructive nature of these choices. I haven't seen Tennessee for a long while now, so I wouldn't know if he continues to make these self-destructive choices.

But as far as I'm concerned, touch wood, I have a feeling that over these last couple of years, I am no longer being tempted to make these kinds of choices, and a kind of warning signal functions in me before I make the choice. I suddenly see how destructive this person can be, and not too late, and then I lose interest. I think that self-destructiveness is something that is an element of the life that we lead in the modern world. We're living in a self-destructive society—a vast amount of pollution. The economy we live in is self-destructive. So this obviously has some effect on the individual. There are other ways of being self-destructive. In the society in which we live drug addiction is a form of self-destructiveness. Look at the vast number of heterosexuals out there who go from one self-destructive relationship to another. And I'm beginning to feel that the society in which we live teaches us to be self-destructive, and that it requires a great deal of self-knowledge or a natural healthiness to escape from this. I have achieved it through self-knowledge. I don't claim to be naturally very healthy, probably anything but. But as one matures one can choose this kind of awareness and no longer allow the society, the economy in which we live, to drive us to self-destructiveness. After all, the history of the United States for the last twenty or thirty years is such a magnificent vision of self-destructiveness. What we are doing to the countryside, what we're doing to our cities, how we've destroyed some of the most beautiful things in the world. I recall what we did in Cambodia. If this isn't self-destructive while at the same time talking about saving democracy, about saving civilization; we destroy it as fast as we can. It was sheer double-talk all along. After all I have been an idealist all my life, and I have every right to be a bit disappointed and a bit bitter today when I see how far we've gone along the path to wars of destruction.

And Paul Goodman was the same. The last time I saw Paul, he was in a very depressed condition, shortly before his death, poor dear; he'd been utterly shattered by the death of his son. His son died in a totally unexpected accident: he went on a vacation mountaineering, slipped, fell, and was killed. And he was a charming, lovely boy, gifted, healthy, whom everybody adored. And Paul never recovered from that. Also, he had after that a vision of what the world in which he was living was actually becoming. It destroyed not only him, but all his hopes and everything. And our last conversations were very depressing conversations about the world in which we are living and the kind of world in which we might be living in another few years.

Paul had been, for a very long time, a very optimistic anarchist. Anarchist in the tradition of Thoreau, a very American tradition and not a politically activist tradition. But a tradition of disbelief in certain institutions, in fact in all institutions. Paul wrote with his brother, the architect Percival Goodman, his book *Communitas* on the ideal, modern urban community proposing a type of community which he believed to be quite possible within his own lifetime. Paul went into psychotherapy and was one of the founders with Fritz Perls of gestalt therapy in America. He was a gay being very open, thinking that this would all lead to a better world. At the time of the Berkeley student riots when Paul came out here and met the leaders of the student movement in Berkeley, he was again very hopeful. And then when I last saw him he had lost hope. Many of the student leaders whom he had admired and encouraged he felt had become rather cynical, destructive persons. Paul was a great believer in education, in our attempting to understand and admire the great works of literature and of art, and was a great believer in their offering us a valid doctrine. And when he saw that so many of these young people, instead of sharing his admiration for the great works and great thinkers, were ready to throw all of that overboard and just sink into a sea of pot smoking, and in fact living like animals instead of like human beings who, after all, have a soul, he was very disappointed. This coincided, this loss of faith in all that he'd sought to achieve and all that he'd sought to teach, with the loss of his son. It was really heartbreaking for me to see him then, because Paul was almost like a brother for me in a way. We had known each other for thirty years and shared so many ideas, and so many ideals, and so many admirations, and had so many friends in common. I still miss him. I often have a feeling of being a survivor who maybe didn't deserve to survive. And I feel in a way like one of my friends who survived Hitler's death camps and said to me that so many of the people who deserved more to survive it had not. And that she felt that she had survived almost on false pretenses. Paul was younger than I, and I have the feeling that he might have achieved much more than I am likely to achieve had he lived to be my age. He's one of the very few real admirations in my life. And the same thing in Ned Rorem's. Ned and I remain devoted to the memory of Paul. We look upon him almost as a kind of saint. We don't put him on a pedestal. He was a great friend and one who could be marvelously good counsel and guidance, a great sense of sympathy with understanding, something very rare. And all those who knew him well miss him in that way. He had his quirks, and he had his peculiar sexual quirks, but who cares about that.

I think that Paul's notion of tactics may have been too much determined by the circumstances of his own life. After all, Paul was basically a metropolitan New Yorker. New York is an extremely sophisticated urban community where one can have the illusion that certain changes are going to occur within one's lifetime, because they would occur if the whole country were like New York. I don't think that Paul knew the grass roots well enough to realize what tremendous prejudices have to be overcome elsewhere.

LEYLAND: And even in New York, too. The city of New York voted down an equal rights bill for gay people.

RODITI: Yes, but in the city of New York, it goes two steps forward and one back. Still, in every respect, the whole situation has changed in New York, much more radically and rapidly than elsewhere. My own attitude toward your own liberation movement is ambivalent, but that's for very personal reasons. I very often think, maybe due to my basic masochism, that if homosexuality became, I won't say legal because that is an absurdity to say that—but fully accepted, I might no longer find it fun to practice it. I have a feeling that in the kind of society in which we live it's damned good to be able to do something which isn't legal. After all, we escape from the phoniness of this society, we express our own individuality and our lack of faith in this society by feeling free to do things that are illegal, and that are not necessarily totally subversive. We escape from the corset in which this society wants to constrict us.

LEYLAND: Even if the laws were changed and it was legal, the attitudes of people would probably not keep pace. I think it will take several generations. Anyway, the main point of the gay liberation movement is not the legalization of homosexual acts. It's a question of seeing gayness in a much wider context within one's life.

RODITI: Certainly. I also tend to feel uneasy about the word "gay." For me, perhaps because I am so much older, the word has certain implications which are unpleasant. I remember in the twenties, the word was not applied to homosexuals. One referred to "gay girls," meaning prostitutes. And then non-homosexuals began to refer to certain types of homosexuals as being gay, implying that they were male prostitutes. They had round heels and were push-overs and could be laid by anyone who wanted. And then this term which was a bit offensive in those days is now generally accepted, more than accepted. It's become a kind of banner, an honor. In the back of my mind is the feeling that the word "gay" is just about as unpleasant as the word "fruit."

LEYLAND: Words change meanings. A word that had bad connotations in one decade can completely change its meaning by the next. The word "black" was probably an insult ten or fifteen years ago, when "colored" or "Negro" was in use. And now "black" is common usage.

RODITI: I see exactly the same evolution there. I was a great friend of Countee Cullen, a major black American poet, who by the way was gay too. One of his closest friends was my friend and we had this relationship which lasted several years, an absolutely adorable Harlem intellectual, who is dead now and who remained a very close friend of mine and of my family for decades after our relationship had ceased for one reason or another. It ceased because we weren't living in the same city, we couldn't live in the same city. For purely material reasons he couldn't come and live in Paris. I couldn't support him; he couldn't get a job there, and I couldn't come to live with him in New York. In my friendships there, I've seen that in the twenties we used the word "colored" and to use the word "Negro" was offensive. Then in the thirties, the word "Negro" became the right term and "colored" was a kind of old-fashioned euphemism. And now "Negro" is the old-fashioned euphemism and "black" is beautiful. It's very strange, this kind of evolution in America in which the term which was offensive and insulting becomes the term which is accepted and of which one is proud.

LEYLAND: To return to Paul Goodman. There seems to have been in his life a dichotomy between his married life and his homosexuality. Is this something you'd care to talk about or do you think it's not important? To what extent is it important to his creativity? If he had been in a situation where the climate was different, if he had come out say in 1970, would he have tended to be living a more homosexual lifestyle than he did?

RODITI: No. When I first met Paul, at the University of Chicago, he was quite frankly homosexual. And at one time he was carrying on two affairs concurrently, with a boy and a girl, both of whom were red-haired, freckled, and in some ways looked remarkably alike. One of them is the mother of his first child, a daughter; Sally was his second wife and the mother of his second and third children—his son who died and his second daughter. During all the years that I knew him, I knew Paul to have only these two significant relationships with women. He may have had a couple of others, passing relationships, but both these women knew all along he was constantly having homosexual relationships. Now as a psychoanalyst, or a psychotherapist, he was also a Reichian. That is to say Paul believed that under certain circumstances it was important to the therapist to have sexual relationships with the patient. If the transference of the patient required it, it should be allowed. I won't say that he practiced this, but this was a belief of his. I remember on one occasion, although Paul sometimes liked to advocate the absurd so I would never never take it literally, Paul had a dog. He was very fond of this dog and he argued on this occasion that if one has a dog and is very fond of the dog, and the dog is very fond of you, there is no reason why you shouldn't have sexual relations with the dog. He felt that love and affection should not be limited to sex nor to species. This was part of his anarchist pansexuality. His whole attitude which was a kind of trancendentalism of the type one finds in the writings of Thoreau; from what one gathers from the way he wrote, he could have an orgasm with a tree practically. Why not? An orgasm with nature. And it was part of his extraordinary, almost mystical pantheism and pansexualism. The doctrine was there, formulated. Whether he practiced it or not, whether he went and had sex with a potato or not, I wouldn't be able to say. But theoretically, it was not absurd to him.

I think that to understand the relationship with these women—that is the concurrent relationship with boys and men—one must realize what friendship and affection meant to him. After all, I can be quite frank, I went to bed with Paul. We were not in love with each other, we were just very fond of each other. And on a couple of occasions, without intending to go to bed together, we had to sleep in the same bed. We had known each other for years, and when we were house guests somewhere, or he'd come and spend an evening with me and for some reason couldn't get back home . . . It was during the war and in New York you couldn't find cabs easily. And one night it was pouring rain and I said, "Paul, you must spend the night here. Phone and say you can't come home and you'll be back tomorrow." We slept in the same bed, and it occurred. And it was the most natural thing from him and for me. We were very fond of each other; we were lying in the same bed; why not? It was an expression of affection and of profound respect for each other, and not simply a momentary desire. This was something which was basic to Paul's character, and in a way basic to mine. I won't say that there are many people that I have that kind of relationship with, unfortunately, because it's very beautiful one.

His loss meant a great deal to the few people who knew him very well. I knew Paul had the gift of bringing out the best in his close friends. He had a marvelous way of bringing us back to the right path, not in terms of morals but in terms of being true to ourselves. If I tended to be going off on a tangential direction, he had a way of criticizing it right, making me realize that I would regret it and bringing me back to what was my true destiny. He had a great gift for guidance. A wonderful source of advice. Curiously, there are three people at the moment writing biographies of him. Last year when I was in New York, I saw one of these biographers who turns out to be someone who isn't gay at all, and he asked me questions about Paul's homosexuality and his marriages. What really puzzled this biographer was not the fact that he could be married and father children and be homosexual, but that Paul could be so frank with his own children about homosexuality. That is very rare. Nowadays it's becoming less rare.

I remember when I was twenty-two I met at a cocktail party once an extremely charming and handsome man who was twenty years older than I and who literally swept me off my feet. He was a foreigner living in a hotel in Paris at the time. And we had a passionate relationship. After about three weeks of it, I discovered that not only was he married, but he had a son my age and sooner or later he would be leaving me to go back to his wife and children. This was a very traumatic experience. We somehow managed to maintain this relationship for about a year during which time I wrote a series of love poems which I published as a book, *Poems for F,* F being his initial. This was for me a very disturbing experience, to fall in love with a man who was obviously in love with me and was married and had a son my age. In that particular social context of forty years ago, this whole relationship was something really catastrophic. It had to remain very secret. Because if it hadn't remained very secret there would have been all sorts of trouble. Nowadays, of course, this kind of relationship can with a certain amount of tact, and in a big city, be something acceptable in a certain sophisticated world, which in those days was impossible. And there are women nowadays who accept that kind of relationship.

I find that in many respects, the evolution of the last forty years, whether here or in Europe, is very satisfactory. We enjoy much more freedom, and there's much less persecution, much less discrimination. We're much more readily accepted. Of course there continue to be areas of our society which are extremely problematic. I happen to have a friend who is a psychiatrist in a county hospital in a very tough industrial city, and she, herself, is lesbian. And while I was dining with her a couple of years ago I asked her what the problem areas were in the kind of hard-hat, redneck society which was that of her practice. And she told me something which really surprised me, that one of the serious problems which caused crackups and hospitalization in the psychiatric wards there was homosexuality. That many of these very aggressively masculine hard hats, rednecks who were married and had children, were basically homosexuals who on some occasion get drunk, get into trouble and then crack up completely. Because there is so much prejudice against it in that type of society that they can't face admitting it to themselves— that they are homosexual and that it happened to them. So that there will continue to be for a long while areas of American life where there will be discrimination and repression and hatred and so on.

I want to talk about observations that I made in the course of a book I wrote about homosexuality. I have lived in a great number of nations or have been there for a considerable length of time. And I've also visited briefly but with almost a sort of anthropologist's eye certain primitive societies. And the thing that struck me is that very often those societies where homosexuality is most widespread—most widely practiced, almost tolerated—also happen to be those societies where the population explosion is greatest. One of the nations which produces the most children, where the population explosion poses enormous democratic and economic problems is India. You have no idea how widespread homosexuality is there. And how generally it appears to be accepted in villages. I won't say in the Europeanized, Anglicized Brahmin upper classes. Another case is Egypt, where the population explosion is terrific, and where homosexuality is very widely practiced, and very openly. Not too much cruising the streets, but anybody who wants to have sex goes to Turkish baths and there are masses of them. You meet all kinds of people there, every class, every type, every age.

Morocco is rather different. There is scarcely a Moroccan who would refuse the chance to have a homosexual relationship. But he is always afraid of other Moroccans knowing that he had it. So they chase after foreigners to a great extent because they are always afraid that if they go to bed with another Moroccan he's going to talk. Algeria is another nation where it is very widespread, where it is obviously part of the natural desire of most men, where they are always seeking relationships, but where there is also a maximum number of children.

I had a lesbian friend, an American, some number of years ago, who was rather an adventurous spirit. I asked her if homosexuality was as widespread among women in Moslem society, because it was very difficult for me as a man to have access. And she told me that she spent six months in Fez, which is the old capital of Morocco. It's also one of the most impenetrable cities; you meet the tradesmen and so on, but it's difficult to get into upper-class families—a very closed world, very traditional. Well, she had somehow managed to get to know some upper-class Arab ladies, at the French hairdresser there. And they had invited her to tea in their harems. And the goings on among these ladies, she said, were fabulous. She could have stayed there for life. She had never been anywhere where she had had such a wild time. I know that Jane Bowles, for instance, had some very easy relationships with Moroccan women, including one rather disastrous relationship which lasted for years.

LEYLAND: Was that relationship with the Moroccan woman who was supposed to have put a curse on her?

RODITI: Yeah. It was horrible. There is something that still puzzles me, this relationship in other societies between the high birth rate and the high incidence of homosexuality. A few years ago I had a Moroccan boyfriend in Paris, and we received a visit of his older half brother, who turned out to be an immensely wealthy businessman from Casablanca. A very stout gentleman in his late seventies, married, and with four children. It never occurred to me that this man could be homosexual. He insisted very much that the next time I am in Morocco I come and see him in Casablanca. I came to Casablanca, made a reservation in the hotel, and he told me, "No no, no. You must come to my apartment." And he put me up in his apartment with the wife and family and all the rest, and everything was all very square and rather boring. I couldn't just get out of it, I had no particular desire, but then I fould myself obliged, on his next trip to Paris, to put him up at my apartment, instead of letting him go to a hotel. And this fat man *flew* at me like that! And I was most embarrassed! Utterly speechless. And then it turned out that all of his life he had had these relationships on the side, and continued to have them.

LEYLAND: Why do you think there is a feeling of shame in a country like Morocco with its long tradition of bisexuality? Is it a Western influence?

RODITI: Oh no. It has something to do with very absurd notions of dignity, with the self-image the Moroccan has of himself. And the Moroccan is brought up to conceive of himself as being much more respectable, in every respect, than he can possibly be. And they are very strict. Practically nobody lives up to all the notions of what is proper.

LEYLAND: There is a sense of machismo in Arab countries, too.

RODITI: Oh, yes a great sense of machismo. I think that machismo in Spain and Portugal is very much a hangover from the Arab occupation.

LEYLAND: And something which comes from Christianity, too.

RODITI: Yes. Islam can be very puritanical too. In a way it's much more puritanical. So puritanical that practically nobody can live up to it. I have a friend who is a rather remarkable man—he's the brother of the first king of Jordan. He was one of the three brothers who had been close friends of Lawrence of Arabia and was the one who did not get a throne. But he was regent in Iraq at one time when the last king of Iraq, the one who was murdered as a minor, was a child, and he was also ambassador of Iraq in London and in several other places. Here was a very sophisticated Arab who had been educated in England, spoke perfect English and was married to a Turkish princess, who had children by his wife, and never that I knew of, had a mistress or a boyfriend. His main interest apart from politics was drinking his whiskey, very British in his way. He told me about once having gone on a diplomatic mission to Saudi Arabia, and how he was a guest in the royal palace there, because in those days there were no hotels. And he had a whole troop of gorgeous slave girls placed at his disposal, for his amusement. And when it was observed that he made no use of these gorgeous slave girls, a similar troop of pretty boys was sent in to be his attendants. And when it was seen that he made no use of those, his hosts were most surprised that he, an Arab prince of a family of wealth, should be utterly faithful to his wife, monogamous. It shows the curious difference, the curious opposition between their puritanism and their laxity.

I must admit that there, too, one can observe an evolution. I notice it especially in Algeria and Morocco, because they're the two Arab countries I know best. They are becoming very westernized, and a kind of anti-homosexual machismo is getting much more widespread. Last summer I was in Tangier. I used to go to the beach every day with a girlfriend who was my house-guest. And there was an incredibly handsome young Moroccan there, and I noticed that my girlfriend had some interest in him, and I took the liberty of going up to him and asking him if he would join us for a drink. Whereupon he became most insulting, go fuck yourself and so on. I wasn't after him, I was just inviting him to join us for the girl. And this would have never happened a few years ago, this aggressive anti-homosexuality, coming out immediately even before I had made any advances. There was no evidence that I was interested in him. He could see that I was with a girl. This was something very strange.

LEYLAND: Are there other areas of your life you'd like to discuss? How do you feel you've integrated your homosexuality into your life, for instance?

RODITI: As far as my life is concerned, I won't say that I make a complete separation between my homosexual life and my professional life. But it so happens that in my professional life, that of a professional interpreter in Western Europe, I find myself associating mainly with women rather than with men, and as a journalist, mainly with perfectly straight men. Most of them know that I'm homosexual; it doesn't seem to bother them in any way. On many an occasion when I've been living with a boyfriend, and I've had to invite colleagues for dinner parties, it was perfectly acceptable. I find that in a limited world of very sophisticated, very educated people, they couldn't care less whether you are homosexual or not. Or this may be an illusion. Most of the women I work with seem to prefer working with a homosexual, because it leads to a perfectly easy working relationship. Much more easy than with a macho, who feels a need to molest them in a way. They're at their job, some of them have their boyfriend or their husband at home, and they don't want to be pestered while at work. And it leads to such a pleasant working relationship that it becomes a rather solid friendship outside of work. I have many friends who are married and with whom I work, and they invite me to dinner with their husbands. The husband isn't jealous, he knows perfectly well I'm a homosexual and a good colleague. And they come and have dinner with me and meet my boyfriend. They invite him with me, they've known him well enough. And it's a pleasant relationship in that the professional life doesn't get mixed up with the emotional life. I find that I've not experienced that to any great extent in America. It's a kind of relationship which is beginning to be possible in big cities. I find one of the things which I dislike in America is the tendency to form minority ghettos.

LEYLAND: Some withdrawal to foster gay community can be healthy.

RODITI: A certain amount of withdrawal is good but there is a point beyond which it becomes unhealthy. There are also absurd things. A few years ago I was flying on a mission for UNESCO to Abidjan, in Ivory Coast, and our plane stopped for an hour or so in the capital of Mali. Out of curiosity I looked at the titles of the books in the bookstore there. And they had nothing but black literature in French. But it also included any title which had the word "black" in it, including a well-known novel called *The Black Manner*, which (in French) means a certain kind of etching. It is a story about Renaissance Europe which had nothing to do with blacks, but the author's style of description was a bit like Rembrandt's rather heavy etchings. The fact that it had the word "black" meant that it was there in that bookstore. And it seems to me that this withdrawal can be very bad intellectually when one sees certain gay people who rush ahead, who buy any goddamned gay book, no matter what tripe it is, and will never read anything that isn't gay.

LEYLAND: Gay chauvinism does exist, and it can be very debilitating intellectually. Gay people should always be culturally open.

It is crucial to have an understanding of the cultural mainsprings of gay people. Just as black people have needed to rediscover their history, so do gay people, without becoming chauvinistic about it. We published an article about how historians and literary critics have suppressed mention of homosexuality in famous writings and texts that have been handed down. Certain passages of ancient writers which mentioned homosexuality were either suppressed or put in Greek, or paraphrased. I think it's crucial that this kind of information become once more available: that we acknowledge those Renaissance poets who wrote love poems to boys, as well as Renaissance poets who wrote love songs to women.

RODITI: Yes. But I think the relationship of this kind of awareness to general culture is not quite the same as the relation of black awareness to general culture. Because in all periods of our Western culture, there have been gay writers and lesbian writers. Take the Renaissance: the gay poets and the lesbian poets had something in common with the non-gay and non-lesbian poets which was a certain kind of Petrarchan Neoplatonism. Black culture is the history of the integration of a racially and culturally entirely different group into our civilization. They are people who have been deprived of their language, to begin with.

LEYLAND: Many gay writers have a real gay sensibility underlying their work. There is a cultural divergence.

RODITI: Their sensibility as a homosexual sensibility is a thoroughly Western sensibility. The Japanese homosexual sensibility has much more in common with the Japanese non-homosexual sensibility than with *our* homosexual sensibility. It's a variant within a given culture. And as such is much more difficult to separate off. Because when you separate it off, unconsciously you are neglecting certain things which we have in common with the non-homosexual. In my case there is something particularly queer and odd, being Jewish: the Jewish religion is in many respects the most anti-homosexual you can imagine. If you read the Bible, masturbation was condemned; Onan was condemned because he masturbated rather than marry his brother's widow. Homosexuals were rejected from the community or stoned. The Jewish religion requires of an orthodox Jew, that every man when he wakes up in the morning goes through a certain ceremony of prayer in which he thanks God for having made him a Jew and a man. Once I was asked by an orthodox Jew how I could somehow bring my being homosexual in harmony with being a Jew. And I made a shocking statement. I said to him that every day I thank God for having made me a Jew and a homosexual, which is almost blasphemous in terms of this prayer. I'm not a religious Jew. In many ways I'm aware of being in the Jewish tradition, but I don't accept the full tradition. At the same time I don't break away from it fully. I certainly wouldn't want to be anything but what I am, especially at this point. The idea of being anything else is absurd. I wouldn't be I, but would be somebody else. I've made my peace with myself, I'm perfectly satisfied with what I am, and God forbid that I should suddenly experience some absurd kind of pentecost with a little flame desecending from heaven to make me straight; God forbid, I'd be lost. But I still feel that as homosexuals we are very much a part of the general Western tradition. And that if we try too hard to affirm a separatist homosexual culture, we are falsifying this tradition which has always included an element of homosexuality, no matter how much repressed.

LEYLAND: I agree it's important not to set up a permanent separatist situation, but I think an element of separatism is necessary until a certain amount of gay cultural identity is realized. The existence of gay creativity and gay artists has often been suppressed by heterosexual scholars.

RODITI: I'm certainly opposed to that kind of falsification of classical texts, but then there's another problem I'd like to discuss: discrimination among homosexuals. For instance, in a country like Spain, where machismo is very strong, the contempt which the active homosexual often has for the passive homosexual is quite real. Or in the Arab countries where the passive homosexual is considered in general as being an utterly degraded creature. In Greece, too nowadays. This kind of discrimination is a form of male sadism. And there are certain types of male homosexuals who are only capable of having sexual relationships with people whom they despise. I've had conversations with women prostitutes who also complained to me of a high percentage of men who go with prostitutes for the pleasure of brutalizing them and insulting them and who are incapable of having a really loving relationship. And this exists to a great extent among homosexuals, too.

LEYLAND: These categories of active and passive are beginning to break down, at least in this country.

RODITI: They are breaking down to a great extent in America, and one no longer hears words like cocksucker used as widely as an insult as one did twenty or thirty years ago. I think things like the Kinsey report have been very useful. Not just the Kinsey report, but all the fallout from it in the next twenty years. I think that is one of the battles we still have to fight, one of the most important ones—to reduce the sadistic hostility which seems to be one of the most frightening elements of sexual relations, whatever they are, in the modern world. And to eliminate the element of exploitation, by the one who thinks that he is stronger of the one he thinks is weaker.

PHOTO © JOHN DE CLEF PIÑEIRO, 1977

NED
ROREM

WORDS AND MUSIC are inextricably linked for Ned Rorem. He has been called "the world's best composer of art songs," yet his musical and literary ventures extend far beyond this specialized field. Rorem has composed three symphonies, three piano concertos, five operas, several ballets and other music for the theater, choral works of every description, and literally hundreds of songs and song cycles. He is also the author of eight books, including four volumes of diaries, and a collection of lectures called *Music from the Inside Out* (Braziller, 1967).

Born in Richmond, Indiana, on October 23, 1923, Rorem early moved to Chicago with his family, where by the age of ten his piano teacher had introduced him to Debussy and Ravel, an experience that "changed his life forever." At seventeen Rorem entered the Music School of Northwestern University. After two years there, he received a scholarship to the Curtis Institute in Philadelphia. Rorem later studied composition under Bernard Wagenaar at Juilliard, where he took his B.A. in 1946 and his M.A. (along with the George Gershwin Memorial Prize in composition) two years later. In New York he was Virgil Thomson's copyist in return for twenty dollars a week and orchestration lessons. He studied with Aaron Copland at the Berkshire Music Center in Tanglewood in the summers of 1946 and 1947. In 1948, his "The Lordly Hudson" was voted the best published song of that year by the Music Library Association.

In 1949 Rorem moved to France, where he lived until 1958. These years as a young composer among the leading figures of the artistic and social milieu of postwar Europe are absorbingly portrayed in *The Paris Diary of Ned Rorem* (Braziller, 1966). This was followed by the books *New York Diary* (1967), *Music and People* (1968), *Critical Affairs: A Composer's Journal* (1970), *Pure Contraption: A Composer's Essays* (1974), *The Final Diary* (1974), and *An Absolute Gift: A New Diary* (1978). In 1976 Rorem received the Pulitzer Prize in Music for his orchestral suite *Air Music*, commissioned and premièred by the Cincinnati Symphony, Thomas Schippers conducting. His music has been performed by virtually every major soloist and orchestra both here and abroad.

THE FOLLOWING INTERVIEW with Ned Rorem was taped by Winston Leyland, editor of *Gay Sunshine*, at Rorem's New York apartment in late October 1973. The interview was edited and revised in May 1974. A profile of Ned Rorem, along with excerpts from his diaries, was published in *Gay Sunshine* no. 17 (March–April 1973), and an excerpt, *Being Alone*, from a later diary appeared in *Gay Sunshine* no. 47 (published 1982 in book format).

Winston Leyland interviews
NED ROREM

LEYLAND: In your *New York Diary* you have an aphorism: "The beautiful have a more drastic challenge than the ugly in aging, for only they must habituate to a change." How do you feel you've met this challenge, now that you've turned fifty, which you've considered a kind of crucial turning point?

ROREM: It's merely an epigram. There's really nothing to add to an epigram because it is its own explanation. The implication is also that I considered myself beautiful when I wrote it, which was twenty-five years ago. Well, I've been fifty for two days and it's less traumatic than thirty. When I was twenty-nine and a half I turned jaundiced with trauma because it was a thing which could happen to anyone but oneself. If you can be thirty, you can die; that I got past, and was willing to die, gave me a new lease on life. There's nothing to add except I'm proud, and I've had a nice life. The difference between me now and, say, fifteen years back, is that I'm more happy. No—happy's not the word. The state of happiness is a stupid state; I'm less miserable. Misery is unbecoming after a certain age and can be controlled consciously, assuming you're in reasonably good health. Nothing's more inelegant than to be unhappily in love after forty, or to show it—to go around crying on people's shoulders. Certain preoccupations replace others with age. It's a favorite topic of the all-knowing Colette: the horror of aging, still falling in love, not being able to adjust to unrequited infatuations and therefore going to pot. Nothing is less graceful than an unhappy person. If the unhappy person is young and handsome, he or she just might get away with tears flowing down those downy cheeks. But I decided one day, okay, I've done all that, I've let myself crack up sentimentally for too long. Let's stop it. There are more pressing concerns. Like, the work must come before the anxiety (which it always did, for that matter). This planet's in too much of a mess for my private vanities to take precedence. So that's my first reaction to fifty. How I'll feel next week I don't know, but for the moment things seem pretty fine. True, I no longer see through a glass darkly, but realize ever more keenly that my heartbeats are numbered. All around me friends are dying off. Yet as the future shrinks the past expands, and the expanse takes on a new significance every day—which is nourishing.

LEYLAND: I didn't know your birthday was two days ago.

ROREM: Yes. Same day as Sarah Bernhardt's, Franz Liszt's, and Johnny Carson's. . . . Again, my little epigram about adapting: a perfect face altered is more dismaying for those who have looked at it than is the alteration of a face they never thought perfect. Auden's face as it aged intrigued but didn't appall people because it always was a crisscross of spider webs. Lana Turner's face disturbs people now because it once existed specifically for being perfect. (Poets don't get face-lifts.) With me, it's not a question of whether I was in fact pretty, but of whether I thought I was. Still, I was smart enough never to let that thought be foremost, although the fact that I even wrote about it so much in the diaries embarrasses me now. I can't think of anything more to say on this.

LEYLAND: Aging seems to be a more traumatic thing for some gay people because of the emphasis which is put on youth in the gay community. You know, the "over-the-hill-at-thirty" syndrome.

ROREM: There's many a well-adjusted homosexual over the age of fifty, and many maladjusted heterosexuals. It just isn't true that gay people are lonelier than ungay people (or whatever the opposite of gay is), and I'm in a position to know.

LEYLAND: I think there's a question of ageism in the gay community to some extent. There are a lot of older, lonely people around who perhaps don't have their work, their art, to uplift them.

ROREM: Well, along with other preoccupations, sex, for instance, as a pastime, doesn't concern me as it used to. The competitive scene of making out no longer seems so urgent. I do like people to respond to me, but to respond to my intelligence more than to my physique. Of course, we all want to be loved for ourselves alone, but none of us are, for the good reason that there's no such animal. I don't put myself in a position to be rejected any longer, and that's a relief. I do see a lot of ageism, for instance, vis-à-vis my own parents, or other older people here and there. Most of the people I frequent regularly are roughly my age, at least here in America. Fortunately, I don't lust for young people, and do not curry their approval.

LEYLAND: In the interview I did with Christopher Isherwood, he talked about his gayness as being crucial to his life as an artist. He gave a quote at the end of the interview to that point: he said that he couldn't imagine himself not being gay. Do you feel the same has been true of your own life, or to what extent has your sexuality been interwoven with your work?

ROREM: How can one know? As an infant, almost from the time I knew how to talk, I knew what I wanted to be. It was just a question of tossing a coin—which kind of artist should I be: a performing musician, or a so-called creative musician? or shall I be a writer, or a dancer, or a whatever? Since I was in America rather than in Europe, which is a country of specialists rather than of general practitioners, I learned you have to be one thing; but even to this day I hate to pigeonhole myself. I'm a composer, but also a performing musician (I give concerts all over the country) and a writer, and more. I never wanted to be what other little boys want to be: a fireman, or Tarzan, or...Oh, I did aspire to be a pastry cook for a while. Still, it never occurred to me that everybody in grammar school wasn't exactly like me; it never occurred to me that when they went home in the afternoon they didn't sit down and play Ravel on the piano, and then try to write pieces that sounded like Ravel. It never occurred to me that they didn't read Hawthorne or Gide. It was a rude awakening—the lack of curiosity I found in my fellow man. By the same token I cannot categorize myself. To be homosexual is too generalizing; I can't say "we," not even "we composers," or "we writers," or "we fifty-year-olds." I say "they." Therefore I can only refer to my *sexuality*. Now a black person is demonstrably black, there's nothing he can do about it. He's black if he's a scientist, he's black as he looks into a microscope, he's black as he reads Plato. We can see that he is. Meanwhile, a homosexual is only homosexual when he's being homosexual. He's not demonstrably so when he's writing music, or when he's thinking about a recipe for carrot cake. Homosexuality is a condition, whereas to be black is not a frame of mind, it's a physical identity.

LEYLAND: I don't agree with you all the way on that. A writer, artist, composer can be (and often is) consciously gay in the act of creating; and a gay sensibility permeates all the work of some writers, for example John Wieners.

ROREM: I don't claim I'm not gay, but my sexuality is only one section of what I am. Certainly it's conditioned me down to my toenails. But as to how it's conditioned me, I'll never know. Let me add that I've never suffered from being what I am, or *particularly* what I am. When I told that to Kenneth Pitchford—who has now become an ultraradical liberationist—he said you *have* suffered, you just don't know it. Well, I've faced far more hurdles for being a composer than for my bedtime inclinations. I feel more discriminated against as an artist in our America than as a queer. The milieu in which I evolved as an adolescent in Chicago was an "artistic" one. My parents, although not swinging people, were and are cultivated and intelligent; we never discussed sex (a case of tact between generations, although there was a lot of gaudy rumpus when I was a kid); still the community was on my side. And even as an artist in this society, if I feel discriminated against, as a composer, I still feel I've been awfully lucky. I've been appreciated for what I am able to do, and appreciation is the food of inspiration.

LEYLAND: Don't you think that perhaps you've not been exposed to as much discrimination as a gay person because of the artistic circles in which you were moving, such as in the fifties in France?

ROREM: France is not all that open-minded, and is also the most heterosexual of European countries. But don't forget, I lived here all through the 1940s. By definition the category to which I have always been drawn is not homosexual so much as literary. Though it's dumb for literati to be antihomosexual, a lot of them are. I mean, Mailer still gets a cheap giggle on TV when he refers to the Marquis de Sade as a faggot. Everybody laughs nervously. Now the nervousness is not because of the word "faggot"; it's because they don't know the Marquis de Sade. Is it conceivable that Mailer would say "nigger" as he says "faggot" for an easy reaction? Well, that doesn't bother me if I'm in a milieu which is not inherently antihomosexual, being literary and thus inherently individualistic, as opposed, say, to a military milieu. It would be no more than vulgar of Mailer to make his quip in my presence. In that sense I wouldn't feel discriminated against. If I were among baseball players and they said it, I would feel, well, what am I doing here anyway? I've nothing in common with them— not because of sexuality but because of education. I've no more in common with them than Kafka or Kissinger do. I may one day suffer from society, but it'll be the suffering of, shall we say, postmenopause....

I do ultimately feel more at ease in a homosexual group than in an essentially straight one. But again, whatever the group, I'm more at home with intelligent than with stupid people. I'm basically shy. That may be hard to believe, because I talk so much, and because I write diaries, which when they first came out were thought of as candid. But the very fact of keeping a diary implies a kind of reticence. In a sense the diarist writes what he is unable to say. As a terribly timid kid I told myself, categorically and calmly: be shy if you want to but no one will pay attention to you. You're as bright as the others in this room, saying their witty empty things. Shyness will get you no place. Yet even now, to speak out at a party means to break through a barrier, which makes me (unjustly) intolerant of people who are shy. If I can conquer it so can they. Shyness surely comes from a person's sexuality, just as everything that a person is contributes to what he produces. May I contradict that by its opposite? Could one say there is such a thing as homosexual music? There are works of literature that I admire terrifically, while feeling they lack a necessary queer spice. That's bigotry in reverse, perhaps, but I mean it. Although I'm attracted toward supermasculinity in humans, I loathe supermasculinity in art. Although I am not attracted toward effeminacy in a person, that's precisely what I admire in art. Which is probably what appeals to me in French art. French homosexuals are not afraid of delicacy. Ballsiness—that is, male defiance—is not an ingredient of twentieth-century European culture. The male artifacts of a composer like William Schuman, a writer like James Jones, a painter like Jackson Pollock are strictly "made in USA." Of course, the greatest art contains both gentleness and savagery. But isn't that also the definition of a true man and a true woman?

LEYLAND: What's your response to the gay liberation movement and its ideology in regard to the oppression of gay people? Do you respond in a negative or positive way to the gay activist movement?

ROREM: I think gay liberation is important. If I haven't done anything about it in a public way it's because I'm a coward. My mother, at the age of seventy-five, stood on street corners to impeach Nixon, to foster abortion, to solicit funds to stop the war in Vietnam. Gay liberation (which we never discuss in any but the most objective way) she's entirely sympathetic with, as is my father. It's something I only kind of enter in with, but whether I'm right or wrong, I'm right for me. The thing is, I am first of all a composer, and anything I can do for any group of people, I want to do as a composer, as Benjamin Britten does with his concerts to raise money for peace in the world. I would willingly give a concert for Gay Liberation. Not as a gay musician necessarily, just as a musician.

Let me put it this way. I'm against Gay Liberation except where it counts. I dislike seeing people stretching virtually every remark, as certain women do, into a sexist remark. Recently in Vancouver to give a concert I read that Jill Johnston was there too, giving a speech. And I said, "Well, I have nothing to do tonight, I'll go listen to her," and I did. Afterward, as we got into the question period, she said, "Nobody's asking me any questions. I usually like some hostility at this point." So I raised my hand and introduced myself and said, "I don't feel hostile, but I'm willing to help get this show on the road. Do you remember that I once sent you a letter that was printed in the *Village Voice*?" She said, "Yes, I know that. I know your book. I know you. You're a sexist." She had the answer before the question was even posed and that was so hopelessly depressing that I simply after half an hour got up and left. We were getting no place. It was not a meeting of minds. I'm for, in other words, Women's Liberation, except as it is misused. Ditto for Gay Lib. But the compassionless infighting is as distasteful as Watergate. There are people, after all, who don't care one way or another about your sex life if they care about you. Not to make an issue of one's penchants doesn't imply one denies them. In my books, I have never said, "I am homosexual." I have simply said "I am sexual." I've never concealed the nature of my love affairs. I've also taken other people's tolerance so for granted that I'm alarmed by any countercurrent. Suddenly there's a new generation who also take it for granted, but far more defiantly.

LEYLAND: This compassionless infighting, as you call it, has occurred too often in the gay movement. In an issue of the gay male feminist journal *Double-F* (happily soon defunct), I was included on a "Gay Enemies" list along with just about every other full-time gay male liberationist in the country. Actually, I was honored rather than hurt. It was like being on Nixon's "Secret Enemies" list.

ROREM: I like your magazine because of your concern with the whole person, and not just the groin nor just flag-waving, if you'll pardon the expression.... To hear these things that you're telling me now about *Double-F* brings bitter tears. Infighting, to me, is a most unhappy thing.

LEYLAND: In your book *Critical Affairs* you say there isn't a homosexual art as such any more than there's heterosexual, female, or black art, although you do say that "art may come from the experience of being these things." You also say that art dealing directly with homosexual experience does not necessarily deepen an understanding of heterosexual relationships. Don't you think that art dealing with homosexual experience deepens our understanding of the homosexual experience? I could mention some of the poetry of John Wieners, Allen Ginsberg, Frank O'Hara—poetry which has certainly deepened my understanding.

ROREM: It doesn't deepen our understanding of homosexuality. It deepens our understanding of art, the human condition. I'm not sure what you mean by homosexual art, but it's a beguiling question and there could be many definitions. A comprehensive editorial on homosexuality is more persuasive, for the so-called average man, than an art work on the subject—whatever that might be. You just mentioned Frank O'Hara. I think if Frank O'Hara were told that his subject was homosexuality, that could come as a surprise to him.

LEYLAND: I don't mean that homosexuality was his subject. I think there was a homosexual sensibility, language underlying all his poems. This comes more to the surface perhaps in some poems in which he was more explicit, such as the poem about visiting a gay bar with friends.

ROREM: That's not quite what you said before. By that token you could say the homosexual sensibility of Hemingway comes to the surface—he is so vitriolically anti-queer that he's obviously queer. So that's a kind of homosexuality too. I thought you were talking about subject matter, not sensibility.

LEYLAND: And subject matter too. In the case of many poets gay subject matter is very important in their writing. John Wieners, for instance, writes many poems on gay themes, or connected with the gay experience in some way.

ROREM: Why say "gay experience"? Why not just say "experience"? Why qualify that any more than you would say that *Romeo and Juliet* is on the heterosexual experience? Why don't you forget the word "gay" in a case of that sort. Insofar as *The City and the Pillar*, for instance, has homosexuality as its theme, it's a bad book. It might be good propaganda but not good literature. Do you think that for President Nixon, the reading of Wieners' poetry would be more convincing than the reading of an essay on the subject?

LEYLAND: I don't think he'd get anything out of John Wieners' poetry *or* out of an essay. Nixon is totally corrupt with zero sensitivity. I think for many gay people, especially when "coming out," reading John Wieners' poetry can be a catalytic experience, can be revelation. It was for me, and I told John that recently.

ROREM: A lot of things "work" that are not "art," yet they can be a great help to men and women who are coming out. Some very intelligent people are just not concerned with art, while many unintelligent people, who are very uptight about sexuality, don't need poetry but therapy. I feel strongly that art doesn't change people. It reinforces what they already know.

LEYLAND: I agree. Poetry did not change me. But it *was* immensely catalytic.

ROREM: As for homosexual subject matter, we can talk about that until the cows come home and never put our finger on what exactly it is. What it is changes with each generation. Let me give you a political example. You have the recording of my *War Scenes*. In 1969, the French baritone Gérard Souzay asked me to write a song cycle for his American tour. I wanted to compose something for him that, with his French accent, wouldn't sound funny. The words of my beloved Frank O'Hara or of John Ashbery were just too colloquially American. Now, the Vietnam misadventure was at its height at that time, so what could I use as a text that would be both good literature and *engagé* which Souzay could put across with his little accent? I wanted to use something to express my concern for this mess we're in. Yet I cannot set current news items to music about bloody injustices. Lots of young poets go on the assumption that "to know where it's at" makes them poets. That war is bad and peace is good does not of itself make literature. Some great poets are terrific bigots. To be a poet does not mean to be right; too many bad poems in the name of peace prove this.

LEYLAND: There's bad music too.

ROREM: Sure. Well, since there's always the question that as a composer I'm going to write bad music, I at least didn't want to set bad verse to it. In 1969 I wanted to set words that had a degree of universality. So I went to Walt Whitman, who had served me well in the past. I didn't want to take verse of his, so I used his Civil War diary, *Specimen Days*, which he kept while he was a medical assistant, writing of his attitudes both tranquil and devastating. The sense of the text could apply not only to the Civil War, but to the Trojan War or to Vietnam, or, as we sit here today, to the war in Israel. Walt's words are not about *the* war, they're about *a* war. They're about generalized strife, applicable to you or to me, to poor and rich and guilty and innocent. Generalized by an individual! So I composed a cycle which is effective, but one of the reasons, perhaps the only reason it's effective, is because Whitman wrote the words. By the same token, not just any bright versifier treating homosexuality can be persuasive; it's how good the treatment is. So that's not homosexual art, that's John Wieners' art, or Whitman's art, or Goodman's art. If it touches a strain in you as a homosexual, that is not because Whitman was homosexual, but because he was a poet.

LEYLAND: I would disagree on that; I doubt that you can separate the two.

ROREM: You mean the mere fact that a poet is a homosexual is going to touch you?

LEYLAND: Not necessarily. Whitman, for example, touches me because he was an insightful poet *and* a gay brother. There's a gay sensibility throughout his writing. A good poet who is not homosexual cannot write really of the homosexual experience. It will not be persuasive at all.

ROREM: Yet the inverse does not held true. I mean, E. M. Forster's weakest book (though I happen to love it) is *Maurice*. It's weak structurally. It's a fairy tale, ah yes sir, with specifically homosexuality as the subject matter. It's a trick, and a fantasy at that. But Forster, or any homosexual, can write of heterosexual experience, because from what do we all learn if not from our heterosexual environs, after all? Remember that chic vogue of criticizing or of digging *Who's Afraid of Virginia Woolf* because the protagonists were drag queens? As if a homosexual can't write about other things! One writes about what one knows, or what one imagines, and Albee is no more a woman than Shakespeare—author of *Macbeth*—was a murderer.

LEYLAND: My point is that successful poems touching on the gay experience are almost always poems that have been written by good poets who happen to be gay—poets who have gotten into their gayness and integrated it into their life, their writing. *Maurice* may be an inferior novel (although that's debatable). But I think it's sad that *Maurice* could not be published while Forster was alive. He did suffer for his homosexuality, and perhaps punished himself by withholding the book during the last decades of his life when it could have been published.

ROREM: I'm very much against censorship, of course, but I do believe that limitations—whether imposed by the artist on himself or by the state, are not a deterrent to communication. Art is form. Does it really make much difference for a novelist? He knows many ways for sidestepping censorship. It's not as though he were a preacher or a journalist. Censorship makes far less difference in questions of art than in questions of daily life. A work of art will come to the fore, censorship or not. Of course an artist needs freedom. But even more, he needs discipline—he's going to set his own limitations in any case. Creation is not solely the spewing forth of unreasoned emotion. Control is the very heart of poetry—to be able to say things within a set framework, or by allusion. I wouldn't presume to define pornography (the definition of pornography changes every three minutes). But in the long run, Sophocles or Tolstoy or even Jane Austen can be very very sexy because their excitation is in context. Hardcore porno, by depicting sex out of context, ends up more wearying than stimulating. Similarly, homosexuality for its own sake proves nothing.

LEYLAND: To return to Walt Whitman, who I gather has been a source of constant inspiration for you. You mentioned in one of your books that you used

Whitman's strophic format, development of ideas, in your tone poem *Eagles.*
You also set five Whitman poems for baritone and clavichord in 1957, and then
there's the setting from *Specimen Days* that you just mentioned. Perhaps you
could talk a little more about Whitman and why he has meant so much to you?

ROREM: Well, I've never musicalized any of his so-called boy poems—unless
they're all boy poems. God knows he was sexual, all sperm and growth, and becoming rather than dying. But I love and need death too, and Whitman essentially is not about death, he's not pessimistic. Like Roethke, who was a most
morbid human—in his poetry he was optimistic and wrote about plant life and
resurgence.

It may be of interest to know how I happened to compose the orchestral tone
poem *Eagles.* It's a nonvocal piece which contradictorily employs a poem rather
than a musical structure as format. Now music cannot be based on, say, sonnet
or ballad or sestina forms because there's no such thing as rhyme in music. Only
words rhyme. What I did there is sort of amusing from a musician's standpoint.
I took a Whitman poem about eagles fucking in mid-air. They clench claws,
start to bleed, gyrate like a wheel, and fall a mile in the air while having a great
orgasm. Then she flies off in her direction and he flies off in his direction, and
the poet, who was watching this during his morning walk along the river, is
somehow changed, and continues to walk. I took each one of those eighteen
lines and translated them into music. Yet music has no literary connotations.
None. Except as it deals directly with words, as in songs. Vocal music is bastard
music, being the illegitimate result of music's rape of poetry. That doesn't mean
bastards can't be healthy and stimulating. If a wordless tone poem has a program, as *Eagles* does or as Richard Strauss's tone poems do, it's only by virtue
of what the composer, in words, tells you it signifies.

To write a song I need good poetry first. Second, it must be my kind of good
poetry. My kind of good poetry as opposed, say, to Pierre Boulez's kind, or
George Crumb's or Lou Harrison's. It has to communicate when sung. That
might sound obvious. Yet another composer has other criteria and may not be
concerned about the words being understood when they're sung. In fact, he
could set them to music disjointly. In Gregorian chant the word "deo" can be
protracted for five minutes. And if you come in late you're lost. Theologically
you know the word is "deo," but it's not the meaning that counts, it's the meaning of the meaning. But I'm interested in the words being understood on a
straight verbal plane as they are sung, so I use them prosodically, as we speak
them. I don't distort words to where you can't understand them, or repeat
arbitrarily words that the poet has not repeated. My kind of good poetry
means, then, that it's got to be fairly easy. I'm not interested in setting T. S.
Eliot, which is a little bit complicated, or Marianne Moore, though I love and
respect them.

LEYLAND: But you did set John Ashbery's work—rather difficult poetry.

ROREM: John Ashbery is complicated but in another way. I did set John Ashbery's "Some Trees" for three voices and piano. Now that's a different concept.
Nobody "understands" Ashbery anyway. I mean, it's not poetry that you understand the same way that you understand, let's say, a Shakespeare sonnet
which has one meaning. It might have puns and things, but it has a specific

message. The elusiveness of Ashbery's poetry is its very nature. The elusiveness of Eliot's poetry is not its nature. An Eliot poem asks you to interpret it, to find references. It dares you to find the key. John Ashbery's poems don't challenge an interpretation. They're asking you to let them flow over your skin. Sensual experience can't be meaningful in any literary way, at least while it's occurring. So music only adds to the fun. Kenneth Koch I've set a good deal of. I just did his opera *Bertha*, which of course is very easy if you know *Bertha*. It's all of the Shakespeare king plays reduced to ten pages: a huge tragic farce in miniature. It's very funny and it's very sad. Very direct too, and all about President Nixon. Bertha, the mad queen of Norway, is so obsessed with invading countries she finally invades her own. We're performing it with a mezzo-soprano, Beverly Wolff, and a little chorus of nine singers. As a play, it makes plain sense. Kenneth's poems don't make sense in the sense of sense, they make sense in the sense of poetry.

LEYLAND: You've also set poems by Paul Goodman.

ROREM: Well, Paul is something quite else—both literal-minded and yet romantic in the expansive nineteenth-century manner. He's sort of my Goethe, the poet I constantly turn to, who constantly satisfies me. And his poetry is just the opposite of his prose writing. It's sentimental, it rhymes, it's non-intellectual. Yet he doesn't say anything in his poetry that he doesn't say in his prose. Because everything that Paul was, was poetry. Like Freud he was a poet first, a thinker second. And I'm sure he thought that way about himself. Paul's approval had much to do with my being an artist today. I'm only one of hundreds of people who felt that. (Here I'm confusing him in both past and present tenses, and he's been dead for over a year. Do poets die? Yes they do, and the meaning of their value alters immediately.)

LEYLAND: He was a catalyst for you when you were in your early twenties?

ROREM: Midteens. Paul was a born Socratic. The two best minds of our time are Paul Goodman's and Wystan Auden's. I single them out—the Compleat Jew and the Compleat Goy—because poets as a rule are not thinkers. Because these two were very well trained, they proposed logical solutions for world problems, and were able to write prose—a sensible prose that was granted authority by virtue of the fact that they were great poets. The prose, say, of a Wilfred Sheed, or a Benjamin DeMott, or of all these clever book reviewers, does not in my opinion have the same force as Auden's or Goodman's, because either they are not poets themselves or they lack a requisite classical background. Auden, unlike Goodman, was not a Socratic type. It was important to Paul that he be surrounded by the young who would listen to him as to the Sermon on the Mount. It wasn't that important to Auden to be personally heard. He might have been the life of the party and assumed everyone would listen while he talked, but he didn't visit the schools and tell people how to raise children or to have proper orgasms or to keep out of the army the way Goodman did. By doing that, Paul did, I think, cheat in a way. It was unfair of Paul, who for many years was a practicing analyst, to try to seduce his cute patients and not the ugly ones. Yet he was a responsible husband and parent and had time for anyone who needed him.

LEYLAND: I met Goodman once very briefly when he came to a small gay-lib-consciousness rap group that we had in Berkeley in 1971.

ROREM: What do you remember him saying?

LEYLAND: He talked a little about gay oppression, what it meant to him and how changes will come about. I remember we disagreed with his reformist approach—that if we wait long enough the laws against gay people will be changed automatically. We felt there needed to be more activism. I respected him immensely, but I also felt that there was too much of a tendency on his part toward being a guru. People reacted a little negatively to that—perhaps a natural reaction among young people.

ROREM: I think gurus are a pain in the neck. They cater to weakness—to grooving rather than to thought. For the general public Paul was a mind rather than a body, which is what gurus are not. God knows he could turn people off. And God knows he was a proselytizer, didn't listen to other people. However, his was such an extraordinary brain that I'm inclined to give him the benefit of the doubt. He did have answers. As for the gay oppression thing, I imagine, between us, it's something that Paul wouldn't have grasped for the simple reason that he grasped it only too well. In the way that I was talking about earlier, he didn't use a word like "homosexuality." Not because he avoided it but because he took it so for granted. Oh, he was so sexual (which I'm not)—always making passes in front of his wife or children even! In principle he was bisexual; in fact his eyes lit up mainly for boys. After I was no longer a boy he grew to see me as a person, then as a rival. Unfair but understandable. Paul's books are full of people who screw each other without asking questions or making problems. Outside the books the problems were whether people were attracted to each other (that is, to him)—not whether they were homosexual! I think that's what he would have assumed your rap group was: not a problem of societal oppression, but sexual beings amongst themselves.

Like many gay people, Paul lacked humor (although Auden had humor). A person can become so great as to be removed from standard questions. Not that young homosexuals have all that much humor, or young anybody. Much of survival I suppose, even living to the age of ten, requires a sense of balance, and humor is balance—seeing two sides of the same coin, or even three. But so is art balance. So is imagination. A lot of artists don't have much humor either (starting with Chaplin, though he is a terrific comic). As Paul grew older, he grew understandably disillusioned with the whole human race; and since with people in any given circumstances he would usually be the wisest, and see them go on making the same mistakes...I can't help but think he died of a broken heart.

LEYLAND: In your book *Critical Affairs*, you say that artists care less about being misunderstood than about being heard, but that we are all misunderstood most of the time. Do you feel this has been true in both your life and music?

ROREM: Gide's famous remark, "Don't be too quick to understand me," is a quip all artists like. When people come up and say, "Oh, I just understand you so well," that makes me feel transparent. Did you misquote a little bit?

LEYLAND: The quote of yours I've got here is "We are all misunderstood most of the time."

ROREM: I do believe it. A work of art, so long as it is art, is never understood. One does not understand art. We understand analyses of art. But we never understand the art any better for the analysis. A real work of art is like the human soul, without finite limits, and changes definition according to who looks at it. So what I meant is not "an artist wants to be understood." What I meant was "he wants not to be misunderstood." Therefore, do not misunderstand him. But I have never read a diagnosis of anything I've ever made that I agreed with. Although I'm pleased, I'm pleased because of the length rather than the insight.

LEYLAND: Is this true of both your writing and your music?

ROREM: Particularly the music. I don't know what my writing is. I don't even know if it's art. I don't even know what art is. But if I'm an artist, it's as a musician. I am a musician who also writes prose, not a prose writer who happens to write music. It's as a musician that I am talking to you. Only as a musician do I have any authority in what I say.

LEYLAND: In *Critical Affairs* you talk about an artist judging his own work under acid. Is that "acid test" meant to be a put-on? Have you taken acid, or is that just a bon mot?

ROREM: It's a bon mot, and I have. I took mescaline three times many years ago, and discussed the first trip at length in *New York Diary.* The only reason for taking taking psychedelics now would be under a control—it is so startlingly informing. I know exactly what I would like to do: an investigation of problems in musical grammar. I would like to discover wherein I have cheated, because we all cheat all the time without knowing it. With each breath we draw we compromise. Life is a compromise, and so is art. But sometimes it's the right compromise. Wrong compromises are cheating, and that's what makes a bad artist out of a bad artist: to take the easy way out, given a set of rules that you've assigned to yourself for constructing this or that piece. You can't always see when you're cheating. Nor do we always know when we're cheating sexually. The human language being already such an artificial situation, we use music to reinforce our artifices. We use it to dissemble rather than to reveal. Musical language is a language of dissemblement. Art is a language of disguise. The artist guards himself and his work. Sometimes he will—I'm mixing my metaphors all over the place, but I hope you follow me—sometimes he will guard himself carefully, sometimes uncarefully, and he can't always know until years later when he looks back and says, "My God, what a good day that was. What a terrific poem that was, and right off the top of my head!" So I would like to hear my own music under LSD and see wherein the seams are closely knit or falling apart. But I say all this as an aside to that essentially cute phrase you just quoted. (Paradoxically, music is sometimes defined as a language—a language not too vague but too precise to be described by words.)

LEYLAND: You mentioned composer Lou Harrison in your book *Music and People,* and you call him one of the most gifted melodists of our century. I had the honor to meet Lou last year—a charming, brilliant man. I spent a weekend with Lou and Bill Colvig down in Aptos, California. Perhaps you'd like to talk a little about his music, or your own music.

ROREM: It's hard for me to talk about my own music. Composers always talk "around" their own music, since that music itself speaks so much more clearly. Presumably. I did the entry for Lou in *Grove's Dictionary* this year so I know his music in depth, as they say. Not that I know all of it, but I've known some of it for a really long time and care about it. That's saying plenty, because I don't like anybody anymore. When people ask, "What American composers do you like?" I always scratch my head and say "Oh God" and Lou Harrison is the only name I can squeeze out. (Naturally there are others.)

LEYLAND: I heard in concert a beautiful, soul-piercing work by Lou last summer—a setting in Esperanto of the Buddhist Heart Sutra. I've long admired his music.

ROREM: Lou Harrison's got wit and that counts for a lot. Nobody has wit anymore. Not even me. He gets in a rut sometimes with those eternal ostinatos—a mannerism I have copied, I fear. But on the whole Lou Harrison has a terrific melodic sense, the sense that most counts, music being all inherently melodic. Which doesn't mean it has to be a simple-minded street song, or a Stephen Foster tune, or even Purcell or Puccini. But any composer worthy of the name is basically a singer. Inasmuch as any author is good, it's not because he deals with homosexuality, but because he's a writer. Inasmuch as a poet is good, it's because he's a poet, not because he's gay. Inasmuch as a composer is a composer, it's not because he's a man or a woman, nor because he's wise and experienced, but because he's got a singer in him trying to get out. All music is song. Now Harrison is a songster if ever there was one. He just reeks of memorable melody. I like him and I like his ideas about a lot of things. Like Paul Goodman, Lou was liberated long before one "was liberated." It must be made clear, though, that both Lou and Paul would have been thought eccentric, not being average people, and highly noticeable. Their sexuality had much to do with it, and certainly their persona had much to do with their sexuality.

To be homosexual today is not eccentric necessarily. A man doesn't have to be a deep intellectual or a mad drag queen today to be homosexual. In New York today he can be a warrior, a truck driver, as well as a maker of women's hats. But eccentricity was a mark of an artist far more in the forties than it is today, and certainly of a homosexual artist. I'm contradicting myself to some extent. To be a pacifist is not particularly unusual, but it was unusual in the thirties and forties, like Lou and Paul. To be intelligent is very unusual any time, and to use one's intelligence to better the world is most unusual of all.

LEYLAND: Maybe you'd like to talk a little bit about Frank O'Hara. You have often set his words to music. What were your feelings about him as an artist?

ROREM: Frank O'Hara was the least selfish of artists. Most artists are out for themselves, like everybody else. They're interested in other people's art only as that applies to themselves. Frank O'Hara was interested in other people's work for its own sake. He could spend hours, months, helping other poets, even bad poets. Or writing blurbs for painters—unsigned blurbs that did nothing for his own posterity. Thus his poetry was generous too—not because it was about other people. He's written an awful lot of lazy junk, but at his best, the split-second on-the-spot poems are good precisely by virtue of being split-second on-the-spot, and they melt your heart. Every time I read it I weep at his poem about Billie Holiday dying, an uncopyable masterpiece that young poets have all tried to copy. Look around at all the imitators of Ashbery, of Koch, of O'Hara! They say, "If Frank can get up and recite a poem that says 'I shit,' so can we." But it doesn't work, because Frank was a poet and they are not. The Masturbation School of Poetry declares: "Anything is valid because it happens to us and we are poets." What makes a poet a poet? It's one thing nobody can define. Frank's poems had at their best the blood of life, and their poems are tubercular, yet the subject matter is identical. He was fun to work with because, in this age of specialists, he adored collaborating in a variety of fields. He collaborated in a tactile way with dancers, painters, novelists, sculptors, other poets. He even collaborated with me and I hate collaboration. My ego doesn't permit me to work gracefully with others. But I did with Frank on two occasions, and happily. Our "Four Dialogues" are not great poetry or great music but they work. And the little poem he wrote on Poulenc's death is lovely, and my music for that works too.

Interestingly, Frank O'Hara was not all that famous while he was alive. He died around the same time as Randall Jarrell, who was an established poet. When a painter dies his property becomes more valuable, because a painting is something that you own. Poetry or music cannot be owned. A composer when he dies is usually forgotten, at least for a while, or becomes immortal. (Bartók was canonized within a week after he died.) The same happens with poets. Frank O'Hara died, and New York City was overrun with widows of all sexes. I've never seen such spiteful behavior. The number of people who acted like barnyard creatures gnashing at each other instead of coming together in a common cause. Each one said, "Frank loved me the most. Frank gave me this poem. It's my poem. Frank wrote that for me."

When you were in Frank's presence, tête-à-tête, you were the only person in Frank's life. You might not think about him the next day, or he might not think about you, but he gave of himself individually to every single person he talked to. And he talked to everyone, important people, unimportant people. He couldn't not talk. He saw the worst minds of his generation destroyed, and the best. It was the same to him. It's not that he loved people but that he made them feel they were worth something. So when there was no more Frank, everybody felt widowed and instead of coming together with benevolence they hated each other for a while. But the hate turned to practicality. The collected works of Frank O'Hara are now out and have sold. His letters are coming out. And other collections. There's a Young Poets' Award now in his name. All of it is very sweet. He has become more famous than Randall Jarrell. He is a cult. I wonder what his reaction would be to this.

In 1970 the Frank O'Hara Foundation said, "Let's give a memorial concert, and ask a bunch of composers to set words of Frank O'Hara to music." They got a slew of Frank's poems and sent that around to a couple dozen composers, and said, "We're having a memorial for Frank at the Whitney Museum; set his poems to music as you would like, and we'll perform them." It failed, of course. If a composer didn't set his words to music while Frank was living, why bother now? Also a lot of it didn't work because the generations change so quickly (as we were saying a while ago). Frank has been dead since 1966. I often think of how Frank would react to Gay Liberation, to women's liberation, or to Susan Sontag, or to his own protégés. Frank is very much situated in my mind, and in many people's minds, as the sixties. He's not a poet of the seventies. Things would be slightly out of focus to Frank if he suddenly came back. None of these composers had a point of view because they were all seventies, and Frank had been dead too long yet not long enough. He spoke with a sixties accent, and they composed with a seventies accent just by virtue of being alive. And that's why it would be interesting to know how Frank would react.

If Frank were alive now he would not be forty, as when he died, but forty-seven. A forty-year-old Frank resuscitated and put into 1973. A forty-seven-year-old Frank would have evolved with the times. Taking the old Frank and putting him in this room with you and me there on that couch, it's possible that not only would he not be able to breathe the air because it's become so polluted (you and I are conditioned to it because we're alive), but he wouldn't know what the hell we were talking about. The issue of Gay Liberation for instance would come as a slap in the face. It would either seem so obvious because it *is* obvious (like anything that's truly needed becomes, after the fact), or so remote he might not comprehend. Of course, that's as vain as asking: how would Bach react to Stravinsky? Bach was a great musician. Stravinsky was a great musician. But that they should thus naturally "understand" each other doesn't follow. Frank O'Hara was lovable and tough. He should not have died, but he did. It was an Irish death. He died talking, and probably drunk. Because he hadn't said all he had to say, his death is a tragedy.

LEYLAND: It would be interesting to hear more on your relationship with Cocteau, although you do go into that somewhat in your books.

ROREM: Everything I know about Cocteau I've already written. That's why I find myself so uninteresting any more: I can just refer you to a page in a book. To meet Cocteau once was to know him, because he was such an outgoing man. He had to be liked. And he also had to spill his seed, so to speak, to disseminate himself indiscriminately throughout the world. He gave of himself to an awful lot of people. All who knew him felt that they were the only person in his life, at least while in his presence, because he exuded a charitable flood of fire. I've only met three or four big people who have such warmth. It may be affectation or opportunism, but it can't be faked.

With Frank it wasn't warmth so much as generosity summed up in the words, "Let me love you, let me help you." With Cocteau it was, "I will labor so you will love me, help me." It takes however as much energy to be loved as to love. A person who wants to be loved must toil at it. Anyone can love. It's harder to be loved than to love: you have to have something a lover doesn't have. Jean Cocteau was loved, and he worked at it, while Frank O'Hara worked at loving. There's the basic difference between them. When Frank died he left mourners of all sexes, each of whom considered themselves his official widow. When Cocteau died he left grandchildren (so to speak), long since weaned and very derisive. Of course, Frank's premature death flung him headlong into a vogue that's still going strong, while Cocteau was out of fashion and forgotten. Cocteau talked and talked, like Tallulah Bankhead. Impossible to get a word in edgewise. Yet he remembered everything you said, and threw it back at you the next time, like Tallulah did. But whereas Tallulah talked without rhyme or reason, and none of her sentences scanned, every Cocteau phrase was a ruby polished right there on the spot for you. Of course he may have pulled out that same jewel for someone else that morning, but while he was there he was shining only for you.

LEYLAND: In your *Diaries* you have written a lot about loneliness and age.

ROREM: I think about loneliness and age, that loneliness is a part of life, though I'm not sure that as one gets older he necessarily becomes more lonely. But loneliness becomes more uncovered—one becomes more aware of it. Loneliness can be good for you. I am fairly self-sufficient and have work that concerns me. May the work continue to interest me for the rest of my life! As to homosexual loneliness (since you asked), again, like heterosexual loneliness it stems from sexual rejection—not from repression so much as from ageism in general. The sad folks in old folks' homes! With each crucial birthday must come a certain accommodation. Can one continue to live—or live with oneself? Male gays often seem more sex-driven than straights. Because sexual intercourse seems proof that one is alive. For better or for worse I feel far less compulsive sexually than I used to. I don't feel I have to prove anything. Were a doctor to say, "Look, you will be very healthy and live to be ninety-eight if you don't have any more sex again ever," it wouldn't be so terrible.

LEYLAND: But would it have been terrible for you say twenty years ago?

ROREM: Sure it would. Whereas I know any number of septuagenarians who would commit suicide if they thought they had to give up sex. My friend J.H., who does not like to be talked about, appeared in my life at an absolute crucial moment, or so he thinks and I do. I might even be dead from alcoholism now. But again, I think sometimes that death can both be willed and willed away. I don't drink now, or smoke, or fuck, or say bad words. I'm impossibly boorish. But I've made choices, and we always get to some extent what we deserve. [*A youngish man enters the room. After a brief introduction he withdraws.*] That's Jim Holmes. He's fifteen years younger than me, although since I'm only attracted to fathers he's a father image. I'm drawn to older types, but that can't go on forever. When I'm ninety-eight I can't only be attracted to people in their hundreds. Well, each to his own fantasies! We are dear friends and I hope that it lasts forever.

That's one thing I wanted to say. The other thing is this: it has to do with my being evasive. There's nothing—nothing—that I don't feel guilty of. It's not unusual; many people feel the same, people from all walks of life. I see myself on trial for my life, accused of crimes that I don't know if I've committed. You know what I'm talking about. If I'm evasive it's precisely because of the governments of this hemisphere. Being too outspoken might be risky. I see myself being tortured in a concentration camp. Perhaps that's one answer to my being cavalier a while ago about oppression. It might be possibly fear of oppression that comes from a certain guilt, that makes me want to be less outspoken. Not just taste, not just a question of good taste, but a terror of the times we inhabit.

LEYLAND: I think you have been outspoken. If the government were to round up known homosexuals sometime in the future, you would definitely be on that list. You speak quite up-frontly about your gayness in the *Diaries*.

ROREM: So it's too late now. Oh, I'm on lots of lists I'm sure, as are my whole family for the measure of things we believe in. It so happens that I am not a champion of any cause except music. I don't think in generalities. I'll sign my name to lists that have to do with peace, but I won't sign anything that will promote any kind of war. I'm not trying to be lofty, I just feel vulnerable. Although I don't feel oppressed, the risk may be just around the corner. And as I say, when they start rounding up people they're going to round up artists too. Artists are not *bien vus*—are not well seen—by revolutionary governments.

LEYLAND: Why do you feel that you've found some stability in a relationship at this point in your life? Your love relationships in the past seem to have been more tumultuous and traumatic.

ROREM: In *The Paris Diary* I talk about an affair with an Italian. He was a delicatessen owner, and hardly a literary giant. My relationships today are less physical. I didn't have much mentally in common with many lovers in the past, but we had a lot in common bodily. I can't imagine spending an evening now, much less a lifetime, with a truck driver. I don't even think about it much, but if I have some sort of "image," it's probably that. I talked in the *Shenandoah* article clearly about my sado-masochistic sexual images. But I need somebody to admire, and also who knows what I'm made of.

LEYLAND: Do you feel this is the first time that you really found that in a relationship?

ROREM: Of course not, no. But time goes by. If I were me now, and wanted to have an affair with the "P" of *The Paris Diary*, who was then twenty-nine, he wouldn't find me attractive—I'm twenty years older—or he might, but I might not find him attractive. One's needs in given situations change as the years roll on, thank God, and I think it has to do with our protective clothing. I'm not especially interested in gorgeous youths or swarthy toughs anymore. So our rhythms alter. J.H. perhaps wouldn't have been the right person, or I wouldn't have been ready ten years ago. There were still wild oats to be sown.

LEYLAND: In *Critical Affairs* you quote Chekhov as saying, "Artists and intellectuals must deal with politics only insofar as it is necessary to put up a defense against politics," and you say in addition, "The past few years"—you wrote this about 1966—"have spawned even fewer genuine works in any form. This I feel is due to the direct alliance of art with the New Left." I disagree with you. In many many cases art *has* been directly inspired by the revolution. Consider Orozco in Mexico, or Soviet literature and music in the twenties, before the clamp-down by Stalin. The artist can't be completely apolitical, because he/she will be among the first to be rounded up when fascism comes.

ROREM: Yes, but what I meant is this: to express honest political ideas in art does not of itself make honest art. Kids who sing rock on a subject matter that's with-it assume that the very with-it-ness makes good music, whereas in fact the words are so simplistic and the music is so gross that there are no longer those levels of complexity inherent to art. That's all I'm saying. People bring up *Guernica*. *Guernica* is not a political work, because it can apply to any war in the world, not just to that specfic war. Picasso did thousands of paintings, of which one was *Guernica*, and sure it's good, but it's not good because it's political any more than the crucifixions of the Renaissance were good because they were religious.

More and more people claim to be artists, who have no métier and no talent, simply because they know how to strum the guitar, because they don't want to go to war, and because they get high on pot. Of course they are right in not wanting to go to war, but their rightness is not automatically musical. That matter is too obvious to need restatement. Not that by definition a subject does or doesn't make art. I'm saying that, just as wars in the name of the Lord are not justifiable (although most wars up until the twentieth century were religious wars), so an artistic effort in the name of Vietnam or Israel or in the name of whatever, is not necessarily art. Art is beyond these frontiers.

For every Orozco there were a thousand people painting lousy pictures on the same subjects. When Mozart lived everyone composed the same kind of music; there was one musical language. He was better than the rest, that's all. There is music which is effective for nonmusical reasons, like military marches. A military march might impel men to walk into battle. Unfortunately it won't inspire them to walk out of battle. If I could write a piece that would inspire an army to turn around and walk away, I wouldn't care whether that was art or not. Music that inspires the masses does seem pretty unsophisticated. When governments are in an emergency art is the last thing they need. To my chagrin, but not to my surprise, the most liberal of Americans politically are the least culture-minded. A Bella Abzug, for example, hasn't made one statement on behalf of the arts, yet she represents this zone of Manhattan from about 100th Street down to the Village. Some of the world's greatest creators inhabit Abzug's zone, yet what has she acknowledged to the United States government in their behalf? Yet God knows she's for the rights of man and I'm all for her. It's people like Rockefeller—jaded, decadent capitalists—who have time for the leisure of art. Alas!

LEYLAND: Aaron Copland was quoted in your *Paris Diary* as saying that your journal expressed the unexpected violent side of your nature, and that your music expresses your serene side. Do you agree?

ROREM: I don't know that I believe it now. At that time I felt less responsibility towards prose writing, and therefore wrote down anything in any order; whereas I felt, being a composer, intense responsibility towards my music. Yet if the arts could express each other we'd only need one art. That's why I write both prose and music, but I truthfully cannot say now whether my music and my prose express the same thing. I don't know what music expresses, that is, music which doesn't have words. However, a composer can't be jailed for subversive ideas in his nonvocal music, though authors can be arrested—have been arrested—for writing certain kinds of prose. In Russia, of course, composers have been arrested for writing certain kinds of music, but it's impossible to label what that music "says." Does a given symphony of Shostakovich represent indecent acts, or political acts, or is it dirty, and if so, how?

LEYLAND: Of course in the case of Shostakovich, he did have political intent in some of his symphonies, such as the *Leningrad* Symphony or Symphonies no. 11 and 12. It is patriotic music for the masses.

ROREM: Again, that's because he explained, in words, what that nonvocal music was meant to represent. Take that same symphony and play it for a class of high school seniors who have never heard of Shostakovich, and explain, "Now Shos-

takovich intended in this last movement to depict the migration of muskrats."
They'd buy that. Music means whatever a composer tells you, in words. Sometimes he even gives it titles, like *La Mer* or *Reformation* Symphony, precisely
because he knows that music doesn't really express literary ideas. It is associa-
tive only through extramusical conditioning—like films on college proms or
dreams.

Being a composer involves a lot more paperwork than being an author. If you
like to generalize, and who doesn't—composers are neater, fussier, more generally collected than any other breed of so-called creative artist. Being a composer
involves not only composition, but copying of that composition, orchestration
of that composition, and the dissemination of that composition, taking it apart,
copying the instrumental parts, and then giving it to middlemen who are performers. All this before it's even published. There's practical menial work that
needs to be done, which poets don't have to do. I once wrote that the main
problem for a poet is how to spend those other twenty-four hours a day. He can
write poetry as he walks along the river. A painter paints his picture, then it's
done. But a composer needs both a performer and listener for his work to exist.
So as a type, he's rather different from a writer. But I'm both of them. The
writer in me drinks, and the composer abstains. The diary represents the
bloody, neurotic, frantic side of me. The music is my pristine, white, controlled
side. A bemusing review of the *Paris Diary* said: "Ned Rorem may well write
of suffering and love and introspection and anxiety, but the fact that he writes
so glibly makes it doubtful that he ever experienced these emotions." Meaning:
if you write well you must be a phony. The reviewer went on to say that in this
era, when Jews have been massacred by the millions in concentration camps,
how can I write as casually as I do about recipes and heartache and abattoirs. It
was a review that I couldn't believe: criticizing me for having style.

LEYLAND: Was the reviewer being paranoid?

ROREM: Well, I suppose he resented my sexual casualness. Homosexuality was
thought frivolous even as recently as 1966. Because the critic didn't want to
censor me outright for loose morals, he accused me of loose politics. Maybe I'm
the paranoid. Nevertheless, the purplest works of nineteenth-century art, say
by Melville or Dostoyevsky or Tchaikovsky, flow forth like so much ecstasy or
vomit, but are always very carefully fabricated. A person writing about his unhappiness is not unhappy during those suspended moments.

LEYLAND: You're talking about a cathartic experience?

ROREM: I don't know if it's cathartic, so much as that the act of projecting onto
paper or canvas the distillation of a feeling precludes, for the duration of that
act, the actual feeling. Artists are in a sense the most self-involved of all people,
socially, but while putting brush to canvas or words to paper or notes to staves,
they become outside themselves; they are thus selfless because momentarily
they don't exist.

LEYLAND: You wrote in one of the *Diaries* that artistic natures tend towards the
Compassionate Left.

ROREM: People often say that artists should stay out of politics. I would agree
if I saw that people in politics were any smarter than artists. Mary McCarthy

contends—and she's no slouch when it comes to politics—that artists may not be more informed than "real people" when it comes to politics, but they do have a knack for smelling rats. Which is why an Auden, while not active politically, had a good sense of the tone of the times. Shelley wrote, "Poets are the unacknowledged legislators of the world," so Auden then wondered how things might be if poets were in the White House. The world would turn into an aristocracy. My generality was that poets tend to be compassionate and left-wing, like painters, since the Industrial Revolution when they were no longer subsidized by courts and things. The bohemian life is theirs. (I'm not speaking about the Andrew Wyeths of this world.) Musicians are more conservative, especially performing musicians. But even composers politically are pretty conservative. I can't think of any painter who is first-rate who could possibly be as monstrous as a Wagner. Writers are a bit of everything, but on the whole they do tend toward the compassionate Left, if not always so compassionate. And even now that is shifting. The very strong school of Jewish writers today is not all that compassionate nor all that left, and what with the war in Israel, Jewish writers can be virulently mean. And is there really, as a WASP like Benjamin DeMott maintains, a Homosexual Mafia in music? It's a terrible thing to say and also untrue. And people talk about "Jewish Mafia" in the arts. The "Goyish Mafia"? Although the *New York Review of Books* is essentially Jewish, it does have some big goy numbers like Gore Vidal and Mary McCarthy. Things are segmented, not all that compassionate, and not even all that left anymore. And that's all I can think to say about that.

LEYLAND: What kind of a lifestyle do you have now that you're living in New York?

ROREM: My health is good but I worry about it constantly. I'm very near-sighted because God wants me not to see. I don't drink anymore or smoke. I'm hooked on sweets and I make pies and cakes and puddings, and I think of them with lust the way others think of salty things like cheese or sex. I work every day, and every one of my actions deals with that work in some manner, this interview for instance. I seldom do anything for the hell of it anymore, having lived so much for the hell of it for so long, and almost dying. (Look how pretty that light comes in now, just as we sit here, just for the past two minutes, there against Jane Wilson's green painting.) I get up every morning at nine. I have very little social life. I don't have fun at parties anymore, because I don't drink. It's boring when everybody else is drunk. And I don't smoke pot. I'm madly stuffy.

LEYLAND: Do you think this is partially true because you've gotten into a more in-depth, continuing relationship?

ROREM: Yes, certainly it has to do with that. On the last page of the *New York Diary* I wrote: Everybody wants success in three areas; he wants success in love, success socially, and success in his trade. Now, any one person can have success in two of those areas simultaneously, but if he has success in all three of those areas he is dancing on the brink. Because with success in love and society, there's no time to get your work done. Success in love and work leaves no time to see other people. If you have success in society and in your work you have no time for the necessary conversation and compassion of conjugal living. So I have given up society; I no longer see many friends whom I think about and love dearly. Of course that happens with everybody as they grow older. I'm a fairly good correspondent with friends all over the world—but it's with anxiety that I get ready for a party, and never a thrill of expectation. My time is filled, therefore, with my work. I visit my parents every week. I cook a lot. I never go to a restaurant, because I loathe the sound of laughter.

LEYLAND: Why?

ROREM: Most laughter is self-conscious and stems from mediocrity. People who laugh too much can't think of any other reaction. Temperamentally it's just their way of reacting; it doesn't mean mirth though, and it does slow down conversation. Anyway I don't go to restaurants or bars, but I spent my youth in them and loved them.

LEYLAND: Looking back on the various love affairs that you've had, what kind of reaction do you have now?

ROREM: I've had six serious love affairs, and remained on good terms with all. I still like everyone I've ever loved. Once love is over, that flaming emotional thing, with me instead of settling into indifference, it settles into a continually glowing ember. "Friendship into love, perhaps, but love to friendship, never." I don't comprehend that old saw. Now, Frank O'Hara just loved to sleep with friends. He was always going to bed with poets and painters and such. My affairs have usually begun with people not met in a, let's say, decent way. People picked up, and not in publishers' offices. People met "abstractly." Those affairs turned into friendship, unfailingly. But the business about friends into lovers is something quite foreign to me.

I'm all for friends doing whatever they want with each other. My generation didn't. I'm not proud of it. It simply *was*. It's absolutely lovely that friends go to bed with each other now, heterosexually or homosexually. But I'm still excited by the anonymous. As soon as I discover how bright or how dull—how *real*—some new person might be, my interest in them changes from carnal to either no interest or to sexless curiosity. I find it hard to link the two, and it's too bad.

Incidentally, four of the six are European. During my Parisian years, if one again can generalize about those things now (because I was younger and my habits were different)—Europeans in the fifties seemed more able to have working love affairs than Americans of that period. By "affair" I mean something worked at by two people, with the necessary—the necessary *sacrifices* that must be made if the pair is not going to spend their days playing tricks on themselves. I don't know about Europe now. But Americans aren't doing so badly.

Speaking of love, did I tell you? One day last year I went to my skin doctor to have a mole removed. It was up by the Metropolitan Museum. I got there early, so before I went in to see him I crossed the street to the Metropolitan and walked around, into the room that had busts of old Roman emperors. One of the emperors was so beautiful, with his ample lips, his wise eyes and his Roman nose and curly hair, that I fell madly in love with him, over the centuries, this Augustus. Then I had my appointment. I went back over to the doctor, and who should be sitting in the outer office but my old friend Kenward Elmslie. I hadn't known he knew this doctor. And I said, "Kenward, what can I do? I'm in love!" And he said, "Oh? Who with ?" And I said, "Well, it's with this Roman emperor, the bust of an emperor, across the street. It's an impossible situation." And Kenward said, "How marvelous to hear someone say they're in love again!" End of story! Not in the least confused, Kenward was pleased only that I should still talk about being in love when young people were all talking about making it, or making out, and so forth, not in terms of affection.

What are twenty-year-olds these days doing? Living together? Are they not living together? My impression is that despite the new permissiveness, there's a lot less promiscuity (as it was named in the forties). During the war, when I think of my own sleeping around, my hair stands on end. The *thousands* of people I went to bed with! Much of that had to do with being a teenager, but it had to do with the war too. Although I was not in the army, I sure had a lot to do with the military. That the world could come to an end—and the sort of urge—I don't know, the urge to propagate, or whatever, there's so much copulation during wartime periods! Yet today these things are not all that untoward. When homosexuality, or sexuality pure and simple, is not an indecent thing, gang bangs seem less urgent. Wouldn't it be pleasant to think that the easing off of promiscuity signified an easing up of international strife?

One heterosexual point of view about homosexual promiscuity is that it is a constant seeking of the unattainable because homosexuality is wrong. Homosexuals, in fact, are not constantly looking for the ideal partner. Anonymity can be so uninhibited, the sex so incredibly fulfilling, that it could never be repeated with the same person, precisely because the next time he would *be* a person. Better to die! In Gide's *Counterfeiters* Olivier does attempt suicide because he had found the ultimate. Homosexuals permit themselves a promiscuity that heterosexuals could not permit themselves in the less permissive days of twenty years ago. Homosexuals could permit it because they already were underground. Promiscuity does not mean hopeless seeking. Promiscuity means: renewal of perfection under different circumstances. Because perfection, by definition, can't be duplicated.

LEYLAND: Do you feel this is true in your own life?

ROREM: Not much anymore. But some of the best sex I ever had was precisely because of the anonymity: when you're no longer a rational being, but a gibbering idiot, throttled by Eros. When everything is the same. Beethoven or Einstein or Groucho Marx or the cashier at a burlesque house are all the same when they're in love. In the sexual act they're equally stupid and ungainly. It's funny-looking to see a person fucking, at least it is to me. To stand off and watch two (or more) people behaving like animals, it's all sort of sweet and ridiculous: great panting bodies rubbing against each other to no apparent purpose. That has nothing to do with scanning verse or city planning. But if the instinct is to become a babbling fool, it's difficult to babble with your peers, and that's why anonymous encounters are more satisfactory.

LEYLAND: Have your views on sex and promiscuity changed radically with increasing age?

ROREM: Well, as I said, sex doesn't mean that much now: the competitive business of making sure you don't go home alone means little, and I'm very relieved. Sex has always been kind of a mental thing with me. I've had a lot in my life, but a lot was to prove that I was desirable, more than out of horniness. It was sufficient sometimes to know that a person wanted me. A lot of my drinking had to do with being able to go to bed with people, being drunk enough to put myself in certain positions.

LEYLAND: Do you feel there was a connection between sexual promiscuity and alcoholism in your own life?

ROREM: Definitely. If you're drunk you're not ashamed of playing a certain role. Shame hangs over me still, a residue that maybe makes me what I am. Do I write the kind of music that I write because of this shame? That's what nobody will ever be able to analyze. It's forever tantalizing as an idea, the relationship between a man's private sexuality and his wordly output. Whether the output is good or bad, its nature can be defined as passive or aggressive, masculine or feminine, dark or light. Too many, for instance, ivory-figurine men compose tough music, and too many tough men (on the surface) compose ivory-figurine music, for one to safely generalize that ivory-figurine music is feminine. I have this endless cobweb of definitions for what is and isn't sexual, feminine, masculine, passive, and such. None of it makes for good art or bad art or even art at all, but it's fun. Surely my point of view about myself sexually has something to do with the "tone" of my work. It has more to do with a musician's work than with a painter's or novelist's who deal in concretes. Except in the case of someone like Christopher Isherwood who writes extremely subjective novels, or Philip Roth on the other side of the fence. But it would be hard to prove that the novels of Balzac or Flaubert or even Dos Passos come out of their sexual behavior.

Kinsey interviewed me and also my parents in 1948. We were all at the same party after a concert. I said, "Oh terrific. I'd love for you to interview me." And he asked, "Do you think I could have your mother and father too?" So I said, "Well, ask them" and indeed they were staying on in New York a couple of days. Kinsey's assistants interviewed them, and Kinsey interviewed me. He was a man of infinite charm, easy to talk to, which had much to do with how he got what he got in his landmark of scientific investigation. Charm or no charm, the interview was standard and lasted the same amount of time for everyone, with the same questions. The questions were so categorized that if you lied on one you'd be tripped up by a later question. After the interview, we discussed homosexuality. I gave him some musical generalities, and I'm curious now, so many years later, how the generalities hold up. For instance, his book should have been titled "Sexual Behavior in the Human *American* Male," because that behavior is not that of the French male, much less of the Moroccan male. It's definitely the American male.

In the forties one could make the following generalizations: organists ninety-five percent homosexual, violinists one percent, pianists fifty percent, cellists and violists zero, harpists less than we might think. (All male harpists were European in those days, and real woman-chasers. Of course ninety-nine percent of harpists are female.) Of composers approximately fifty percent. In the pop world, female vocalists were all drugged and sapphic, while the males were all drunk and straight. (Today that is really quite changed.) And I gave Kinsey my reasons as much as I could figure them out. Organists were of a WASP family makeup that lent itself to homosexuality as it was then thought to be bred. String players were in those days mostly Jewish and the Jewish family did not tend toward the homosexual, particularly in the nonsoloist area. Orchestra players are simply never homosexual. If a violinist today is queer (which is very rare) he is inevitably a soloist and probably Gentile, but the violinist who plays in the string section of the orchestra just isn't.

Composers, during the fifties, what with the sterility of twelve-tone music being revived, were neither heterosexual nor homosexual, they just were not sexual. (I'm speaking of composers who came of age in that period, in their twenties.) They didn't look it and didn't act it. Now, I don't think composers worry about what they are. And there are many heterosexual organists, both in America and in Europe. Indeed, all French organists are heterosexual. Does this sound flippant? I don't mean it to be. It's neither important nor unimportant. Today, organists in America are about seventy-five percent homosexual and a lot of them in closets because they're in small towns. Art in Europe is not considered a sissy thing. It has to do with the Catholic past, and the church is not sissy.

LEYLAND: There's a certain amount of camp that gay people are attracted to in the church—ecclesiastical drag. I went through it myself in my own seminary past: cassocks, vestments, incense. My gay sensibility—at that time still nascent—thrived on the aesthetic aspects of Roman ritual.

ROREM: Less in Europe. Take your average Catholic in Europe. It may be ecclesiastical drag to us, but it isn't to him—it's life and death. And I would venture to say that the clergy, just like the organists, in Europe are far less gay than in America. We may find it a camp because art is still a silly thing for us. Therefore we use phrases like "ecclesiastical drag." Even if we're not Protestant, in America we inhabit a Protestant ethic. So all the gold and silver and perfume and incense and saints and confession of the Roman church became for us a thrill so untenable we write it off as camp.

LEYLAND: When I was in the Roman priesthood several years ago, I certainly didn't consider the rituals of the church as just camp. I became radicalized at that time (influenced especially by Dan Berrigan, Merton, and Teilhard de Chardin). I left the ecclesiastical structure in the sixties because I reacted against the stylized ritual of the church and ecclesiastical fascism, partly because of my desire to really implement my pacifist views, my horror at the church's complicity in the genocide of Vietnam, also my desire to explore my own gayness. But I do feel that the church would be a good deal better off if it were able to acknowledge the homosexual camp aspect of ritual, vestments and so forth. Perhaps such an attitude might help to liberate gay clerics. There are more closet cases in the Roman clergy that anyone would believe—I would guess up to sixty percent.

But to return to Kinsey: did he do research on the sexuality of artists?

ROREM: Kinsey wanted to do a book on the sexuality of artists and he certainly had the archives in Bloomington—hordes of goodies that should be revealed sometime. One cannot generalize about male ballet dancers any longer. Too many are presumably well-adjusted family men and not all that interested. The ballet scene has changed. The organ scene has to some extent changed in America. The pop scene has changed—because first of all there are no more woman pop singers, except Barbra Streisand. I can't think of a single gay male pop singer except maybe Johnny Ray or Johnny Mathis.

LEYLAND: Or David Bowie and Lou Reed. Mick Jagger of the Rolling Stones also tries to project a bisexual image—not too convincingly I might add.

ROREM: Yes. He projects that image but I'll bet he's not. He's too flamboyant about pretending to be. If he were, he wouldn't do it quite that way. What Mick Jagger is, is not a camp. He thinks he is but he isn't. Camp is a homosexual sensibility with a soupçon of weariness. A heterosexual in drag thinks he is a camp, but he can't bring it off—perhaps from lack of pathos. Camp also implies a certain sophistication, whereas Mick Jagger is a child in a tantrum. Precisely that innocence keeps him from being a camp. A drag queen is saying, "Get me, I am a woman," while Mick Jagger is saying, "Get me, I'm pretending to be woman and isn't it a scream?"

LEYLAND: In the gay scene now there are people who are into "genderfuck" who are not into "Look at me, I'm a woman." They're into drag for itself and for political reasons. We printed an article on this in issue number 21. I know a number of people in San Francisco who are into genderfuck drag on an everyday basis. It's a new, completely different kind of approach.

ROREM: To go onto a stage and people applaud—the very idea that they're there for me is already so absolutely insolent! For any public performer the fact that people should watch and listen to him hawk his wares! There's a chutzpah in arranging to be clapped for, even through playing Bach. To perform for people could be thought of as active, but also very passive. It's like being possessed when people applaud you, being possessed to perform music for people. There's no such real thing as a passive act or an active pass. It's what goes through your head. Is to blow somebody passive? Is the blower the fucker or fuckee? To my mind, he's being fucked, what with that male member discharging into his body! To be fucked, in other words, as a woman is being fucked. Now that's a passive grammatical construction in English. But like anyone with any brains I know perfectly well that women have teeth in their cunts. That cunt, grasping the cock, draining it of its virility, and leaving it limp. A cunt is a most aggressive organ, in a sense that a cock is not. But again, it's what goes through your head. If you're being fucked in the ass what are you doing? Are you devirilizing the man? Or being possesed by him? So all of those things—those definitions about who is what in a given relationship, I disclaim in my own psyche. The same goes for drag queens, some of whom lift their skirts and bugger truck drivers. You just never know. Had I not early reaped appreciation in a comparatively dignified way by writing music and sometimes going out and performing it (that's so carnal that I feel almost like Mick Jagger) I too might be in drag today. At the corner delicatessen, too. Everyone likes to get in costume. Even Nixon sponsors drag for the White House guardsmen—or whatever they're called.

LEYLAND: He is in drag himself. That visage and the bourgeois garb.

ROREM: A very gloomy drag, and dangerous too. The drag of Dracula!

LEYLAND: You said earlier that you dislike macho literature.

ROREM: Yes. I loathe macho literature like Lowry's *Under the Volcano,* which is considered a masterpiece. Faulkner is a mystery to me. I mean, why it is considered good is a mystery to me. I don't see that greatness there. I do see tackiness in Hemingway, and do feel that that comes out of his macho thing. But if a Hemingway type excites me in a man-to-man encounter, I find that the work that comes from that is terrible. Whereas fruity types don't send me in a sexual way. But if I'm not attracted toward what used to be called effeminacy, I love delicacy and nuance and looking at things from a great distance. Of course now that isn't really femininity at all, and women writers can be extremely (Mary McCarthy for one) what we used to call masculine. All those things are now melding in such a way that one can no longer distinguish between the sexes, and that's perhaps good. It's happened I think that now in the English language females are writing better prose than men, in both England and America. I wouldn't say the same in poetry, but I would say that in painting and English literature women are certainly as good as if not better than men. Someone like Colette who writes with great elegance has as good a sense of construction as any man who ever lived.

LEYLAND: Music or composing has been pretty much a male preserve, more so than writing. There've been very few women composers. I can think of Clara Schumann, Germaine Tailleferre, Peggy Glanville-Hicks, a few more.

ROREM: Well, I once wrote in an essay called "Ladies' Music" that women composers today are no worse than men composers.

LEYLAND: I wanted to ask you also if you knew Paul Bowles. I've admired his fiction and his music for some time. I just saw a preview in Los Angeles of a one-hour color film about Bowles, made in Morocco.

ROREM: Why doesn't somebody make a film on me before it's too late? Nobody's ever done that and I'm dying to be in a movie. And now I can't be young in a movie anymore. Paul Bowles doesn't know it, but he's been a big influence on me. He's one of the most original Americans since the twenties. His music is quite underrated. I wrote a little essay on his autobiography scolding him nicely and saying I wish he would write more music. But he has one of the most unusual minds, and his wife Jane is—was—surely one of the most intriguing writers of any sex who ever lived. Paul and Jane Bowles, in the thirty years I've known them, have never ceased to interest me. Paul was the first real live composer I ever met. I was fifteen at the time, in Taxco, and so our age difference was big enough for me to look up to this person. I'd never known a composer who had published music and had it performed. Little did I realize that he would become the weird Paul Bowles and end up writing those fairly good novels. He's a most valuable individual and everyone should talk about him more. They don't because he lives away, because he gave up the American rat-race competition scene. He went to live in Morocco on his own terms.

LEYLAND: Since we're talking about literary personalities (and why not a little gay gossip), did you know Gore Vidal?

ROREM: We see each other every three or four years. I like and agree with everything about him except his style, which is a little aloof for me. He's sort of aloofed himself into a corner with his blasé shrieks of doom. (If one can speak of blasé shrieks.)

LEYLAND: He was on the Dick Cavett show just a few nights ago advertising his new book, *Burr*.

ROREM: He's pretty good on those shows. I once asked him, "Why are you so good on those shows?" and he answered, "Ostensibly I'm there to plug a new book. So I come out and sell my book for two minutes, and then go on to really important things, like ecology or Vietnam, rather than constantly saying I, I, I like those vocalists who just opened at the Rainbow Grill." Gore talks about things bigger than himself. It gives him a certain lasting quality. I like that quality. He's not all that self-involved, considering his whole career. He's good-looking, and makes the most of that, but he's used it for entrée to valuable people. Gore's known everybody and gotten a great deal out of them, and his vanity is not essentially sexual. I mean, he's a very sexy number, and he likes a lot of sex, and likes to talk about it. But essentially he writes not about himself. Imagine writing a novel on Aaron Burr, for God's sake! A homosexual writing a novel on Aaron Burr, or on the Washington political scene! That's rare. Homosexuals are usually too self-directed to turn toward politics. I'm speaking of another time and place, because some American homosexuals are political now, but much of that has to do solely with gay politics. Gore's politics is more general. For instance, he's specifically against Nixon or Buckley, or any right-wing or conservative party, considering he's an aristocrat to the manor born, rather than a gay liberationist which he probably is too. But he's barking up a broader tree.

LEYLAND: I suppose I shall have to ask the inevitable question about your narcissism. This is one thing you've been criticized for in regard to the diaries. Not that narcissism is necessarily negative.

ROREM: I'm not more narcissistic than anyone else. I just admit to it. I'm not very interested in my own person.

LEYLAND: You do look much younger than you are. I suppose you've been told that throughout your life.

ROREM: That's nice to hear. Everybody likes to hear that. But I'm not out to prove to anyone that I'm younger than I am. I'm not interested in clothes and so forth, though I want to be loved as well as liked. But mostly, I want to get my work done. That has always come first. The rest has been pure decoration, and admittedly I've at various points confected certain personages for myself. But I'm not necessarily like that. I'm a nicer person than I make myself out to be.

PHOTO BY EDWARD HART, 1977

SAMUEL
STEWARD

SAMUEL M. STEWARD was born in Woodsfield, Ohio, in 1909. He was educated at Ohio State University, receiving his B.A., M.A., and Ph.D. (1934) from that institution. He taught English literature at Washington State College (from which he was dismissed in 1936 for writing a novel termed "racy") and in Chicago until 1954. He forsook teaching to become a tattoo artist for approximately the next fifteen years until his retirement in 1970.

His published writing includes several scholarly articles in such publications as PMLA, *Sewanee Review, French Review, Romanic Review, Commonweal,* and the *London Times Literary Supplement.* He has published one novel *Angels on the Bough* (1936) and a collection of short stories, *Pan and the Firebird* (1930). His *Chapters from an Autobiography* appeared in 1981.

Under the pen name of "Phil Andros" he wrote six paperback gay pornographic novels of literary merit: *The Joy Spot* (1969), *My Brother, the Hustler* (1970), *San Francisco Hustler* (1970,) *When in Rome, Do...* (1971), *Renegade Hustler* (1972), and *The Greek Way* (1975). More than a hundred gay short stories and essays have appeared since 1958 in various publications in Switzerland, Denmark, Germany, and the United States under a variety of pen names: Phil Andros, Ward Stames, Donald Bishop, John McAndrews, Philip Young, etc. Eighteen of these stories were published as a hardcover book under the title *$tud* (1966)—later reissued in two paperback editions. Recent gay stories by Phil Andros have appeared in *Gaytimes* and *Drummer* magazine. His account of meetings with Lord Alfred Douglas and André Gide, included in the present interview, originally appeared in the Arts & Letters supplement to *GaysWeek*, a New York gay newspaper.

Samuel Steward's friendship with Gertrude Stein and Alice B. Toklas began with a correspondence in 1932 and continued after Gertrude Stein's death until that of Alice Toklas in 1967. The first actual meeting with them was in 1937 when he was invited to Bilignin (France) for two weeks; he visited there again in 1939. He continued to see Alice B. Toklas every year from 1950 until her death. The Stein letters to him were given to Yale University at the request of Alice Toklas. Toklas's letters to Steward were deposited at the Bancroft Library of the University of California at Berkeley. In 1977 Houghton Mifflin published *Dear Sammy: Letters from Gertrude Stein & Alice B. Toklas.* This book also includes a 177-page memoir written by Steward about his relationship with Stein and Toklas.

Gay Sunshine editor Winston Leyland taped the present interview at Samuel Steward's Berkeley home in May 1978. This is its first publication.

Winston Leyland interviews
SAMUEL STEWARD

LEYLAND: Could you speak about your early life?

STEWARD: I was born in the southeastern corner of Ohio in a small town called Woodsfield. While I was working for the *World Book Encyclopedia*, an authority who composed a new article on the state for our major re-writing called that particular section the most backward and undeveloped in the United States. It's very hilly country, a few miles from the Ohio river, where once we went to watch Gloria Swanson film *Showboat* many years ago. Our town had about 1800 people in it and never changed. It used to have a narrow-gauge railroad but even that disappeared after a while, and a bus ran back and forth between Barnesville, which was the next largest town. Then the bus stopped, and there was no way to get to Woodsfield except by car. Its physical isolation was indicative of its artistic, aesthetic, and intellectual isolation as well.

I went through high school there. Then two aunts of mine (my mother had died when I was about six, and my father, a weak man, did not count at all in my upbringing) moved in 1927 to Columbus, Ohio, so that my sister and I would have a place to live while she went through high school and I went through college at Ohio State University.

It was in the university that I began to "expand" although I already knew what I was. A copy of the second volume of Havelock Ellis's studies, the one on *Sexual Inversion*, had already fallen into my hands earlier in Woodsfield, with the result that—oh, I had a dandy time, with the football team, the basketball team, the athletic coach—and many others. This was when I was about sixteen or seventeen. The lack of sophistication and knowledge of homosexuality among the townspeople made my life fairly easy there. I was not teased much about my proclivities; rather, I was made use of much to my pleasure and delight. Oddly enough, I found two or three classmates who reciprocated. They never thought of themselves as queer or fairies, but I was convinced that I was one very early, and had little trouble with sexual identity—all thanks to Havelock Ellis.

The leading figure at Ohio State University for me was Professor Clarence Andrews, who had written *The Innocents of Paris,* a volume about his love for that city. It was the vehicle for Maurice Chevalier's first American movie. I remember that entering freshmen had to write an essay on a topic of their choice to see in what level English class they belonged. I chose Walt Whitman, and said a lot of things about his homosexuality. This put me under the eye of Professor Billy Graves, a harmless elderly non-practicing homosexual who loved to caress young men. And strangely enough, got away with it, although some of his fraternity brothers talked and joked about him.

Andrews had also been in Gertrude Stein's circle and had visited her salon. As a matter of fact, he was one of the two men who had expelled Hemingway when Hemingway was drunk one night at Gertrude's. I think perhaps that may have been one of the reasons that Gertrude and Hermingway fell out, because Hemingway could not stand the disgrace or the shame or the mortification of being bodily thrown out of Gertrude's salon. But Andrews would go to Paris to lose himself in the darkly romantic (to us) life of the city, and then return to teach six months at Ohio State, talking about Gertrude Stein, of whom very little was known at that time, 1927 or 1928; and we would always run to the library to see what we could find out, but—not very much about Gertrude.

LEYLAND: So you went through college with lots of gay experiences?

STEWARD: Yes, there were really lots of homosexuals on campus and we found each other soon enough. In downtown Columbus there was a little artistic enclave on Long Street, where we met a lot of kindred souls. There was a great Junoesque lesbian named Marie Anderson who had case on Garbo. I remember meeting someone who said, "I've seen you walking across the campus with Marie Anderson, and I thought 'I'd like to know him, because I imagine he spends all afternoon dipping long yellow ladyfingers into purple tea' "

LEYLAND: Where did you go after you finished at the university?

STEWARD: After that I went out west to teach, first for a year at a little college in Helena, Montana, called Carroll College, and then on the next year to the State College of Washington at Pullman, which has some new name by now, I guess. And while I was at Washington State I had a novel published, *Angels on the Bough. Angels* had one hidden homosexual character in it, but that was 1936 and you could not write openly. All I could do was create the character called Jan Halliday in *Angels,* and just suggest that he was homosexual and unhappy, and filled with a great many other minor conflicts regarding his mother, so that his eventual accidental death, falling down the stairwell, could be motivated without any feeling of sin or suicide because of his homosexuality.

A little firm in Caldwell, Idaho, called Caxton published the book. It was not very well known but nonetheless the novel got a nice review in the *New York Times;* I would not have thought Caxton able to reach that far, but they did. And Gertrude Stein liked *Angels.*

LEYLAND: Where did you get the title "Angels on the Bough"?

STEWARD: The title comes from William Blake. In one place he says that he was walking through the fields one day when he saw a tree full of angels sitting on the bough. It's a kind of handling of the theme that Wilder used in *The Bridge of San Luis Rey*—whether things happen by accident or design—and the lives of these eight or ten persons in my novel come together, cross, and affect each other, and finally unwind.

LEYLAND: You also wrote another book around this time called *Pan and the Firebird.*

STEWARD: Yes, although that was earlier, about 1930, and it was published by a "friend." At any rate, he arranged for its publication—a small private publisher in New York City named Henry Harrison. It was a series of sketches that I had written in a creative writing class of Andrews's. They were largely influenced by James Branch Cabell who was to the 1920s what Tolkien was to the 1960s and the modern day, but the sketches in *Pan* were very forthrightly homosexual, and there were lots of little Cabellian tricks—the firebird's name, for instance, was "Kircp" and it doesn't taske much rearranging of the letters to come up with something else. Or the lovers Nomad and Saihtyp, if you spell them backwards. Or the "Libation to a Dead God" which was addressed to Valentino. It seems odd to me now, looking back, and I am somewhat astounded at the frankness evident in that small book. The homosexuality of it was noticed by two or three reviewers.

LEYLAND: And then around the same time your book *Hero and Leander* was published?

STEWARD: No, I just started to write that, talked it over with Gertrude, and she didn't like it very much, so I abandoned that. *Angels on the Bough* got me fired from the State College of Washington because the president had one of his henchmen read it, and he reported that it was "racy." It did have a lady of the evening in it—but very tame, the whole thing, reading like *Little Women* by today's standards. Anyway, the "racy" character, the prostitute, got syphilis, her payment for her sins. At any rate, I was fired after the graduation ceremonies were over, in 1936, and despite the fact I'd been given a contract for the following year.

As a result of my complaining to the American Association of University Professors, an investigation by the Committee on Academic Freedom and Tenure was conducted; they published a report in their bulletin exonerating me and condemning the administration for stifling creative work by the faculty. So I moved on to Chicago and spent many years teaching English literature there at two small sectarian universities. After a few years I was able to concentrate more on the modern fields, which I liked better. I interrupted my teaching career to spend two years on a major rewriting of the *World Book Encyclopedia*.

LEYLAND: It was around this time that you made your first trip to France?

STEWARD: Yes, in 1937. It was a sort of literary pilgrimage. One of the curiosities of that trip was a visit to Lord Alfred Douglas.

LEYLAND: Could you tell us about your meeting with Bosie (Lord Alfred Douglas) including the events that led up to it?

STEWARD: At Ohio State University in the early 1930s, there was a group of us who prided ourselves on being very sophisticated and *au courant*—alert and intellectual and all the rest. By the standards of those days we possibly were those things but measured by today's patterns we were only groping towards the kinds of esoteric knowledge and experience that are old-hat, even corny, to the young of the moment.

My particular channel was a literary one. In 1932, after starting the correspondence with Gertrude Stein, her answers to my letters put me just a notch above my competitors. Such success started me writing letters of appreciation and flattery to many of the authors I admired. My list of replies, expanding, came to include Thomas Mann, Van Vechten, Cabell, Undset, Morley, O'Neill, Freud, Housman, Yeats, Wescott, Wilder, Gide, and others. The trick to getting a response, I found, was to say something intelligent about an author's work, and *never to ask for anything* in my letter, not even a reply. It worked.

Naturally, whenever a literary figure came to the campus to lecture, we were all there en masse—to hear John Cowper Powys declaim like thunder, and James Stephens read Keats in a murmurous whisper—and in 1934 to listen to Hamlin Garland, who wrote *A Son of the Middle Border*, give us the October reminiscences of his long career. He was a pleasant silver-haired giant, by then somewhat diminished in reputation and obscured by men like Hemingway and Dreiser and Sinclair Lewis. But during the course of his lecture he mentioned that he had known Whitman, and that electrified me.

Afterwards I went up on the stage to speak to him. "Did you really know Whitman?" I asked in awe.

"Yes," said the patriarch. "I was very little, but he shook my hand and laid his hand on top of my head."

"Well, Mr. Garland," I said with the brash bravado of youth, "I've shaken your hand, but may I put my hand were Whitman laid his?"

He was somewhat taken aback, but he smiled.

"I want to be linked in with Whitman," I stammered, feeling my face grow red.

"Of course," he said, and bowed his head slightly. I put my left hand on his silver mane. Someone giggled, and I escaped sweating into the auditorium.

That was the genesis of the idea. The next day I wrote to Lord Alfred Douglas, finding his address in *Who's Who*. And in due time a letter from him arrived, chatty and somewhat avuncular, asking who I was and telling me about his latest book, *The True History of Shakespeare's Sonnets*. I answered, saying that I was a student working on my doctorate, and that I would try to find a copy of his book somewhere in the States. He replied that he would be glad to send me a copy but he would have to charge me for it since all his author's copies had been given out. I sent him a draft for two pounds sterling, and waited.

The book arrived. It contained the "dedication" of a full page in his handwriting, with the statement that he had corrected two misprints.

It soon became obvious from his inquiries, at first veiled and then direct, that what Lord Alfred was really looking for was someone who could help him find an American publisher for the *True History;* and I had to confess to him that I had no ties or any influence in the publishing world. And at that point our correspondence dwindled and died until three years later, 1937, when I made my first trip to Europe, a kind of literary pilgrimage to visit Gertrude Stein at her invitation, and Thomas Mann and André Gide and Romain Rolland, all of whom seemed to be a little curious about me. I wrote again to Lord Alfred and received a short note from him, asking me to come down to Hove to call on him should I find the time while in London.

I must honestly admit that I had no interest whatsoever in Lord Alfred Douglas as a person or a writer, but only in the fact that he and Oscar Wilde had been lovers; and that back in those shrouded days the name of Wilde had a magic all its own for us who had to live without the benefits of liberation or exposure of our wicked lives. Besides, I was in my twenties and by then Lord Alfred was sixty-seven, and in anyone's book that's *old*. To go to bed with him was hardly the most attractive prospect in the world—it was terrifying, even re-pulsive. But if I wanted to link myself to Oscar Wilde more directly than I was linked to Whitman, there was no other way to do it.

That possibility seemed remote. After Wilde's death, Lord Alfred had ranted and raved (in print) in his defense of Wilde—and then suddenly changed. He had married in 1902 and become a Roman Catholic in 1911, and thus put behind him all such childish things as fellatio, mutual masturbation, sodomy, and so on.

When I got to London I established myself in a small hotel on Suffolk Place called Garland's (which seemed a curious omen to me after the Hamlin Garland experience) and after seeing the sights of London, telephoned Lord Alfred.

His voice was high-pitched and tinny over the phone. He seemed cordial enough, and invited me down to a tea on the afternoon of two days hence. And on that day, extremely nervous, I found my way to the great blackened ugly skeleton of Victoria Station and took the train to Brighton in Sussex, which was next door to Hove where he lived, connected in those days (and perhaps still) by a kind of boardwalk along the sea-front.

My nervousness increased on the way down. He was a lord of the realm, son of the Marquess of Queensberry. I must remember not to mention the names of Robert Ross, Frank Harris, André Gide—and a host of others who had been involved in controversy with him—nor even that of Winston Churchill, who had sued Lord Alfred for libel and won, with Lord Alfred spending six months in Wormwood Scrubs as a penalty, all this while he had been editor of *Plain Speech*. And I must not talk about the Jews or mention Gertrude Stein, for he was often very obviously anti-Semitic, even in print.

What, in heaven's name, could we talk about at all?

I found out when we met. The only safe topic was Lord Alfred Douglas.

His address gave me no trouble; the station-master said that it was not far, a fifteen-minute walk from Brighton past the flimsy pavilions dingy with the sea-air. I turned a corner and found myself facing a block of flats, perhaps in Regency architecture, little plots and gates and short sidewalk entrances. It was hardly Coleridge's countryside "enfolding sunny spots of greenery," nor Wordsworth's "pastoral farms green to the very door," but it was pleasant and British and the sort of dwelling I was used to seeing in British movies.

He opened the door himself—a man of medium height with hairline receding a bit on the right side where it was parted, and the somewhat lackluster straight mousy hair falling down towards his left eyebrow. The red rose-leaf lips beloved by Wilde had long since vanished; the mouth was compressed and thin, pursed somewhat, and the corners turned slightly downwards. I looked in vain for a hint, even the barest suggestion, of the fair and dreamy youth of the early photographs with Wilde. None was visible. The skin of his face had not suffered the dreadful slackening of the flesh that goes with age; it seemed rather to be of the type that grows old by stretching more tautly over the bones, until—at the end—a skull-like face results. Yet the skin was not stretched tightly enough to pull out the fine network of tiny wrinkles that entirely covered his face and neck.

"Do come in," he said, but then instead of standing aside to let me precede him, he turned and walked ahead of me into the flat, leaving me to shut the door. He looked at me closely and waved to a chair. "Do sit down," he said.

It was a pleasant room with many glass-doored bookcases, a kneehole desk with inlaid leather top, and books and papers strewn carelessly on it. There were three or four chairs, rather grimy white curtains at the windows, and a general air of disorder and confusion—crowding, perhaps—everywhere.

I had been in England just long enough to perceive that most British conversation was all form and no content, a kind of boneless thing, a sort of pingpong game played without balls. There were no awkward gaps; it ran on and on, pegged to the flimsiest topics—the scenery, the weather of today and yesterday and tomorrow.

Perhaps to put me at ease but more likely to sound me out, Lord Alfred launched into that kind of talk, with a literary flavor. Hemingway was a prurient cad, and Dos Passos a proletarian, probably a Communist (like all left-wingers). Americans do not get enough exercise, and skyscrapers are too too utterly dreadful. Marriage is a mockery in America. If there is war, the only decent thing for America to do will be to come to Britain's aid immediately; we waited too long in the war of 1914-18—and of course as Rudyard Kipling pointed out (had I read his poem about that, the one that began "At the eleventh hour they came"?) America then took all the credit for winning.

On and on... I received a detailed account of the ten or eleven lawsuits he had been involved in, the trouble he had had over the money of his inheritance, his youthful passions for horse-racing and gambling, his poetry (how much of it had I read, rilly?)—thank you for saying it, yes, he *was* probably England's greatest living poet. Masefield was a poetaster, a hack who had sold his birth-right, who had never written a good line after 1930 when he was made poet laureate; George Russell ("Æ") wrote mystical trash... And of course Yeats and the other Irish ones—well, you couldn't really call them British poets, now could you?

The pale blue eyes were never still, nor were his hands, nor his feet—for he was continually crossing and recrossing his ankles or tapping his shoe against a nearby chair-leg.

"I suppose," he said suddenly, "you want to hear all about Oscar Wilde and myself!"

By then I think I had analyzed him enough to know that I must disclaim all interest. "Not necessarily," I said with a rather wan smile. "I've read everything that you have written on the subject, and the work of several others... "

"Including, I suppose," he said in a fierce voice, "the evil canards and lies of persons like Robbie Ross and Frank Harris and that unspeakable sod André Gide."

"Well, yes... " I said lamely.

"Lies, all lies," he said hoarsely, and rose to pace around the room. Had he lived later, doctors would have called him hyperkinetic. He gestured towards the untidy desk. "I am doing a final book on it," he said. "I think I will call it 'The Summing-Up.' "

Suddenly he sat down again, the storm having passed. "Shall we have a spot of tea?" he asked.

"That would be nice."

I took milk in my tea, largely because it was there and it helped to disguise the taste of the brew, which I hated. With the tea he served a small plateful of pink cakes, disastrously sweet, with small silver pellets sprinkled on the top, possibly silver-plated buckshot to judge from the internal content.

He never stopped talking—a long monologue in which "As a poet I" and "As an artist I" recurred again and again. He seemed not ever to realize the extent to which he revealed his violent prejudices and hates, nor the immaturity of his view of himself. For it became obvious before very long that he had never really grown up. He remained psychologically (and in his own eyes perhaps physically) still the radiant and brilliant adolescent beloved by the gods. He was a man of vast essential egotism yet burdened with a well-concealed inferiority, aggressively insistent on his social position, glossing over his repeated failures in business, and furious with Lord Beaverbrook ("essentially a commoner, donchaknow") for turning down the publication of his poems in the *Evening Standard,* grudge-holding for real and fancied slights, damning White's Club for closing its doors to him . . .

As for homosexual leanings and entanglements—that had all been given up when he became a Catholic, oh yes. He still got hundreds of letters from curiosity seekers and homosexuals and he could have his pick of any of thousands (my ears and armpits flamed), but that was all finished. Sins of the flesh were obnoxious and uninteresting.

(I did not know at the time of his liaison with "D.E."—a young person with whom he was infatuated after his wife left him—and all this after he had become Catholic! These initials were those used by André Gide in telling me, later in 1937, that Alfred Douglas had become enamored of "une personne" [feminine gender, but referring in French to either a male or female] and had been to bed with him/her. There were actually at least two recorded liaisons; the first with an American girl in 1913 who with jewels and money offered to help Lord Alfred in one of his many litigations, and with whom in his *Autobiography* he admits "a loss of innocence." The second was a male, a young man sent down from Oxford for low grades, who always introduced himself as the reincarnation of Dorian Gray; and whose camping and good looks and "butterfly devotion" delighted Lord Alfred for over a year (1925). It was to this young man that Lord Alfred addressed a poem; "To —— with an Ivory Hand Mirror." Whether the initials "D.E." belonged to the American girl or the British Oxonian can presumably never be determined.)

The more he talked, the more I saw the possibility of linking in with Oscar Wilde fading, along with the afternoon sun. Yet I did not give up. It was inconceivable to me that any man who had spent approximately the first forty years of his life in homosexual activity could have lost his leanings completely on joining the Catholic church. It still seemed to me, as we said in the Midwest, "Once one, always one."

And then, since this was still in my drinking days, a happy thought: *in vino veritas.*

"Perhaps you will accompany me," I said, "to a nearby pub so that I may buy a round of drinks for us."

He waved his hand. "Hardly necessary, m'boy," he said. "All we need is here. Scotch? Gin and bitters? Sherry?"

"Gin, please." I had learned to love it warm.

And that did it. Within an hour and a half we were in bed, the Church renounced, inhibitions overcome, revulsion conquered, pledges and vows and British laws all forgotten. Working away, head down, my lips where Oscar's had been, I knew that I had won. After I had finished my labors and settled back, his hand stole down to clamp itself around me. It began to move gently. Still moving his hand up and down, he spoke; "You really needn't have gone to all that trouble. This is almost all Oscar and I ever did with each other."

Genuinely astonished, I stammered: "B-b-but... the poems, and all... "

"We used to get boys for each other," he said. "I could always get the workers he liked, and he could get the intellectual ones I preferred. We kissed a lot, but little more."

I got to Brighton for the ten o'clock train that night. Lord Alfred never wrote to me again, nor I to him. He died in 1945.

After meeting Douglas I went on to Paris, and fiddled around there a good deal as one does on a first trip, meeting a good many persons. By that time I could speak French fairly well, still not too fluently.

LEYLAND: I understand you met André Gide during your stay in Paris. Could you talk about that meeting?

STEWARD: His name is nearly forgotten today for some reason, but André Gide was one of the first writers of the twentieth century who dared openly to confess his homosexuality in print. He produced two classics of homosexual literature: *The Counterfeiters* and *The Immoralist*, as well as a very early Platonic dialogue on the subject—*Corydon*—in 1911. Unabashed, he could write—and be accepted for writing—a haunting sentence about the Arab boys whom he loved: "More precisely, I was attracted to them by what remained of the sun on their brown skins"; and could in 1920 say in print: "In the name of what God or what ideal do you forbid me to live according to my nature?... My normal is your abnormal, and your normal is my abnormal." These were strong statements indeed for those early years, especially when it is remembered that despite France's reputation for tolerance, the basic tradition in that country was heterosexual, that of a man for his wife and mistress. Homosexuality, when it occasionally reached the public press, was referred to as an "outrage of manners/taste" (*outrage des mœurs*).

I had been in correspondence with him, and it was only natural that on this, my first trip to Europe, Monsieur Gide should be included. Although in my callow literary judgment of the time Gide did not measure up to the other "greats," he was nonetheless important to me, because his brave and brilliant stand for homosexuality was like a lighthouse in those dark and stormy days of the 1930s. His writing lacked the realism of today, of course (such language was not used in those days), but it had talent, skill, comprehension, and understanding of the human heart. To many, Gide's writing was thin, but to me in my twenties he was one of the first knights of Camelot.

It is difficult to say what was in my mind that muggy Parisian afternoon in August when I sought out his address on the rue Vaneau, climbed a flight of stairs, and very timidly rapped at the door. I was quite nervous and a little frightened.

Neither Gide nor a maid answered my knock. Instead it was an eighteen-year-old Arab boy. He was like a very handsome young Roman, dark and bronze-like with splendidly chiseled nose and mouth, and (to borrow a phrase from Wilde's letters) the tents of midnight were folded in his eyes; moons hid in their curtains. His face rose like a classic sculpture above the straight lines of his white burnoose, and on his head was a tasselled red *chéchia*, a fez.

"I am expected by Monsieur Gide," I gulped in French.

"*De la part de qui?*" His teeth gleamed in a curve of white. "Who is it?"

I was so taken with him that all French momentarily deserted me, but it soon came back. I gave him my name and he asked me to come to wait in the study. I sat down, dumbstruck by his beauty, and he disappeared.

It was a very untidy room with piles of books here and there—stacked on the floor and filling many shelves. A decrepit old typewriter stood on the scarred desk, and the windows were closed with louvered shutters. A moment's panic rose in me, for what I do not know; a feeling, a subcurrent of something almost evil and mysterious. Perhaps it was just the heat, or the claustrophobic sensation induced by the shuttered room.

And then André Gide entered. He was a tall slightly stooped man in his late sixties, wearing a shabby old unbuttoned brown cardigan sweater that sagged from somewhat narrow shoulders. His shirt had no collar, but was secured at the neck below his mobile Adam's apple by a brass collar stud. The face was sensitive and thin-lipped, and he was nearly bald save at the back of his head. His cheekbones were high and hollowed underneath—the sort of face in which Lombroso would have seen Gide's troublesome puritan-Protestantism reflected.

"Monsieur," he said, shaking hands with the usual short sharp French snap. "I am enchanted to meet you." And then he looked around the room. "This is not an inviting place to talk. Let us retire to another room which may be more comfortable."

It was one of those characteristic long French "railroad" apartments, with rooms opening on each side of a central corridor. In one of them with an open door sat the young Arab who had let me in, nearly naked and cross-legged on a bed, sewing a fine seam in his burnoose which he had removed and laid across one knee.

"What an extraordinarily handsome young man," I murmured to M. Gide.

"Yes," he said in English, "he is one of the most beautiful creatures I have ever seen." He smiled. "I speak a little the English. If he hears a compliment one cannot live with him . . . the rest of the day." Then he switched to French again. "In here," he said, opening another door at the end of the hall.

It was an amazing room. It had a huge circular bed draped with a pink satin coverlet, and frilly curved canopy at one end. Circular beds were very rare indeed in 1937.

Gide sat down in a noisy wicker chair with his back towards the windows. "I hope the monsieur will excuse me," he said. "The light is painful to my eyes."

He had the habit of a small cough which constantly interrupted his speech—not exactly asthmatic, but dry and a little rasping. "It is a great pleasure to meet Americans. My books seem to be more popular in your country than in mine. And I thank you for your letters. They have been most moving . . . most flattering.

"Thank you very much." I said. "Yes, your work is very popular in the States," adding that in a course in the modern novel I taught his *The Counterfeiters* and much admired its experimental structure.

He smiled. "I wanted to call the translation *The Coiners,* but Madame Knopf said that such a term would not be as well understood."

"We have just finished reading your *Return from the USSR,*" I said.

"And that too," he said. "I thought 'Back from' would be more forceful than 'Return' but once again Madame Knopf said no. Women are strong in America. One wonders whether she or her husband is the publisher."

"You were gravely disappointed with Russia," I said.

"Ah!" he said, striking his forehead with the palm of his hand. "That is hardly the word. I was profoundly... disillusioned. So much there, so wonderful, so fascinating. I went there expecting to find the new race—the handsome young men, the workers... and all I found was a state headed for the worst kind of dictatorship of the few, those high in the party,. And no freedom at all in sexual matters, except marriage and divorce. It has gone the way of all great centralized powers." He smiled again. "I apologize, but your country must be included. Have you been to the Exposition yet?" he asked.

I nodded.

"Then you have seen the two pavilions—Russia with its façade, the hammer and sickle confronting the German eagle and the swastika directly across the way. I find it extremely symbolic. And it will be all too short a time, I fear, until Germany and Russia do really confront each other. It will be Armageddon; we will all be destroyed."

I thought that perhaps it would be wise to try to turn him to another topic. "What do you think of American writers?"

"I like many of them," he said. "There is Steinbeck—such simplicity and understanding. And empathy with his characters. His *Cannery Row* is beautiful."

"And *The Grapes of Wrath*?"

"I did not like that so much. It was very painful."

"*The Immoralist* was a painful book too," I said. "At least for some of us. You had the courage to speak out about the 'problem' here in France when no one else dared touch the subject. What do you think of Hemingway?" I went on like an inquiring reporter.

The Gallic hand vibrated in front of my face. "No, no," he said forcefully. "He is too... too physical. One can see through the hairy chest. He is a poseur; he pretends to be a man but all the time struggles against what he really is—else why the overwhelming male friendships in all his works?"

I wanted to get the word out of him. "Do you mean you think him homosexual?"

Gide smiled and shrugged. "It is not for me to say."

"What other writers do you like?"

"Faulkner. He did a spendid piece of work in *Sanctuary*, but nothing since. And Dos Passos is interesting. Some critics claim he is a disciple of mine. And Michael Gold—such feeling, such pity for the Jews."

"Gold has been very much against us all," I said. "Do you like Dreiser?"

"I can't read him. He is too... lumpy. Too ungrammatical."

I smiled to hear the titan of American letters so easily disposed of. "A lot of critics feel that the floral period of the American novel was the 1920s," I said. "Wharton, Wilder, Hemingway, Willa Cather... "

"Who is Cather? I have not heard of him."

I explained gently that it was a woman, and then asked, "Have you ever thought of coming to America?"

"I am afraid of New York," he said.

"A lot of people are," I said, "but they would be very kind to you."

"Ah, yes... perhaps *too* kind. I would like to go incognito but that is not possible. Even in Russia I was recognized. I do not think I would be physically able to stand your great country."

Shifting topics a bit, I told him that I had seen Lord Alfred Douglas in England. His eyebrows went up.

"A dreadful man," he said. "A shocking man."

"Will you ever write any more about Wilde and Lord Alfred?" I asked.

"When that point in my journals is published," he said, "there will be more perhaps. But in *Si le Grain ne Meurt* I said most of what I wanted to say."

It was a short interview but I did not want to tire him. "Your *chef-d'œuvre*," I said, holding out a French edition of *The Counterfeiters*. "Would you be kind enough to sign this for me?"

"Delighted," he said. "It is always flattering." He took the book and inscribed an elegantly phrased sentiment, pausing to make sure of the exact spelling of my name. At the door, he said "Au revoir" and then delivered himself of a short speech deploring the lack of an exact American equivalent for the expression. "I hope that you will come to see me again when I am recovered from my recent travels."

I assured him that I would. He took my address at the Hotel Récamier and promised to give me a *coup de téléphone* soon.

I thanked him, not expecting to hear from him again. But about ten days later, the *patronne* at the hotel, much impressed, told me that Monsieur Gide had phoned and left a message which said: "Can you come this evening at nine o'clock?"

Nothing in the world could have stopped me. Gide himself met me at the door. "I have a little surprise for you," he said, handing me an inscribed copy of his novel, *Les Caves du Vatican*.

"I am overwhelmed," I said.

"Ah, but that is not really the surprise," he said. "Come with me."

Once again we went down the long corridor towards the room with the circular bed. He half-opened the door and I went in, and then to my amazement he closed the door again with himself on the outside.

Lighted only by the frilly little pink tulip-lamp on the bed-table the young Arab who had opened the door for me on my first visit sensually stretched his naked limbs on the bed and smiled, and held out his arms in invitation.

"I am Ali," he said.

Small wonder that I have never forgotten the works of André Gide.

LEYLAND: Where did you go after meeting Gide?

STEWARD: After my stay in Paris I went down to the southeast of France at Gertrude Stein's invitation to visit her and Alice at Bilignin, and spent a couple of weeks there with the two of them. And after that, on to Zurich where Thornton Wilder was writing *Our Town*. Gertrude gave me a note of introduction to him, and we met; then I went on to Küsnacht to meet Thomas Mann and had lunch with the whole Mann family there.

LEYLAND: I understand you had a brief affair with Thornton Wilder.

STEWARD: Yes. Let me first say something about a curious little literary footnote regarding Thornton Wilder. I met him for the first time with Gertrude's introduction in hand, and Thornton gave me a great lecture about "normalizing" myself or at least on how to handle my homosexuality and learning to live with it, and a lot of advice about meeting the problem; reading the great homosexual writers of the past. We talked all evening and walked all night in the rain. We walked and walked getting wetter and wetter, but Thornton had to show me where Tristan Tzara had begun Dadaism by reading laundry lists into poetry, and then he had to show me the house where Nietzsche "in great loneliness" had written *Zarathustra*—and then he insisted we stay up until dawn to hear the bells of Zurich as Max Beerbohm had described them.

Well, that was in my drinking days, and I kept going into every café we passed. My feet were getting wet and so was I, and I kept hollering for an umbrella. When daylight came I went home to dry out and fell into bed and slept all day, but Thornton went to his hotel and wrote the last act of *Our Town*, which begins with the graveyard scene with umbrellas. He confessed later that he had "struck a match on me," and that the graveyard-umbrella scene came from my complaining about the walk in the wet.

LEYLAND: Had Thornton Wilder been basically homosexually oriented in his life up to this time or bisexual?

STEWARD: Entirely homosexually oriented. And after one of his "lectures" to me we fell into bed, he using the old "Princeton first-year" business of *frottage*, or being a *fricator* or whatever you prefer, and after five or six thrusts he pleasured himself, got up and used the towel and said "Didn't you come? Didn't you come?" And the answer of course was no. The casual acquaintance I had with Thornton went on for many years after that until it was broken up by the war, and by various other things.

LEYLAND: Did you ever live with him at any time?

STEWARD: No. It was just a passing thing. In a life that had to be very circumspect, I suppose, I was just a contact—his Chicago piece.

LEYLAND: To what extent had Wilder integrated his sexuality into his life?

STEWARD: I think perhaps that he had not integrated it at all—that it was an entirely separate thing. Gertrude once said that Thornton had a curious division in his personality, that he loved the gypsy world of the theater, and all that went with it and all the people in it, and then just as he was about to let go of himself, the red traffic light of his New England puritanism would come on, and the green would go off. Everything would stop. I think that was quite true. He never discussed sex. Even in his writing all sexual activity seems to be done behind your back and is not to be talked about at all. It was a sort of low animal release, no more than that. In his work—for example *Theophilus North*—the boy and girl go upstairs to the bedroom, the door shuts behind them, and a new chapter begins on the next page. He simply cannot write, or perhaps think, about sexual things. Or else he does it with a kind of tongue-in-cheek attitude as in *The Matchmaker, the Merchant of Yonkers*, ending up as *Hello, Dolly!* or the very early novel, the pure-fool one called *Heaven's My Destination*.

LEYLAND: Then you went to meet Thomas Mann in Switzerland, also in 1937?

STEWARD: Yes. I had lunch with him and the whole family—even the Great

Dane, which seemed to me to be about seven feet high. Frau Katia Mann spoke English, the others German or French. It was certainly a multilingual experience. Frau Mann, Erika, Klaus were there—and I've forgotten the name of the other one. Klaus, I guess, was the one who committed suicide.

After lunch we retired to his study where we had a very long literary discussion, in French; my German was nonexistent. I told him that I thought *The Magic Mountain* was the greatest novel of the twentieth century, and that having read it, I found that instead of diminishing in perspective as time went by, as so many things do, it grew larger each year. I asked him if he were ever going to do a sequel to it (a foolish question, certainly, but I was young) and he said no, he had said everything he wanted to in that one. And finally I asked him what he thought the theme of the greatest novel of the century might be, since he very modestly disclaimed the statement of mine that I thought *Der Zauberberg* the greatest. He pondered the question for a while and then said, "The need of everyman for solitude versus his desire for companionship, and the desire for solitude versus his need for companionship." He was very kind. He signed a couple of books for me including my favorite *Der Tod in Venedig*, and I went my way. Our correspondence lasted for many years after that, even after he came to America to live. He was always polite and charming—the complete gentleman.

LEYLAND: Did you feel that there was an overtly homosexual side to Thomas Mann?

STEWARD: Yes, indeed—oh, my yes. The way he describes the friendship between Hans Castorp and his cousin Joachim in *The Magic Mountain* certainly leaves very little to the reconstruction of the imagination, because it's *there*.

LEYLAND: Perhaps he had a lifestyle similar to that of John Addington Symonds—married, but also capable of having affairs with male friends?

STEWARD: Yes, I had the feeling all through that day's experience—it was even underlined by the way he put his arm around my shoulders as I was leaving. I of course did nothing overt with him. I was quite discreet, because really I was quite in awe of him.

LEYLAND: Turning to Gertrude Stein—Most of her early biographers ignored the homosexual dimensions in her work and in her life. Such a conspiracy of silence is undoubtedly due either to homophobia or lack of appreciation of the gay sensibility. More recent biographers have tried to be more open.

STEWARD: I think it was Richard Hall who once referred to her lesbianism as the "worst kept secret of the twentieth century." Almost everyone who has any sophistication at all or any acquaintance with her life, her lifestyle, and her life with Alice certainly must have known all along that it was a lesbian relationship.

And the biographers—Linda Simon when she wrote her biography of Alice Toklas in 1977 was very forthright about it, and James Mellow when he wrote *Charmed Circle* did not withhold anything. So the major biographers have come to accept it and talk and write about it. I kept quiet about it because I had not written anything for a long time and was lazy about it; and secondly Gertrude said "twenty years after I die" which would have made it 1966, so I was only ten years beyond that when I got around to writing the memoir in *Dear Sammy*. The most superb job was done by Richard Bridgman in *Gertrude Stein in Pieces*. Sutherland in his critical study in 1951 did not mention her lesbian nature at all; neither did Elizabeth Sprigge in her superficial life of Gertrude, and Brinnin barely skims over the surface of it. Bridgman's work on Stein is really a *tour de force* because he never knew either of them, not being of that generation. But he merely took her writing and from it drew out the whole picture perfectly and beautifully. His book appeared in 1970, and there were no more secrets after that. It remains, along with Donald Sutherland's book, the best critique of Gertrude Stein.

LEYLAND: During one of your visits to Bilignin, Gertrude asked you: "Are *you* queer or gay or different?" And then she said (I am quoting her words from your book *Dear Sammy*): "We are surrounded by homosexuals, they do all the good things in all the arts. When I ran down the male ones to Hemingway it was because I thought he was a secret one. If Shakespeare had had a psychiatrist we would never have had the plays or sonnets. I like all people who produce and Alice does too. And what they do in bed is their own business, and what we do is not theirs. We saw a part of all this in you, but there was a dark corner and we were puzzled, and now we have the right answer, haven't we?" Did you get the impression that Gertrude usually spoke so openly with her gay friends?

STEWARD: No, not at all. I'm sure she never—or very rarely—talked about it. Why in the world she would have chosen me to talk about it is a mystery. You know, when I saw Thornton in Zurich, I asked him if Gertrude and Alice were lesbians. Later Gertrude laughed about it. The thing is—well, perhaps it lies in the adjective that Gertrude once used about me; she said I was a "motherable" person. One reviewer of *Dear Sammy* called me Gertrude's "spiritual son." Maybe I triggered her maternal instinct and that led her to discuss it. But I'm sure she never discussed it with Thornton, nor with Bravig Imbs or George Platt Lynes who had come to her and surrounded her. I know she never discussed it with Cecil Beaton or Francis Rose. I know she didn't with Donald Sutherland because he said so—and really, I don't know why she picked me, unless it was that I seemed discreet and had grown very close to her. In two weeks, alone with them, you have no idea how very *close* one could come to them in sixteen hours a day.

LEYLAND: I understand that at times Gertude and Alice had a stormy relationship.

STEWARD: Well, there were frictions—nothing very serious. But small abrasive situations arose sometimes regarding household matters. Alice would say, "Now Lovey, don't do that, don't sit in that chair. It's not good for your back. Sit over there." And Lovey would go and sit over there. Once in a while there was some grumbling on Gertrude's part. I remember she spoke once about "Alice's nagging me all the time" but she said it jokingly. As far as serious ruptures, I think there were none at all. There were periods when the love lay fallow, I suppose didn't show itself in any way, but they were always models of decorum in every way to Francis and myself as well. They were like two Victorian ladies who didn't approve too much of modern ways. They certainly didn't like drinking and drunks. Alice smoked all the time and Gertrude didn't, and Gertrude didn't like that very much. She would wrinkle her nose at the sight of an overfilled ashtray.

LEYLAND: Do you know whether they had any friendships, close or otherwise, with lesbian writers such as Natalie Barney?

STEWARD: There are several stories about Natalie, and Virgil Thomson is responsible for one story about Gertrude's asking where Natalie Barney got all her tricks, at which point Alice is supposed to have said, "Oh, she picks them up from the toilets of the Louvre Department Store." There were some lesbian writers in their circle of friends. I don't know how many of them are still alive. Marie Laurencin, the painter, is gone now, and I'm not sure about some others. But actually you didn't see so many women hanging around as you saw males. During their American tour, they met and made a good many female friends, but how many of them were lesbian I have no way of knowing.

LEYLAND: One thing so very beautiful about both of them was that their lesbianism, their sexuality, was so well-integrated in their lives and their work.

STEWARD: Yes, that's very true. They were perfectly integrated. And the fact that it had begun in the early years of the century and lasted so long, continuing without interruption even until Gertrude's death in 1946. Astounding. And then, of course, it went on even after death. Alice just became the custodian of the legend, the custodian of Gertrude's greatness. Until her own death in 1967.

LEYLAND: Did Gertrude or Alice ever talk to you about the repressed homosexuality of Hemingway aside from what Gertrude said to you on a couple of occasions mentioned in *Dear Sammy*?

STEWARD: No not really. I think that Scott Donaldson of the College of William and Mary has written something about Hemingway in that regard, but I haven't seen it yet. Carlos Baker in his definitive life of Hemingway merely brushes the topic, which Edmund Wilson had suggested as early as *The Wound and the Bow*—a thing that made Hemingway very angry indeed. Gertrude, however, made several small references to his homosexuality; they were always a bit denigrating, and they were also always suggestive of the fact that she didn't really know. Or care. Alice one day said something about the Chevalier d'Eon—the woman of the courts of Louis XV and XVI who wore male dress until ordered to do otherwise—and Gertrude said, "Yes, and if Ernest had been alive then he would have worn the same kind of clothes" which was a pretty direct statement.

LEYLAND: Perhaps Hemingway didn't know himself.

STEWARD: That I think is largely true. I had one remark in *Dear Sammy* about what a he-man he was, and Gertrude put her thumb to measure about halfway down her little finger and said he was really about that big, and then we talked a little about compensation and that was all she said at that time.

LEYLAND: In one of her conversations with you Gertrude said "Creating is not remembering but experiencing. It is to look and to hear and to write—without remembering. It is the immediate feelings arranged in words as they occur to me. But only a very small number of artists reveals a sensitivity to materials and to the world in general. That is, I mean, acting according to their experiencing and to be really living and creating." Which writers did she feel had this sensitivity?

STEWARD: If I remember correctly, that statement followed a discussion of Hart Crane's poetry, and I think she enlarged it by an illustration to Willa Cather as well as by one to Edith Wharton. I would be reluctant to hazard a guess about any others.

LEYLAND: For many years, as you say in your book, Gertrude and Alice were friends it with French Catholic writer Henri Daniel-Rops. Then all of a sudden there was a break in the relationship around the time of World War II. What actually happened? Daniel-Rops strikes me as being somewhat of a snob, and rather right-wing.

STEWARD: Yes, that's true, and I think he was homosexual as well, although Madeleine, his wife, never gave any indication she knew it. I never heard anything about it from either Gertrude or Alice, although Alice once said: "Can she [Madeleine] not know the truth?" About Henri, that is. But I think what happened—and this again is supposition, although it is fairly borne out by a few things that Alice said to me in the fifties or sixties—is that Gertrude had become enamored of Madeleine Rops, and Alice did not like it at all—was jealous, really, and that was the reason for the break-up. Nothing definite was said; it was just the little stories that Alice would tell of the Daniel-Rops, long after Gertrude had died. For example; Henri Daniel-Rops made a great deal of money on a popular life of Jesus which he wrote, which was published in many different editions—even de luxe—and then the two of them showed up at a function in Paris, with Madeleine wearing a mink stole, at which point François Mauriac came up and stroked the mink stole lovingly and said: "Cher Jésus, cher Jésus." Alice always got great deal of delight out of telling little stories like that about the two of them, always with a faint malice. Putting two and two together, I think it was really that, Gertrude's attraction to Madeleine, because Madeleine was truly a beautiful woman—vivacious, highly-colored, attractive, and *bien-faite,* well-made, which is one of the highest compliments the French can pay.

LEYLAND: In one of her conversations with you, Gertrude mentions her book *G.M.P.* which has the section "A Long Gay Book." It would appear that Gertrude was using the word "gay" in its homosexual meaning long before it came into common usage. Am I right?

STEWARD: Yes, I think so. And in her piece "Miss Furr and Miss Skeen" from *Geography and Plays* in 1922, she quite definitely uses "gay" to mean homosexual. And she used it when she asked me the question that bowled me over that day; "Are *you* queer or gay or different or 'of it' as the French say, or whatever they are calling it nowadays?"

LEYLAND: Which are your favorites among the writings of Gertrude Stein?

STEWARD: That's almost impossible for me to answer. I like many of her early things—*Lucy Church Amiably,* some of her *Tender Buttons*; some of her more arcane and hermetic things I still don't understand and probably never will. I don't expect to in my lifetime. I know her work *in extenso* pretty well, but I really don't know it in depth—as for example Thornton Wilder knew it (what a pity he never wrote anything about her except the introductions to various volumes!) or as Bridgman investigated it in his book. Some of her light and lilting lyrical pieces are very nice—there are sections in *Alphabets and Birthdays* I find very charming, and also in *Bee Time Vine* there are nice passages.

LEYLAND: Some of the portraits perhaps?

STEWARD: Yes, my all-time favorite short piece, I think, is "A Valentine to Sherwood Anderson" one of the few that she recorded. Perhaps my fondness for that lies in the fact that one can still hear that golden wonderful voice speaking the valentine and that has helped me to like it so much. And also "A Completed Portrait of Picasso." So there is a fairly large number of pieces that I enjoy and return to again and again like the long passage about "When they are a little older" that occurs in *A Long Gay Book*. I have seen people actually turn pale as Gertrude in that passage approaches the point at which they find themselves at present in their lives.

LEYLAND: Gertrude also wrote a portrait of you in her *Alphabets and Birthdays* (Yale University Press, 1957), after she had discovered that you were allergic to many foodstuffs. We'll print it here in full, since I'm sure many of the readers of this interview would enjoy it:

And now for S.

Sammy and Sally and Save and Susy.

Sammy had his aunt and his aunt had Sammy and his aunt's name was Fanny and Fanny had Sammy.

Sammy was his name and he was funny and he had an aunt Fanny and she was funny.

Sammy could not eat bread or potatoes or chocolate or cake or eggs or butter or even a date, if he did he fainted away, that was his way, a very funny way but it was Sammy's way. His aunt Fanny was not funny that way, but she was funny in another way, wherever she saw a cat or dog a turtle or a bird or a third, a third of anything she had to turn away. She was funny that way.

But Sammy had his aunt Fanny and aunt Fanny had her Sammy.

A lemonade perhaps or a beefsteak, or a plate or a but dear me no not ice cream, he could not eat cream, nor a birthday cake, he could eat the candles but not the cake, poor dear Sammy.

Sample and example.

His Aunt Fanny did not care that Sammy could not share what she ate, she just went on cooking and eating and Sammy just went on looking and fainting. They were very funny Sammy and his Aunt Fanny. Poor dear Sammy.

And in spite of all Sammy grew tall tall enough to go to school.

In school they were taught

Sample and example.

There was a pretty girl and she had a curl and her name was Sally. They called her pretty Sally and she was a sample. And then there was Sammy there just was Sammy poor dear Sammy and he was an example.

And then one day pretty Sally in play asked Sammy to come to her house on her birthday.

Sammy did.

There was a great cake with frosting and a date and Sammy feeling faint said he could not eat icing or the date or cake but he could eat candles if they were to be given. But no said Sally oh no don't you know, and if we did not burn them I would not have my next one not my next birthday, oh naughty Sammy wants to take my next birthday away.

Now you may think this is a funny story but not it is true, anybody even you could know Sammy poor dear Sammy and his Aunt Fanny, he lives there too and it is true all the story of Sammy all the story of his Aunt Fanny all the story of Aunt Fanny all the story of Sammy is true. Poor dear Sammy.

*　　*　　*

LEYLAND: In the 1950s you resigned your position as a university professor and became a tattoo artist. Would you like to talk about that?

STEWARD: Yes. In 1952 I was completely fed up to the water-level with university teaching. The students got dumber each year and had less of an associational background. I mentioned in *Dear Sammy* that there came one year when in an entering freshman class of forty, not one person had ever heard of Homer, but three-fourths of them knew how to change a sparkplug, even the girls. So finally I decided that that was not for me. The last five years of teaching were really loathsome. I thought I had better get out of teaching. I didn't know what to do, I had been trained for that and nothing else, and so I overlapped teaching with my first two years of tattooing—which gave rise to a great many interesting situations. I taught myself, largely, but got lessons from an old grand master of the art in Milwaukee, Amund Dietzel. It was a drop-out thing, which nowadays happens all the time but in the 1950s it was a little unusual, to stop university teaching and become a tattoo artist. I enjoyed the double life, having already enjoyed a double life up until then with my homosexuality. I would finish my classes at the university at four o'clock in the afternoon, go downtown to south State Street—the highest class skid row in Chicago (Madison was lowest, Clark Street just above that, and State Street the classiest one). It was down there in an old arcade called Playland, right next to the Pacific Garden Mission where Billy Sunday was converted, in a little shack attached to an interior wall of the arcade, that I first started to tattoo. And I used to practice on the skin of winos—you'd give them a dollar, and they were very happy: they not only had a new tattoo but enough money for their daily jug of wine.

But when you come right down to asking me, it's difficult to answer beyond this. It was not self-destructive, as Alice said. I just wanted to get out of teaching since I felt it was going nowhere; and higher education today seems to bear me out. Nothing was happening in the classroom. If two people responded, if the curtain went up, that is, on the great world of art or drama or literature or music for two persons in the course of a year—well, that was some reward, but not very much.

LEYLAND: How long did you work as a tattoo artist?

STEWARD: I worked from about 1952 to 1963 in Chicago, when they changed the law in Illinois so that you had to be twenty-one to get tattooed; a move that cut out all the boot sailors from the Great Lakes Naval Training Center. Then I went up to Milwaukee with Cliff Raven and tattooed there on weekends for a year, and in 1965 came to California and had a shop in Oakland under my *nom d'aiguilles*, Phil Sparrow, from '65 to 1970. Then I got mugged or strong-armed three times in my shop and gave up in 1970 before getting a bullet or knife in the ribs.

LEYLAND: I understand that you kept a journal for Kinsey during your period as a tattoo artist. Was it also partly a sexual journal?

STEWARD: Yes, it turned out to be, after I had found and isolated about thirty-two major motivations for getting tattooed, the aspect of tattooing in which Kinsey was especially interested. Twenty-five of those motives were purely, or impurely, sexual, and the others utilitarian, like social security numbers. The motives ranged all the way from an assertion of masculine status through the act of possession or sexual identity, to an existential or "forever" act, as Sartre defines it; one that can't be undone. Other motivations were such things as narcissism, the pseudo or incomplete narcissism in which the person thinks he can further beautify his body by decoration; whereas the complete narcissist knows that he doesn't want to spoil his pretty pink body with a decoration. Then there's the manhood initiation rites, a tattoo substituting for what used to be the graduation from knickers to long pants, or your first communion, or something like that; now our culture has no manhood initiation rites unless you'd count cigarettes, pot, or alcohol. Or a compensation motive: a tattoo being a relief for feelings of inadequacy or loss of a limb; or imitation. After seeing the Robert Mitchum movie *Night of the Hunter*" everybody wanted "Love" and "Hate" written on the first phalanges of the fingers. Or a farm-wife having seen a TV movie in which a girl had a small butterfly tattooed on the shoulder would come in for one like it. Or the macho thing with the Marlboro ads, which gave us the greatest trouble: the man in the ads had an eagle or other symbol on the back of his hand; and no ethical tattoo artist would ever tattoo on the face or hands. Tattooing is really a very curious business. And then there was exhibitionism, pure and simple; I didn't know until two or three years into tattooing why so many boys always got tattooed on the left biceps. Do you know why? So they could hang the arm out the car window while driving, and impress the girls.

LEYLAND: What has your life been like in the past few years?

STEWARD: Oh, it's been very happy. I've been a pornographer. I've written six or seven novels under the name of Phil Andros, and one hardcover collection of Phil Andros short stories, called *$tud*. Actually, I had begun to write again in the late 1950s under the gentle and persistent prodding of Rudolf Burkhardt, or Rudolf Jung—he used both names—who was English editor for *Der Kreis* ("The Circle") in Zurich. He got me started to writing again—first, little essays and then short stories in *Der Kreis* from about 1958 until it suspended publication in 1967. ("Our work is now done," they said—meaning that the climate of acceptance of homosexuality was changing. But actually they ran into financial difficulties...) Rudolf published a great many of my poems and stories and essays, under various pen names.

LEYLAND: I have in my library a small anthology called *Four from the Circle*.

STEWARD: It contains one of my stories, "Third Movement," under the name of Philip Young. I made a bibliography of my "works" and ephemera a couple of years ago for the Kinsey people and was surprised to see so many things scattered through *Der Kreis*, and the astounding number of pen names, perhaps ten or twelve. Then Rudolf put me in touch with Kim Kent in Copenhagen, who at that time was publishing *eos* and *amigo*, with stories in Danish, English, and German. I created for him the character of Phil Andros, which is of course a world play of Greek origin: "philos," love, and "andros," of man—thus either "man-lover" or "lover-man."

Phil Andros was a hustler, but an intelligent one; a cut above the ordinary. The *$tud* volume contained about eighteen stories collected from *eos* and *amigo*.

LEYLAND: You wrote several articles for the Danish magazines also?

STEWARD: Yes, on all sorts of topics: the "leather-mania," the bull-market in America, the Negro homosexual, tattooing. And then Kim Kent published what in America had appeared under the title of *The Joy Spot* as *Ring-Around-the Rosy*, a trilingual—German, Danish, English—version of six interconnected stories, a sort of Schnitzlerian *Reigen* or *La Ronde* or *Hands-Around* thing, the first episode of which had circulated for many years in typescript as a literary translation of the famous series of drawings of the motorcyclist picking up the farm-boy; then episode two had the motorcyclist and a homosexual, and so on. *The Joy Spot* was published by arrangement with Le Salon in San Francisco.

I've often said that I wrote them for my own amusement, and to bring pleasure to lonely old men in hotel rooms at night. Actually, it was rather fun, having created a character like Phil Andros who was literate and intelligent—another sort of John Rechy, I suppose—and who reacted to people instead of being just a hustler who was paid and then departed, a person who enjoyed a sort of intellectual and emotional give-and-take. The stories are, I think, fairly sensitive and illuminating about homosexuals in general. But a lot of homosexual readers are so revolted, turned off by the idea of hustling, that a great many readers would not even bother with the stories because Phil was a hustler. This was somewhat annoying but not enough to send me spinning downward.

LEYLAND: There are elements of S&M in much of your writing done under the pen name of Phil Andros, for instance in the stories published in the S&M magazine *Drummer*. To what extent has this particular form of sexuality been part of your own life?

STEWARD: Long ago, shortly after World War II ended, I found myself interested in the sado-masochistic phenomenon, which even in the 1920s we called "Sadie-Maisie." And long before S&M became ritualized, codified, hardened in a patterned stimulus and response, Phil Andros found himself following the scent of a leather jacket on a drizzling night in Chicago, following for blocks, perhaps, and finally daring to approach. In those days before S&M became the voluntary game it is today, we never knew whether that leather jacket would leave us alive or not. We took fearful chances, especially when we asked a straight, or a drunk, or a drunk straight to whip us. I experimented with S&M for a period of about ten years, gradually abandoning it as my adjustment to my homosexuality became better balanced and less guilt-ridden.

LEYLAND: Do you agree with John Rechy's statement in his *Gay Sunshine* interview that people interested in S&M are reactionary, the "self-haters of the gay world," or do you side with those who think pain can be an added dimension and can be part of a growth relationship?

STEWARD: With neither one, exactly. Before the apologists for S&M began to explicate the phenomenon so painstakingly, or to explain it simplistically as "self-hate," I think there was a more subtle possibility. Man has always needed heroes, and certain areas in history are notable for the lack of them. S&M did not begin in the immediate postwar period, of course, but it gained a powerful impetus at that time. We were searching for heroes. And certain forces were removing the hero from the scene—the growth of the matriarchy, chronicled by Philip Wylie in *Generation of Vipers*, the cult of Momism. And secondly, the growth of automation; the Hero in his aspect of breadwinner disappears. And finally, the Hero as warrior vanishes. What good are his bow and arrow, his shotgun, his TNT, against the little killing sun of Hiroshima?

Pain as an "added dimension, and part of a growth relationship"? It seems to me that perhaps the M's are merely looking for their lost Hero. The complicated fabric of the ritual of the leather bar merely conceals the small and lonely cry for something to admire, at least so it seems to me. Homosexuality is not all self-hate, or guilt-feelings, or love, or domination or submission, or any one thing; it's a many-branching path, down which we are all walking.

LEYLAND: Have you ever had any extended love relationships in your own life?

STEWARD: No, never. One misses it, of course, when one grows old; a companion by the hearthside would be nice. But I have resisted it because I shirked the responsibility. For a while in my life I was quite bisexual, even during that period when I knew Gertrude. During the interview Kinsey did with me, he said, "Why don't you stop fooling yourself and forget about the other side?—although I guess I had largely done so already.

The "Ackerley syndrome" hit me about two years ago with this little long-haired dachshund who had to be destroyed just last week. I loved that little bullnecked, barrelchested, bandylegged, black-and-tan beast more than most members of my family. And believe me, baby, it really broke me up when he had to be put away. I had written several thousand words, about half a novel, about the dog and the various owners he had had before coming to me, but I didn't know how to end it. Now, unfortunately, I have an ending.

As homosexuals our emotional lives are broken into many pieces. When we find something —a living object—which can give us unswerving devotion, unquestioning love, over the years, we tend to open ourselves completely. If we have nothing living, then we tend to collect objects that have meaning for us—as Newman did, gathering souvenirs of laurel leaves, sentimentalizing over his old blue cloak.

LEYLAND: So you have been a loner?

STEWARD: A loner, quite definitely. I have always been convinced that perhaps a basic component of the homosexual matrix is the butterfly syndrome—always looking for the Ideal Friend, always searching for new shepherds in our pastures. We're with one for five dirty minutes, and then we're on to the next, looking for the man of our dreams, and a permanent "arrangement." I think that's one of the saddest things in Ackerley's autobiography — his search for the ideal. There's a lot in that novel of mine on this topic.

You see, we who grew up in the twenties, thirties, forties, and fifties never had the support of groups or movements; it's difficult for the young today to realize this. Once someone asked me why I was not "politically involved with my oppressed gay brothers and sisters during the Depression"!! Hell, we were involved with staying alive! There were no political movements at all. We all felt set apart, individuals. We got all the sex we wanted, but marching?! Where to? Who would dare march? The young of today have no conception at all of the lives we had to lead — furtive, hidden — but joyously hedonistic just the same. Involved? What was there to get involved in? We learned how to "detach" ourselves for our own self-protection. We learned what Keats meant by "negative capability" — the refusal to accept a universe reducible to a neat $x^2 + y^2$ formula, content to live in the midst of doubts and uncertainties and secrets without any irritable reaching out after facts or reasons. We all let a little fog rise around us, to conceal us — and thus not categorized, not pigeonholed, not stereotyped — we enjoyed a really perfect form of freedom. We developed our inner resources carefully over the years, knowing the day would come when we would need them, when we were old — a stock of memories to sustain us, a sort of masochistic resignation towards Time which is the greatest of all sadists.

I really don't know how basic it is. Some people do need companionship; others seem to get along all right alone. I would not be averse to companionship but I've had to train myself along other lines. Right now, as you grow older you go out less. It would be nice I suppose to have a man around the house but if not, you settle for a dog.

LEYLAND: How do you feel about the question of age as you've grown older? Do you feel at ease?

STEWARD: I've forced myself to feel at ease because there isn't anything to be done about it. I hate it, I hate every bit of it, I hate the dreadful slackening of the flesh, the deposits of calcium in the tissues, and everything else which is an accompaniment of age. I will not be a Pollyanna about it, and I will not never refer to myself as "s****r c*****n" as most people refer to us old farts — er — fogeys. The problem of a homosexual growing old is one that everyone has to meet in his own way. If we can reach the goal when experience has multiplied itself to such an extent that one is no longer under any compulsions of any kind toward persons or things or situations — a truly *detached* person — that seems to be a freedom worth aiming for. When old age had freed him from sexual desire, Sophocles said he felt he had been liberated from a mad, tyrannical master. Of course, the hell arises when the libido stays constant and the body deteriorates.

I really have no greatly helpful advice for anyone growing old as a homosexual — aside perhaps from keeping busy. I was forty-six when I broke from teaching and went into tattooing; and that's a helluva time to break. But I can honestly say that I had more fun, enjoyed myself more during the tattoo years, than at any other time in my life. Some persons struggle against taking orders; luckily, even during the teaching years, then certainly in tattooing and also in writing, I have been my own boss, and that has been very pleasant. I think if you're inventive enough you can do it — avoid the pitfalls of depression and too much looking into mirrors.

PHOTO BY HAJIME SAWATARI, 1976

MUTSUO
TAKAHASHI

MUTSUO TAKAHASHI (b. 1937, northern part of Kyushu) has published the following books of poetry: *Mino, My Bull* (1959), *Rose Tree: False Lovers* (1964), *Sleeping, Sinning, and Falling* (1965), *You Dirty Ones, Do Dirtier Things* (1966), *Ode* (1971), *King of the Calendar* (1972), *Verbs: I* (1974), and *Myself or Selfportraits* (1975). His first novel, *Twelve Perspectives*, was published in 1970, and followed by a collection of novellas, *Holy Triangle*, in 1970, and a novel, *Zen's Pilgrimage*, in 1974. In 1976 he published two collections of essays, *On Unknown Poesie* and *Reading Hell*.

Takahashi writes deliberately, often employing rarely used words and phrases, and that is why, as he says in the interview, he is associated with the late Yukio Mishima. He works with an advertising agency in Tokyo.

Translations of Takahashi's poems (by Hiroaki Sato) were published in the book *Poems of a Penisist* (Chicago Review Press, 1975). See also *Orgasms of Light: The Gay Sunshine Anthology* (1977)

KEIZŌ AIZAWA (b. 1929), who interviewed Takahashi, studied English at Tokyo University and has so far published nine books of poetry; his *Collected Poems* came out in 1974. He began writing poems after reading Shakespeare's sonnets, and the poems in his first collection, *Mad Virgin's Songs* (1961), were in fourteen lines.

This interview was translated from the Japanese by Hiroaki Sato, and originally appeared in *Gay Sunshine* no. 31 (Winter 1976/77).

Keizo Aizawa interviews
MUTSUO TAKAHASHI

MUTSUO TAKAHASHI's house is in Setagaya Ward, one of Tokyo's representative residential areas. Built about fifty years ago, ten years after the great Kanto earthquake, the Western-style, two-story house is surrounded with a grove of trees which have dark-blue foliage in the summer. At the entrance door is hung a wooden plaque that says "Zenzai Kutsu," Zenzai's Cave. Zenzai, or Boy Sudhana, was a wealthy man's son who is said to have visited fifty-three wise men, then met Samanthabhadra, and decided to see the enlightenment. Another wooden board hung on a pillar says "Kōdō Kyo." One meaning of the phrase is the "dwelling of a wild boy or monster." Both inscriptions seem to symbolize the essence of the poet, Mutsuo Takahashi. A distinguished scholar lived his last ten years in the house, but it's already eight years since Mr. Takahashi settled down in it, and his presence permeates every nook and corner. The hour of dialogue I had there one evening toward the end of July, while a light shower started and stopped, stopped and started, was, may I say, densely Takahashi-esque. —K.A.

AIZAWA: I am your friend, and that makes it difficult for me to sit down and ask you formal questions. Fortunately, though, I have here *Poems of a Penisist* that Hiroaki Sato translated, so I'd like to start off from there. I've long respected you as a poet, and I think *Poems of a Penisist* is a selection of extremely good poems and a very good starting point for knowing Mutsuo Takahashi. Now, the word "penisist" in the title, is that a word you coined?

TAKAHASHI: Once, when I was in the middle of writing *Ode*, I was drinking at a bar in Shibuya. A young man began talking to me and said, "Mr. Takahashi, aren't you a *penisist*?" I don't remember how I responded then, but thought the word "penisist" interesting and used it in the "Afterword." Several years later— after *Ode* was published—when I saw the same man again, I said, "You used the word *penisist*, and I've used it in my writing." He said, "I don't remember using such a word." I think I heard the word for sure, but if he really didn't say it but I heard it, then it has truly got to be a "revelation." [*Laughter.*]

AIZAWA: I think "penisist" is a very interesting word. It has a feeling, say, of a *penis insisting*. When it's used in the title of a book, it seems to add to the insistence.

TAKAHASHI: It was certainly I who used the word in the "Afterword," but it was the translator, Mr. Sato, who made it part of the title. I felt some resistance halfway through and offered an opinion that perhaps all the poems might better be represented by *Ode*, for example, but Mr. Sato said firmly, "No, this title has an absolutely fresh feeling and has no such problems of imagery as you're afraid of." Well, now, first of all, that book of translated poems is, if anything, Mr. Sato's work, and I don't have any confidence at all about the feeling of English words, so in the end I took him at his word. I now think the title is all right as it was decided on. Because, I must say, my view of art, my view of life is condensed in the word "penisist."

AIZAWA: That's right, because one could add that a penisist's "insistence" holds together all of your writings. About this word, would you elaborate on it? If "homosexuality" means a male's love of a male as a male, it will lead as a matter of course, spiritually and physically, to the praising of the phallus, I think. Does that mean, in short, it isn't pederasty?

TAKAHASHI: I wrote about it in the "Afterword" to *Ode* in some detail, but I'll explain it once again, more plainly. I'd say penisism is homosexuality that doesn't involve the anus. What I think is this: homosexuality with the interference of the anus can't but end up a parody of the sex between a man and a woman. You know, in the anus, though for good reasons, the principle of pleasure exists. On the other hand, the oral cavity doesn't have the kind of pleasure that the anus does. To say it doesn't may be going too far, but its pleasure isn't something as defined as that of the anus. It should rather be thought of as nonpleasure, I think. This non-pleasure must be the essence of homosexuality. In other words, what comes out not between phallus and anus, but between phallus and oral cavity is homosexuality, but in this case too, the essence of homosexuality is not on the side of the phallus, but on the side of the oral cavity, and the way I see it, the essence, as is, is appropriate for the essence of humanity. I'm saying that I take the emptiness of the oral cavity as the symbol of the imperfection of human existence. And I take the phallus, which is the object that the oral cavity hopes to hold to complement its emptiness with, as the symbol of the absolute other, which is perfect. So the essence of homosexuality, and of humanity, must for all its worth be on the side of non-pleasure, of the oral cavity. Here, as you see, is some influence of the great modern rabbi, Martin Buber.

AIZAWA: You mean, *I and Thou.*

TAKAHASHI: Yes. But recently, a French theologian has said that *I and Thou* is only going halfway. In French, it's *Moi et toi*, isn't it, but that still isn't enough, the theologian says. "I" and "the other" are not equal in their relation, but "I" continues to be absolutely lower than "the other" in position, and that is the only way of being in which the imperfection of "I" can be complemented by the perfection of "the other."

AIZAWA: Wasn't the original title *Ich und Du?* There's no appropriate Japanese phrase for it. It can't be *Ore to omae.*

TAKAHASHI: Not *Ore to omae*, but it could be *Wastashi to anatasama*, though to put it that way gives it a sado-masochistic feeling; I mean it in a more spiritual, more metaphysical sense. So *watashi* or "I" is always the "I" on the receiving side. Can this "I" grow to be on the giving side? That is not possible. In the first place, the giving "I" — such a modifier-and-the-modified relation — is self-contradictory. The giver is always "the other."

AIZAWA: Does that mean that "receiving " will lead to "receiving pain"?

TAKAHASHI: The content of what is received could, of course, be pain, but I think ultimately it is joy that's received.

AIZAWA: You have a poem called "Myself in the Manner of Christopher" in *Selfportraits,* one of your books of poems published after *Ode.* In the poem, which is based on the legend of Saint Christopher, the child the speaker carries on his back, though infinitely light, becomes infinitely heavy, and before he knows it, the child who is supposed to be being carried on his back is carrying Christopher. Does that mean not receiving pain but receiving joy?

TAKAHASHI: The poem has a line, "at the pinnacle of ugly embarrassment, with the youth on my shoulders I topple." In other words, the infant that *I* was carrying on my shoulders had turned, before I knew it, into a young man, so I was embarrassed and toppled. This toppling can be said to be toppling from receiving pain to receiving joy. Will this toppling ever become a toppling from receiver to giver? The answer is no. Because receiving pain and receiving joy are the same in receiving. Rather, through the toppling process the content that is received acquires depth.

AIZAWA: In that sense too, I think your metaphor in the poem is superb. I really think that for the poem alone Christopher should remain a saint. Recently, you know, the Vatican has taken him out of the rank of saints on the ground that it's doubtful that he existed historically.

TAKAHASHI: I agree. For Christopher Street in New York too.

AIZAWA: Your mention of New York reminds me of your story, *A Legend of a Holy Place.* I don't think it's been translated into English, but isn't its setting New York, although the word New York doesn't appear once in the novel?

TAKAHASHI: Yes, it's completely New York.

AIZAWA: When I read the novel I thought of various things. It's basically a story of New York, but it's blended with a story of Rome, and the two stories make up the inside and outside of a wall—a fascinating superimposition. And at the center of the story of New York is the image of a peephole on the wall of a health club, and that is very skillfully superimposed on the relation between New York and Rome. Another thing: with *Holy Place* I feel your novel greatly changed. I mean, before it, you have this excellent novel called *Twelve Perspectives,* but that's in the form of a memoir. Then there's this novel called *Holy Promontory.* In this one too, you appear. That changed a little in *Holy Triangle* and changed decisively in *Holy Place,* I think.

TAKAHASHI: The protagonist still appears in the form of "I," but that "I" can be anybody.

AIZAWA: "I" stopped being the same as Mutsuo Takahashi, and this arbitrary "I" goes on various pilgrimages in New York. I take it that the novel is a springboard on which Takahashi the poet becomes Takahashi the novelist, and I'm greatly interested in what's coming after it.

TAKAHASHI: I don't know whether I'm a poet or a prose writer, and I don't know if I've become a prose writer with *A Legend of a Holy Place.* But I can say this much: I wrote the novel because of my stay in New York in 1971, which lasted only about forty days, but it had a great meaning for me. Rilke, you know, talks about his Russian experience. I don't mean to compare myself with Rilke, but for myself the New York experience in me is no less, if not more, important that the Russian experience in Rilke. If I hadn't been to New York at that time, I am quite confident that I wouldn't be what I am now.

AIZAWA: Would you be specific about it?

TAKAHASHI: During the short period of forty days I was there, a friend of mine had the lock to his apartment broken and another friend was robbed of all the money he had at knifepoint one night. Some of my other friends, though they had doormen, had four or five locks on the door and were still frightened, terrified. Even during the daytime, if you walk about the streets you don't know that you won't be killed by a bum, they said. As far as danger goes, that's the most dangerous place, but there's no other place where man's evil side is so openly exposed. In the sense that there is an undeniable element of evil in man, I felt that New York was truly a human city.

AIZAWA: Is your New York the real New York? If New York like that really existed, I think it would be wonderful. But if I walked in Christopher Street, I'm not sure that the sort of things (that happen in *Holy Place*) would happen to me...

TAKAHASHI: I should say that the real New York is either much nicer or much lousier. That's the New York I felt and experienced. Wherever I go, I seem more or less to run into the kind of things I wrote about in that novel, but perhaps in New York things were extreme.

AIZAWA: What strikes me about you is that wherever you go, and in any situation, you bump into its very essence. You may not mean to or make a tour of "evil" places, but you run into them. You don't mean to meet this or that sort of person, but end up running into him. If I may put it this way, you always meet a "guidance."

TAKAHASHI: I feel I'm not the only one, that everybody is running into all sorts of things just as I am.

AIZAWA: That can also be said of your most recent novel, *Zen's Pilgrimage*. If *A Legend of a Holy Place* is a tour of evil places in New York based on the legend of St. Christopher in Christianity, *Zen's Pilgrimage* can be said to be a tour of evil places in Tokyo based on the legend of Zenzai Dōji (Boy Sudhana) in Buddhism. Since I live in Tokyo too, I should be running into the kind of mysterious scenes that are in the novel, but that rarely happens. If there are so many of these mysterious scenes, I'd think Tokyo and Japan would be wonderful.

TAKAHASHI: I am somewhat dissatisfied with *Pilgrimage*. My dissatisfaction is, first, that as a piece of literature it's far from perfect, and, second, that I failed to describe even one tenth of what I experienced. It should be at least ten times as interesting as it is now.

AIZAWA: That's far out. Normally, there isn't much to experience, but the writing is supposed to make it great. But you go the other way and say that experiences are more wonderful. In any case, you take a train and have an encounter, you go to a public bathhouse and have an encounter, you walk in a park and have an encounter, you stay at an inn and have an encounter...As if your appearance makes the world swirl around you...

TAKAHASHI: About that, I'd rather have you think this way: this world or universe is composed of erotic equations. These erotic relations don't have to be limited to human beings, but can be between human being and tree, between human being and landscape, or between a human being and the weather of a certain day. Anyway I'd like you to read the novel as a symbol of a world composed of such erotic equations.

AIZAWA: Hearing us talk like this, some people may think Mutsuo Takahashi is a terribly lecherous fellow, but as far as I know you as a friend, this isn't so. You digest every experience completely and change it into a noble language. I think that among the contemporary poets you have the most exalted Japanese at your command.

TAKAHASHI: Thank you very much.

AIZAWA: Generally, people with meager experiences write so badly. But you are different. In the case of *Ode*, too, you must have put in it various experiences, but what you have come up with is, I feel, an encyclopedia of metaphors in Japanese—though no one has called it that.

TAKAHASHI: But in that sense, *Ode* to is full of things I'm dissatisfied with and I'd like to rewrite it carefully, putting a lot of time into it. I don't mean to say that I'd throw away *Ode* as it is; it would be left as it is, so that later those interested could compare the first and second versions.

AIZAWA: Recently, John Nathan's *Yukio Mishima*[1] came out and is talked about quite a bit. In it Nathan mentions the illustrator Tadanori Yokoo and the poet Mutsuo Takahashi as the two talented men Mishima discovered during a certain period. What actually happened? To be more precise, how did it come about that he wrote the afterword to your third book of poems, *Sleeping, Sinning, and Falling*?

TAKAHASHI: It was perhaps two years after I came to Tokyo at the age of twenty-four, I published my second book of poems, *Rose Tree: False Lovers*, and sent some of the copies to various people. To Mr. Mishima, too, I sent a copy. It apparently attracted his attention; I got a call from him. In those days, I was at an advertising agency called Nippon Design Center, and one day, toward the end of the day's work, the receptionist told me, "You have a call from Mr. Mishima." For a moment I didn't know who she meant. Immediately, this husky voice was asking, "My name is Yukio Mishima. Are you Mr. Takahashi?" He said, "It's so difficult to get hold of you." He explained that he had called me six times. Then he asked, "Are you going to be free tomorrow?" I checked my schedule and, unfortunately, it was full. So he went on to ask, "How about the day after tomorrow?" That wasn't good either. He said "Then today?" I said, "It's quite all right today," and he said, "Well then, I'll reserve a private room at the Chinese restaurant First Tower. Would you wait for me there?" When I went to the Chinese restaurant First Tower and was ushered into the private room, the maître d' came and said, "Mr. Mishima has just given us a call and said that he'll be late by about six minutes." I was looking at the clock on the wall, and exactly six minutes behind the time, he came in saying, "Hello, hello." After the dinner, we began talking about *Rose Tree: False Lovers,* and went on to talk about what Shuntarō Tanigawa kindly wrote in the afterword. Mr. Mishima said he understood well what Mr. Tanigawa said, but that he wouldn't write like that. So I said I was going to put out my next book of poems soon, would he mind writing an afterword to it? He was kind enough to say he'd be glad to. For the six years after that until he died, we were friends.

AIZAWA: He always watched for young people's writings and read them carefully, didn't he?

TAKAHASHI: I understand Mr. Mishima was a person who was not born fair and therefore was fair. A person who, because he was not born fair, decided to be fair and became more fair than those born fair—that's the way I understand Mr. Mishima's critical attitude. This critical attitude of his had a lot to do with his *masuraoburi* or virile way;[2] he was not born masculine and so tried to be masculine. As a result, I think, he became more masculine than those born masculine. As a whole, I think Mr. Mishima went about using the opposing power as his leverage. So the richness of his literature is the result of the poverty of his experience—though to put it this way may be too cruel to him.

AIZAWA: I think he was a person one should feel sorry for. Walking in the streets, watched by people, he was pleased that they were conscious of him as Yukio Mishima, but because he was conscious that he was being watched, he couldn't do what he wanted to do. It was after his death that your *Zen's Pilgrimage* came out, but he really wanted to go about in the world like that. About his works, as I reread them I find many that are lousy. What do you think of *Forbidden Colors*[3] for example?

TAKAHASHI: *Forbidden Colors* is one of his novels that I like a good deal, in which his true character comes out, but I didn't like his famed *Temple of the Golden Pavilion,*[4] for example. So I said to him, "I don't like *Golden Pavilion.*" And his reply was, "Oh you don't you don't."

AIZAWA: You would say something he wouldn't like but he wouldn't argue back.

TAKAHASHI: He wouldn't. That was admirable... Perhaps he had self-confidence, but I think he knew well his weakness or, say, his negative sides.

AIZAWA: So, that's why in his last years when he was made a laughing stock about his activities and Wang Yang-ming's principles,[5] he wouldn't twitch a muscle.

TAKAHASHI: As a joke or seriously, I too was once asked to join his Shield Society.[6] He asked me, "If I told you to die, would you?" so I replied, "No."

AIZAWA: Weren't you for a time obsessed by the Ise Shrine?[7]

TAKAHASHI: I am still greatly interested in the Ise Shrine. But that doesn't mean that I am a Nationalist. If you trace Japan to its essence, you are bound to hit on the Ise Shrine, so I'm interested in it as one way man, or say, universe, or existence, can be.

AIZAWA: You also have Catholic interests. Is your interest in the Ise Shrine part of your attempt to understand Catholicism?

TAKAHASHI: Not necessarily. Rather, both the Ise Shrine and Catholicism are for understanding man, universe, or existence.

AIZAWA: I began with Mr. Mishima. His allusions include both Greek tragedies and Buddhism, but I wonder if he had a mystic sensitivity. Take his play, *The Fall of the House of Suzaku*. In it the "noble" thing turns out to be the emperor. If he had had a mystic sensitivity, this sort of stupid thing wouldn't have happened.

TAKAHASHI: I don't think Mr. Mishima did not have a mystic sensitivity. What happened, I think, is that he continued to refuse the mystic inclination, the religious quality in himself.

AIZAWA: Perhaps that was his modernism. Talking about modernism, you're somehow not poisoned by it.

TAKAHASHI: I don't understand that very well, but I do dislike modernism or things modern, instinctively. What's modern may be new now but as time goes on it becomes the most dated, I feel. That's why on every occasion I say I hate the phrase, modern poetry. Why is the adjective, modern, necessary? What's wrong about simply calling it poetry? I'm determined never to be a "modern" poet.

AIZAWA: You often say, "The word descends." What is the relation of this concept to homosexuality?

TAKAHASHI: The relation is quite deliberate.

AIZAWA: Your concepts, "The word descends" and "The word stays," are quite hard to understand, I'm afraid.

TAKAHASHI: That's probably because you are too concerned with modernity. If you put yourself away from what's modern, you'll see the word is originally something that descends.

AIZAWA: Do you mean "Wordspirit"⁸ by that?

TAKAHASHI: We don't have to specify it as "word spirit." Looking back on our childhood, I think we see very well that the word is something that descends, or something that comes from far to near. The word is, at the same time, the world... Because when the world comes toward us it always comes in the form of a word. When we are born, we don't know the world, the word. We come to know it, I think, because the word called world, or the world called word, comes toward us. And I think that the relation between the word and us is very erotic in the Platonic sense. That's why I understand the word, the world, as the phallus that comes into the penisist's empty mouth and fills it.

AIZAWA: In the case of Mishima, he probably thought that the word is not something that descends, but something that a man manipulates.

TAKAHASHI: I think he did. And that's where he and I decisively differ. For a period I too was inclined to think that the word was there to be manipulated.

But I decided that the idea was wrong, and have since then told myself many times to get at accurate expressions rather than resplendent expressions. Some seem to think that I belong to Mishima's school, but in the attitude toward literature and the world, we are quite opposite.

AIZAWA: To go back a little, *Twelve Perspectives* is an autobiographical account of your childhood, where, it seems to me, the prototypical sexual experiences have the potentiality of going to both homosexual and heterosexual love. But the potentiality has ended up one-sided. Was there any determining factor to it?

TAKAHASHI: As far as a factor goes, I think the only thing we can say is that the factor was my bisexuality. You met this person, had that experience, and so you've become what you are—that's coincidental. You could say that without having met such and such a person you'd still be what you are anyway. I feel it's a destiny you're born with.

AIZAWA: You've been hooked on homsexuality since childhood, and you've been trying to explain "the word" in relation to, or perhaps through, the metaphor of homosexuality. Have you had this awareness of "the word that descends," like homosexuality, since you were quite young?

TAKAHASHI: The word that descends—to be precise, The Word in capital letters—I began to use consciously when I got to know Catholicism. But this just means that I became clearly conscious of it at that time. Even before then, I think I unconsciously had an awareness of The Word. Because I did, I jumped to Catholicism the moment I knew of it.

AIZAWA: When did you know of it?

TAKAHASHI: Just before graduating from college, I had consumption and went to a clinic. Right near the clinic there was a church called Stella Marina, and Brother Joseph Tsuda was there. Mr. Tsuda is the best teacher I've ever had in my life, and I was awakened by him to Catholicism. But I had, before then, read about it, so I think meeting Mr. Tsuda was also predestined.

AIZAWA: I have heard about Mr. Tsuda's wonderful personality from other people too. The thing is to come across people like that. I have a feeling that a poet molds his life by meeting a terrific person at a critical moment as you did, and I think that's a great grace. Don't you feel that way yourself?

TAKAHASHI: If I didn't feel more or less like that, I wouldn't be writing poems [*Laughter*], though after self-confidence comes a terrible loss of it so that I want to disappear completely . . .

AIZAWA: A grace is also a curse.

TAKAHASHI: Sometimes I come to feel that I don't even have that curse, that I must be a banal, irremediably lousy human being.

AIZAWA: Jonah. That miserable prophet.

TAKAHASHI: Terrible, but blessed with grace, as he should be.

AIZAWA: So his is a curse, isn't it?

TAKAHASHI: But I suspect there's no one as happy as he is. Because there are so many people who act right and still suffer badly. Isn't Jonah the very proof that The Word descends?

AIZAWA: In a most appropriate moment The Word descends—it's fantastic.

TAKAHASHI: I don't know European literature very well, but I can't help feeling that they basically have this belief or faith that The Word descends. The way I see it, when such thinking is denied, Rilke's idea of "manual labor" appears. In Japan there was from the outset no such idea as "The Word descends," so Rilke's theory of "manual labor" was, I'm afraid, accepted as nothing more than commonplace.

AIZAWA: In Japan, hasn't there continously been the attitude to the word that it's to be manipulated?

TAKAHASHI: I think it has been shared by Ki no Tsurayuki (?-945), Fujiwara no Teika (1162-1241), and all the others. Saigyō (1118-90), too, though related to Buddhism, is suspect. All in all, the only one who had something close to a religious feeling toward words is Matsuo Bashō (1644-94), I think. The Edo period (1600-1868) is when literary language collapsed, and things like Fujitani Mitsue's (1768-1823) theory of "word spirit" came out. I think you can call Motoori Norinaga (1730-1801) a believer in "word spirit." I suggest that Bashō had grasped the theory on a more erotic dimension, though of course in a Platonic sense. To put it in the manner of *The Symposium*, the word and the world, which were originally one, split into two in the Edo period; accordingly, Bashō, who had the sharpest sensitivity of the age, worked in the belief or faith that the word is the world. This, I don't think, is unrelated to his homosexuality.[9]

AIZAWA: Bashō was born with an extremely erotic sensitivity to words.

TAKAHASHI: There's no evidence that homosexuals are artistically superior to heterosexuals, but I think there is some point of contact for the homosexual and the artistic. Again to put in in a Platonic way, the homosexual's is a sex kicked out of the world's generative development, an alienated sex. So it has a strong desire to become connected once again with the world's generative development. When the desire becomes artistic impulse, the impulse may be fiercer, more to the point than the heterosexual's. At least, homosexuals are more keenly aware than heterosexuals that words are erotic beings.

AIZAWA: Words come out of the mouth, the mouth is an eating organ for maintaining the body. And it is into this same mouth that the phallus pushes in . . .

TAKAHASHI: Words can't but be erotic.

AIZAWA: It seems none of the contemporary poets, other than you, are consciously writing poems on the basis of that particular awareness. Japanese premodern and modern poets have been and are writing poems in a world so utterly unrelated to the eroticism of words. Some of their subjects are erotic, but their words are devoid of eroticism. I wonder how such Japanese poets take you. I know *you* don't give a damn for them.

TAKAHASHI: My feeling is thank you very much for leaving me alone [Laughter]. When a criticism accurately appreciating my poetry comes out, I should of course be glad, but that, too, I feel, is coincidental.

AIZAWA: Don't homosexuals somehow consider you their spokesman?

TAKAHASHI: I'm not sure about that. I myself don't feel that I'm writing especially for them, and they probably sense that too. At the moment homosexuality is my main subject, but that's because I consider it most appropriate to express my relation to the world. It's quite possible that my subject will change in the future.

AIZAWA: You mean that homosexuality is there as a lever with which to comprehend the relation between the world and you, that with it as a lever you can overturn the world. The failure of Mishima's *Forbidden Colors*, I think, is that it doesn't have the awareness of this lever.

TAKAHASHI: That I'm homosexual seems like a sure thing—I've associated with myself for nearly forty years—but that too is coincidental, and it isn't something that I must treasure for the rest of my life. As far as I am homosexual, it's been the easiest thing to do to explain my relation to the world through homosexuality. For one thing, my mode of expression has been the first person singular. But in the future I may move to the third person, and if that happens, I won't have to express the world through homosexuality ... It's possible to express it totally non-sexually, and being erotic doesn't by itself mean being sexual. Homosexuality should not only be homosexual but also homoerotic. Come to think of it, that the penisist is of the oral cavity type and of the non-pleasure type may suggest that he is rather more homoerotic than homosexual.

AIZAWA: Does that mean that homoeroticism is ascetic?

TAKAHASHI: I think it does—that if homosexuality is obscene or licentious, homoeroticism is ascetic. Putting it that way, we can say that Japan has a homoerotic tradition. For example, there's *bushidō* (warrior's way). The book Mr. Mishima liked a great deal, *Hagakure*,[10] the most radical philosophical treatise on bushidō—in it is a statement, "The best way of loving is to love in secrecy." It means supreme love is the one in which you suffer, not telling the person you love that you do. If this love was meant to be loyalty to the master, it is truly homoerotic, isn't it? Couple it with the famous dictum, "The essence of bushidō is to die," and the homoeroticism of bushido is almost complete. In George Bataille's sense, too.

AIZAWA: I'd like to go further into the first person and third person bit...

TAKAHASHI: You said I have changed since *A Legend of a Holy Place*. Well, if it's really a change, the change is still going on. In *Holy Place* too, the protagonist is "I," even though "I" may not be the same as Mutsuo Takahashi. But I have a hunch that not "I" but "he" will become the protagonist. Before then, though, a period may be necessary when "I" and "he" coexist or compete with each other. In *Holy Place*, Antonio is that "he," and in *Zen's Pilgrimage* there appear many "he's." However, these "he's" are all void. In the competing period, "he" and "I" must fight with each other, because "he" is "substantial" as the phallus, whereas "I" is void as the oral cavity.[11]

AIZAWA: Tell me what you are writing now.

TAKAHASHI: For the last several years I've been taking notes for a novel I plan to write. Its subject is the Japanese mythological hero Yamato Takeru.[12] Yamato Takeru is going to be the "he." Is he going to be the protagonist? Well, "I," who is his adversary, will be juxtaposed to him. It will be more precise to say that the protagonist will be the conflict between "he" and "I." Surely, in contrast to the substantial "he," "I" is merely void. But it's also a fact that because "I" is void, "he" is substantial—that's the way it'll be structured. The setting is modern Tokyo; in Azabu, Tokyo's high-class residential area, an imaginary slope called Yomotsuhira Saka—meaning an incline leading to hell—will be set up. There, on a night that may be described as the darkness of creation, the writer "I" encounters the protagonist Takeru—that is, the protagonist of an epic the writer is planning—and the drama begins. Perhaps, Takeru should be called the material for a protagonist rather than the protagonist, for it is a misunderstanding on "my" part or by "my" imagining that Takeru becomes Yamato Takeru. But "I" becomes too involved with Takeru as he is, the plan for an epic is dropped and the relation between "I" and Takeru itself becomes a substitute for the epic. "I" and Takeru compete with each other to be the material for the writer. Takeru dies in the end, "I" goes blind and decides to live in retirement, and so Takeru, as Yamato Takeru, changes completely from material to protagonist or is made into a literary work. That's the outline. If this represents the period I meant where "I" and "he" compete, it may later become possible for me to set up "he" as the protagonist, pull myself behind him, and write in the third person. When that happens it will no longer be necessary to openly make homosexuality my subject. Because, then, the only thing needed will be for my feeling as a writer for "him" the protagonist to remain homosexual, and that feeling can remain hidden inside me as part of the writer's creative psychology.

AIZAWA: But during the competing period, homosexuality is going to have a somewhat important weight, isn't it?

TAKAHASHI: I think that the central theme of the novel will be homoeroticism rather than homosexuality. That's because the novel is, in a word, an analysis of what creative writing is all about, and in my case I take the creative act as a pseudo-childbirth in that the writer loves his protagonist's material, becomes impregnated by its semen, and gives birth to the protagonist. And this act, I think, is possible basically not through licentiousness but through asceticism. By nature, literary works are born in ascetic space. So the sexual relationship between "I" and Takeru must ultimately end up unsuccessful.

AIZAWA: How about the poems you are writing now?

TAKAHASHI: A group of poems that I may call *Kingdom* is now in progress, though I've so far written only the first and last poems. As for the structure of the group, it begins with the king's poem and ends with the queen's poem. Between them there will be twenty to thirty poems of the people. There will be poems of the minister, the slave, the prostitute, the merchant, and the alien. The idea is to make a kingdom with all of them. With this group of poems, in fact the third person that I've been discussing may already have started to walk.

AIZAWA: It's somewhat interesting that your poetry is getting rid of "I" before your novel does.

TAKAHASHI: This may have something to do with the Japanese "I-novel" tradition.[13] But it's highly doubtful that in poetry "I" came first. In Greece, what existed at the outset were epics told in the third person, and the advent of "I" in Archilochus was a great revolution. In that sense my move from the first person to the third may be a return home. Then too, to abandon the first person and to concentrate on the third person has much to do with being a penisist as we discussed in the beginning. To abandon the first person is to make "I" infinitely void. In that sense, the third person may be represented with the phallus. The phallus, which comes from far, is also the material for the phallus. To receive it in the oral cavity and turn it into a perfect phallus, that is, the third person, by making a mold of the oral cavity, is the job of the first person, or even better, the job of the non-first person.

AIZAWA: How would you compare the relation between phallus and oral cavity with traditional homosexual relations—for example, the relation between the lover and the loved in ancient Greece?

TAKAHASHI: The relation between the lover (*erastes*) and the loved (*erómenos*) is the same as that between *nenja* (homosexual partner) and *shōnen* (boy) in Japan—in short, it's a matter of old and young. The lover must be older, and the loved, younger. As for the shapes, the lover is the phallus, and the loved, the anus—there's that fixed combination there. But the relation between oral cavity and phallus, or the relation between penisist and penis, can't be that. In the case of the lover and the loved, the loved boy, when he grows up, may have his own loved one. But the penisist never becomes the penis. The oral cavity is eternally an oral cavity and can not possibly become a phallus. Accordingly, the penis, which is the penisist's partner, can be older or younger. One thing could be said, though: since the penis must, for all its worth, be a substance that fills the void of the penisist, it has to be young, powerful, and beautiful, regardless of its age. The penis, however, always remains a semblance and no more. My understanding of the penisist has at its root an understanding that man is essentially void. This is to say that to be a penisist is the most human way of living, and the penis is there as the substance that fills the void innate to man—as the substitute of God.

AIZAWA: How does that jibe with your religious standpoint? I thought homosexuality is banned in Catholicism.

TAKAHASHI: In the sense that I have not been baptized, I can't call myself, in the precise sense, a member of the faithful. But in the sense that I believe in most of the Catholic doctrines, I may call myself a faithful member. Why do I believe in them? Because I think that Catholicism explains most rationally the meaning of this world, the meaning of my being in this world. As for homosexuality, Catholicism surely doesn't recognize it. Even the recent Vatican *litterae encyclicae*, though sympathetic, ultimately declares it abnormal. I hear that some progressive Catholic priests expressed their objection to this. The important question is whether or not declaring a homosexual person abnormal saves him, because, I think, the essence of a religion lies in salvation, not in condemnation. My understanding is that we have reached a point where the homosexual problem can't be solved just by banning it. Then, what shall I do about the discrepancy between my believing in Catholicism and my being homosexual? In the end, sooner or later, I think I'll have to settle this problem. At the same time, the time will come when the Vatican too must settle the matter one way or the other. And that won't be too far in the future.

AIZAWA: I see. To conclude this interview, I can perhaps say that your writings from now on may be different in content from those in the past. You'll use the third person, and homosexuality may recede to the back. But at the base of your writing activities there will always be the first person, that is, your own homosexuality, and that will continue to exert leverage.

TAKAHASHI: After all, I can't change my essential part. That is, as it were, my fate. And it is impossible for me to relate myself to the world in any other way than through my own destiny.

TRANSLATOR'S NOTES

1. The Japanese translation of John Nathan's superb *Mishima: A Biography* (Little, Brown, 1974). The reference to Takahashi and Yokoo occurs on pp. 194-195. In the afterword referred to, Mishima says, "Mr. Takahashi was exempted from the human principle that every young boy grows up to be a young man... he did not have to go down to the bottom of the sea, down to the depth of female genitalia, which many a young man mistakes for a philosophy, mistakes for profundity."
2. Characterization that the classicist scholar and poet Kamo no Mabuchi (1697-1796) made about ancient Japanese literature.
3. Translated by Alfred H. Marks (Alfred A. Knopf, 1968).
4. Translated by Ivan Morris (Charles E. Tuttle, 1959).
5. Wang Yang-ming (1472-1529), founder of the Idealist school of Ming Confucianism, contributed greatly to the theoretization of Japanese *bushidō*, warrior's way. See Ivan Morris's *Nobility of Failure* (Holt, Rinehart & Winston, 1975), pp. 193-198; the book, tacitly dedicated to Mishima, is excellent.
6. A paramilitary "army" of about one hundred men that Mishima set up as a "symbolic force to protect the Emperor." See *Nobility of Failure*, pp. 181-182, and *Mishima*.
7. The most important Shinto institution where Amaterasu, female deity and ancestor of the imperial family, is enshrined.
8. The ancient Japanese believed that words had magic powers. The idea was elaborated by scholars and poets in later periods.
9. The names referred to here are given the Japanese way, the family name first.
10. *Hagakure* ("hiding under foliage") is an eleven-volume discourse on bushidō by Yamamoto Jōchō, completed in 1716. Yamamoto was a retainer of the Saga clan. See Nathan's *Mishima*, pp. 223-224.
11. For "void" and "substantial," see the afterword to *Ode*, which is translated in *Poems of a Penisist*.
12. Perhaps the finest and most readily available introduction to Yamato Takeru is Chapter 1 of Morris's *Nobility of Failure*.
13. "I-novels" are dominantly autobiographical. They first developed under the influence of Naturalism and are usually categorized—at least by Japanese critics—as a genre peculiarly Japanese.

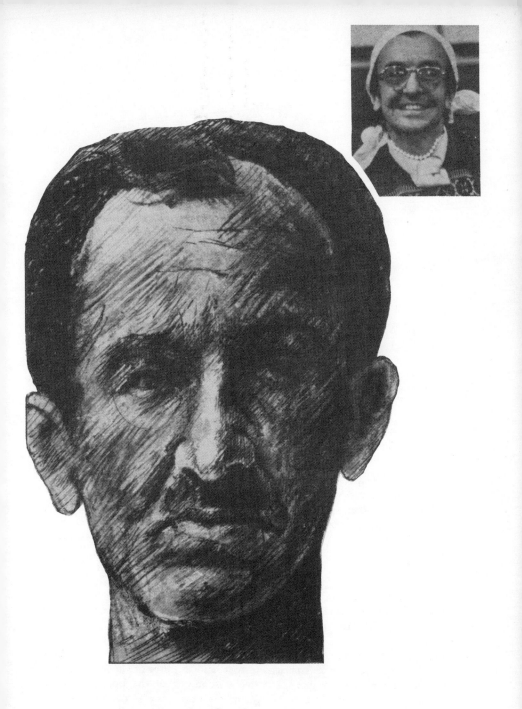

JOHN
WIENERS

JOHN WIENERS was born in Boston in 1934. He attended Black Mountain College under the tutorship of Charles Olsen and Robert Duncan and co-founded the magazine *Measure*. *Hotel Wentley Poems* (1958) brought him acclaim, and selections from his work appeared in the 1960 anthology *New American Poetry.* His other books of poetry include: *Ace of Pentacles* (1964), *Pressed Wafer* (1967), *Asylum Poems, Nerves* (1970), *Selected Poems* (1972). The Good Gay Poets, Boston, have published his books *Playboy* (1972) and *Behind the State Capitol or Cincinnati Pike* (1975). He was imprisoned for awhile in Massachusetts State Hospital (see his poem "Children of the Working Class" in *Orgasms of Light*). Wieners has been involved in the gay liberation movement for several years as a staff member of *Fag Rag*.

THE PRESENT INTERVIEWS were conducted in Boston by Charley Shively (born 1937), poet, professor of American history, and an editor of *Fag Rag*, a national gay liberation cultural journal. Shively is author of the poetry chapbook *Nuestra Señora de los Dolores* (1975), and his work has appeared (as has that of Wieners) in the two gay anthologies *Angels of the Lyre* and *Orgasms of Light*. The first interview was taped on February 8, 1973, and originally appeared in *Gay Sunshine* no. 17 (Spring 1973). The second was taped in March 1977, and is previously unpublished.

Charley Shively interviews
JOHN WIENERS

I

Sʜɪᴠᴇʟʏ: Maybe we might talk a little about mental hospitals. We've been to some of the mental patient liberation meetings.

Wɪᴇɴᴇʀs: We could get a little more actively involved in this. I would say that the homosexual is repugnant, repelled by others, even in the insane asylums. They're looked on as somewhat apart, more extravagant in gestures and mannerisms. Most of the women are oversized, usually with masculine characteristics. And the men seem to be underdeveloped as to an ideal manhood. I suppose they are in those institutions just because we have created stereotyped roles of what people should look like; what they should wear; how they should converse. Because these individuals fill none of these roles, they're incarcerated.

You definitely notice this with women in the hospital; their appearance would probably imperil the ordinary citizen on the street. They are usually heavy and wear the close-cropped hair style imposed on them by the institution. Although they have beauty salons for those who wish to go out of their way, that's only after two or three months of medication.

You have little will to bother with yourself in the hospital — other than to get to breakfast or a few hours of television or avoiding a fight with another patient and avoiding being noticed and therefore chastized by a nurse or orderly.

So the individual sense of particularity is sapped within ninety days. Resentment and outrage are chained down — I wouldn't say removed — just repressed through the medication or regimentation, the identical clothing. Your own goods are taken away or if they are returned, they're labeled with your name. If you're lucky, you get a locker or place, but they get mixed up with other patient's clothing; and if you don't want a fight, they're worn by someone on the ward. They just need something different from the standard apparel.

I've been in several state hospitals; Medfield State (January-July, 1960) in Mass.; Metropolitan State (March-August, 1961) in Mass.; Central Islip (June-Sept., 1969) on Long Island; and Taunton State (April Fool's Day-May 31, 1972) in Mass. I've only been in a private sanatorium for a couple of months, and I have no recollection of it.

Sʜɪᴠᴇʟʏ: Because of electric shock?

Wɪᴇɴᴇʀs: Yes, that's where I had electric shock. Coming East from San Francisco in 1959 I had stopped off in Washington D.C. and didn't have enough money to go all the way home. So I checked into a hotel there and called Frank O'Hara (I can remember that). I asked for money to get to New York City. He got me in touch with Barbara Guest. I barely recollect that, and receiving funding in advance, money coming from the anthology *New American Poetry* by Donald Allen.

In New York City I went to visit Allen Ginsberg. He wasn't home, and I can remember waiting up in his hallway. It was very cold and I was improperly dressed. I had probably taken something in New York that reduced my memory even less because I had been on opium all the way across the country on the train ride. That leaves the mind in a reduced state of perception and observation. You don't have the same self-protective faculties after you've used narcotics. The senses that the human organism has equipped itself with to take care of itself, to protect itself; diet; companionship. These all dissolve. I'd had two or three years of steady marijuana and peyote daily. In New York I didn't have these things. My senses had become utilized in a new way through the use of marijuana; that exertion probably tired the accepted, everyday cognitions of public appearance and communication. I was living in a visionary state so that eventually the conscious faculties were being used to a minimum.

It was all a hallucinatory trip. I remember being with some young Jewish fellow in New York trying to find LeRoi Jones. I was sort of making these excessive grasps toward his genitalia—really seeking out for somebody to love, somebody to have a relationship with, and he was willing to go along up to a point. We'd been traveling together for a few days on the streets of New York.

Finally we did get to LeRoi's apartment. I don't remember too much. Some of it's coming back. They say I just sat in a chair, wouldn't talk to anybody, took some unworthy manuscripts of my own from the past and burned them. This rather shocked people, I think.

I guess I was hosted by Irving Rosenthal at the time. He called up my mother and told her I was coming home on the bus and she should meet me. I don't know whether I had a beard then or not. I did have longer hair than was accepted at that time—short hair was still in style except for artists and pacifists.

SHIVELY: Your book, *Asylum Poems*, and the recent poem "Children of the Working Classes," written at Taunton, are some of my favorite ones. Do you think publishers are uncomfortable at publishing material like that?

WIENERS: No, but I think they have come in vogue. Anne Sexton has popularized poems about mental breakdown, as has Sylvia Plath, and both came out and made public statements of their content at that time. Mostly using Robert Lowell as their example for their efforts. You could also include W. D. Snodgrass, I think, who wrote *Heart's Needle*—the breakdown of a man and wife. Poems about mental illness were always popular. There was, of course, Tennessee Williams' *Streetcar Named Desire*—all of his themes have to do with hallucinatory states of unreality.

SHIVELY: You were visiting the state psychologist yesterday, weren't you?

WIENERS: Yes, and coming back on the bus from Plymouth was such a deadening influence. It just turned me to murder and rage. As it turned dark you could see on the highway all the way back to Boston about twenty-three hundred automobiles streaming in a steady line from Boston proper all the way down to Quincy—going into those marshlands that offer nothing to promote the human spirit. I was so glad to come back to the city proper. People leave the heart of the state where more things could be offered to them to develop themselves as adults, as citizens, and they go into areas that offer them nothing but isolation and suspicion, and they run for it.

SHIVELY: You've usually lived in the city, haven't you?

WIENERS: Well, I lived in the same suburban environment where I grew up for twenty years. I was educated in towns. After I was twelve, I had to accept the misery of the South End daily and the slumland. I was exposed to that and found it thrilling.

SHIVELY: I've never found that much resonance from the countryside. Do you get any? Like when you lived in Hanover, Mass., you had trees and yards...

WIENERS: I like to be somehow on a hill, on a slope and I don't mind it so much. I don't like flatlands, and the South Shore is nothing but a descent into the coast. If the population or architects were awakened... Robert Duncan has something about the last fifty years of architecture being dominated by Freud.

Just the irritation of having, after a full day's work, to drive on that in-human expressway, with nothing but machines at breakneck speed, with total strangers—rather than coming into society where you would have so much really up-and-coming activity around you and possibly a more positive ac-quaintance with your own desire to be sociable.

SHIVELY: Maybe that landscape near Newark on the New Jersey Turnpike? It's just smoke.

WIENERS: That's what they're creating; that's almost a reflection, a reverse image. But I'm sure all of our capital cities suffer this mass flight, five days a week. No one goes to the theater any more; the concerts are in barren, deserted mausoleums, the cities turn into rot and decay.

SHIVELY: What about Black Mountain? Is that really a mountain? a hill?

WIENERS: Yes, a hill slopes, stretched right up from the community to about two hundred fifty feet—sheer mountain, forested, with copperheads and streams and a lake. It was rather flat before the hill coming in. Black Mountain, North Carolina—the town itself—was hilly, not straight as the expressways. There's no pleasure there like human contemplation, just a direct line to—I don't want to say oblivion, but to abeyance. Not to get mixed up in anything, not to get involved in our society, not to become a different person than you are.

SHIVELY: You often call yourself a Black Mountain poet. Do you feel you are that rather than a New York poet or a Boston poet or a San Francisco poet?

WIENERS: I am a Boston poet. I was thinking this morning why I get so irritated with some political opportunists. My whole ideation was towards a Robert Lowell type, a sort of Yankee man of leisure, rather than to the radical... they just lack the literary aura. This Brahmin Robert Lowell thing, I think, goes back a couple of hundred years; he wrote about Mt. Vernon Street, just around the corner—that gives me reinforcement. I've heard people speak in disfavor of him, but he's a better writer in his contribution and substance of poetry; he is more intricate. But he treats homosexuals in his poetry in a demeaning and denigrating way—as if they were societal outcasts, irregularities.

SHIVELY: You talked about some of the establishment, academic poets who are all being driven into suicide with the collapse of their inspiration or something.

WIENERS: Well, the loss of their audiences is one thing. Since you bring that up, I immediately think of Randall Jarrell. But on the revolutionary side, there would be d.a. levy too. There may be more than just a man of letters who threw in the rag in Randall Jarrell. John Berryman is another, who possibly wasn't equal to the content of what he felt he had to write, to be successful. He had embarked upon a course of, say, psychological disorientation, and yet he was not that kind of person, by vernacular, I don't think he was equal to the revolution of logic that's occurred and that's depicted in his verses.

The establishment loomed greater to me as a youth because there were minor practitioners all over their universe. They've gone under or their modes have beome altered. People are probably just as intimidated by the highly accepted writers that we now count ourselves in the company of today. Theirs are the books we buy for our library—those writing in a similar *esprit*.

Let's get back to that question about the academic poets, either by suicide or no longer writing as much as they once did, having reached a nil point. Fortunately, I think the poets who are now involved still stimulate the young enough so that *they* are capable of writing. The academics haven't been able to, as fully. It was imitating another form that was sterile and artificial. It wasn't classic but it was stuffy, academic—bucking for power in their posts within a salaried environment.

SHIVELY: You can get that bucking for power and position in "underground" poetry.

WIENERS: We don't offer them salaries, that's the great thing. If they get a commercial success or salary, they know they've closed their shop for seventy-five percent of their readers almost automatically; the young will then distrust them inordinately. America has been so burdened over with success that we're mistrustful of it.

SHIVELY: I've heard you talk before about your sources. What were your earliest people that you cared for when you were in college just starting?

WIENERS: I cared for Edna St. Vincent Millay until the man I worked for in the catalogue department at Boston College Library told me Emily Dickinson was a far greater poet; that Edna was a bit too popular, too available, and I found that to be true. By the time I got to be thirty Emily Dickinson had transcended her. But she was my first poet. And then I liked all the women poets: Elinor Wylie, Sara Teasdale and H.D. as well, initially through anthologies.

SHIVELY: There are so many pompous men poets who put themselves up as heads of coteries, rulers, sort of politicians. It's interesting that you responded first to women poets.

WIENERS: Yes, and to their observations of nature, to their love feeling and to an abbreviation of expression.

SHIVELY: It was interesting when Allen Ginsberg introduced you to Chögyam Trungpa, Rinpoche. He said, "I want to introduce John Wieners, he's a shy poet and that's a contradiction in terms, a 'shy poet.'"

WIENERS: I think Robert Creeley is a shy person still and has developed a set of verbal defenses as a means of escape... the needs of his imagination.

SHIVELY: When did you first meet Creeley?

WIENERS: In 1955 I drove from Black Mountain College back to Washington D.C. with him and Charles Olson, Joe Dunn, Carolyn Dunn and Dana, my lover, who was driving. Robert had spent an evening there talking to Franz Kline. In Washington we dined and there were government officers there that Charles had spotted. From Washington we went on to New York where they (Robert and Charles) both left, rather rudely. And later I saw Robert in San Francisco, where he visited with his second wife Bobbie—around 1958. He'd met her in New Mexico when she was working for a radio station as a D.J.

SHIVELY: You have great affection for Creeley. When did that develop?

WIENERS: Not more than for the late Charles Olson. But I always admired Robert in a sexual attraction, and in San Francisco in 1959 I would think of him in a pure, admiring way doing his work in Placitas, New Mexico. He idealized the development of the poem for me; and then later I became enamored with him briefly in Annisquam [in Massachusetts on Cape Anne] when he paid a visit to our house where I was living with a woman in the summer of 1966 and announced himself outside the front door as "Robert Greene." He moved to Buffalo in 1965 after Charles Olson left and drove me back from Canisius College one evening from a lecture by Samuel Noah Kramer. And I envisioned myself as his wife getting into the car in the darkness. Ever since then I have become infatuated with him.

That night he read me an essay by Cyril Connolly in an English newspaper mentioning my name. Later he arranged for our reading together at the YMHA poetry center in New York City and at Bard College. He taught me in his course at the Harvard Summer School last June (1972). He refuses to write to me and conditionally sleeps without me. There is a poem of Creeley's that ends: no longer to love or be loved which was never the question. One man, only one, and not to be here. This place he finds himself alone.

SHIVELY: Perhaps you could talk about Frank O'Hara and your work together in the Poets Theater in 1956.

WIENERS: Yes. [O'Hara] was on a grant and wrote some of his most poignant verses of absence those spring days along the Charles River, Cambridge. He was obviously a campy person; I felt at once at home with him—drawn to his sophistication, his knowledgeability of the New York art world. He offered me a job to come to New York to write reviews for *Art news*. I said I didn't have any experience; on the boat to Provincetown he said, "That's just the point." He had that kind of humor that was just a bit disrespectful. Any kind of freedom that we now know in our lives was taking ground in the conversation and mores of involved writers and artists meeting in bars, museums and lofts—out of bounds one might say. There's an image of professional success in Frank O'Hara that's sadly missing in the New York world of today's cocktail party.

SHIVELY: His irreverence is what excites me so much. There are so many pompous people, particularly males in "professional" positions in poetry.

WIENERS: Yes, self-protective machinery. They don't ever want to get caught with their pants down.

SHIVELY: When did you first meet Robert Duncan?

WIENERS: I don't want to ignore Duncan because he has been put out to sea and has been inundated by the gay liberation movement as if he'd never even existed. There's a lot of material coming out for popular perusal, far too immediate to stir the roots of the really deeply thinking so-called "deviates."

In 1944 Duncan wrote "The Homosexual in Society." It was in Dwight MacDonald's *Politics* and was followed up with a letter, "The Politics of the Unrejected." This is part of a letter I received from Duncan yesterday:

"With the way words have of drawing us into their depths, that term 'liberation' that is so much the jargon of the day (so that while the bosses of the U.S. —which to our sorrow includes *us,* and to our enduring wrath—move in on Asia burning and exterminating as they go, it is called 'liberating') does draw us deeper into searching out for ourselves true liberation. And the word *gay* will be searcht out until it rings painfully true to us."

I first met Duncan in Boston on Charles Street in 1956 after I had become associated with the Poets Theater. He was with Robin Blaser, a friend of his from early school days; they'd studied the Renaissance together with Ernst Kantorowicz. There's a poem about this, "Among my friends, love is a great sorrow" in *Heavenly City, Earthly City,* from Berkeley of that period, 1946.

So, Duncan was a leader of that undergraduate group. He was on his way to teaching at Black Mountain College in North Carolina, and I was returning from there; so we had that in common. When I met him I thought I had never met such a fabulous creature. He started recounting about Mary Butts. He had all the effeminacies of a bar habitué but it was truly more than that—a rush of language that sprang out of his mouth. His conversation was far from *sotto voce* as well; it was very effeminate and loaded with authority. We had stopped at Sharaf's to eat, and ostentatious is hardly the word.

SHIVELY: Was Sharaf's then a gay restaurant?

WIENERS: Yes, it was a place mainly for regulars and underaged persons who couldn't go to bars; it located them in proximity to the Public Gardens, a heavy cruising place, "Queens' Row." They would promenade up and down Charles Street in front of Sharaf's; they wouldn't go much further—down to Mt. Vernon, then over to Beacon Street, the Esplanade, over to the Cafeteria—for the under twenty-one. You could also go down towards Boylston St. sort of cruising around. Possibly you could get a beer without anyone paying too much attention to it at Playland. Meet a friend, go to the bar where he'd buy you a bottle of beer. And you could stand in a dark corner and drink it.

So we would get to know our own kind and we could go out for a ride with some older gentleman to the beach or something that was good enough. Men waiting in parked cars on Beacon St. and getting out; sitting on the benches in the Gardens. They said those bricks were known around the world!

SHIVELY: Yeah, you have some of that in your preface to Steve Jonas's *Transmutations.*

WIENERS: Yes, that was written when the area was still current.

SHIVELY: When did you come out?

WIENERS: I think I was a homosexual a lot younger than I was able to re-member—when I was able consciously to remember. It was possibly from the dawning of communicative powers, even before that. I mean communicating in more than a few words, but in actual sentences. I would think just before pre-schooling, possibly with the advent of kindergarten. As I said in the Electric Generation interview (Philadelphia *Drummer*, January, 1973). It wasn't when my brother made me touch his cock; then I was about eight. I can remember that as an intellectual thing as well, but this was almost a first new awakening through a known effeminate in our neighborhood, who I somehow received some sensual pleasure from and I realized that this sort of climactic feeling came from such a person. I can remember running up as a little boy to a little grove of trees on top of an abandoned lot and waiting for him to show up; he was a teen-ager then. I've seen him since on the trolley; he probably lives in the same neighborhood. My brother knew him; he may have dallied with him, I don't know. But I waited trembling, just looking all over because I knew there was something whispered about.

I didn't hang around with kids outside my house too much; they were too rough, too raucous, too noisy, too loud. He was known to them. I had decided to hunt him out in a place in the park where we played. It wasn't until I decided to actively be a homosexual that I had any idea social stigma revolved about him. Then I had to choose between that and organized religion and a possible salvation after death. Even to lose that—my salvation—I decided I would forgo it—for the sake of being frequently in the company of persons who quali-fied as professionally competent. Of course, I'm a Capricorn and that means a great deal to me!

Also I had been having numerous sexual experiences with "one of the boys" in the neighborhood down the street—a Harvard graduate who had been struck with polio at his senior prom. He had a library, taught me to read *Forever Amber, Gentlemen Prefer Blondes;* he showed me my first copy of *Life* maga-zine. While I was looking at it one day, he said to me, "I think some day you'll break out of this," meaning the neighborhoood, a mediocre society. He was then over fifty and had a plastic leg.

SHIVELY: What about your first love affair?

WIENERS: With Dana? He was very good looking. Of course, I really had to throw myself down at his feet to make him my lover. He was having a marriage or relationship with somebody else. I just had to abandon all my adolescent feelings toward him to hold him and to bind him through protestations of love. But somehow he fell.

SHIVELY: It lasted several years?

WIENERS: From 1952 to 1958. He's married now and has children. He was five years older than I, so he would have been twenty-one then. He was a strong twenty-one. We went to Provincetown; we wore twin blouses. It was very much a masculine/feminine part-role. He wanted his lover to be his Mrs., sort of, to provide the home. But that was just taken for granted.

SHIVELY: Do you think you'll ever have another lover like that?

WIENERS: Well, it lasted long enough so that even now in wished for love, in solitude, I feel that I was gratified through some sort of interrelationship with a god or hero and that I was given the privilege of a passion returned. And it doesn't make me quite so needy toward satisfaction now in my late thirties and beginning my middle years. I don't feel that I must have a new young lover to keep up my image in society or my own ego. I feel that it's something I've submerged myself to knowing that I was doing it for just that purpose so that I would have an affair at the very beginning.

It may be unlucky to speak of it in the present, but I feel in later life too that I will again be blessed with a deep understanding of a sincere relationship in maturity.

SHIVELY: Have you ever thought about a living relationship with a whole group of people?

WIENERS: I'm not against that at all. But I'm rather temperamental. I'm very aware of other persons' tensions and feelings, and I always wish to respect that. I wouldn't like to get into circumstances where to protect myself I would have to hurt someone else. I don't know whether or not I'm constructed for community living. If the house were large enough and had at least two exits I think I would be able to do it, and if I had a room apart of my own. I would like to share meals with others. I would like to have a common living room where I could sit in the evening and talk with three or four lovers; an ideal situation; and also be exposed to the interests of others and to the struggles they make in the world. I look toward other people for what they bring to themselves.

[John had brought out the scrapbook with Dana's picture; we looked at some of the other memorials from the past—giggling over some triumphs and sorrows. Some pages had been smashed with a candlestick—in a fury at one disappointment, John had once tried to destroy the book.]

SHIVELY: You've got a lot of pictures of movie stars.

WIENERS: Yes, I grew up with them in my bedroom with my whole wall covered with fan magazine covers; it was like the wallpaper. I had ten feet of page clippings from screen magazines. So it must have been more than my older sister's taste. My mother's too. She never missed a movie; once a week she'd go to the Mattapan theater to get a free dish. She had to call up someone to accompany her; she'd never go alone. Once a week, that was her relaxation, escape.

SHIVELY: You're also keen as well on female vocalists. When did you first hear Billie Holiday?

WIENERS: On records in 1946. On a Commodore ten-inch disc with the songs, "I Cover the Waterfront," "Yesterdays," "Strange Fruit," "He's Funny That Way," "Georgia on My Mind," etched thereupon and at the same time a recording of Greta Keller likewise plaintively soulful. I know that was on Atlantic and they had a very painted mannequin figure for the cover, very bold red lips, very tightly coiffured hair on both these performers as possibly long white evening gloves with greens and blues for their costumes.

I think Billie's cover was just her own beige face painted on the jacket, taken from a photograph with the moon rising behind same. But the reds were very bold on the cover. And at twelve years old I was drawn to that. At the same time I had heard a Judy Garland side called, "Love, Love Is Just a Moment's Madness." [John sings the whole song.] I empathized with that a great deal until I knew I would give over my own future to the act of love—and similarly to a decision not fully realized until years later, in a choice of poetry.

SHIVELY: Once when you were reading you said that you could hear the words in some of your poems in song.

WIENERS: I once wrote in a notebook that I can see the unknown words written in my brain; since a lot of mental confusion is cleared up, that's less common in my practice that it was then when I was less of a verbal person.

But we were talking about how music stays in the mind involuntarily. Automatic osmosis through one's perceptions to retain what you see and hear. I still like to hear music without having anything played on the phonograph. I want to tell you an anecdote: In Buffalo once, I used to keep the radio near the pillow; being wakened from a nap I reached up to turn off the radio which I thought had been playing for the past fifteen minutes and discovered that the radio hadn't been on at all! My framework was able to incur the actual transcriptions of broadcasting and communication without the devices necessary.

SHIVELY: How important are your dreams for your poems?

WIENERS: They seize the waking day, but I've never been able to transpose them into my poems.

SHIVELY: Celia Gilbert, a Boston poet, said some poets must now spend their time sleeping, since it's so fashionable to use dreams in poetry.

WIENERS: That's not wholly true in my case. I analyze first, waking *and* sleeping; sometimes, I analyze my relations to things, persons, to prior events.
[John was still thumbing through his scrapbook and came upon a photo of a friend, Jennifer, a professional "exotic" or "stripper."]

WIENERS: That's Jennifer; we traveled from San Francisco to Boston together. It was with her that I first took heroin. She was arrested right around the corner here on Cambridge Street one night when I went up miraculously to visit Charles Olson. I had decided to leave their place casually. They had received a lot of illicit drugs from a drugstore break. A musician in Boston brought the narcotics over. I just got up off the couch and said I was going to visit Charles. Later on that night there was a knock on the door and a man with a lumber jacket was standing there—a young, good looking fellow. And Jennifer, not knowing who he was, but thinking she knew who he was because he was so familiar with the milieu in which she traveled. I had introduced her to Kerouac a few weeks before. He was of that social qualification or identification. They all had heavy trials and received suspended sentences on probation. The front pages of the *Record American* had headlines: "Stripper Nabbed in Drug Arrest."

Ed Dorn called me this morning, and I told him I thought X— and Y— were cops to bag us and that shocked him. They have an altogether different physiognomic, physiological response when they become interested in some*thing* from when we become interested in something. There's also intellectual lacunae in them that I have wondered about for years. Why these gaps? I've come to the

conclusion that it's a different state of the mind, that it's an analytic quality, analytic process of the intellect that is being used to evaluate, record the information there being transmitted. There's nothing wrong with having cops as part of
your audience, but they do put other people behind bars and they enforce laws
that reduce our liberation and our liberties.

SHIVELY: The worst police maybe aren't the people that are just immediately
getting money from the police department or the FBI. There's a whole tribe of
policemen.

WIENERS: I said to Ed Dorn: they're not the kind of cops that actually go out
and arrest people. (Maybe Z— is.) And it's usually narcotics they're interested
in, or gambling, or organized underworlds. But I think they're the kind of
police that turn in records to whatever agencies collect such information; and
they in turn learn to train young officers in the government agencies and send
them into the field as decoys for us sitting ducks. They not only deal with ourselves but they know others, more important because of this information; and
as we get older, they can take more advantage of us, bring us more pain more
disease. So, I figure their job is to funnel more information in as to what's going
on, what characterizes outlaws and us. And maybe get information on basic
structural patterns for the future when possibly our course of work is even
more radical.

I have this proselytizing aspect to my character that I would imagine too that
someone might even give up the police work after awhile if they become a convert to our ideals, our kind of thinking, so I tell them the "truth."

One point I know is factual—when Raffael de Gruttola started talking about
anarchism the other night at the Stone Soup Gallery. His knowledge of it comes
from authentic sources in the Italian community. When he began to talk, there
was an altogether different response from those three persons (X, Y, Z) in that
room. Z's eyes lit up; X's body became more tense. When Ralph started naming
names and unknowingly talking about his uncle, saying there was still smug-
gling of political prisoners in the U.S., they couldn't have been more happy
than they were given the plot. And then of course, afterwards—I know it's just
putting them in a position were they could be introduced to insurgent elements
of our society.

SHIVELY: And also, you can notice that they don't feel themselves but they
watch other people feel and manipulate other people's feelings; they don't participate in the circle themselves.

WIENERS: It's a manipulation. And even if they aren't cops, I would think this is
a police procedure anyway, a form of police provocation. But even if they are
not doing it, one wonders how inside information passes.

Of course, the revolution of the movement hasn't been quelled at all really by
police harassment in the United States; excepting perhaps cases like John
Sinclair or the obscenity trial of Ed Sanders' [magazine] *Fuck You!* I don't actually think they were mass-media set ups; it's just that when you do get into a
social situation, the government through its local constabulary seems to crack
down on you almost immediately.

SHIVELY: I wonder if it's like people who have taken various forms of drugs and
those who haven't?

WIENERS: To give them this extra awareness?

SHIVELY: Yeah.

WIENERS: Well, I think that at least the Narcotics Bureau through its employees takes as many drugs as the persons who are rounded up by them and imprisoned. That's always been bandied around.

SHIVELY: But it just doesn't open them up?

WIENERS: Well it does. They have a very good time for themselves. It was reported in the *New York Times* that there was a plot by narcotics agents to set up Allen Ginsberg as an innocent target for dealing.

After I talked with Ed Dorn I lay down and thought for three quarters of an hour how and why I would be an object of police persecution? Could they have set up these mental hospitalizations over the years? Could I have been duped into putting myself into a circumstance where my whole mind would be on the books for the psychologists and therefore part of government property?

The only reason I could think of was my homosexuality. I went to Washington in 1954 with my lover. Then, after Atlanta, we went to Provincetown and stayed at Captain Jack's Inn. There was a purge going on at the same time, well publicized in local and Boston newspapers. Even Archbishop Richard Cushing came out with a statement against homosexuality at this time. There was this church person at the Inn where we stayed who liked Dana very much and who could have been a police person as well as continuing his other "activities."

Just putting my name into whatever offices there are either here in Boston or Washington, saying "disreputable homosexual," would have been enough to keep files open over the years. Then when you begin publishing homosexual documents or even getting into print at all, they apply pressure. Especially if you are a Catholic in various ways by all kinds of drugs that can be detrimental to you, through the hands of your friends or by even giving you money so that you can do things to involve other people. If they can't actually manipulate arrests and imprisonments for fear of arousing suspicion against themselves at least they can provide the means so that your power among your associates will be questioned and they can retain the power. As in the case of Timothy Leary, where the government wanted to maintain power over the distribution of LSD against its coming from private sources among the counterculture. There are other instances.

Those offices are only staying in operation because there's something they've got to do. They can't waste government money, literally. They have to turn in results. And even if they can't act on what information they're getting, in a series of years they can train men to be at least equal to the efforts that we are trying to push: furthering the rights of poor people, or "unnatural" sexual acts.

SHIVELY: Have you ever been arrested?

WIENERS: Yes, twice. Once I stayed two weeks in the Manhattan Tombs awaiting trial on credit cards. I called my mother for bail and she said, "Well, I don't know, Jackie." I was really crestfallen. But she stayed on the telephone while I was crying, from the Tombs. She said, "Your father and I haven't been getting on so well lately." This was because they were moving to a new house in Hanover, something that he didn't go for too much at their age.

SHIVELY: What about your mother and father?

WIENERS: I have very warm feelings toward my mother. I was duly blessed by her person, her embrace toward the world. She loved a good time, entertainment, people; she loved to socialize, converse. She was very aware of fronts, persons who were a bit intractable; she felt that. She had respect for the town in which she lived for its conventions and proprieties as long as you didn't upset them and draw attention towards yourself. She liked eccentricity up to a point; if it was employed by the person rather than employing the person or if it was out of control, she would become easily frightened. But if a person could harmonize his idiosyncracies and make something out of them—it was all quite a utilitarian stance towards the values of her community. If a person got a bad name, was scandalous, noticed, they were reprimanded—in her mind, and small talk.

I remember my uncle John who came home after World War II with a male companion, and my mother brought it to our attention; she didn't approve. She went into the living room and found the friend combing his hair in front of a mirror, and she had a few remarks on that—her witty Irish tongue.

Nonetheless, she would offer aid in her mind and I would imagine in a real sense of the word to somebody who manifested need. So I likewise feel that what I'm doing is to increase those feelings in others so that they no longer have to regard themselves as tramps, deviates, guttersnipes or aberrations.

My mother lived to be sixty years of age, was born in Maine, worked as a waitress and housecleaner and was a parts worker in a defense factory during the war. She was very good at mathematics. She had a duplicity of more than one role in her own characteristic feelings for both men and women. She also worked in the Walter Baker chocolate factory; that's where she met my father when she was eighteen.

My father was born in South Boston in 1903 and was a laborer with the highway (what they'd call the WPA during the Depression), was uneducated and spent the last thirty years of his life as a maintenance man in downtown Boston.

SHIVELY: You dedicated your *Asylum* poems to him.

WIENERS: Yes, because when I was born he was committed to the Taunton State Hospital for assaulting another patient with a chair at the Boston Psychopathic Hospital. He was being treated for alcoholism.

SHIVELY: He had quite a temper?

WIENERS: Mostly induced by drink. But he had a charitable nature and was always reliable for an emergency. He'd come through for you if you needed him. He was rather content to stay set where he was; he had an insecure youth and was the youngest of six children. He was the baby of the family—that's what they used to say of him. All of his brothers and sisters also had large expansive natures. He was never one to inhibit any kind of dissatisfaction, but he was a bit shy, carping towards his family. Later, I think he felt compelled to be our father. As he spoke of it in his last year, he would have liked to have bought a trailer after his wife died and become an itinerant wandering around the whole country.

JOHN WIENERS | 273

II

Wieners: This is John Wieners in conjunction with Charley Shively preparing a tape for Winston Leyland's *Gay Sunshine Interview Anthology* upon March 27th, 1977. We are sitting in Cambridge, Massachusetts, across the river from the New World Damascan City Capitol, comparable in estimation of Morocco to Casablanca. A question that might serve the interests of readers in California is: How to take a meeting ground and turn it into hard times.

Shively: I wonder about the importance of meeting ground, geography, place or residence in your work. *The Hotel Wentley Poems, Hotels,* and *Behind the State Capitol or Cincinnati Pike* all have a lot of geography. How important is geography or the turning of locations into a meeting place of terror?

Wieners: For self-inhabitation, so that we would think of the new world in New England and the publishing outpost of San Francisco strictly as Wild Bill Hickock's, Sheriff or Marshall's office on Sundays, and leave the back yard even less confident. Comradeliness: 'cause men are men, and Hickock has a definite function in the 19th century, or did, to evaporate the miscellaneous, extraneous, inveterate confusion between South and East.

Shively: Well, what was it like for you to go from the East to Wild Bill, and Polk Gulch and Land's End?

Wieners: Oh my dear! Your mother just lost her buckskin and trappings altogether! I lost my virginity, choosing New Jersey as an Eastern outlook and Mr. Bronco Buster in the Latin American renegade fashion of dirt.

Shively: Was there any dirt in San Francisco?

Wieners: I was too young to enjoy *Hell on Frisco Bay,* but I would assume that I never got raped less, even though if I had to choose anyone to do it it would be the postage stamp variety that Hell is endowed with around the Golden Gate Bridge in regards to, say, how it manifests itself to the two of us through the Shah presumably of Iran or Ladin. You weren't stationed during the armed terrorist confrontation known as World War II in Europe? or did you serve overseas?

Shively: No, I was never in the army, although I like sailors, soldiers and marines. Were there lots of sailors and military people in San Francisco in the late fifties?

Wieners: Laconically, immutably mufti late fifties, and then as a whole unlike the Good Samaritan, who turned the majority of Americans into hairdressers.

Shively: Do you have any desire to return to San Francisco?

Wieners: Since I don't need the Pharaoh that they call Kay Starr until the moon of Mitzi. Yes.

Shively: What were the baths and bars like in the fifties?

WIENERS: Like Fatty Arbuckle. They had Louise de Roachment passing for the Blue Fox. Like Peter Stenile in the Garden. They couldn't find enough supporting players except for Sally Rand, Sister Kenney and Steve McQueen that the sobriquents had evacuated to Hinduism and began drowning drachmas like Graham or Gallipoli. The majority proselytize; a minority masturbate.

SHIVELY: How long were you in San Francisco when you were there?

WIENERS: Two years.

SHIVELY: That's a long time.

WIENERS: Sort of like Joey Brown down and out at the bottom of Bagdad.

SHIVELY: What was that?

WIENERS: Defeat.

SHIVELY: You split with your lover when you went to San Francisco, didn't you?

WIENERS: Well, I've got a confidence, wiped-out confidence.

SHIVELY: Is that San Francisco generally, broken-hearted memories?

WIENERS: It's like waking up with a can of Spam in a desert outpost and finding out an insurance neophyte and the H-bomb dictated Mecca.

SHIVELY: Mecca dictated Alcatraz or Treasure Island?

WIENERS: No, absolutely only North Beach. As far as Irene and Wally, or John Ryan at the Place of J. Bagel's shop, Chinatown, Marian, the Cellar, Shig at City Lights, Enrico's, Vesuvio's, Barbary Coast, the Black Cat... those were the focal points: Finocchio's and the Tenderloin District, Market Street, Comradeship, the Palace, the Fairmont, Nob Hill, the Mark Hopkins Hotel, Penthouse.

That's when I decided to give the old Guard the heave-ho and take to the streets. Winding up at Land's End in their chauffeur-controlled limousines: Sutros snitching lifts via cable cars as a flood/blow job. *So* near the ocean that one's atmosphere or health immediately clears up, one's attitude. Atmosphere! Dietrich says that I would—not knowing she was such a sunbird—I would change my rectal suppository for a good night on the town.

SHIVELY: Did you do a lot of nights on the town in San Francisco?

WIENERS: In search from hunger. Well, you know the stars that they call bedridden are so much younger than one actually has been informed. It was girls who lent themselves to my escapades, who kept my spirits from flagging. The real hoity-toity tigresses, much like Baby Jane in the early sixties and Nico on the Canadian border. Then too, specifically, Baby Jane around New York and Irene Nicholson had some attention, as they oughter, for keeping a foot in the door.

But bathtub gin can sour if it's kept in the same locality, so broadening my horizons, I took schooling and a desire to taste some of the nectar of the Big Apple, found its clearly faded hauteur, blonds (platinum preferably) or redheads.

SHIVELY: After you had written and then published *The Hotel Wentley Poems* (San Francisco, 1958, Auerhahn Press)—was that like *A Star Is Born?* Did everyone recognize them right away for what they truly were?

WIENERS: No, it's more like the *Village Voice* in the hands of *The Manhattan Review of Unnatural Acts,* when Joan Bennett and Wendy Hiller and Dick Haymes commanded the echelon of Dick, Wendy and Joan of Times Square Korean. Sally go 'round the roses *de troit* Victorian crosses. That's how I came to regard *The Hotel Wentley Poems,* in the heraldry of an Easter Island, Tidewater Billy.

SHIVELY: Can you say anything about the publication of *Behind the State Capitol or Behind the Cincinnati Pike* [Good Gay Poets, 1975]? Has it made any difference in your being?

WIENERS: No, I find that the 1500 copies count down to a position that the prime minister at the present date in the hitherlands has yet to equal—after two world wars in the twentieth century—the assault made upon the French aristocrat and the Greek Nubian just doesn't tally up to anything more than a Bert Parks on "This Is Your Life."

   J. W. used to shack up in Hyde Park with a dwarf by the name of Baily—Marie Antoinette Williams was her name and she used to work in the *Condemned at Altoona* on Chinese fortune cookies—that's what *The Hotel Wentley Poems* bring out of the Polk Gulch area—a sense of after-dinner addresses much as a mistress of ceremonies at a state smoker might say running down a back stairs to the maid with the head of John the Baptist in a bed pan. It's like what Spengler called Oswald or Anita Bryant in Florida, "Come On Down the Weather's Fine," or it's a killing in Rome.

SHIVELY: On the after-dinner speech; I'm wondering do you think about your audience?

WIENERS: No! The audience is parasitic—they are prostitutes, panderers, pimps and pigs. You have to write for each category—the four P's: pigs, prostitutes, panderers and pimps. They don't amount to more than the preterpari Simone used to stock for a beauty parlor and the poet is nothing more than the premonitions that come off of Palm Beach when Art Rimbaud was put into exile at the whim of Farouk. Fortunately the prime minister or the curate or the rector have demonstrated themselves to be incapacitated for anything besides profit.

SHIVELY: What do you think of poetry readings now?

WIENERS: Up against the biggest fraud that's been pulled upon the fools of since our Lady of Health gave up her chastity to the moon. Much like Judas sought anything other than Jesus.

SHIVELY: Well, they were kissing in the dark.

WIENERS: Sanitationally speaking. What was evidenced in the airport this afternoon was nothing that could be accounted as sacerdotal only sacrilegious.

SHIVELY: On the sacerdotal—Do you think it was important for you to have been raised a Christian? A Roman Catholic?

WIENERS: I'm not a counter-revolutionist. I'm not a Populist, I'm not a Popist, Papist; I'm not a coward; I'm not a jack of London Platinum Blond; I'm not a Martha Rae Harlow; I'm not an orphanage; I'm not a New Orleans shahville or Claire Trevor warmonger.

It's definitely important to go to school and learn that platinum dowagers are nothing less than Communists or that the impersonators to the true art of prostitution are San Francisco tubs like Hickock or Shallop or Landrey's.

Zoa and the Cabala come down to nothing more than Bing Crosby's Bobcats. Christians imply a disavowal of Delilah and a kind of dedication foreign to what's taking place in the terms of Dedham and Dodge City.

SHIVELY: The Christians do have faults.

WIENERS: Well they have the faults Las Vegas has when it forgets about Havana or that Dolly has when she remembers that her cash register can never equal the bar hops or flies. How many times have the douche bags from Denmark called themselves wolves? In other words when you're past your prime you're the prime minister of Israel or you're a papal mistress impersonating...

SHIVELY: The Apocalypse?

WIENERS: Perth Amboy...puda...

SHIVELY: Then who are you impersonating?

WIENERS: I'm hankering after Hopalong Cassidy.

SHIVELY: Well, we started with a Wild Bill. What about Billy the Kid in San Francisco?

WIENERS: I guess he got evicted as Paramount Pictures from Universal International. It's just a loss of allegiance. You come up to a paraplegic and say, "Is a silver spoon still down your throat?" and you find that "No, it's been garnisheed."

SHIVELY: A pretty face carries you a long way.

WIENERS: There's nothing better than a comely appearance unless you're catamitic as I fear Virginia Hill was caught blank in Casablanca when her credentials ate away any energies that a non-existent education loomed as Lana Turner lost all of her maturity before becoming Mickey Rooney.

SHIVELY: What do you think about the relationship between the wardrobe (or clothing) and poetry?

WIENERS: Like Frederick's of Hollywood?

SHIVELY: Or *Women's Wear Daily.*

WIENERS: Hmm. Well, I don't find that I save my last copies as I feel the garment district when it believes in Yves St. Laurent bridges the lewdness that has done nothing more than bring to public acclaim that a pig is a prize for piss pots.

SHIVELY: Oh, pigs have their virtues. What're you doing now as far as the literary scene goes?

WIENERS: Well, I'm trying to raise enough dimes to pay for Twentieth Century Fox.

SHIVELY: Mitzel said if it weren't for you there'd be no movie stars. You're keeping them all alive in your mind.

WIENERS: It's like I'd say Judy Garland dropped her pants for Billy's Jane. Judy Garland dropped her pants for petty larceny—that's what Mitzel means.

SHIVELY: What is James Dean then?

WIENERS: A hermaphrodite in the living room without Tilly Loach.

SHIVELY: Where do we go from here?

WIENERS: Well, we try to unravel the word Gallup Poll, come down through Sal is a repetition of "l" and "l"—that's what Polly Adler sells.

SHIVELY: That's quite a way to go; that's even better than an airport.

WIENERS: You've faith to come up to snuff with *The Manhattan Review of Unnatural Acts* and say because I did not wear the best pajamas that I should lose my maidenhead to Midway Island or I should surrender my soupçon for Santa Margritta de Genoa or Salome or Carmen or Sadie Thomson or Lucretia Borgia (Cesare Borgia's niece) should cause a broken heart as a whore.

SHIVELY: Do you have anything to say about glory holes? Or glory?

WIENERS: I only wish them on Dowell a jerk like Morey with children between their legs and they're nothing more than Jury Street Journeymen. I mean specifically a crown prince jade and a German witch without the "h" and Donald has lost his happiness, his holiness for the Agah headwear much like an anthropologist beckoning to the human race for consignment to its indiscriminate conglomerates. The lifespan of a single individual doesn't measure up to what Madison Avenue calls the Ku Klux Klan.

TOM MEYER (LEFT) AND JONATHAN WILLIAMS, CUMBRIA, 1978

JONATHAN
WILLIAMS
•
THOMAS
MEYER

JONATHAN WILLIAMS (b. 1929, Asheville, N. Carolina) occupies the dual position of poet and publisher. As head of Jargon Society, since founding it in 1951, he has impresarioed the literary careers of a diverse group of writers by publishing their work. As poet, Jonathan's works include *Mahler* (1969); *An Ear in Bartram's Tree* (1969); *Blues & Roots / Rue & Bluets* (1971); *The Loco Logodaedalist in Situ* (1972); *Imaginary Postcards* (Trigram Press, London); *Adventures with a Twelve-Inch Pianist Beyond the Blue Horizon* (1973); *gAy BC's* (Finial Press); *Pairidaeza* (Jargon Books); *Elite/Elate: Selected Poems 1971–75*; and *Get Out*, selected and new poems (1982). His *Celestial Centennial Reverie for Charles Ives (The Man Who Found Our Music in the Ground)* appeared in the sixth issue of *Parnassus*. For several years Jonathan Williams has shared his life with poet Thomas Meyer. They live part of the year in Corn Close, a centuries-old cottage in Yorkshire (Northern England) and the remainder traveling, and in Highlands, North Carolina.

THOMAS MEYER (b. 1947, Seattle, Washington) received his A.B. in English at Bard College. His first book of poems, *The Bang Book*, was published by Jargon in 1971. There followed *Poikilos* (1972), *O Nathan* (1973), *Umbrella of Aesculapius* (1975), *Uranian Roses* (1977), *Staves Calends Legends* (1979), and *Sappho's Raft* (1982). His poems also appear (along with those of Jonathan Williams) in the two gay anthologies published by Gay Sunshine Press, edited by Winston Leyland: *Angels of the Lyre* (1975) and *Orgasms of Light* (1977).

INTERVIEWER JOHN BROWNING writes: "The following interview [Yorkshire, England, 1974] was eight days in the making. Early on we decided against the kind of mindless chatter induced by tape-recorded sessions. Being writers, Jonathan and Tom felt that the logical medium was the typewriter. So I typed out my questions, which were found and answered throughout various times of the day. As the visit progressed, the line diminished between interview and event—the event of relationship. Therefore this interview serves not only as a record of these poets' thoughts, but also as an organic process of feeling as it occurred in the 'working holiday' of a threesome.

"I first met Jonathan and Tom as a senior English student at Wake Forest University, where Jonathan was poet-in-residence. Those short three months introduced notions of discipline, confidence, hilarity, and decadence, accompanied by doses of Mahler, Bette Midler, jazz, and other lubricants of the spirit; I offered Elton John, cosmic fickleness, and fruitiness-in-general. As a result, I moved to London upon graduation in 1973, where I witness the comings and the goings of this transatlantic and very divine couple."

This interview originally appeared in *Gay Sunshine* no. 28 (Spring 1976).

John Browning interviews

JONATHAN WILLIAMS
& THOMAS MEYER

B ROWNING: Pardon the Queen's rhetoric, but what do you boys like doing?

MEYER: At twenty-seven, most or *first* of all I like getting fucked. I never knew how to honestly answer that kind of "let's get serious" question when people sprung it on me. Never, until now. I like opening up. I like all the tensing and relaxing of muscle and meat that fucking demands. I want *it* (in this case, a cock) inside me, going deep. Getting fucked gives me that feeling of openness, receptivity and that fantastic sense of pulling something inside myself.

WILLIAMS: What they call these days a "heavy" question to start with, John. Being forty-five as opposed to Tom's twenty-seven has at least two consequences I am aware of. One is that I was brought up in an up-tight generation and surrounded by many persons (gay or covertly so) who radiated the feeling that being fucked was "unmanly" and demeaning. A macho thing, I suppose, and as Ginsberg remarked in a previous *Gay Sunshine* interview: Sheriff Dickey, there are really worse things in American life than getting fucked in the ass. Amen. Trouble is: by my age it's difficult to alter the pattern—not that I am not prepared to try. Lovemaking can get pretty tiresome if the partners are only able to do this or that as some abstract principle. Surely it does all have to do with passion, and the person involved on the particular occasion. There are means, hopefully, of learning to accommodate lovers and relaxing one's sphincters. Drugs, exercises, devices, etc. Still, Tom's preference just stated tends to be the pattern we get into. . . . Second point about the age difference. There is a very eloquent book called *Phallos* by the Danish psychoanalyst Thorkil Vang- gaard (Jonathan Cape, London, 1972). One kind of fucking of men is clearly to dominate enemies and degrade them. The other is the important one, which has come down to us from Dorian times: ". . . it is the semen of the man, adminis- tered to the boy per anum, which is the carrier of his *arete*." *Arete* is a complex word, meaning nobility, manly character, adult strength, loving regard, etc. Hence, a rite of passage with all the force of religion—the way one carries one's ideas over into another's person. . . . Not to go on at much more length, but the question does have its load. Jacking off remains (solitary or in company) one of the great releases. I imagine because it goes back to boyhood and simplicity and this is an area that all artists continue to tap, continue to work out of . . . cock- sucking— well, that's part of the repertory too, but not very often. Urologia, sir, and enema-freakery, I, thus far at least, leave to those with more refinement than my simple tastes.

BROWNING: Your answers would indicate a fairly male/female-ish sort of setup, sexually, anyway. True? And if so, would you characterize your roles in living together as "marriage"?

MEYER: True. And the answer to your second question is yes. But (or as they say in Rome, *ma*—holding that *a* as long as possible) let me say something about marriage. Very early in our relationship or "marriage" (at honeymoon phase, before we settled in one place long enough to live our daily lives together) Jonathan invoked in a letter to me the image of The Divine Couple. The same day a friend handed me a book of erotic Indian art which fell open in my hands to a plate showing The Divine Couple. That cinched it for me. I knew that my commitment to Jonathan and his to me—our vow—married us, not one to another but to something so simple yet so powerful as two bodies: a couple. A *divine* couple, that word divine there meaning holy, special, sacred, cultivated, or simply the ordinary no longer ordinary but made *conscious*. That *marriage* usually means a biological man and a biological woman honestly never occurred to me. I saw us as linked to a third thing and through that linkage participating in a, dare I say, ritual relationship. Pretty heady stuff but I assure you (and I know Jonathan can tell you so) that I tell you *true*. I put none of it on, I just see it like that.

BROWNING: And the male/female aspect of it?

MEYER: Yeah, male and female, both of them present, not as roles but as polarities. Whatever the physical circumstances or limitations of our sexual acts, I never feel like *the* man or *the* woman. If anything, I sense an emphasis in the moment on either the passive or the active, the thrusting and the receiving. As though my ass became a fist jacking a cock off. . . . Getting fucked has nothing in my mind or body to do with laying back and just taking it.

WILLIAMS: The words male and female must have been invented by the same crowd that talks about Truth and Beauty—abstractions that can be made to pay off commercially and politically when spoken out of the moola-side of the mouth. A friend of mine in London says he was just filling in a form to get a visa to America to work in a university library on some special assignment. There is a little box to tick that indicates: "White, Black, Other." Why don't they have a similar tripartite section for sex: "Male, Female, Other"? I have one friend who loves to call me Super-Butch; another who likes to say that I am one of the last Great White Southern Ladies. Until we learn to laugh at ourselves and at the foibles of our friends, we are of little use.

BROWNING: Well then, if you're not exactly married, does that mean we can all go to bed together now and fuck this interview?

WILLIAMS: Gosh all hemlock and land sakes, Mr. Interviewer, to react like Ma Perkins used to on NBC Radio. It's only 2:20 in the afternoon on this dark, vile, Yorkshire Wednesday. You must observe local amenities, although it is rumored the local amenities demand that a Yorkshireman only takes his clothes off on a Friday evening. We can all go to bed *later* if the spirits are way up high and the flesh is not weak, but I have twelve letters to write, have to do the dusting, have to drag the dustbins down the lane to tomorrow's dawn pickup, and, like I say, not even sheepfarmers would do any shagging before sundown. Tennessee Williams likes to say he never drinks before six (in the morning). But that is in the land of the gardenia, not here in the thistles, nettles and dock.

BROWNING: Is that a typical domestic procedure? Who does the work here?

MEYER: Jonathan, you know as well as I do that farmers shag sheep when the flesh moves 'em, not when they finish cutting hay or shoveling muck... in other words, when it feels right. However, I can understand how these twelve letters call out, and how the dust and dustbins have the right to make their demands. No one in his right mind wants to settle down to a cozy threesome with someone or thing nagging at him. Sorry, John, you wanted to know what?

BROWNING: I think I was after something about who does the housework, but now that you mention it, threesomes are as well a way of life, are they not? How do your various communal exploits affect your own relationship—sexual and otherwise—with each other?

MEYER: Okay, housework first. Generally, I see to those things that need day-to-day attention: dishwashing, cooking, keeping a mild sense of order around us. Jonathan, on the other hand, undertakes the big projects, like washing all the windows, or a once-a-week scrubdown. The same applies, almost in reverse, to Jargon Society business. Jonathan spends most of the day at his desk working on that and I sit down once or twice a week to answer whatever letters I can, or deal with the pile of unsolicited manuscripts and such. That seems basically our "routine." It has its interruptions: guests, sudden unexpected demands and unprecedented reversals. At this point in time, it also sustains us both as poets and makes a place and a time for us to write poems and to keep those fires burning on our hearth.

WILLIAMS: Lordy, John Browning, it looks like it's time for Parson Williams to put on his black sackcloth and ashes and deliver another too-lengthy sermon. Some questions really deserve books, not paragraphs. Still, role-playing is another modern cant. I abhor abstractions and try to live my life in a world of particular responses. One thing at a time, one person at a time—the old-fashioned bohemian anarchist position, if you like. I drive a car very well, so I do the driving. Tom cooks in the two-star Michelin class if he feels required to, and has the time to; the kitchen is his domain. Again, to bring in the difference in age; it sets up two situations: (1) I tend to get the "literary" attentions, since I've been at it since 1951, when he was four years old. This does not mean he is not every bit as committed to his work as I am, or that it is "less" in any way. I can't translate from the Anglo-Saxon, the Greek, the ancient Hebrew. He can. These differences allow us to pursue the same devotional occupations without getting in each other's hair. Very very difficult, if two men are closer in age and approach to words.... (2) In social situations any handsome 27-year-old is going to get more "scenic" attention than an aging, severe 45-year-old. I don't know whether gay people are more sensitive and less hung up on age than so-called straight people? I doubt it. (I don't like these tiresome words *gay* and *straight* either, but am so disinterested in all politics outside the house that I put up with them, like most of us have to.) Anyway, I think we can now go on to the second part of your question, as I see it: i.e. "communal exploits."

Kenneth Rexroth used to regale the young poets clustered at his San Francisco salon with such ancient wisdom as: "*Never fuck your friends*" and "*Never go up a dirt road without a raincoat.*" Well, yes and no, one learns.... Paul Goodman, in useful contrast to Kenneth, pursued just about anything with two legs and a pulse and knew that this "love" people were always complaining they didn't have and were seeking could often be generated by some friendly, playful action in bed. Surely it's true that people stand very revealed during sexual encounters, though I would argue that I can often tell as much about a man (or a woman) by watching them listen to a poem, respond to music, play poker, play volleyball, etc. Still, there are occasional times when it is hospitable to invite friends, old or new, into our bed—one or two or three. The sextet remains a mystery. Five people, dining and conversing, is an optimum figure—concentration is held and prattle doesn't have to ruin conversation. In a threesome nobody gets "undivided" attention, but that is not a bad thing. One maybe learns a little about generosity and sharing and feeling threatened. And no one is not left out. The basic human question is clearly: what's in it for me? If one is isolated in a cold bedroom, reading the ghost stories of M. R. James, while some dishy friend is fucking one's companion in life beyond a partition, the psychic distress can get fierce. Loss is a menace to most of us, and no amount of theory about trust and a couple's integrity can lay that specter. At least not for me. Most of us, after all, have been brought up in parental households where years of bickering and rage and coldness have made us horribly vulnerable and ever fearful of losing a relationship which we have constructed of male partners—as a hopeful positive alternative to the child's misery before heterosexual parents. I may be naïve, but my observation is that most men treat each other more sensitively and kindly than they do women— and I'm not talking gay or straight here.

Just one more thing about this group sex. Guy Davenport has been writing to me about some of the theories of utopian sexuality of Charles Fourier, about whom we still know so very little because French philosophers have suppressed most of the text all these years. Fourier seems to have based his society on sexual joy, and joy is a word seldom on the minds of drones like philosophers. He thought everybody should come six times a day. Three or four times with your friends or lovers; twice a day with anyone in the community needing *affection*. Like Richard Nixon, Strom Thurmond, James Dickey or Lawrence Welk— if they asked you nicely. Interesting thought: the body and one's absolute inability to unarmor the body and give it to a community—that as the basis of a society instead of Law or Commerce or Nationalism, etc. Davenport has a preliminary story in his new volume, *Tatlin!*, related to Fourier and Sam Butler.

MEYER: Something about that last question, John. A phrase stuck in my mind, sort of sat there while I listened to Jonathan. You said something about threesomeness as a way of life here at Corn Close. The threesome thing disturbed someone who came and stayed with us earlier this summer, On the way to the train early the morning he left, he turned to me and said: "I think you're playing with fire introducing a third person into your relationship." He said that out of concern and respect for both of us and our home. Right then an odd, slightly botched sentence out of the introduction to *Mastering the Art of French Cooking* came out of my mouth, like an answer I guess: "Train yourself to handle fire; this will save time." If Jonathan feels like Parson Williams, I feel like Madame Roo, Clairvoyant and Housewife. I told him then that I always felt our threesomes as foursomes. When Jonathan and I climb into bed with a third person, I always think someone else gets into bed with us . . . some other presence. And when I set a table for three people I usually have to stop myself from putting out four glasses, four plates, etc. That—for whatever worth it has—

arises as the first thing that stands revealed, as Jonathan said, during such sexual encounters, and specifically during a threesome. Four or five people in bed gives me something of the same weird sensation, but then I feel at sea or in the dark . . . in a nice way, a very nice hide 'n' seek way.

BROWNING: There is much talk here about this business of "being threatened." Just what is it that constitutes a threat to ourselves and our relationships? It seems you both have a way of identifying a threatening situation. But where do you go from there? Do you modify the circumstance so that it doesn't threaten, or is a change of attitude called for?

WILLIAMS: Less Abstraction, please. I am a poet and a man who lives by Catullus' little song, *Odi et Amo!* Which I like to translate in bluegrass style: I love and I hate, and that's all she wrote. . . . Which is risky, and passion can tear lots of things to tatters, like another man said. Risky, yes, but the necessary risk, and I inveigh constantly against those Laodicean folks Saint Paul yelled at: "I spew thee out of my mouth, for ye are neither hot nor cold." Sex is one form of heat; poetry another. Our encounters are never entered without openness. Sneakiness is a threat that ultimately ruined an earlier ten-year relationship I once had—and coldness came in upon me like a plague. Sex, as I said earlier, indicates a lot of a man's character in a rush. Those who are greedy, predatory, hoping to break up my relationship with Tom, are soon found out. "Fun and games" is, to me, part of the idiom T.C.B. (taking care of bodily business), getting one's ashes hauled. Black people have had an imaginative and clear language for some of the uses of sex for a long time. Every new encounter is precisely that. Poetry is about paying close attention to the particulars and not going moralistic, diffuse, intellectual, remote. "Every man in his life makes many marriages," said Sherwood Anderson. Not with lovers only, but with beloved plants, hills, sacred places, animal spirits, rivers, etc. What was it Whitman said: "I shall plant male friendship thick as trees along the rivers of America." That's close to it.

MEYER: Yes, Jonathan, it makes me very happy to find this interview the occasion for our "witnessing" each other in the presence of a third person—right now, here in this library, in this house and in this dale. A sacrament of sorts, a holy threesome out of which there gathers a Holy Smoke, or Ghost, or . . .

BROWNING: I can only affirm by experience the openness and generosity which marks your work, your hosting, and your friendships. But being only a visitor hot off the London ways and means, it occurs to me that remoteness or isolation here might have its more frustrating moments. Are you ever bored?

MEYER: Winter here can make the heart bleak, and things go much slower then; they vegetate or brood. Remoteness and isolation function as seasonal for me, they characterize my winter: a time of year that causes a certain withdrawing somewhere inside me. At eighteen, when I left Seattle to go to Bard, I really left "The City." Even Winston-Salem, the last urban place I lived in—or we lived in, last year for almost five months—makes me see myself as a Country Mouse, as a visitor to cities. I went through a period from about eighteen to twenty-five of hating or rejecting cities. Even in London I had a hard time sleeping at night—always was glad to get back to Corn Close.

BROWNING: Has this changed any?

MEYER: Yes, I begin to feel a change in me, an acceptance of cities, their noises, their weather, their demands—all quite different from the noises, weather and demands of a place like Annandale, Highlands, or Dentdale. It took a lot of depression and unhappiness to learn that the energy I have in summer turns into its opposite in winter. I found myself frustrated in winter or late autumn, year after year—fearful of losing my "powers": my ability to write, my sexiness, my tan, my sunny self, my ease in situations. Tied into that kind of knot by the shift of seasons, I rarely experienced "boredom," basically because when "threatened" (the threat there a loss...the loss of what? identity, I guess), I push harder or am pushed harder. Whatever causes boredom caused in me a franticness, a willfulness, and the need to take drastic steps. In such situations, I forced myself, I forced my poems, my sex life.... The gradual unfolding of a situation, the waiting or giving up into the immediate situation and its demands played no active or conscious part in my life—or in the way I went about living what I considered my life. And I begrudged or fought everything that I considered irrelevant to my life as a poet, a lover, a man. It made me very bitchy at times, mostly with Jonathan. It made me exasperated with his way of getting things accomplished which struck me as too slow, too relaxed. Last autumn everything turned black in my life. Something inside me simply broke and, feeling it break, I assumed I lost a certain wholeness: I considered myself an absolute failure on all counts. So I just gave up, or gave up my plan to write vital, original poems, my plan to dazzle the world with my glittering presence, and sat up late into the night reading. Sometimes not even going to bed, but listening to the house creak and waiting for birds to start up just before dawn; for me, washing the dishes at three in the morning became all the great poems I planned to write and the fame I sought. It represents, in its *Reader's Digest* way, "my most favorite moment" in Dentdale. Three variations stir in my head, three variations of a theme that beckons me like a poem:

> *I break*
> *I break in two*
> *I break into*

That thing broke inside me, broke me in two, shattered me (or the me I saw myself as) but it went on to break *into* something else and break into me. I often thought I might explode, but never for a minute expected to implode. If that makes any sense?

BROWNING: This comes very close to my advocacy of "risk" and "investment," that there are times when, with others or with self, a nearly blind play is called for. We take what little information we have, and coupling it with our compulsive, if obsessive, intuitive notions, play the last and unmarked card. The fear is understandable, since we seem for a moment to be left with an empty hand. But surely to be optimistic is to know that by experience such gambles pay high and fascinatingly unpredictable returns. I suppose that for such an attitude to be genuine, the cost must not be counted, that nothing is to be expected from our out-giving ventures. But I think it need not be this serious, especially as it involves other people. Everyone expects sooner or later to achieve reward in some way from relationship.

My favorite moment is when that wavelength is locked between the eyes of

I and thou, and for a suspended infinity, it all happens, it all occurs in one big time wash. Such has been the case with the four lovers of my life. Through the visual a complete sort of memory is exchanged, and a future realized, all in the present tense, so whole and radiant that neither word nor gesture is needed. Of course, this is only the beginning, and might seem vague and romantic to you. I must admit, however, a certain kind of thrill in the disillusion that can follow such encounters. And this is where investment comes in—when that cosmic intensity dissolves, and one is left with the more practical considerations of time and space, i.e., Do I want to live with this person, smell his farts, witness his own unrevealed monster, spend my money on him, etc. These processes do not, it seems to me, contradict the glamor of that initial love fantasy; they mediate it, they translate it into a history which I think all relationships desire. The mundane aspects of living together ease the pressure of the demanding, often consumptive force of love, and likewise, the love transforms the boring affairs of existence. But the important thing here, in this moment I speak of, is the interplay of life and death. In each instance, it was as if before ever really knowing each other, we communicated a certainty that even death could not sever so strong an attraction. This "problem" being solved with the ritualistic affirmation that "we will be in heaven together," it is the working out of a lifetime which is left. The sacred and the secular are unified in that promise, which may have been signaled in something so simple as a wink and a nod, or in my experience, a glare. Is this anything like the circumstance of your meeting?

WILLIAMS: Glory be to gay old Orfeo, John. That is another one of your Profound Numbers.

Tom and I met because of poetry. And, frankly, that is the ultimate concern. We are *devoted*, and, as Basil Bunting was saying here the other day: "Sex and money are bugger-all; the only reason we make works of art is because of what they used to call 'The Glory of God.'" Basil is an atheist of Quaker persuasion. I am a disciple of Orpheus and of Priapus, yet almost became an Episcopal minister. Anyway, I got left in Aspen, Colorado, in a snowbank in February 1968 by a poet whom I felt I literally had "invented," which is hardly fair to his talents, but that is the way I conceived it. It was, after all, a matter of ten years. Within a few weeks, Fate (i.e. one's luck and one's gumption) introduced me to another Budding Poet, playing at being waiter in a frenchified restaurant and recovering from unfortunate drug and sex problems at Brown University. *Alors.* I spent six months lavishing everything on this bruised adolescent: money, attention, hope, affection. I wrote a journal of poems (revolving, oddly, around the music of Edward Elgar) to him. What did he turn out te be? Aloof, freaked out, to use the current common parlance. I fear I shall have to say he was simply a cockteaser—and spoiled. Certainly he invested very little.

Six months of that and I was climbing walls that didn't even exist. I wrote to a friend, Gerrit Lansing, and tried to ask, coolly: "Gerrit, doesn't anybody write honest gay poetry these days?" He supplied a name (Tom Meyer), to whom I wrote and received a reply in book-length poem called *The Bang Book*. It was to my taste and I accepted it for publication without even asking for a publicity picture in the Golden Boys tradition. Were my motives devious? No, lad, they were not. I publish gays, straights, stockbrokers from Greenwich, one Communist, a whole mess of fucked-up characters more or less like ourselves.

Anyway, I liked the *The Bang Book* for its words and for its theme—and let the queens and cynics scream forever: the words were the point. Sex is not much more important than okra... you may quote me on that. It's generally less glutinous as well.

I was in September 1968 starting a post as poet-in-residence at the Maryland Institute College of Art. It transpired that there was a festival of Carl Ruggles' music coming up in Vermont. I phoned Bard College (where Tom was a senior) and announced to Robert Kelly, his wife, et al. (including his student, Tom Meyer) that I would be driving up to New England for the occasion. They were welcome to come along. Accordingly, one Friday I dismissed my charges early and headed the vw up the interstate to Bard. Kelly couldn't accompany us, but his former wife could, and in walked Thomas Meyer. Blond, quiet, "complicated." We drove on to Bennington and stayed with a professor friend of mine in his lovely house about twenty-five miles north of the campus. *Alors*, after driving eight hours on American freeways, a few drinks, etc., I was in no condition to do anything to anybody. I collapsed into a bedroom, gleefully isolated by my host, while he put on his Spider Drag and dragged Mr. Meyer off to his attic lair. The script did not seem to be reading right, but I was too fucked out to take much notice. ... By next evening, lechery and sanity had returned, and I thought benignly in my heart of hearts: look, baby, fuck this shit, this is my move; fuck this predatory "friend" and the delicate prey I had put on his plate, albeit inadvertently. Thus, I grabbed Mr. Meyer from the midst of Saturday night dinner prattle and talked a little turkey. Three orgasms later, at seven in the morning, we had established that *something* was to be established. The presumption seems to have been correct, say I, pompously, but securely.

Thinking about what has gone before in this exchange of ours leads to me to the obvious conclusion that it is very different from the previous interviews in *Gay Sunshine*. Viz., little in-group gossip. I will not tell you what happened the night Jack Spicer and I shared a motel room in Fort Bragg, California, after hours of pinball among drunken Finns. I won't tell who knocked on my apartment door at eight a.m. Christmas morning, San Francisco, 1954, except that it wasn't Gregory Corso, thank God. And even a New Year's Eve party at the Living Theater, where Ned Rorem met me and remembered I'd once called him the most vapid composer in America in the *Black Mountain Review*—that doesn't have to tell all—we don't need to talk poetry and contemporaries. That material, at least in my case, is available in *Vort Magazine* and other interviews.

I'll end throwing out a barrage of nouns—things, persons, places I find kinship with, find a sacramental relationship with. It is a familiar list, for I value tradition and I have one of my own that is thousands of miles wide and thousands of years old: Ogata Korin, Mae West, Mount LeConte, Sergei Rachmaninov, Chopin, Samuel Palmer, Basho, Thomas Jefferson, the Nantahala Mountains, R. B. Kitaj, Theakston's "Old Peculiar" strong Yorkshire ale, Maker's Mark, Charles Ives, Ingleborough Hill, *Shortia galicifolia*, Ralph Eugene Meatyard, Harry Partch, Cotman, Lorine Niedecker, Tassajara, Marvell, Wm Bartram, Bewick, Satie, Corondum Hot Springs, Albert Pinkham Ryder, George Lewis, Vladimir Horowitz, Gaston Bachelard, Clarence John Laughlin, Levens Hall, Highland Park single malt, Restaurant F. Point, skillet corn pone from water-ground meal, Mervyn Peake, Ross MacDonald, Cautley Spout, Monte Acute, Geoffrey Grigson, Mahler, Robert Duncan, *Franklinia alatamaha*. That's a start. Tom Meyer is a good place to stop.